Cameron Denver

AUTOBIOGRAPHY OF
DR. ALEXANDER CARLYLE

Dr Alexander Carlyle
from a Miniature.

THE
AUTOBIOGRAPHY OF
DR. ALEXANDER CARLYLE
OF INVERESK
1722—1805

EDITED BY JOHN HILL BURTON
NEW EDITION, WITH MANY ADDITIONAL NOTES

T·N·FOULIS
London & Edinburgh
1910

September 1910

Printed by MORRISON & GIBB LTD., *Edinburgh*

PREFATORY NOTE

In the "advertisement" to the original edition, the editor says: "The reader will soon discover that this is a work requiring no introduction to his attention. Indeed, whoever catches a glimpse of the attractions of the interior, will not be disposed patiently to listen to any details intended to detain him on the threshold." While this is so, it may not be out of place in this new edition to give the reader a brief sketch of the history of the family to which the author of this extraordinary biography belonged. It will at least enlighten him, at the outset, with regard to many allusions to family associations and connections continually cropping up in the narrative; while it will explain the author's predilection for "the company of his superiors," which some of the parishioners of Inveresk raised against him as unbecoming in their minister.

Dr. Carlyle did not require, like the governess at Balcarres, who, anxious to parade a "lang pedigree" before her "superiors," instructed her brother in the Herald Office at Edinburgh to prepare a family tree beginning with Fergus the First of Scotland,

and indicating the several families she wished introduced. His was without doubt a family of great antiquity reaching back to, if not before, the Norman Conquest, and one which was closely allied by marriage to
King Robert the Bruce.* The Carlyles—de Karliolo,
Carleile, or Carlisle, as the name was variously spelt
—were a Cumberland family originally, who held property there and in Yorkshire, and were of considerable
authority in the county, and the city of Carlisle from
which the name was derived. In common with other
notable families on the southern border, the Carlyles
early began to add small properties in Scotland to
their English lands, and thus acquired a dual interest
in the border country. From their position in the
north they were employed by the English monarchs
on service to the Scottish Court, but such service did
not prevent them occasionally deserting their royal
masters in a raid on Scotland, for on one occasion,
at least, we learn that a Robert de Carlisle had to
appear before Henry II., and pay peace money for
having joined King William of Scotland, promising at
the same time allegiance to Henry for the future.

While still holding allegiance to the English
throne, the family associated themselves with the
cause of the Bruces, Lords of Annandale, and
through their influence gradually increased the
extent of their property in that district, which till
then was confined to the parish of Cummertrees,

* A full account of the Carlyle family will be found in Sir J.
Balfour Paul's *Scots Peerage*.

where centuries later Dr. Carlyle's father was minister before he was translated to Prestonpans. But it was in the days of King Robert the Bruce that Sir William de Carlisle, having married the King's sister, Margaret, finally threw off the English allegiance, joined the Scots, and thereby forfeited his English estates. For this and other services rendered to Bruce further lands in Annandale were granted to Sir William and his lady, and the family rose to great importance in the country. Following this valiant knight were several generations who took no great part in public affairs, but through mortgages, as in the case of the Limekilns property, or otherwise, apparently added considerably to the family estates until nearly one-half of Annandale was under their control.

Towards the end of the fifteenth century the family again comes into prominence in Scottish history in the person of Sir John de Carlisle, who was Keeper of Threave and Lochmaben Castles ; was sent on a mission to France by James the Third ; and for the active part he played in suppressing the Douglas rebellion, was raised to the peerage as Lord Carlyle of Torthorwald. Of his three successors in the peerage little is recorded. On the death of the fourth Lord Carlyle the greater part of the estates passed into the possession of his granddaughter, but only after long litigation which greatly depleted them. This lady married a Douglas of Parkhead, and her Carlyle properties were ultimately merged in those of Douglas of Drumlanrig, first Earl of Queensberry. With the loss of their property the family did not relinquish their right to the title, although they discontinued the use of it, until towards the end of the eighteenth century the direct male line of the Barons Carlyle of Torthorwald became extinct.

A great-grandson of the Sir William de Carlisle of Bruce's day, nephew of the first Lord Carlyle, obtained from his uncle a charter of the lands of Bridekirk, and became the ancestor of that branch of the family which terminated with Dr. Alexander Carlyle's death. The Bridekirk family do not emerge in Scottish public affairs; but in the reign of Charles I., one member of it, Ludovick, held a position at Whitehall as Groom of the Privy Chamber, and later Keeper of Richmond Park, while he also made some reputation as a playwright. On his retirement from office in England, he purchased the estate of Newpark, near Annan, and close to the Bridekirk property. His son Ludovick, born in 1647, was the father of Mr. William Carlyle, minister of Cummertrees and later of Prestonpans, and the grandfather of the author of this Autobiography.

In the course of his narrative Dr. Carlyle makes frequent reference to his relationship to the Jardines of Annandale—his father and mother being both related to branches of that family—and earlier in their history we find the family became connected by marriage with the Johnstones, who were repre-

sented in Dr. Carlyle's day, and were his great friends,
by Sir James Johnstone of Westerhall and Sir
William, who, on his marriage, assumed the name of
Pulteney.

Recognising, therefore, the position his family for
centuries had occupied in the south of Scotland,
and their close association with the powerful border
clans of Douglas, Jardine, and Johnstone, we can
realise his appreciation of the "company of his
superiors" in which by "right of lineage, by culture
and talent, by dignity of manner and vivacity in
conversation," Dr. Carlyle naturally took his place,
and fulfilled his part in a manner rare among the
clergy of the first half of the eighteenth century.

In the Supplementary Chapter by John Hill
Burton will be found an explanation of the nature
and conditions of the materials placed in his hands
for the original publication, and the manner in which
he thought fit to execute the trust confided in him.
Every reader of the Autobiography will regret, with
Dr. Hill Burton, that the gifted author did not live to
complete his story; while at the same time, also, it
will be admitted that what he has left is a unique
picture among the many that have come down to us
of the life and manners of the period in which he
lived.

The Publisher would here wish to express his
indebtedness to Colonel Bell for placing the original

MS. of the Autobiography at his service, by which he was enabled to correct one or two minor slips in the original issue ; for the use of the first draft of the Autobiography—the " Recollections "—from which further interesting notes have been added to this edition ; and, finally, for his kind permission to reproduce for the first time the miniature portrait of Dr. Carlyle which forms the frontispiece to the volume.

SUMMARY OF CONTENTS

CHAPTER I

CHAPTER II

CHAPTER III

SUPPLEMENTARY CHAPTER

AUTOBIOGRAPHY OF

DR. ALEXANDER CARLYLE

CHAPTER I

1722–1736   AGE, BIRTH TO 14

HAVING observed how carelessly, and consequently how falsely, history is written, I have long resolved to note down certain facts within my own knowledge, under the title of *Anecdotes and Characters of the Times*, that may be subservient to a future historian, if not to embellish his page, yet to keep him within the bounds of truth and certainty.

I have been too late in beginning this work, as on this very day I enter on the seventy-ninth year of my age ; which circumstance, as it renders it not improbable that I may be stopped short in the middle of my annals, will undoubtedly make it difficult for me to recall the memory of many past transactions in my long life with that precision and clearness which such a work requires. But I will admit of no more excuses for indolence or procrastination, and endeavour (with God's blessing) to serve posterity, to the best of my ability, with such a faithful picture of times and characters as came within my view in the humble and private sphere of life, in comparison with that of many others, in which I have always acted ; remembering, however, that in whatever sphere men act, the agents and instruments are still the same, viz. the faculties and passions of human nature.

The first characters which I could discriminate were those of my own family, which I was able to mark at a very early age.   My father was of a moderate understanding, of ordinary learning and accomplishments for the times, for he was born in 1690 ; of a warm, open, and benevolent temper ; most faithful and diligent in the duties of his office, and an orthodox and popular orator.   He was entirely beloved and much caressed by the whole parish.*   My mother was a person of superior understanding, of a calm and firm temper, of an elegant and reflecting mind ; and considering that she was the eldest of seven daughters and three sons of a country clergyman, near Dumfries, and was born in 1700, she had received an education, and improved by it, far beyond what could have been expected. Good sense, however, and dignity of conduct, were her chief attributes. The effect of this was, that she was as much respected as my father was beloved.

They were in very narrow circumstances till the stipend was largely augmented in the year 1732.

* He was minister of the parish of Prestonpans.

Two of the judges, who were his heritors, Lords Grange and Drummore, came down from the bench and pleaded his cause.* And the estate of the patron, then Morison of Prestongrange, being under sequestration, it was with little difficulty that a greater augmentation than was usual at that period was obtained; for the stipend was raised by it from £70 to £140 per annum.

In the year 1729, the good people had a visit from London that proved expensive and troublesome. It was Mrs. Lyon, a sister of my father's, and her son and daughter. Her deceased husband was Mr. Lyon of Easter Ogill, a branch of the Strathmore family, who had been in the Rebellion 1715, and, having been pardoned, had attempted to carry on business in London, but was ruined in the South Sea [Scheme.]

* His heritors—that is to say, proprietors of land in his parish liable to contribute to the payment of his stipend.—J. H. B.

One of the advantages of the increased stipend is recorded by the author in his *MS.Recollections*: " In the overflow of wealth my father took it in his head to make me a small apartment to study in. This was a little hole off the dining-room. . . . This dining-room was the apartment in which my mother received her morning visitors, and she being without dispute the wisest woman in the parish, and had still pretensions to be handsome although turned thirty, she was resorted to for advice by all the women of the parish, high and low. In this secret cell I heard perfectly whatever was going on in the parish, whether it was the expected marriage of a daughter, or the reformation of a prodigal son or unfaithful husband. Whatever occasioned doubt or perplexity, or required advice, were laid before my sagacious mother. This made me master of all the secrets of the parish, and wonderful to tell, I did not abuse this casual confidence into which I fell so prematurely, for, as I was never very inquisitive into other people's affairs, I was no fool when I found out things by accident."

This lady, who came down on business, after a few weeks went into lodgings in Edinburgh, where she lost her daughter in the smallpox, and soon after returned to my father's, where she remained for some months. She was young and beautiful, and vain, not so much of her person (to which she had a good title) as of her husband's great family, to which she annexed her own, and, by a little stretch of imagination and a search into antiquity, made it great also. Her son, who was a year and a half older than myself, was very handsome and good-natured, though much indulged. My father was partial to him, and I grew a little jealous. But the excess of his mother's fondness soon cured my father of his; and as I was acknowledged to be the better scholar of the two, I soon lost all uneasiness, and came to love my cousin most sincerely, though he intercepted many of the good things that I should have got.

Not long after this, another sister of my father's came down from London, who was a widow also, but had no children. She stayed with us for a year, and during that time taught me to read English, with just pronunciation and a very tolerable accent—an accomplishment which in those days was very rare. Long before she came down, I had been taught to read by an old woman, who kept a school, so perfectly, that at six years of age I had read a large portion of the Bible to a dozen of old women, who had been excluded the church by a crowd which had made me leave it also, and whom I observed sitting

on the outside of a door, where they could not hear.
Upon this I proposed to read a portion of Scripture
to them, to which they agreed, and set me on a tomb-
stone, whence I read very audibly to a congregation,
which increased to about a score, the whole of the
Song of Solomon. This would not deserve to be noted,
but for the effect it had afterwards.*

There lived in the town and parish of Prestonpans at this time several respectable and wealthy
people—such as the Mathies, the Hogs, the Youngs,
and the Shirreffs. There still remained some foreign
trade, though their shipping had been reduced from
twenty to half the number since the Union, which put
an end to the foreign trade in the ports of the Firth
of Forth. There was a custom-house established here,
the superior officers of which, with their families,
added to the mercantile class which still remained,
made a respectable society enough.

The two great men of the parish, however, were
Morison of Prestongrange, the patron, and the Honourable James Erskine of Grange, one of the Supreme Judges. The first was elected Member of Parliament for East Lothian in the first Parliament of
Great Britain, although the celebrated Andrew Fletcher of Saltoun was the other candidate.

But Government took part with Morison, and

* " This first attempt to preach made a great noise, and I was
dubbed by the vulgar a minister already selected and set apart
by the Lord. The caresses I met with on this account were not
to my taste, for I did not feel any merit in having read a few chapters, and I did not like to be a minister."—*MS. Recollections.*

Fletcher had only nine votes. Morison had been
very rich, but had suffered himself to be stripped by
the famous gambler of those times, Colonel Charteris,
whom I once saw with him in church, when I was
five or six years of age ; and being fully impressed
with the popular opinion that he was a wizard,
who had a fascinating power, I never once took
my eyes off him during the whole service, believing
that I should be a dead man the moment I did.
This Colonel Charteris was of a very ancient family
in Dumfriesshire, the first of whom, being one of
the followers of Robert Bruce, had acquired a great
estate, a small part of which is still in the family.
The colonel had been otherwise well connected, for
he was cousin-german to Sir Francis Kinloch, and,
when a boy, was educated with him at the village
school. Many stories were told of him,* which would
never have been heard of had he not afterwards been
so much celebrated in the annals of infamy. He was
a great profligate, no doubt, but there have been as
bad men and greater plunderers than he was, who
have escaped with little public notice. But he was
one of the Runners of Sir Robert Walpole, and
defended him in all places of resort, which drew the

* A story of Charteris' avarice is told by the Hon. John Crawford writing to his sister the Hon. Peggy Crawford. He says:
" Mr. Cummin, the minister, attended him on his death-bed ; he
[Charteris] asked at his sister, who is exceedingly mean, what he
should give him ; she replied that it was unusual to give anything on such occasions. ' Well, then,' says Charteris, ' let's have
another flourish from him,' so calling for prayers. So you see
he died as he lived."

wrath of the Tories upon him, and particularly sharpened the pens of Pope and Arbuthnot against him. For had it not been for the witty epitaph of the latter,* Charteris might have escaped in the crowd of gamesters and debauchees, who are only railed at by their pigeons, and soon fall into total oblivion. This *simple* gentleman's estate [Morison's] soon went under sequestration for the payment of his debts. He was so imaginary and credulous as to believe that close by his creek of Morison's Haven was the place where St. John wrote the Apocalypse, because some old vaults had been discovered in digging a mill-race for a mill that went by sea-water. This had probably been put into his head by the annual meeting of the oldest lodge of operative masons in Scotland at that place on St. John's Day.

My Lord Grange was the leading man in the parish, and had brought my father to Prestonpans from Cumbertrees in his native county Annandale, where he had been settled for four years, and where I was born. Lord Grange was Justice-Clerk in the end of Queen Anne's reign, but had been dismissed from

---

* The epitaph begins: "Here continueth to rot the body of Francis Charteris, who, with an inflexible constancy, and inimitable uniformity of life, persisted, in spite of age and infirmity, in the practice of every human vice except prodigality and hypocrisy: his insatiable avarice exempted him from the first, his matchless impudence from the second;" and ends: "He was the only person of his time who could cheat with the mask of honesty, retain his primeval meanness when possessed of ten thousand a year, and having daily deserved the gibbet for what he did, was at last condemned to it for what he could not do."

that office in the beginning of the reign of George 1., when his brother, the Earl of Mar, lost the Secretary of State's office, which he had held for some years. After this, and during the Rebellion [of 1715], Lord Grange kept close at his house of Preston, on an estate which he had recently bought from the heirs of a Dr. Oswald, but which had not long before been the family estate of a very ancient cadet of the family of Hamilton. During the Rebellion [of 1715], and some time after, Lord Grange amused himself in laying out and planting a fine garden, in the style of those times, full of close walks and labyrinths and wildernesses, which, though it did not occupy above four or five acres, cost one at least two hours to perambulate. This garden or pleasure-ground was soon brought to perfection by his defending it from the westerly and south-westerly winds by hedges of common elder, which in a few years were above sixteen feet high, and completely sheltered all the interior grounds. This garden continued to be an object of curiosity down to the year 1740, insomuch that flocks of company resorted to it from Edinburgh, during the summer, on Saturdays and Mondays (for Sunday was not at that time a day of pleasure), and were highly gratified by the sight, there being nothing at that time like it in Scotland, except at Alloa, the seat of the Earl of Mar, of which indeed it was a copy in miniature.

My Lady Grange was Rachel Chiesly, the daughter of Chiesly of Dalry, the person who shot President Lockhart in the dark, when standing within the

head of a close in the Lawnmarket, because he had
voted against him in a cause depending before the
Court.* He was the son or grandson of a Chiesly,
who, in *Baillie's Letters*, is called Man to the famous
Mr. Alexander Henderson ; that is to say, secretary,
for he accompanied Mr. Henderson on his journey
to London, and having met the Court somewhere on
their way, Chiesly was knighted by Charles I. ; so
that, being a new family, they must have had few
relations, which, added to the atrocious deed of her
father, had made the public very cool in the interest
of Lady Grange. This lady had been very beautiful,
but was of a violent temper. She had, it was said,
been debauched by her husband before marriage ; and
as he was postponing or evading the performance of
his promise to marry her, it was believed that, by
threatening his life, she had obtained the fulfilment
of it.

It was Lord Grange's custom to go frequently
to London in the spring ; and though he seemed
quiet and inactive here, it was supposed that he resented his having been turned out of the Justice-

* It was not, strictly speaking, a decision of the Court that in-
furiated Chiesly, but a finding in an arbitration. He was desirous,
and thought himself entitled, to leave his wife, with whom he had
quarrelled, and his children, to starve. The question of his lia-
bility for their support having been referred to President Lockhart and Lord Kemnay, they found him bound to make his family
an allowance. It may be proper to explain that Grange and his
wife were not Lord and Lady in the English sense, as a peer and
peeress, but by the custom of Scotland, which gives " Lord " to
a judge, and used to give " Lady " to the wife of a landed proprietor.—J. H. B.

Clerk's office in 1714, and might secretly be carrying on plots when at London. Be that as it may, he had contracted such a violent aversion at Sir Robert Walpole, that having, by intrigue and hypocrisy, secured a majority of the district of burghs of which Stirling is the chief, he threw up his seat as a Judge in the Court of Session, was elected member for that district, and went to London to attend Parliament, and to overturn Sir Robert Walpole, not merely in his own opinion, but in the opinion of many who were dupes to his cunning, and his pretensions to abilities that he had not.* But his first appearance in the House of Commons undeceived his sanguine friends, and silenced him for ever. He chose to make his maiden speech on the Witches Bill, as it was called ; and being learned in dæmonologia, with books on which subject his library was filled, he made a long canting speech that set the House in a titter of laughter, and convinced Sir Robert that he had no need of any extraordinary armour against this champion of the house of Mar.† The truth was, that the man had neither learning nor ability. He was no lawyer, and

* A Bill to regulate elections in Scotland was then passing, and Walpole added to it a clause disqualifying Judges of the Court of Session from sitting in Parliament, for the purpose, it was said, of keeping Erskine out.—J. H. B.

† The " Act to repeal the statute made in the first year of King James I., intituled 'An Act against Conjuration, Witchcraft, and dealing with evil and wicked Spirits, except so much thereof,'" etc., was passed early in the session of 1735. Unfortunately, we have no account of any debate on the measure, and thus lose Erskine's speech, which was probably curious, for the vulgar superstitions of the day seem to have taken fast hold on him, and his diary is full of

he was a bad speaker. He had been raised on the
shoulders of his brother, the Earl of Mar, in the end
of the Queen's reign, but had never distinguished
himself. In the General Assembly itself, which many
gentlemen afterwards made a school of popular eloquence, and where he took the high-flying side that
he might annoy Government, his appearances were
but rare and unimpressive ; but as he was understood
to be a great plotter, he was supposed to reserve himself for some greater occasions.

In Mr. Erskine's annual visits to London, he had
attached himself to a mistress, a handsome Scotch-
woman, Fanny Lindsay, who kept a coffeehouse
about the bottom of the Haymarket. This had come
to his lady's ears, and did not tend to make her less
outrageous. He had taken every method to soothe
her. As she loved command, he had made her factor
upon his estate, and given her the whole management of his affairs. When absent, he wrote her the
most flattering letters, and, what was still more flattering, he was said, when present, to have imparted
secrets to her, which, if disclosed, might have reached
his life. Still she was unquiet, and led him a miser-

dreams, prognostics, and communings with persons supernaturally
gifted. The tenor of his "canting speech" may perhaps be inferred
from the following testimony borne in 1743 against the same Bill, by
the Associate Presbytery : " The penal statutes against witches
have been repealed by the Parliament, contrary to the express
law of God ; by which a holy God may be provoked, in a way of
righteous judgment, to leave those who are already ensnared to
be hardened more and more, and to permit Satan to tempt and
seduce others to the same wicked and dangerous snares."—J.H.B.

able life. What was true is uncertain ; for though
her outward appearance was stormy and outrageous,
Lord Grange not improbably exaggerated the violence
of her behaviour to his familiar friends as an apology
for what he afterwards did ; for he alleged to them
that his life was hourly in danger, and that she slept
with lethal weapons under her pillow. He once
showed my father a razor which he had found concealed there.

Whatever might be the truth, he executed one of
the boldest and most violent projects that ever had
been attempted since the nation was governed by
laws ; for he seized his lady in his house in Edinburgh,
and by main force carried her off through Stirling
to the Highlands, whence, after several weeks,
she was at last landed in St. Kilda, a desolate isle
in the Western Ocean, sixty miles distant from the
Long Island. There she continued to live to the
end of her days, which was not before the year
17—, in the most wretched condition, in the society
of none but savages, and often with scanty provision
of the coarsest fare, and but rarely enjoying the comfort of a pound of tea, which she sometimes got
from shipmasters who accidentally called.* Lord
Grange's accomplices in this atrocious act were be-

* She was carried off in 1732 ; and after being detained about
two years in the small island of Hesker, was conveyed to St. Kilda.
On the affair getting wind, she was afterwards removed to Harris,
where she died in 1745, before the arrangements for obtaining her
release, and a full inquiry into the affair, could be completed.—
J. H. B.

lieved to be Lord Lovat and the Laird of M'Leod, the first as being the most famous plotter in the kingdom, and the second as equally unprincipled, and the proprietor of the island of St. Kilda. What was most extraordinary was, that, except in conversation for a few weeks only, this enormous act, committed in the midst of the metropolis of Scotland by a person who had been Lord Justice-Clerk, was not taken the least notice of by any of her own family, or by the King's Advocate or Solicitor, or any of the guardians of the laws. Two of her sons were grown up to manhood—her eldest daughter was the wife of the Earl of Kintore—who acquiesced in what they considered as a necessary act of justice for the preservation of their father's life. Nay, the second son was supposed to be one of the persons who came masked to the house, and carried her off in a chair to the place where she was set on horseback.*

This artful man, by cant and hypocrisy, persuaded all his intimate friends that this act was

---

* In a letter by Lady Grange quoted in vol. x. of the *Transactions of the Society of Antiquaries*, she says, "'Twas Lord Lovat and Roderick M'Leod that stole me." On the other hand, Lord Lovat defends himself on this charge in a characteristic letter quoted by Hill Burton: " As to that about my Lady Grange, it is a much less surprise to me, because they said ten times worse of me, when that damned woman went from Edinburgh, than they can say now ; for they said it was all my contrivance . . . but I defyed them as I do now, and do declare to you, upon my honour, that I do not know what has become of that woman, where she is, or who takes care of her ; but if I had contrived and assisted, and saved my Lord Grange from that devil, who threatened every day to murder him and his children, I would not think shame of it before God or man."

necessary for the preservation of her life as well as of his ; and that it was only confining a mad woman in a place of safety, where she was tenderly cared for, and for whom he professed not merely an affectionate regard, but the most passionate love. It was many years afterwards before it was known that she had been sent to such a horrid place as St. Kilda ; and it was generally believed that she was kept comfortably, though in confinement, in some castle in the Highlands belonging to Lovat or M'Leod. The public in general, though clamorous enough, could take no step, seeing that the family were not displeased, and supposing that Lord Grange had satisfied the Justice-Clerk and other high officers of the law with the propriety of his conduct.

From what I could learn at the time, and afterwards came to know, Lord Grange was in one respect a character not unlike Cromwell and some of his associates—a real enthusiast, but at the same time licentious in his morals.*

He had my father very frequently with him in the evenings, and kept him to very late hours. They were understood to pass much of their time in prayer, and in settling the high points of Calvinism ; for their creed was that of Geneva. Lord Grange

* Lord Grange was the lay head of the Ultra-Presbyterian party, and has been commemorated by its historian, Robert Wodrow (*Analecta*, vol. ii.), who notes on one occasion that " he (Grange) complains much of preaching up mere morality, and very little of Christ and grace." On another occasion he is represented by this historian as complaining that " he was extremely abused by not a few at Edinburgh, and represented as a hypocrite."

was not unentertaining in conversation, for he had a great many anecdotes which he related agreeably, and was fair-complexioned, good-looking, and insinuating.

After those meetings for private prayer, however, in which they passed several hours before supper, praying alternately, they did not part without wine ; for my mother used to complain of their late hours, and suspected that the claret had flowed liberally.*

* [Those meetings might partly be calculated to keep Grange free of his wife's company, which was always stormy and outrageous. I remember well that when I was invited on Saturdays to pass the afternoon with the two youngest daughters, Jean and Rachel, and their younger brother John, who was of my age, then about six or seven, although they had a well-fitted-up closet for children's play, we always kept alternate watch at the door, lest my lady should come suddenly upon us ; which was needless, as I observed to them, for her clamour was sufficiently loud as she came through the rooms and passages.]

In the *Recollections* there is the following account of an interview with the lady :—

" I had travelled half a mile westwards to the Red Burn, which divides Prestonpans from its suburbs the Cuthill, and was hovering on the brink of this river, uncertain whether or not I should venture over. In this state I was met by a coach, which stopped, and which was under the command of Lady Grange. She ordered her footman to seize me directly and put me into the coach. It was in vain to fly, so I was flung into her coach reluctant and sulky. She tried to soothe me, but it would not do. She had provoked me on the Sunday, by telling my father that I played myself at church, that she had detected me smiling at her son John (exactly of my age), and trying to write with my finger on the dusty desk that was before me. She was gorgeously dressed : her face was like the moon, and patched all over, not for ornament, but use. For these eighty years that I have been wandering in this wilderness, I have seen nothing like her but General Dickson of Kilbucho. In short, she appeared to me to be the lady with whom all well-educated children were acquainted, the Great Scarlet Whore of Babylon. She landed me at my

Notwithstanding this intimacy, there were periods of half a year at a time when there was no intercourse between them at all. My father's conjecture was, that at those times he was engaged in a course of debauchery at Edinburgh, and interrupted his religious exercises. For in those intervals he not only neglected my father's company, but absented

father's door, and gave me to my mother, with injunctions to keep me nearer home, or I would be lost. This, however, drew on a nearer connection, for the two misses, who had been in the coach, came down with John, who was younger than them, and invited me to drink tea with them next Saturday : to this I had no aversion, and went accordingly. The young ladies had a fine closet, charmingly furnished, with chairs, a table, a set of china and everything belonging to it. The misses set about making tea, for they had a fire in the room, and a maid came to help them, till at length we heard a shrill voice screaming, ' Mary Erskine, my angel Mary Erskine ! '

" This was Countess of Kintore afterwards, and now very near that honour. The girls seemed frightened out of their wits, and so did the maid. The clamour ceased ; but the girls ordered John and me to stand sentry in our turns, with vigilant ear, and give them notice whenever the storm began again. We had sweetcake and almonds and raisins, of which a small paper bag was given me for my brother Loudwick, James, Lord Grange's godson, who came last, being still at nurse. I had no great enjoyment, notwithstanding the good things and the kisses given, for I had by contagion caught a mighty fear of my lady from them. But I was soon relieved, for my father's man came for me at seven o'clock. The moment I was out of sight of the house, I took up my paper bag and ate up its contents, bribing the servant with a few, for Loudwick was gone to his native country to die at our grandfather's. When I read the fable of the ' City Mouse and Country Mouse,' this scene came fresh to my memory. What trials and dangers have children to go through ! "

The *Recollections* also give the following story of Lady Kintore :—

" Lord's Grange's daughter Mary, Countess of Kintore, was truly a beautiful and lively woman, but had the misfortune to be married to a lord, little better than a changeling. She had no children. They lived most part of the year in Aberdeenshire in

himself from church, and did not attend the sacrament—religious services which at other times he
would not have neglected for the world. Report,
however, said that he and his associates, of whom a
Mr. Michael Menzies, a brother of the Laird of
St. Germains, and Thomas Elliott, W.S. (the father

the country, which being but desolate she tired excessively. To
amuse herself she contrived to make her lord's valet fall in love
with her and brought him even to a declaration. My lord, dull
as he was, took offence ; my lady observed that he was jealous,
and told him frankly that the young man had declared his passion,
which she had laughed at, but made this condition that he should
not be turned away, as it would ruin the poor young man. My
lord consented, but grew more and more jealous and irksome.
She wanted only a pretence for leaving him, and went to Edinburgh, to consult her father, she said. The lad, who grew restless
with irresolution and jealousy, soon followed her. And by the
interposition of the father a treaty for a separation commenced ;
but Kintore, not yet cured of his passion for his wife, and having
but a small estate, stood out upon terms. He visited her daily,
however, and they were civil to each other. By a contrivance of
her father, however, as it was believed, to whom every guileful
plot was at that time ascribed, the poor fool of a husband was
entirely defeated. She asked him to come to breakfast one
morning, when she had a female friend or two with her. As they
did not retire after breakfast, my lady asked him to go into her
dressing-room and mend or make her a couple of pens, and she
would come to him. She did so very soon. He had laid down
the penknife on the table ; she, on some short altercation between
them which she brought on, took up the knife and gave herself a
very slight cut in the back part of her neck. She shrieked immediately. The two friends broke in, who found her lord in the act
of wresting the knife from her hand, looking timid and dismayed
and terrified beyond all conception. She exclaimed that he had
attempted to murder her—he that never killed a fly all his life.
The father, who not far off, soon appeared on the scene, and
threatening a justiciary process for an assault with an intention
to murder, soon prevailed with the simpleton of an Earl (now completely cured of love for his wife) to agree to a deed of separation
with a handsome allowance for his wife."

of Sir John Elliott, physician in London), were two,
passed their time in alternate scenes of the exercises of religion and debauchery, spending the day
in meetings for prayer and pious conversation, and
their nights in lewdness and revelling. Some men
are of opinion that they could not be equally sincere
in both. I am apt to think that they were, for
human nature is capable of wonderful freaks. There
is no doubt of their profligacy ; and I have frequently
seen them drowned in tears, during the whole of a
sacramental Sunday, when, so far as my observation
could reach, they could have no rational object
in acting a part.* The Marquess of Lothian of
that day, whom I have seen attending the sacrament at Prestonpans with Lord Grange, and whom
no man suspected of plots or hypocrisy, was much
addicted to debauchery. The natural casuistry of

* Grange kept a diary, a portion of which was printed in 1834,
under the title, *Extracts from the Diary of a Member of the College
of Justice.* It tends, on the whole, to confirm Carlyle's view of
his character ; but it is drier reading than one would expect from
the self-communings of a man whose character was cast between
extremes so wide apart, and whose career had been so remarkable.
Along with the hankering after dreams and prophecies already
alluded to, it contains chiefly accounts of his conduct and views in
the proceedings of the church courts. It mentions some pieces of
conduct on his own part, which, if not criminal, would not then,
or now, be deemed very consistent with honour—as, for instance,
how he examined a private diary kept by the family tutor, in
order that he might see what was said therein about himself and
his household ; and the result, as people who pursue such in-
vestigations usually find, was not agreeable. Each reader will
judge for himself how much sincerity there is in the following extract from the diary :—" I have reason to thank God that I was
put out from the office of Justice-Clerk, for beside many reasons

the passions grants dispensations with more facility than the Church of Rome.

About this time two or three other remarkable men came to live in the parish. The celebrated Col. Gardiner bought the estate of Banktoun,* where Lord Drummore † had resided for a year or two before he bought the small estate of Westpans, which he called Drummore, and where he resided till his death in 1755.

The first Gardiner, who was afterwards killed in the battle of Preston, was a noted enthusiast, a very weak, honest, and brave man, who had once been a great rake, and was converted, as he told my father, by his reading a book called Gurnall's *Christian Armour*, which his mother had put in his trunk many years before. He had never looked at it till one day at Paris, where he was attending the

from the times and my own circumstances, and other reasons from myself, this one is sufficient—that I have thereby so much more time to employ about God and religion. If I consider how very much more I have since I was neither concerned in the Court of Justiciary nor in the politics, how can I answer for the little advances I have made in the knowledge of religion ? If, while I have that leisure, I be enabled, through grace, to improve it for that end, I need not grudge the want of the £400 sterling yearly : for this is worth all the world, and God can provide for my family in his own good time and way " (p. 34).

* The original name of the estate was Olive Stob. When Colonel Gardiner purchased it from the Hamilton family in 1733, he changed the name to Banktoun. It adjoined the battlefield of Prestonpans, and a monument in front of the house records the death of Colonel Gardiner.

† Hew Dalrymple, second son of Sir Hew Dalrymple of North Berwick, Lord President of the Court of Session. He took the title of Lord Drummore when he was raised to the Bench in 1726.

Earl of Stair, who was ambassador to that court from the year 1715 to the Regent's death, when, having an intrigue with a surgeon's wife, and the hour of appointment not being come, he thought he would pass the time in turning over the leaves of the book, to see what the divine could say about armour, which he thought he understood as well as he. He was so much taken with this book, that he allowed his hour of appointment to pass, never saw his mistress more, and from that day left off all his rakish habits, which consisted in swearing and whoring (for he never was a drinker), and the contempt of sacred things, and became a serious good Christian ever after.

Dr. Doddridge has marred this story, either through mistake, or through a desire to make Gardiner's conversion more supernatural, for he says that his appointment was at midnight, and introduces some sort of meteor or blaze of light, that alarmed the new convert.* But this was not the

* [" He thought he saw an unusual blaze of light fall on the book while he was reading, which he at first imagined might happen by some accident in the candle. But lifting up his eyes, he apprehended, to his extreme amazement, that there was before him, as it were suspended in the air, a visible representation of the Lord Jesus Christ upon the Cross, surrounded on all sides with a glory ; and was impressed as if a voice, or something equivalent to a voice, had come to him, to this effect (for he was not confident as to the very words), ' Oh, sinner ! did I suffer this for thee, and are these the returns ? ' But whether this were an audible voice, or only a strong impression on his mind equally striking, he did not seem very confident ; though, to the best of my remembrance, he rather judged it to be the former."—Doddridge's *Remarkable Passages in the Life of Colonel Gardiner*, § 32.]

case ; for I have heard Gardiner tell the story at least three or four times,* to different sets of people—for he was not shy or backward to speak on the subject, as many would have been. But it was at mid-day, for the appointment was at one o'clock ; and he told us the reason of it, which was, that the surgeon, or apothecary, had shown some symptoms of jealousy, and they chose a time of day when he was necessarily employed abroad in his business.

I have also conversed with my father upon it, after Doddridge's book was published, who always persisted in saying that the appointment was at one o'clock, for the reason mentioned, and that Gardiner having changed his lodging, he found a book when rummaging an old trunk to the bottom, which my father said was Gurnall's *Christian Armour*, but to which Doddridge gives the name of *The Christian Soldier ; or, Heaven Taken by Storm*, by Thomas Watson.† Doddridge, in a note, says that his edition of the story was confirmed in a letter from a Rev. Mr. Spears, in which there was not the least difference from the account he had taken down in writing the

* " The leading circumstances I have frequently heard him repeat when only my father and I, and the Rev. Mr. John Glen, his son's tutor were there, though Dr. Doddridge in his account has varied the circumstances."—*Recollections*.

† " *The Christian in Complete Armour ; or, A Treatise on the Saints' War with the Devil :* wherein a discovery is made of the policy, power, wickedness, and stratagems made use of by that enemy of God and his people ; a magazine opened from whence the Christian is furnished with special arms for the battle, assisted in buckling on his armour, and taught the use of his weapons—together with the happy issue of the whole war.—By WILLIAM GUR-

very night in which the Colonel had told him the
story. This Mr. Spears had been Lord Grange's chaplain, and I knew him to have no great regard to truth,
when deviating from it suited his purpose; at any rate,
he was not a man to contradict Doddridge, who had
most likely told him the story. It is remarkable
that, though the Doctor had written down everything
exactly, and could take his oath, yet he had omitted
to mark the day of the week on which the conversion
happened, but, if not mistaken, thinks it was Sabbath.
This aggravates the sin of the appointment, and
hallows the conversion.

The Colonel, who was truly an honest, well-meaning
man and a pious Christian, was very ostentatious;
though, to tell the truth, he boasted oftener of his
conversion than of the dangerous battles he had been
in. As he told the story, however, there was nothing
supernatural in it ; for many a rake of about thirty
years of age has been reclaimed by some circumstance
that set him a-thinking, as the accidental reading of
this book had done to Gardiner. He was a very skil-
ful horseman, which had recommended him to Lord

NALL, A.M., formerly of Lavenham, Suffolk. 1656–62." Three
volumes quarto. *The Christian Soldier ; or, Heaven Taken by
Storm*, one of many works written by Thomas Watson, one of the
non-juring clergy driven out by the Act of Conformity, appears to
be very rare ; it is not in the list of its author's works in Watt's
Bibliotheca. Doddridge, before he wrote his well-known *Remarkable Passages*, had preached and published a funeral sermon on
Colonel Gardiner, which he called *The Christian Warrior Animated
and Crowned*—an evident assimilation to the title of Watson's
book.—J. H. B.

Stair as a suitable part of his train when he was ambassador at Paris, and lived in great splendour. Gardiner married Lady Frances Erskine, one of the
daughters of the Earl of Buchan, a lively, little, deformed woman, very religious, and a great breeder.
Their children were no way distinguished, except the
eldest daughter, Fanny, who was very beautiful, and
became the wife of Sir James Baird.*

Lord Drummore, one of the Judges, was a second
or third son of the President Sir Hew Dalrymple, of
North Berwick, a man very popular and agreeable
in his manners, and an universal favourite ! He
was a great friend of the poor, not merely by giving
alms, in which he was not slack, but by encouraging
agriculture and manufactures, and by devoting his
spare time in acting as a justice of peace in the two
parishes of Inveresk and Prestonpans, where his
estate lay, and did much to preserve the peace of
the neighbourhood, and to promote the peace of the
country. It were happy for the country, if every man
of as much knowledge and authority as the Judges are
supposed to have, would lay himself out as this good
man did. By doing so they might prevent many a
lawsuit that ends in the ruin of the parties. Lord
Drummore had many children.

Mr. Robert Keith of Craig, who was afterwards
ambassador at many courts, and who was a man of
ability and very agreeable manners, came also about

* Fanny became the wife of Sir William Baird, fifth baronet of
Saughton.

this time to live in the parish.* His sons, Sir Robert
Murray Keith, K.B., and Sir Basil Keith, were afterwards well known.†

There lived at the same time there, Colin Campbell, Esq., a brother of Sir James, of Arbruchal, who
was Collector of the Customs ; and when he was
appointed a Commissioner of the Board of Customs,
George Cheap, Esq., became his successor, a brother
of the Laird of Rossie, all of whom had large families
of seven or eight boys and girls, which made up a
society of genteel young people seldom to be met
with in such a place.

When I was very young, I usually passed the
school vacation, first at Mr. Menzies', of St. Germains, and afterwards at Seton House, when the
family came to live there upon the sale of their
estate. I was very often there, as I was a great
favourite of the lady's, one of the Sinclairs of Stevenson,‡ and of her two daughters, who were two or

* Under the title of " Felix," a brief but interesting sketch of
Ambassador Keith will be found in Mrs. Alison Cockburn's
Letters and Memoirs of her Own Life, with notes by T. Craig-
Brown.

† Abundant information about this family will be found in the
Memoirs and Correspondence of Sir Robert Murray Keith, 1849.
The elder Keith was ambassador at Vienna, and subsequently at
St. Petersburg, during the revolution which placed the Empress
Catherine on the throne. His wife was the prototype of Scott's
sketch of Mrs. Bethune Baliol. The son, Sir Robert, was the am-
bassador in Denmark who saved Queen Caroline Matilda, George
III.'s sister, from the fate to which she was destined on account of
the affair of Struensee.—J. H. B.

‡ " That the lady of St. Germains liked my company I need not
wonder, for then I only listened and her tongue never lay, for

three years older than I was. These excursions from home opened the mind of a young person, who had some turn for observation.

The first journey I made, however, was to Dumfriesshire, in the summer 1733, when I was eleven years of age. There I not only became well acquainted with my grandfather, Mr. A. Robison [minister of Tinwald], a very respectable clergyman, and with my grandmother, Mrs. Jean Graham, and their then unmarried daughters ; but I became well acquainted with the town of Dumfries, where I resided for several weeks at Provost Bell's, whose wife was one of my mother's sisters, two more of whom were settled in that town—one of them, the wife of the clergyman, Mr. Wight, and the other of the sheriff-clerk. I was soon very intimate with a few boys of this town about my own age, and became a favourite by teaching them some of our sports and plays in the vicinity of the capital, that they had never heard.*

she was truly as eloquent as her nephew, the first President Dundas."—*Recollections.*

* On this journey it was that I first witnessed an execution. There was one Jock Johnstone who had been condemned for robbery, and, being accessory to a murder, to be executed at Dumfries. This fellow was but twenty years of age, but strong and bold, and a great ringleader. It was strongly reported that the thieves were collecting in all quarters, in order to come to Dumfries on the day of the execution, and make a deforcement as they were conducting Jock to the gallows, which was usually erected on a muir out of town. The magistrates became anxious ; and there being no military force nearer than Edinburgh, they resolved to erect the gallows before the door of the prison, with a scaffold or platform leading from the door to the fatal tree, and

At this time, too, I made a very agreeable tour round the country with my father and Mr. Robert Jardine [minister of Lochmaben], the father of Dr. Jardine, afterwards minister of Edinburgh. Though they were very orthodox and pious clergymen, they had, both of them, a very great turn for fun and buffoonery ; and wherever they went, made all the children quite happy, and set all the maids on the titter. That they might not want amusement, they took along with them, for the first two days, a Mess John Allan, a minister who lay in their route, with whom they could use every sort of freedom, and who was their constant butt. As he had no resistance in him, and could only laugh when they rallied him, or played him boyish tricks, I

they armed about one hundred of their stoutest burgesses with Lochaber axes to form a guard round the scaffold. The day and hour of execution came, and I was placed in the window of the provost's house directly opposite the prison : the crowd was great, and the preparations alarming to a young imagination : at last the prison-door opened, and Jock appeared, enclosed by six town-officers. When he first issued from the door, he looked a little astonished ; but looking round a while, he proceeded with a bold step. Psalms and prayers being over, the rope was fastened about his neck, and he was prompted to ascend a short ladder fastened to the gallows, to be thrown off. Here his resistance and my terror began. Jock was curly-haired and fierce-looking, and very strong of his size—about five feet eight inches. The moment they asked him to go up the ladder, he took hold of the rope round his neck, which was fastened to the gallows, and, with repeated violent pulls, attempted to pull it down ; and his efforts were so strong that it was feared he would have succeeded. The crowd, in the meantime, felt much emotion, and the fear of the magistrates increased. I wished myself on the top of Criffel, or anywhere but there. But the attempt to go through the crowd appeared more dangerous than to stay where I was, out of sight of thought it but very dull entertainment. Nor did I much approve of their turning the backsides of their wigs foremost, and making faces to divert the children, in the midst of very grave discourse about the state of religion in the country, and the progress of the gospel. Among the places we visited was Bridekirk, the seat of the eldest cadet of Lord Carlyle's family, of which my father was descended. I saw, likewise, a small pendicle of the estate which had been assigned as the portion of his grandfather, and which he himself had tried to recover by a lawsuit, but was defeated for want of a principal paper. We did not see the laird, who was from home; but we saw the lady, who was a much greater curiosity. She was a very large and powerful virago, about forty

the gallows. I returned to my station again, resolving manfully to abide the worst extremity.

Jock struggled and roared, for he became like a furious wild beast, and all that six men could do, they could not bind him ; and having with wrestling hard forced up the pinions on his arms, they were afraid, and he became more formidable ; when one of the magistrates, recollecting that there was a master mason or carpenter, of the name of Baxter, who was by far the strongest man in Dumfries, they with difficulty prevailed with him, for the honour of the town, to come on the scaffold. He came, and, putting aside the six men who were keeping him down, he seized him, and made no more difficulty than a nurse does in handling her child : he bound him hand and foot in a few minutes, and laid him quietly down on his face near the edge of the scaffold, and retired. Jock, the moment he felt his grasp, found himself subdued, and became calm, and resigned himself to his fate. This dreadful scene cost me many nights' sleep.

N.B.—The greater portion of this narrative is taken from the *Recollections*, where it is more fully, and, as it seemed to the Editor, more picturesquely told, than in the note appended by the author to his Autobiography.—J. H. B.

years of age, and received us with much kindness and
hospitality ; for the brandy-bottle—a Scotch pint—
made its appearance immediately, and we were
obliged to take our *morning*, as they called it, which
was indeed the universal fashion of the country at
that time. This lady,* who, I confess, had not many
charms for me, was said to be able to empty one of
those large bottles of brandy, smuggled from the Isle
of Man, at a sitting. They had no whisky at that
time, there being then no distilleries in the south of
Scotland.†

The face of the country was particularly desolate,

* Miss Swan of Auchencraig, wife of William Carlile of Bridekirk.
† This interview is thus related in the *Recollections* :—

"The laird was gone to Dumfries, much to our disappointment ; but the lady came out, and, in her excess of kindness,
had almost pulled Mr. Jardine off his horse; but they were
obstinate, and said they were obliged to go to Kelhead ; but
they delivered up Mess John Allan to her, as they had no farther
use for him. I had never seen such a virago as Lady Bridekirk,
not even among the oyster-women of Prestonpans. She was like
a sergeant of foot in women's clothes ; or rather like an over-
grown coachman of a Quaker persuasion. On our peremptory
refusal to alight, she darted into the house like a hogshead down
a slope, and returned instantly with a pint bottle of brandy—a
Scots pint, I mean—and a stray beer-glass, into which she filled
almost a bumper. After a long grace said by Mr. Jardine—for it
was his turn now, being the third brandy-bottle we had seen since
we left Lochmaben—she emptied it to our healths, and made the
gentlemen follow her example : she said she would spare me as I
was so young, but ordered a maid to bring a gingerbread cake
from the cupboard, a luncheon of which she put in my pocket.
This lady was famous, even in the Annandale border, both at the
bowl and in battle : she could drink a Scots pint of brandy with
ease ; and when the men grew obstreperous in their cups, she
could either put them out of doors, or to bed, as she found most
convenient."

not having yet reaped any benefit from the union of
the Parliaments ; nor was it recovered from the
effects of that century of wretched government
which preceded the Revolution, and commenced
at the accession of James. The Border wars and
depredations had happily ceased ; but the borderers,
having lost what excited their activity, were in a
dormant state during the whole of the seventeenth
century, unless it was during the time of the grand
Rebellion, and the struggles between Episcopacy
and Presbytery.

On this excursion we dined with Sir William
Douglas of Kelhead, whose grandfather was a son
of the family of Queensberry. When he met us in
his stableyard, I took him for a grieve or barnman,
for he wore a blue bonnet over his thin grey hairs,
and a hodden-grey coat. But on a nearer view of
him, he appeared to be well-bred and sensible, and
was particularly kind to my father, who, I understood, had been his godson, having been born in the
neighbourhood on a farm his father rented from
Sir William. My father's mother, who was Jean
Jardine,* a daughter of the family of Applegarth, had
died a week after his birth in 1690. His father lived
till 1721.

---

* " By this lady he (Dr. Carlyle's father) was connected with
the family of Queensberry of which Sir William (Douglas) was a
branch. For the Jardines had twice married daughters of that
house. My father passed much of his youth at Jardine Hall, for
his mother dying when he was an infant, he resided there with an
aunt who kept house for Sir John Jardine."—Recollections.

In the evening we went to visit an old gentleman, a cousin of my father's, James Carlyle of Brakenwhate, who had been an officer in James II.'s time, and threw up his commission at the Revolution rather than take the oaths. He was a little fresh-looking old man of eighty-six, very lively in conversation, and particularly fond of my father. His house, which was not much better than a cottage, though there were two rooms above stairs as well as below, was full of guns and swords, and other warlike instruments. He had been so dissolute in his youth that his nickname in the country was Jamie Gaeloose. His wife, who appeared to be older than himself, though she was seven years younger, was of a very hospitable disposition. This small house being easily filled, I went to bed in the parlour while the company were at supper. But, tired as I was, it was long before I fell asleep ; for as my father had told me that I was to sleep with my cousin, I was in great fear that it would be the old woman. Weariness overcame my fear, however, and I did not awake till the tea-things were on the table, and did not know that it was the old gentleman who slept with me till my father afterwards told me, which relieved me from my anxious curiosity. After breakfast our old friend would needs give us a convoy, and mounted his horse, a grey stallion of about fourteen and a half hands high, as nimbly as if he had been only thirty. Not long after he separated from us, I took an opportunity of asking my father what had been the subject of a very earnest conversation he had had the evening before, when they were walking in the garden. He told me that his cousin had pressed him very much to accept of his estate, which he would dispose to him, as his only surviving daughter had distressed him by her marriage, and he had no liking to her children. My father had rejected his proposal, and taken much pains to convince the old gentleman of the injustice and cruelty of his procedure, which had made him loud and angry, and had drawn my curious attention. He died three years after, without a will, and the little estate was soon drowned in debt and absorbed into the great one, which made my father say afterwards that he believed he had been *righteous overmuch*.

This was the first opportunity I had of being well acquainted with my grandfather, Mr. Alexander Robison, who was a man very much respected for his good sense and steadiness, and moderation in church courts. He had been minister at Tinwald since the year 1697, and was a member of the commission which sat during the Union Parliament. He was truly a man of a sound head, and in the midst of very warm times was resorted to by his neighbours, both laity and clergy, for temperate and sound advice. He lived to the year 1761, and I passed several summers, and one winter entirely, at his house, when I was a student. He had a tolerably good collection of books, was a man of a liberal mind, and had more allowance to give to

people of different opinions, and more indulgence
to the levities of youth, than any man I ever knew
of such strict principles and conduct. His wife,
Jean Graham, connected with many of the principal
families in Galloway, and descended by her mother
from the Queensberry family (as my father was, at a
greater distance by his mother, of the Jardine Hall
family), gave the worthy people and their children
an air of greater consequence than their neighbours
of the same rank, and tended to make them deserve
the respect which was shown them. When I look
back on the fulness of very good living to their
numerous family, and to their cheerful hospitality
to strangers—when I recollect the decent education
they gave their children, and how happily the
daughters were settled in the world ; and recollect
that they had not £70 per annum besides the £500
which was my grandmother's portion, £100 of which
was remaining for the three eldest daughters as they
were married off in their turns, it appears quite surprising how it was possible for them to live as they did, and
keep their credit. What I have seen, both at their
house and my father's, on their slender incomes, sur-
passes all belief. But it was wonderful what moderation and a strict economy was able to do in those days.

In my infancy I had witnessed the greatest trial
they had ever gone through. Their eldest son, a
youth of eighteen, who had studied at Glasgow
College, but was to go to the Divinity Hall at
Edinburgh in winter 1724, to be near my father, then

removed to Prestonpans, went to Dumfries to bid farewell to his second sister, Mrs. Bell, and left the town in a clear frosty night in the beginning of December, but having missed the road about a mile from Dumfries, fell into a peat pot, as it is called, and was drowned. He was impatiently expected at night, and next morning. My brother and I had got some halfpence to give him to purchase some sugar-plums for us, so that we were not the least impatient of the family. What was our disappointment, when, about eleven o'clock, information came that he had been drowned and our comfits lost ! This I mention merely to note at what an early age interesting events make an impression on children's memories, for I was then only two years and ten months old, and to this day I remember it as well as any event of my life.*

Two years after this journey into my native

* [Here it may not be improper to relate an extraordinary incident to show how soon boys are capable of deep imposture. There was a boy at school in the same class with me whose name was Mathie. He was very intimate with me, and was between eleven and twelve years old, when all at once he produced more money than anybody, though his mother was an indigent widow of a shipmaster, and continued only to deal in hoops and stakes for the support of her family. This boy having at different times showed more money than I thought he had any right to have, I pressed him very close to tell me how he had got it. After many shifts, he at last told me that his grandfather had appeared to him in an evening, and disclosed a hidden treasure in the garret of his mother's house, between the floor and the ceiling. He pretended to show me the spot, but would never open it to me. He made several appointments with me, which I kept, to meet the old gentleman, but he never appeared. I tried every method to make him confess his imposture, but without effect. After some time, I heard that he had robbed his mother's drawers.]

country, which had the effect of attaching me very much to my grandfather and his family, and gave him a great ascendant over my mind, I was sent to the College of Edinburgh, which I entered on the 1st of November 1735.* I had the good-luck to be placed in a house in Edinburgh where there was very good company ; for John, afterwards Colonel Maxwell, and his brother Alexander, were boarded there, whose tutor, being an acquaintance of my father's, took some charge of me. John Wither-spoon, the celebrated doctor, was also in the house ; and Sir Harry Nisbet of Dean, and John Dalrymple, now Sir John of Cranstoun, not being able to afford tutors of their own, and being near relations of the Maxwells, came every afternoon to prepare their lessons under the care of our tutor.

The future life and public character of Dr. Wither-spoon are perfectly known. At the time I speak of he was a good scholar, far advanced for his age, very sensible and shrewd, but of a disagreeable temper, which was irritated by a flat voice and awkward man-ner, which prevented his making an impression on his companions of either sex that was at all adequate to his ability. This defect, when he was a lad, stuck to him when he grew up to manhood,† and so much

* [We had a very good master at Prestonpans, an Alexander Hannan, an old fellow-student of my father's, whom he brought there, and who implicitly followed his directions. He possessed excellent translations of the classics.]

† " His manner was inanimate and drawling ; but the depth of his judgment, the solidity of his arguments, and the aptitude with which they were illustrated and applied, never failed to produce

roused his envy and jealousy, and made him take a road to distinction very different from that of his more successful companions.

John Maxwell was remarkably tall and well made, and one of the handsomest youths of his time, but of such gentle manners and so soft a temper that nobody could then foresee that he was to prove one of the bravest officers in the allied army under Prince Ferdinand in the year 1759.

Sir Harry Nisbet was a very amiable youth, who took also to the army, was a distinguished officer and remarkably handsome, but fell at an early age in the battle of Val [?].

The character of Sir John Dalrymple, whom I shall have occasion to mention afterwards, is perfectly known ; it is sufficient to say here that the blossom promised better fruit.*

I was entered in Mr. Kerr's † class, who was at that time Professor of Humanity, and was very much master of his business. Like other schoolmasters, he was very partial to his scholars of rank, and having two lords at his class—viz., Lord Balgonie and Lord Dalziel—he took great pains to make them (especially the first, for the second was hardly osten-

a strong impression on the Assembly."—Somerville's *Memoirs of my Life and Times.*

 * The author of the *Memoirs of Great Britain and Ireland,* in which so much light is thrown on the history of the later Stewarts and the Revolution period.—J. H. B.

 † Mr. Kerr was Professor of Greek in King's College, Aberdeen, and was transferred to the Humanity Chair in Edinburgh University in 1734.   He died in 1741.

sible) appear among the best scholars, which would
not do, and only served to make him ridiculous, as
well as his young lord. The best by far at the class
were Colonel Robert Hepburn of Keith ; James
Edgar, Esq., afterwards a Commissioner of the
Customs ; * Alexander Tait, Esq., Clerk of Session ;
and Alexander Bertram, of the Nisbet family, who
died young. William Wilkie the poet and I came
next in order, and he (Mr. Kerr) used to allege long
after that we turned Latin into English better than
they did, though we could not so well turn English
into Latin ; which was probably owing to their being
taught better at the High School than we were in
the country. I mention those circumstances because
those gentlemen continued to keep the same rank in
society when they grew up that they held when they
were boys. I was sent next year to the first class of
mathematics, taught by Mr. M'Laurin,† which cost
me little trouble, as my father had carried me through
the first book of Euclid in the summer. In this
branch I gained an ascendant over our tutor, Pat.
Baillie, afterwards minister of Borrowstounness,
which he took care never to forget. He was a very
good Latin scholar, and so expert in the Greek that

* An account of " Commissioner Edgar " will be found in Kay's
Edinburgh Portraits.—J. H. B.

† Professor M'Laurin, the youngest son of the Rev. John
M'Laurin, minister of Glenderule, was born at Kilmodan in 1698.
Entering Glasgow University in his eleventh year, he took his M.A.
degree at the age of fifteen, was appointed Professor of Mathe-
matics in Aberdeen University at nineteen, and transferred to
Edinburgh in 1725.

he taught Professor Drummond's class for a whole winter when he was ill. But he had no mathematics, nor much science of any kind. One night, when I was conning my Latin lesson in the room with him and his pupils, he was going over a proposition of Euclid with John Maxwell, who had hitherto got no hold of the science. He blundered so excessively in doing this that I could not help laughing aloud. He was enraged at first, but, when calm, he bid me try if I could do it better. I went through the proposition so readily that he committed John to my care in that branch, which he was so good-natured as not to take amiss, though he was a year older than I was. At the end of a week he fell into the proper train of thinking, and needed assistance no longer. Mr. M'Laurin was at this time a favourite professor, and no wonder, as he was the clearest and most agreeable lecturer on that abstract science that ever I heard. He made mathematics a fashionable study, which was felt afterwards in the war that followed in 1743, when nine-tenths of the engineers of the army were Scottish officers. The Academy at Woolwich was not then established.

CHAPTER II

I was witness to a very extraordinary scene that
happened in the month of February or March 1736,
which was the escape of Robertson, a condemned
criminal, from the Tolbooth Church in Edinburgh.
In those days it was usual to bring the criminals
who were condemned to death into that church, to
attend public worship every Sunday after their con-
demnation, when the clergyman made some part of
his discourse and prayers to suit their situation; which,
among other circumstances of solemnity which then
attended the state of condemned criminals, had no
small effect on the public mind. Robertson and Wilson
were smugglers, and had been condemned for robbing
a custom-house, where some of their goods had been
deposited; a crime which at that time did not seem,
in the opinion of the common people, to deserve so
severe a punishment. I was carried by an acquaintance to church to see the prisoners on the Sunday
before the day of execution. We went early into the
church on purpose to see them come in, and were seated

in a pew before the gallery in front of the pulpit. Soon after we went into the church by the door from the Parliament Close, the criminals were brought in by the door next the Tolbooth, and placed in a long pew, not far from the pulpit. Four soldiers came in with them, and placed Robertson at the head of the pew, and Wilson below him, two of themselves sitting below Wilson, and two in a pew behind him.

The bells were ringing and the doors were open, while the people were coming into the church. Robertson watched his opportunity, and, suddenly springing up, got over the pew into the passage * that led in to the door in the Parliament Close, and no person offering to lay hands on him, made his escape in a moment—so much the more easily, perhaps, as everybody's attention was drawn to Wilson, who was a stronger man, and who, attempting to follow Robertson, was seized by the soldiers, and struggled so long with them that the two who at last followed Robertson were too late. It was reported that he had maintained his struggle that he might let his companion have time. That might be his second thought, but his first certainly was to escape himself, for I saw him set his foot on the seat to leap over, when the soldiers pulled him back. Wilson was immediately carried out to the Tolbooth, and Robertson, getting uninterrupted through the Parliament Square, down the back stairs, into the

* " Robertson, crossing the church, passed close by the head of the pew where I was."—*Recollections.*

Cowgate, was heard of no more till he arrived in
Holland. This was an interesting scene, and by filling
the public mind with compassion for the unhappy
person who did not escape, and who was the better
character of the two, had probably some influence in
producing what followed : for when the sentence
against Wilson came to be executed a few weeks thereafter, a very strong opinion prevailed that there was
a plot to force the Town Guard, whose duty it is to
attend executions under the order of a civil magistrate.

There was a Captain Porteous, who by his good
behaviour in the army had obtained a subaltern's
commission,* and had afterwards, when on half-pay,
been preferred to the command of the City Guard.
This man, by his skill in manly exercises, particularly
the golf, and by gentlemanly behaviour, was admitted
into the company of his superiors, which elated his
mind, and added insolence to his native roughness, so
that he was much hated and feared by the mob of
Edinburgh. When the day of execution came, the
rumour of a deforcement at the gallows prevailed
strongly ; and the Provost and Magistrates (not in
their own minds very strong) thought it a good
measure to apply for three or four companies of a
marching regiment that lay in the Canongate, to be
drawn up in the Lawnmarket, a street leading from
the Tolbooth to the Grassmarket, the place of exe-

* " He was a common soldier in Queen Anne's wars, but had got
a commission for his courage."—*Recollections.*

cution, in order to overawe the mob by their being at hand. Porteous, who, it is said, had his natural courage increased to rage by any suspicion that he and his Guard could not execute the law, and being heated likewise with wine—for he had dined, as the custom then was, between one and two—became perfectly furious when he passed by the three companies drawn up in the street as he marched along with his prisoner.*

Mr. Baillie had taken windows in a house on the north side of the Grassmarket, for his pupils and me, in the second floor, about seventy or eighty yards westward of the place of execution, where we went in due time to see the show ; to which I had no small aversion, having seen one at Dumfries, the execution of Jock Johnstone, which shocked me very much.† When we arrived at the house, some people who were looking from the windows were displaced, and went to a window in the common stair, about two feet below the level of ours. The street is long and wide, and there was a very great crowd assembled. The execution went on with the usual forms, and Wilson behaved in a manner very becoming his situation. There was not the least appearance of an attempt to rescue ; but soon after the executioner had done his duty, there was an attack made upon him, as usual on such occasions, by the boys and

* " He was heard to growl as he passed down the Bow [West Bow] : ' What ! was not he and his Guard fit to hang a rascal without help ! ' "—*Recollections.*

† See above, p. 25, note.

blackguards throwing stones and dirt in testimony of their abhorrence of the hangman. But there was no attempt to break through the guard and cut down the prisoner. It was generally said that there was very little, if any, more violence than had usually happened on such occasions. Porteous, however, inflamed with wine and jealousy, thought proper to order his Guard to fire, their muskets being loaded with slugs; and when the soldiers showed reluctance, I saw him turn to them with threatening gesture and an inflamed countenance. They obeyed, and fired; but wishing to do as little harm as possible, many of them elevated their pieces, the effect of which was that some people were wounded in the windows; and one unfortunate lad, whom we had displaced, was killed in the stair window by a slug entering his head. His name was Henry Black,* a journeyman tailor, whose bride was the daughter of the house we were in. She fainted away when he was brought into the house speechless, where he only lived till nine or ten o'clock. We had seen many people, women and men, fall on the street, and at first thought it was only through fear, and by their crowding on one another to escape. But when the crowd

* " Henry, being of a jocular humour, had been laughing at the people who fell in the street, which he imagined was only through fear. On the second fire his jokes were laid at once, when his companions jogging him perceived his head was bleeding."— *Recollections*.

In the *Caledonian Mercury* appears the name of Henry Graham, tailor in the Canongate, shot through the head while looking out at a window.

dispersed, we saw them lying dead or wounded, and had no longer any doubt of what had happened. The numbers were said to be eight or nine killed, and double the number wounded ; but this was never exactly known.

This unprovoked slaughter irritated the common people to the last ; and the state of grief and rage into which their minds were thrown, was visible in the high commotion that appeared in the multitude. Our tutor was very anxious to have us all safe in our lodgings, but durst not venture out to see if it was practicable to go home. I offered to go ; went, and soon returned, offering to conduct them safe to our lodgings, which were only half-way down the Lawnmarket, by what was called the Castle Wynd, which was just at hand, to the westward. There we remained safely, and were not allowed to stir out any more that night till about nine o'clock, when, the streets having long been quiet, we all grew anxious to learn the fate of Henry Black, and I was allowed to go back to the house. I took the younger Maxwell with me, and found that he had expired an hour before we arrived. A single slug had penetrated the side of his head an inch above the ear. The sequel of this affair was, that Porteous was tried and condemned to be hanged; but by the intercession of some of the Judges themselves, who thought his case hard, he was reprieved by the Queen-Regent.* The

* " Having been a golfing companion of President Forbes, Lord Drummore, and other persons of rank and consequence, application was made for a respite to Queen Caroline, then Regent."— *Recollections.*

Magistrates, who on this occasion, as on the former, acted weakly, designed to have removed him to the Castle for greater security. But a plot was laid and conducted by some persons unknown with the greatest secrecy, policy, and vigour, to prevent that design, by forcing the prison the night before, and executing the sentence upon him themselves, which to effectuate cost them from eight at night till two in the morning ; and yet this plot was managed so dexterously that they met with no interruption, though there were five companies of a marching regiment lying in the Canongate.

This happened on the 7th of September 1736 ; and so prepossessed were the minds of every person that something extraordinary would take place that day, that I, at Prestonpans, nine miles from Edinburgh, dreamt that I saw Captain Porteous hanged in the Grassmarket. I got up betwixt six and seven, and went to my father's servant, who was thrashing in the barn which lay on the roadside leading to Aberlady and North Berwick, who said that several men on horseback had passed about five in the morning, whom having asked for news, they replied there was none, but that Captain Porteous had been dragged out of prison, and hanged on a dyer's tree at two o'clock that morning.

This bold and lawless deed not only provoked the Queen, who was Regent at the time, but gave some uneasiness to Government. It was represented as a dangerous plot, and was ignorantly connected with a great meeting of zealous Covenanters, of whom many still remained in Galloway and the west, which had been held in summer, in Pentland Hills, to renew the Covenant.   But this was a mistake ; for the murder of Porteous had been planned and executed by a few of the relations or friends of those whom he had slain ; who, being of a rank superior to mere mob, had carried on their design with so much secrecy, ability, and steadiness as made it be ascribed to a still higher order, who were political enemies to Government. This idea provoked Lord Isla,* who then managed the affairs of Scotland under Sir Robert Walpole, to carry through an Act of Parliament in next session for the discovery of the murderers of Captain Porteous, to be published by reading it for twelve months, every Sunday forenoon, in all the churches in Scotland, immediately after divine service, or rather in the middle of it, for the minister was ordained to read it between the lecture and the sermon, two discourses usually given at that time.   This clause, it was said, was intended to purge the Church of fanatics, for as it was believed that most clergymen of that description would not read the Act, they would become liable to the penalty, which was deposition.   By good-luck for the clergy, there was another party distinction among them (besides that occasioned by their ecclesiastical differences), viz., that of Argathelian and Squadrone, of which political divisions there were some both of

* Lord Islay was Archibald, brother of John, fourth Duke of Argyle, and succeeded him in the Dukedom in 1743.

the high-flying and moderate clergy.* Some very
sensible men of the latter class having discovered
the design of the Act, either by information or
sagacity, convened meetings of clergy at Edinburgh,
and formed resolutions, and carried on correspondence through the Church to persuade as many as
possible to disobey the Act, that the great number
of offenders might secure the safety of the whole.
This was actually the case, for as one-half of the
clergy, at least, disobeyed in one shape or other, the
idea of inflicting the penalty was dropped altogether.
In the mean time, the distress and perplexity which
this Act occasioned in many families of the clergy,
was of itself a cruel punishment for a crime in which
they had no hand. The anxious days and sleepless
nights which it occasioned to such ministers as had
families, and at the same time scruples about the lawfulness of reading the Act, were such as no one could
imagine who had not witnessed the scene.

The part my grandfather took was manly and
decided ; for, not thinking the reading of the Act
unlawful, he pointedly obeyed. My father was very

* The term " Argathelian " is new to the Editor, but the
meaning is obvious. " Argathelia " is the Latin name of the
province of Argyle, and the word doubtless applied to those who
favoured that unlimited influence in the affairs of Scotland exercised by the family of Argyle before the ascendancy of Lord
Bute. The name of "Squadrone" had been long used to
designate a public party professing entire independence. The
"ecclesiastical differences" concentrated themselves in a dispute,
of memorable importance to the Church of Scotland, called " The
Marrow Controversy," from one party standing by, and the other
impugning, Fisher's *Marrow of Modern Divinity*.—J. H. B.

scrupulous, being influenced by Mr. Erskine of Grange, and other enemies of Sir Robert Walpole. On the other hand, the good sense of his wife, and the consideration of eight or nine children whom he then had, and who were in danger of being turned out on the world, pulled him very hard on the side of obedience. A letter from my grandfather at last settled his mind, and he read the Act.

What seemed extraordinary, after all the anxiety of Government, and the violent means they took to make a discovery, not one of those murderers was ever found. Twenty years afterwards, two or three persons returned from different parts of the world, who were supposed to be of the number ; but, so far as I heard, they never disclosed themselves.*

In my second year at the College, November 1736, besides attending M'Laurin's class for mathematics, and Kerr's private class, in which he read Juvenal, Tacitus, etc., and opened up the beauties and peculiarities of the Latin tongue, I went to the Logic class, taught by Mr. John Stevenson, who, though he had no pretensions to superiority in point of learning and genius, yet was the most popular of all the Professors on account of his civility and even kindness to his students, and at the same time the most useful ; for

---

* Charles Kirkpatrick Sharpe has a characteristic bit of gossip to relate regarding the Porteous mob: " People of high rank were concerned in the affair. My great-grandfather, Lord Alva, told my grandfather that many of the mob were persons of rank—some of them disguised as women. Lord Haddington for one, in his cook-maid's dress."—Wilson's *Reminiscences of Old Edinburgh.*

being a man of sense and industry, he had made a judicious selection from the French and English critics, which he gave at the morning hour of eight, when he read with us Aristotle's *Poetics* and Longinus *On the Sublime*. At eleven he read Heineccius' *Logic*, and an abridgement of Locke's *Essay* ; and in the afternoon at two—for such were the hours of attendance in those times—he read to us a compendious history of the ancient philosophers, and an account of their tenets. On all these branches we were carefully examined at least three times a-week. Whether or not it was owing to the time of life at which we entered this class, being all about fifteen years of age or upwards, when the mind begins to open, or to the excellence of the lectures and the nature of some of the subjects, we could not then say, but all of us received the same impression—viz., that our minds were more enlarged, and that we received greater benefit from that class than from any other.* With a due regard to the merit of the Professor, I must ascribe this impression chiefly to the natural effect which the subject of criticism and of rational logic has upon the opening mind. Having learned Greek pretty well at school, my father thought fit to make me pass that class, especially as it was

* " The truth is, that it is universally known in this part of the country, that no man ever held a Professor's chair in the University of Edinburgh who had the honour of training up so many young men to a love of letters, and who afterwards made so distinguished a figure in the literary world as Dr. Stevenson. He died in 1775, and bequeathed his library to the University."—Bower's *History of Edinburgh University*.

taught at that time by an old sickly man, who could seldom attend, and employed substitutes.

This separated me from some of my companions, and brought me acquainted with new ones. Sundry of my class-fellows remained another year with Kerr, and Sir Gilbert Elliot, John Home, and many others, went back to him that year. It was this year that I attended the French master, one Kerr, who, for leave given him to teach in a College room, taught his scholars the whole session for a guinea, which was then all that the regents could demand for a session of the College, from the 1st of November to the 1st of June. During that course we were made sufficiently masters of French to be able to read any book. To improve our pronunciation, he made us get one of Molière's plays by heart, which we were to have acted, but never did. It was the *Medecin malgré lui*, in which I had the part of Sganarelle.

Besides the young gentlemen who had resided with us in the former year, there came into the lodging below two Irish students of medicine, whose names were Conway and Lesly, who were perfectly well-bred and agreeable, and with whom, though a year or two older, I was very intimate. They were among the first Irish students whom the fame of the first Monro * and the other medical Professors had brought over ; and they were not disappointed. They were sober

* Dr. Monro was appointed Professor of Anatomy in 1720. In the year referred to by Dr. Carlyle his pupils numbered 131, the largest attendance since his appointment.

and studious, as well as well-bred, and had none of
that restless and turbulent disposition, dignified with
the name of spirit and fire, which has often since made
the youth of that country such troublesome members
of society.   Mr. Lesly was a clergyman's son, of Scottish extraction, and was acknowledged as a distant
relation by some of the Eglintoun family.   Conway's
relations were all beyond the Channel.   I was so
much their favourite both this year and the following,
when they returned, and lived so much with them,
that they had very nearly persuaded me to be of
their profession.   At this time the medical school of
Edinburgh was but rising into fame.   There were not
so many as twenty English and Irish students this
year in the College.   The Professors were men of
eminence.   Besides Monro, Professor of Anatomy,
there were Dr. Sinclair,*

I was in use of going to my father's on Saturdays
once a-fortnight, and returning on Monday ; but this
little journey was less frequently performed this winter, as Sir Harry Nisbet's mother, Lady Nisbet, a
sister of Sir Robert Morton's, very frequently invited
me to accompany her son and the Maxwells to the
house of Dean, within a mile of Edinburgh, where we
passed the day in hunting with the greyhounds, and
generally returned to town in the evening.   Here I
had an opportunity of seeing a new set of company
(my circle having been very limited in Edinburgh),
whose manners were more worthy of imitation, and

* *Sic.*   He seems to have intended to add other names.—J.H.B.

whose conversation had more the tone of the world. Here I frequently met with Mr. Baron Dalrymple,* the youngest brother of the then Earl of Stair, and grandfather of the present Earl. He was held to be a man of wit and humour ; and, in the language and manners of the gentlemen of Scotland before the Union, exhibited a specimen of conversation that was so free as to border a little on licentiousness, especially before the ladies ; but he never failed to keep the table in a roar.

Having passed the Greek class, I missed many of my most intimate companions, who either remained one year longer at the Latin class, or attended the Greek. But I made new ones, who were very agreeable, such as Sir Alexander Cockburn of Langton, who had been bred in England till now, and John Gibson, the son of Sir Alexander Gibson of Addison, both of whom perished in the war that was approaching.†

In summer 1737 I was at Prestonpans ; and in July, two or three days before my youngest sister Jenny was born, afterwards Mrs. Bell, I met with an accident which confined me many weeks, which was a shot in my leg, occasioned by the virole of a ramrod having fallen into a musket at a review in Musselburgh Links, part of which lodged in the outside of

* George Dalrymple of Dalmahoy, who married Euphame, eldest daughter of Sir Andrew Myrton, Bart., of Gogar. He died in 1745.

† "Gibson at the siege of Carthagena and Cockburn at the battle of Fontenoy. Jenny Stewart, the beauty, afterwards Lady Dundonald, was engaged to Gibson, but his father forbade and sent him abroad."—*Recollections.*

the calf of my leg, and could not be extracted till after the place had been twice laid open, when it came out with a dressing, and was about the size of the head of a nail. This was the reason why I made no excursion to Dumfriesshire this summer.

Early in the summer I lost one of the dearest friends I ever had, who died of a fever. We had often settled it between us, that whoever should die first, should appear to the other, and tell him the secrets of the invisible world. I walked every evening for hours in the fields and links of Prestonpans, in hopes of meeting my friend ; but he never appeared. This disappointment, together with the knowledge I had acquired at the Logic class, cured me of many prejudices about ghosts and hobgoblins and witches, of which till that time I stood not a little in awe.

The next session of the College, beginning in November 1737, I lodged in the same house and had the same companions as I had the two preceding years. Besides Sir Robert Stewart's Natural Philosophy class, which was very ill taught, as he was worn out with age, and never had excelled,* I attended M'Laurin's second class, and Dr. Pringle's Moral Philosophy, besides two hours at the writing-master to improve my hand, and a second attendance on Mr. Kerr's private class. The circle of my acquaintance was but little enlarged, and I derived more agreeable amusement from the two Irish students, who returned to

* He became a regent in 1703. His father was Sir Thomas Stewart of Coltness.

their former habitation, than from any other acquaintance, except the Maxwells and their friends. My acquaintance with Dr. Robertson * began about this time. I never was at the same class with him, for, though but a few months older, he was at College one session before me. One of the years, too, he was seized with a fever, which was dangerous, and confined him for the greater part of the winter. I went to see him sometimes when he was recovering, when in his conversation one could perceive the opening dawn of that day which afterwards shone so bright. I became also acquainted with John Home † this year, though he was one year behind me at College, and eight months younger. He was gay and talkative, and a great favourite with his companions.

I was very fond of dancing, in which I was a great proficient, having been taught at two different periods in the country, though the manners were then so strict that I was not allowed to exercise my talent at penny-weddings, or any balls but those of the dancing-school. Even this would have been denied me, as it was to Robertson and Witherspoon, and other clergymen's sons, at that time, had it not been for the persuasion of those aunts of mine who had been bred in England, and for some papers in the *Spectator* which were pointed out to my father, which seemed to convince him that dancing would make me a more accomplished preacher, if ever I

* Afterwards Principal of Edinburgh University.
† Author of *Douglas* and other plays.

had the honour to mount the pulpit. My mother too, who generally was right, used her sway in this article of education. But I had not the means of using this talent, of which I was not a little vain, till luckily I was introduced to Madame Violante, an Italian stage-dancer, who kept a much-frequented school for young ladies, but admitted of no boys above seven or eight years of age, so that she wished very much for senior lads to dance with her grown-up misses weekly at her practisings. I became a favourite of this dancing-mistress, and attended her very faithfully with two or three of my companions, and had my choice of partners on all occasions, insomuch that I became a great proficient in this branch at little or no expense.* It must be confessed, however, that, having nothing to do at Stewart's class, through the incapacity of the master, and M'Laurin's giving me no trouble, as I had a great promptitude in learning mathematics, I had a good deal of spare time this session, which I spent, as well as all the money I got, at a billiard-table, which unluckily was within fifty yards of the College. I was so sensible of the folly of this, however, that next year I abandoned it altogether.

Dr. Pringle, afterwards Sir John, was an agree-

* " The partner I had for most part was Miss Jenny Watson. She was a beautiful girl, who afterwards married Alexander Rocheid, the brother of Sir David Kinloch. Jenny was a fine dancer, and I was envied; but I would have rather had one of the three or four Miss Cants. . . . Dame Janet was haughty and reserved, and all the rest turned away from her."—*Recollections.*

able lecturer, though no great master of the science he taught.* His lectures were chiefly a compilation from Lord Bacon's works; and had it not been for Puffendorf's small book, which he made his text, we should not have been instructed in the rudiments of the science. Once a-week, however, he gave us a lecture in Latin, in which language he excelled, and was even held equal to Dr. John Sinclair, Professor of the Theory of Medicine, the most eminent Latin scholar at that time, except the great grammarian Ruddiman. The celebrated Dr. Hutchison of Glasgow, who was the first that distinguished himself in that important branch of literature, was now beginning his career, and had drawn ample stores from the ancients, which he improved into system, and embellished by the exertions of an ardent and virtuous mind. He was soon followed by Smith, who had been his scholar, and sat for some years in his chair; by Ferguson at Edinburgh; by Reid and Beattie, which last was more an orator than a philosopher; together with David Hume, whose works, though dangerous and heretical, illustrated the science, and called forth the exertions of men of equal genius and sounder principles.

I passed the greater part of this summer (1738) at my grandfather's, at Tinwald, near Dumfries,

* The youngest son of Sir John Pringle of Stitchell, where he was born in 1707. He practised as a physician in Edinburgh, while he held the chair of Moral Philosophy, which he clearly considered a secondary subject. He afterwards became well known in scientific circles in London, and was President of the Royal Society.

who had a tolerably good collection of books, and where I read for many hours in the day. I contracted the greatest respect for my grandfather, and attachment to his family ; and became well acquainted with the young people of Dumfries, and afterwards held a correspondence by letters with one of them, which was of use in forming my epistolary style.

A new family came this year to Prestonpans ; for Colin Campbell, Esq., the brother of Sir James of Arbruchal [Aberuchill], had fallen in arrears as Collector of the Customs, and was suspended. But his wife dying at that very time, an excellent woman of the family of Sir James Holburn, and leaving him eight or nine children, his situation drew compassion from his friends, especially from Archibald, Earl of Isla, and James Campbell of St. Germains, who were his securities, and who had no chance of being reimbursed the sum of £800 or £1000 of arrears into which he had fallen, but by his preferment. He was soon made a Commissioner of the Board of Customs, an office at that time of £1000 per annum. This deprived us of a very agreeable family, the sons and daughters of which were my companions. Mr. Campbell was succeeded by Mr. George Cheap,* of the Cheaps of Rossie in Fife, whose wife, an aunt of the Lord Chancellor Wedderburn, had just died and left a family of eight children, two of them beautiful girls of sixteen or

* "On the death of Mr. George Cheap, Mr. Colin Campbell's youngest son, Archibald, who had been a lieutenant in the 42nd Regiment, was appointed Collector at Prestonpans."—*Recollections.*

eighteen, and six sons, the eldest of whom was a year older than I, but was an apprentice to a Writer to the Signet in Edinburgh. This family, though less sociable than the former, soon became intimate with ours; and one of them very early made an impression on me, which had lasting effects.*

In November 1738 I again attended the College of Edinburgh; and, besides a second year of the Moral Philosophy, I was a third year at M'Laurin's class, who, on account of the advanced age and incapacity of Sir Robert Stewart, not only taught Astronomy, but gave us a course of experiments in Mechanics, with many excellent lectures in Natural Philosophy, which fully compensated the defects of the other class. About this time the choice of a profession became absolutely necessary. I had thoughts of the army and the law, but was persuaded to desist from any views on them by my father's being unable to carry on my education for the length of time necessary in the one, or to support me till he could procure a commission for me, as he had no money to purchase; and by means of the long peace, the establishment of the army was low. Both these having failed, by the persuasion of Lesly and Conway, my Irish friends, I thought of surgery, and had prevailed so far that my father went to Edinburgh in

* " The girls were both as handsome as possible, especially the younger, who was born for my perdition, for from the moment I saw her, I loved her with a constancy of adoration which was not surpassed by that of Petrarch for his Laura."—*Recollections.*

the autumn to look out for a master in that profession.*

In the mean time came a letter from my grandfather, in favour of his own profession and that of
my father, written with so much force and energy,
and stating so many reasons for my yielding to the
wish of my friends and the conveniency of a family
still consisting of eight children, of whom I was the
eldest, that I yielded to the influence of parental
wishes and advice, which in those days swayed the
minds of young men much more than they do now,
or have done for many years past. I therefore consented that my name should this year be enrolled in
the list of students of divinity, though regular attendance was not enjoined.

On the 13th of January 1739, there was a total
eclipse of the moon, to view which M'Laurin invited
his senior scholars, of whom I was one. About a
dozen of us remained till near one o'clock on the

* "I drew up with them [Leslie and Conway], and they had
almost induced me to be a doctor, had not the dissection of a
child, which they bought of a poor tailor for 6s., disgusted me
completely. The man had asked 6s. 6d., but they beat him down
the 6d. by asserting that the bargain was to him worth more
than 12s., as it saved him all the expense of burial. The hearing
of this bargain, together with that of the dialogue in which they
carried it on, were not less grating to my feelings than the dissection itself. Before that I had been captivated by the sight
of a handsome cornet of the Greys, and would needs be a soldier ;
but my father having no money to purchase a commission for
me, and not being able, he said, to spare as much money per
day as would make me live like a gentleman, although Colonel
Gardiner said he would recommend me for a cadet in a very good
regiment, I desisted from this also."—*Recollections*.

Sunday morning, when the greatest tempest arose
that I remember. Eight or ten of us were so much
alarmed with the fall of bricks or slates in the
College Wynd, that we called a council of war in a
stair-foot, and got to the High Street safe by walking
in file down the Cowgate and up Niddry's Wynd.

I passed most of the summer this year in Dumfriesshire, where my grandfather kept me pretty
close to my studies, though I frequently walked in
the afternoons to Dumfries, and brought him the
newspapers from Provost Bell, his son-in-law, who
had by that time acquired the chief sway in the
burgh, having taken the side of the Duke of Queensberry, in opposition to Charles Erskine of Tinwald,
at that time the Solicitor. George Bell was not a
man of ability, but he was successful in trade, was
popular in his manners, and, having a gentlemanly
spirit, was a favourite with the nobility and gentry
in the neighbourhood. He had a constant correspondence with the Duke of Queensberry, and retained his friendship till his death in 1757. What
Bell wanted in capacity or judgment was fully compensated by his wife, Margaret Robison, the second
of my mother's sisters, and afterwards still more by
my sister Margaret, whom they reared, as they had
no children, and who, when she grew up, added beauty
and address to a very uncommon understanding.
During the period when I so much frequented
Dumfries, there was a very agreeable society in that
town. They were not numerous, but the few were

better informed, and more agreeable in society, than any to be met with in so small a town.

I returned home before winter, but did not attend the College, though I was enrolled a student of divinity. But my father had promised to Lord Drummore, his great friend, that I should pass most of my time with his eldest son, Mr. Hew H. Dalrymple, who, not liking to live in Edinburgh, was to pass the winter in the house of Walliford, adjacent to his estate of Drummore, where he had only a farmhouse at that time, with two rooms on a ground-floor, which would have ill agreed with Mr. Hew's health, which was threatened with symptoms of consumption, the disease of which he died five or six years afterwards, having been married, but leaving no issue.

Mr. Hew H. Dalrymple had been intended for the Church of England, and with that view had been educated at Oxford, and was an accomplished scholar ; but his elder brother John having died at Naples, he fell heir to his mother's estate. He was five or six years older than I, and being frank and communicative, I received much benefit from his conversation, which was instructive, and his manners, which were elegant. With this gentleman I lived all winter, returning generally to my father's house on Saturdays, when Lord Drummore returned from Edinburgh, and went back again on Monday, when I resumed my station. We passed great part of the day in November and December planting trees round the enclosures at Drummore, which, by their appearance at present,

prove that they were not well chosen, for they are very
small of their age; but they were too old when they
were planted.   After the frost set in about Christmas,
we passed our days very much in following the greyhounds on foot or on horseback, and though our evenings were generally solitary, between reading and
talking we never tired.   Mr. Hew's manners were as
gentle as his mind was enlightened.   We had little
intercourse with the neighbours, except with my
father's family, with Mr. Cheap's (the Collector), where
there were two beautiful girls, and with Mr. Keith,
afterwards ambassador, whose wife's sister was the
widow of Sir Robert Dalrymple, brother of Lord
Drummore.   They were twins, and so like each other,
that even when I saw them first, when they were at
least thirty, it was hardly possible to distinguish
them.   In their youth, their lovers, I have heard
them say, always mistook them when a sign or watch-
word had not been agreed on.   Mr. Keith was a very
agreeable man, had much knowledge of modern history
and genealogy, and, being a pleasing talker, made an
agreeable companion.   Of him and his intimate friend,
Mr. Hepburn of Keith, it was said that the witty
Lady Dick (Lord Royston's daughter) said that Mr.
Keith told her nothing but what she knew before,
though in a very agreeable manner, but that Hepburn
never said anything that was not new to her,—thus
marking the difference between genius and ability.
Keith was a minion of the great Mareschal Stair, and
went abroad with him in 1743, when he got the com-

mand of the army.   But I observed that Lord Stair's
partiality to Keith made him no great favourite of
the Dalrymples.   Colonel Gardiner had been another
minion of Lord Stair, but being illiterate, and considered as a fanatic, the gentlemen I mention had no
intimacy with him, though they admitted that he was
a very honest and well-meaning brave man.

My father had sometimes expressed a wish that I
should allow myself to be recommended to take
charge of a pupil, as that was the most likely way to
obtain a church in Scotland ; but he did not press
me on this subject, for as he had been four years in
that station himself, though he was very fortunate
in his pupils, he felt how degrading it was.   By that
time I had been acquainted with a few preceptors,
had observed how they were treated, and had contracted an abhorrence of the employment—insomuch
that, when I consented to follow out the clerical profession, it was on condition I should never be urged to
go into a family, as it was called, engaging at the same
time to make my expenses as moderate as possible.

This was the winter of the hard frost which commenced in the end of December 1739, and lasted for
three months.   As there were no canals or rivers of
extent enough in this part of the country to encourage
the fine exercise of skating, we contented ourselves
with the winter diversion of curling, which is peculiar
to Scotland, and became tolerable proficients in that
manly exercise.   It is the more interesting, as it is
usual for the young men of adjacent parishes to con-

tend against each other for a whole winter's day, and
at the end of it to dine together with much jollity.

I passed the summer of this year, as usual, in the
neighbourhood of Dumfries, and kept up my connection with the young people of that town as I had
done formerly. I returned home in the autumn, and
passed some part of the winter in Edinburgh, attending the divinity class, which had no attractions, as the
Professor,* though said to be learned, was dull and
tedious in his lectures, insomuch that at the end of seven
years he had only lectured half through Pictet's *Com-
pend of Theology*. I became acquainted, however, with
several students, with whom I had not been intimate,
such as Dr. Hugh Blair, and the Bannatines, and Dr.
Jardine, all my seniors ; Dr. John Blair, afterwards
Prebendary of Westminster ; John Home, William
Robertson, George Logan, William Wilkie, etc.
There was one advantage attending the lectures of a
dull professor—viz., that he could form no school, and
the students were left entirely to themselves, and
naturally formed opinions far more liberal than those
they got from the Professor. This was the answer I
gave to Patrick, Lord Elibank, one of the most learned
and ingenious noblemen of his time, when he asked
me one day, many years afterwards, what could be

* Dr. Goldie, minister of Edinburgh, and in 1754 elected
Principal of Edinburgh University. It was during his Moderator-
ship of the General Assembly, and on his casting vote to "proceed"
to inflict the higher censure, that Ebenezer Erskine and other
ministers were deposed and formed the body of dissenters known
as " Seceders."

the reason that the young clergymen of that period
so far surpassed their predecessors of his early days in
useful accomplishments and liberality of mind—viz.,
that the Professor of Theology was dull, and Dutch,
and prolix. His lordship said he perfectly understood
me, and that this entirely accounted for the change.

In summer 1741 I remained for the most part at
home, and it was about that time that my old schoolmaster, Mr. Hannan, having died of fever, and Mr.
John Halket having come in his place, I was witness
to a scene that made a strong impression upon me.
This   Mr. Halket had been tutor to Lord Lovat's
eldest son Simon, afterwards well known as General
Fraser. Halket had remained for two years with
Lovat, and knew all his ways. But he had parted
with him on his coming to Edinburgh for the education of that son, to whom he gave a tutor of a superior
order, Mr. Hugh Blair, afterwards the celebrated
Doctor.* But he still retained so much regard for
Halket that he thought proper to fix his second son,
Alexander Fraser, with him at the school of Prestonpans, believing that he was a much more proper hand

* Lord Lovat was connected with Dr. Patrick Cumming of
St. Giles, and before fixing on Dr. Blair as his son's tutor, had
hoped to place him with Dr. Cumming. Writing in 1739, Lord
Lovat says: "All this makes me resolve positively to have my
son educated after my own manner ; that is a true Scotsman
and a Highlander. . . . And if I could prevail with you as my
relative to accept of him, that I would settle him with you ; and,
if you refused to receive him, I would endeavour to settle him
with Mr. Kerr, Professor of Humanity, who is my friend."—Burton's *Life of Lovat*.

for training an untutored savage than the mild and elegant Dr. Blair. It was in the course of this summer that Lovat brought his son Alexander to be placed with Halket, from whom, understanding that I was a young scholar living in the town who might be useful to his son, he ordered Halket to invite me to dine with him and his company at Lucky Vint's, a celebrated village tavern in the west end of the town.

His company consisted of Mr. Erskine of Grange, with three or four gentlemen of the name of Fraser, one of whom was his man of business, together with Halket, his son Alexander, and myself. The two old gentlemen disputed for some time which of them should say grace. At last Lovat yielded, and gave us two or three pious sentences in French, which Mr. Erskine and I understood, and we only. As soon as we were set, Lovat asked me to send him a whiting from the dish of fish that was next me. As they were all haddocks, I answered that they were not whitings, but, according to the proverb, he that got a haddock for a whiting was not ill off. This saying takes its rise from the superiority of haddocks to whitings in the Firth of Forth. Upon this his lordship stormed and swore more than fifty dragoons ; he was sure they must be whitings, as he had bespoke them. Halket tipped me the wink, and I retracted, saying that I had but little skill, and as his lordship had bespoke them, I must certainly be mistaken. Upon this he calmed, and I sent him one, which he was quite pleased with, swearing again that he

5

never could eat a haddock all his life. The landlady told me afterwards that as he had been very peremptory against haddocks, and she had no other, she had made her cook carefully scrape out St. Peter's mark on the shoulders, which she had often done before with success. We had a very good plain dinner. As the claret was excellent, and circulated fast, the two old gentlemen grew very merry, and their conversation became youthful and gay. What I observed was, that Grange, without appearing to flatter, was very observant of Lovat, and did everything to please him. He had provided Geordy Sym, who was Lord Drummore's piper, to entertain Lovat after dinner ; but though he was reckoned the best piper in the country, Lovat despised him, and said he was only fit to play reels to Grange's oyster-women. He grew frisky at last, however, and upon Kate Vint, the landlady's daughter, coming into the room, he insisted on her staying to dance with him. She was a handsome girl, with fine black eyes and an agreeable person ; and though without the advantages of dress or manners, she, by means of her good sense and a bashful air, was very alluring. She was a mistress of Lord Drummore, who lived in the neighbourhood ; and though her mother would not part with her, as she drew much company to the house, she was said to be faithful to him ; except only in the case of Captain Merry, who married her, and soon after went abroad with his regiment. When he died she enjoyed the pension. She had two sons by Drummore and one by Merry. One of the first was a pretty lad and a good officer, for he was a master and commander before he died. Lovat was at this time seventy-five, and Grange not much younger ; yet the wine and the young woman emboldened them to dance a reel, till Kate, observing Lovat's legs as thick as posts, fell a-laughing, and ran off. She missed her second course of kisses, as was then the fashion of the country, though she had endured the first. This was a scene not easily forgotten.

Lovat was tall and stately, and might have been handsome in his youth, with a very flat nose. His manner was not disagreeable, though his address consisted chiefly in gross flattery and in the due application of money. He did not make on me the impression of a man of a leading mind. His suppleness and profligacy were apparent. The convivium was not over, though the evening approached. He conveyed his son to the house where he was to be boarded, for Halket had not taken up house ; and there, while we drank tea, he won the heart of the landlady, a decent widow of a shipmaster, and of her niece, by fair speeches, intermixed with kisses to the niece, who was about thirty, and such advices as a man in a state of ebriety could give. The coach was in waiting, but Grange would not yet part with him, and insisted on his accepting of a banquet from him at his house in Preston. Lovat was in a yielding humour, and it was agreed to. The Frasers, who were on horseback, were sent to Edinburgh, the boy was left with his dame, and Lovat and Grange, and Halket and I, went up to Preston, only a quarter of a mile distant, and were received in Grange's library, a cube of twenty feet, in a pavilion of the house which extended into a small wilderness of not more than half an acre, which was sacred to Grange's private walks, and to which there was no entry but through the pavilion. This wilderness was said to be his place of retreat from his lady when she was in her fits of termagancy, which were not unfrequent, and were said by his minions to be devoted to meditation and prayer. But as there was a secret door to the fields, it was reported that he had occasionally admitted fair maidens to solace him for his sufferings from the clamour of his wife. This room had been well stored with books from top to bottom, but at this time was much thinned, there remaining only a large collection of books on dæmonologia, which was Grange's particular study. In this room there was a fine collection of fruit and biscuits, and a new deluge of excellent claret. At ten o'clock the two old gentlemen mounted their coach to Edinburgh, and thus closed a very memorable day.*

* " In 1748, Lord Grange was so much reduced in London that he accepted of two guineas from Robert Keith, then living with Marshall Lord Stair. By my lord's application, he got a pension of £200. On his wife's death he married his old mistress, Fanny Lindsay, and brought her down to Preston, when he still had the house and about 50 acres of land. Lord Prestongrange's lady and my mother were the only two ladies who visited her, having been wheedled into it by the old gentleman, who to his other talents added a very irresistible species of flattery. Fanny took pet on not being visited, and made him return to London

In the following winter—viz., November 1741—I attended the Divinity Hall at Edinburgh again for three or four months, and delivered a discourse, *De Fide Salvifica*, a very improper subject for so young a student, which attracted no attention from any one but the Professor, who was pleased with it, as it resembled his own Dutch Latin.

The summer 1742 I passed at home, making only a few excursions into East Lothian, where I had sundry companions. My father, ever attentive to what he thought was best for me, and desirous to ease himself as much as possible from the expense of my education, availed himself of my mother's being a relation of the Hon. Basil Hamilton—for their mothers were cousins—and applied to the Duke of Hamilton for one of the bursaries given by Duchess Ann of that family in the former century to students in divinity to pass two winters in Glasgow College, and a third in some foreign university, the salary for the first two years, £100 Scots annually, and for the third, £400 ; which might have been competent as far back as 1670, but was very far short of the most moderate expense at which a student could live in 1742.* But I was pleased with this plan, as it opened a prospect of going abroad. The presentation was obtained, and my father and I set out on horseback for Glasgow in the beginning of November, and arrived there next fore-

again, where in a year he died in obscurity, not being then so much thought of as to be despised or hated."—*Recollections.*

* A hundred pounds Scots are equivalent to £8, 6s. 8d. sterling. —J. H. B.

noon, having stayed all night at Mr. Dundas's of
Castle Cary, on the old Roman wall. My father immediately repaired to the College to consult with an
old friend of his, Mr. Dick, Professor of Natural Philosophy, how he was to proceed with his presentation.
I was surprised to see him return after in a great
flurry, Mr. Dick having assured him that there was no
vacant bursary, nor would be till next year. The
next object was how to secure it, in which we were
both much interested—my father, to prevent my
deviating into some other employment ; and I, for
fear I should have been forced to become tutor to
some young gentleman, a situation which, as I then
observed it, had become an object of my abhorrence.
Several of my companions had the same turn of mind;
for neither Robertson, nor John Home, nor George
Logan were ever tutors. We thought we had observed
that all tutors had contracted a certain obsequious-
ness or *bassesse*, which alarmed us for ourselves. A
little experience corrected this prejudice, for I knew
many afterwards who had passed through that station, and yet had retained a manly independency
both in mind and manner.

After a hasty dinner, we took our horses by four in
the afternoon, and riding all night by the nearest road,
which was as bad as possible, we arrived in Edinburgh
by eight in the morning. My father dressed himself,
and went down to the Abbey, where, to his great joy,
he found that Duke Hamilton was not set out for London, as he was afraid he might have been, and obtained

a promise that the presentation should be renewed next year.

In compensation for this disappointment, I passed the greatest part of this winter at my grandfather's, at Tinwald, where I read for many hours of the day, and generally took the weekly amusement of passing one day and night at Dumfries, where I met with agreeable society, both male and female.

I returned to Edinburgh in March, and attended the Divinity Hall for a few weeks. Living at Edinburgh continued still to be wonderfully cheap, as there were ordinaries for young gentlemen, at fourpence a-head for a very good dinner of broth and beef, and a roast and potatoes every day, with fish three or four times a-week, and all the small-beer that was called for till the cloth was removed. In the summer I passed some time in East Lothian, where by accident at that period there were no less than a dozen young scholars, preachers, and students in divinity, who generally met there on the presbytery day. For two or three times we dined with the presbytery by invitation ; but finding that we were not very welcome guests, and that whatever number there were in company they never allowed them more than two bottles of small Lisbon wine, we bespoke a dinner for ourselves in another tavern ; and when the days were short, generally stayed all night. By this time even the second tavern in Haddington (where the presbytery dined, having quarrelled with the first) had knives and forks for their table. But ten or twelve years before that time, my father used to carry a shagreen case, with a knife and fork and spoon, as they perhaps do still on many parts of the Continent. When I attended, in 1742 and 1743, they had still but one glass on the table, which went round with the bottle.

Very early in the afternoon, Mr. Stedman, a minister in the town, and one or two more of the clergymen, used to resort to our company, and keep up an enlightened conversation till bedtime. The chief subjects were the deistical controversy and moral philosophy, as connected with theology. Besides Stedman, Murray and Glen almost always attended us.*

John Witherspoon was of this party, he who was afterwards a member of the American Congress,† and Adam Dickson, who afterwards wrote so well on Husbandry. They were both clergymen's sons,

* Mr. Edward Stedman was second minister of Haddington, and a man of very superior understanding. He it was who first directed Dr. Robertson how to obtain his leading in the Church, and who was the friend and supporter of John Home, when he was in danger of being deposed for writing the tragedy of *Douglas*. It was Stedman who, with the aid of Hugh Bannatyne, then minister of Dirleton, and Robertson, conducted the affairs of the presbytery of Haddington in such a manner that they were never able to reach John Home, till it was convenient for him to resign his charge.

† After being minister at Beith and Paisley, Witherspoon went to America, where he became Principal of Princeton College, N.J., in 1768. He took part in framing the first constitution of New Jersey in 1776, in which year he was a member of Congress and was active in support of the Declaration of Independence. He continued to hold political positions till the settlement of American Independence in 1783, when he resumed his duties in Princeton College. He died in 1794.

but of very different characters ; the one open, frank, and generous, pretending only to what he was, and supporting his title with spirit ; the other close, and suspicious, and jealous, and always aspiring at a superiority that he was not able to maintain. I used sometimes to go with him for a day or two to his father's house at Gifford Hall, where we passed the day in fishing, to be out of reach of his father, who was very sulky and tyrannical, but who, being much given to gluttony, fell asleep early, and went always to bed at nine, and, being as fat as a porpoise, was not to be awaked, so that we had three or four hours of liberty every night to amuse ourselves with the daughters of the family, and their cousins who re- sorted to us from the village, when the old man was gone to rest. This John loved of all things ; and this sort of company he enjoyed in greater perfection when he returned my visits, when we had still more companions of the fair sex, and no restraint from an austere father ; so that I always considered the auster- ity of manners and aversion to social joy which he affected afterwards, as the arts of hypocrisy and am- bition ; for he had a strong and enlightened under- standing, far above enthusiasm, and a temper that did not seem liable to it.*

* Thomas Hepburn, a distinguished minister, who died minister of Athelstaneford, and was born and bred in the neighbourhood, used to allege that a Dr. Nisbet of Montrose, a man of some learning and ability, which he used to display with little judg- ment in the Assembly, was Witherspoon's son, and that he was supported in this opinion by the scandalous chronicle of the country. Their features, no doubt, had a strong resemblance,

It was this summer that my father received from Mr. Keith (afterwards ambassador) a letter, desiring that I might be sent over to him immediately. He had been sent for by Lord Stair, and went to Germany with him as his private secretary. This was after the battle of Dettingen. But I knew nothing of it for some years, otherwise I might probably have broke through my father's plan. When Lord Stair lost the command of the army, Mr. Keith lived with him at London, and had a guinea a-day conferred on him, till he was sent to Holland in 1746 or 1747 as Resident. His knowledge of modern history, and of all the treaties, etc., made him be valued.

but their persons were unlike, neither were their tempers at all similar. Any likeness there was between them in their sentiments and public appearances might be accounted for by the great admiration the junior must have had for the senior, as he was bred up under his eye, in the same parish, in which he was much admired. Whether or not he was his son, he followed his example, for he became discontented, and migrated to America during the Rebellion, where he was Principal of Carlisle College, Pennsylvania, for which he was well qualified in point of learning. But no preferment nor climate can cure a discontented mind, for he became miserable at one time because he could not return.

CHAPTER III

IN November 1743 I went to Glasgow, much more opportunely than I should have done the preceding year, for the old Professor of Divinity, Mr. Potter, who had been a very short while there, died in the week I went to College ; and his chair, being in the gift of the University, was immediately filled by Mr. William Leechman, a neighbouring clergyman, a person thoroughly well qualified for the office, of which he gave the most satisfactory proof for a great many years that he continued Professor of Theology, which was till the death of Principal Neil Campbell * raised him to the head of the University. He was a distinguished preacher, and was followed when he was occasionally in Edinburgh. His appearance was that of an ascetic, reduced by fasting and prayer ; but in aid of fine composition, he delivered his sermons with such fervent spirit, and in so persuasive a manner, as captivated every audience.† This was so much the case

* Mr. Neil Campbell was minister of Roseneath, and through Argyll influence was appointed Principal of Glasgow University in 1728 in succession to Principal Stirling. He died in 1761.

† A portrait of Leechman, from a painting by W. Millar, very

that his admirers regretted that he should be withdrawn from the pulpit, for the Professor of Theology has no charge in Glasgow, and preaches only occasionally. It was much for the good of the Church, however, that he was raised to a station of more extensive usefulness ; for while his interesting manner drew the steady attention of the students, the judicious choice and arrangement of his matter formed the most instructive set of lectures on theology that had, it was thought, ever been delivered in Scotland. It was, no doubt, owing to him and his friend and colleague Mr. Hutcheson, Professor of Moral Philosophy, that a better taste and greater liberality of sentiment were introduced among the clergy in the western provinces of Scotland.

Able as this gentleman was, however, and highly unexceptionable not only in morals but in decorum of behaviour, he was not allowed to ascend his chair without much opposition, and even a prosecution for heresy. Invulnerable as he seemed to be, the keen and prying eye of fanaticism discovered a weak place, to which they directed their attacks. There had been published at Glasgow, or in the neighbourhood of Dr. Leechman's church, in the country, before he came to Glasgow, about that period, a small pamphlet against the use of prayer, which had circulated amongst the inferior ranks, and had made no small impression, being artfully composed. To counteract this poison

characteristic, and in harmony with this description, is prefixed to an edition of his Sermons : London, 2 vols. 8vo, 1789.—J. H. B.

Leechman had composed and published his sermon on the nature, reasonableness, and advantages of prayer; with an attempt to answer the objections against it, from Matthew, xxvi. 41. In this sermon, though admirably well composed, in defence of prayer as a duty of natural religion, the author had forgot, or omitted to state, the obligations on Christians to pray in the name of Christ. The nature of his subject did not lead him to state this part of a Christian's prayer, and perhaps he thought that the inserting anything relative to that point might disgust or lessen the curiosity of those for whose conviction he had published the sermon. The fanatical or high-flying clergy in the presbytery of Glasgow took advantage of this omission, and instituted an inquiry into the heresy contained in this sermon by omission, which lasted with much theological acrimony on the part of the inquirers (who were chiefly those who had encouraged Cambuslang's work, as it was called, two years before), till it was finally settled in favour of the Professor by the General Assembly 1744.* Instead of raising any anxiety among the students in theology, or creating any suspicion of Dr. Leechman's orthodoxy, this fit of zeal against him tended much to spread and establish his superior character.

* *Cambuslang's Work :* Revivals in the Parish of Cambuslang in Lanarkshire in the year 1742. They were the occasion of abundant controversy ; but the fullest account of them will be found in *Narrative of the extraordinary Work of the Spirit of God at Cambuslang, Kilsyth, etc.*, written by Mr. James Robe and others.—J. H. B.

I attended Hutcheson's class this year with great satisfaction and improvement. He was a good-looking man, of an engaging countenance. He delivered his lectures without notes, walking backwards and forwards in the area of his room. As his elocution was good, and his voice and manner pleasing, he raised the attention of his hearers at all times ; and when the subject led him to explain and enforce the moral virtues and duties, he displayed a fervent and persuasive eloquence which was irresistible. Besides the lectures he gave through the week, he, every Sunday at six o'clock, opened his class-room to whoever chose to attend, when he delivered a set of lectures on *Grotius de veritate Religionis Christianæ*, which, though learned and ingenious, were adapted to every capacity ; for on that evening he expected to be attended, not only by students, but by many of the people of the city ; and he was not disappointed, for this free lecture always drew crowds of attendants.

Besides Hutcheson and Leechman, there were at that period several eminent professors in that university ; particularly Mr. Robert Simson, the great mathematician, and Mr. Alexander Dunlop, the Professor of Greek. The last, besides his eminence as a Greek scholar, was distinguished by his strong good sense and capacity for business ; and being a man of a leading mind, was supposed, with the aid of Hutcheson, to direct and manage all the affairs of the University (for it is a wealthy corporation, and has much business), besides the charge of presiding over literature, and maintaining the discipline of the College.

One difference I remarked between this University and that of Edinburgh, where I had been bred, which was, that although at that time there appeared to be a marked superiority in the best scholars and most diligent students of Edinburgh, yet in Glasgow, learning seemed to be an object of more importance, and the habit of application was much more general. Besides the instruction I received from Drs. Hutcheson and Leechman, I derived much pleasure, as well as enlargement of skill in the Greek language, from Mr. Dunlop's translations and criticisms of the great tragic writers in that language. I likewise attended the Professor of Hebrew, a Mr. Morthland,* who was master of his business. I had neglected that branch in Edinburgh, the professor being then superannuated.

In the second week I was in Glasgow I went to the dancing assembly with some of my new acquaintance, and was there introduced to a married lady who claimed kindred with me, her mother's name being Carlyle, of the Limekiln family. She carried me home to sup with her that night, with a brother of hers, two years younger than me, and some other young people. This was the commencement of an intimate friendship that lasted during the whole of the lady's life, which was four or five and twenty years. She was connected with all the best families in Glasgow and

* Mr. Charles Morthland was appointed to the chair of Oriental languages in 1709, and held it till his death in 1744.

the country round. Her husband was a good sort of
man, and very opulent ; and as they had no children,
he took pleasure in her exercising a genteel hospitality.
I became acquainted with all the best families in the
town by this lady's means ; and by a letter I had procured from my friend James Edgar, afterwards a Commissioner of the Customs, I also soon became well
acquainted with all the young ladies who lived in the
College. He had studied law the preceding year at
Glasgow, under Professor Hercules Lindsay,* at that
time of some note. On asking him for a letter of
introduction to some one of his companions, he gave
me one to Miss Mally Campbell, the daughter of the
Principal ; and when I seemed surprised at his choice,
he added that I would find her not only more beautiful
than any woman there, but more sensible and friendly
than all the professors put together, and much more
useful to me. This I found to be literally true.

The city of Glasgow at this time, though very in-
dustrious, wealthy, and commercial, was far inferior to
what it afterwards became,† both before and after the
failure of the Virginia trade. The modes of life, too,
and manners, were different from what they are at
present. Their chief branches were the tobacco trade

* Professor Hercules Lindsay was the first Professor of Law
to deliver lectures on the *Institutes of Justinian* in English.

† " In a word, 'tis one of the cleanest, most beautiful, and best
built cities in Great Britain."—Defoe's *Tour*, 1727.

" Glasgow is, to outward appearance, the prettiest and most
uniform town that I have ever seen, and I believe there is nothing
like it in Britain."—Burt's *Letters from the North of Scotland*
(published 1754).

with the American colonies;* and sugar and rum
with the West India. There were not manufacturers
sufficient, either there or at Paisley, to supply an out-
ward-bound cargo for Virginia. For this purpose
they were obliged to have recourse to Manchester.
Manufactures were in their infancy. About this time
the inkle manufactory † was first begun by Ingram
& Glasford,‡ and was shown to strangers as a great
curiosity. But the merchants had industry and stock,
and the habits of business, and were ready to seize
with eagerness, and prosecute with vigour, every new
object in commerce or manufactures that promised
success.

Few of them could be called learned merchants;
yet there was a weekly club, of which a Provost
Cochrane was the founder and a leading member,
in which their express design was to inquire into
the nature and principles of trade in all its branches,
and to communicate their knowledge and views
on that subject to each other. I was not acquainted
with Provost Cochrane at this time, but I observed
that the members of this society had the highest
admiration of his knowledge and talents. I became

---

* " The tobacco lords distinguished themselves by a particular
dress, like their Venetian and Genovese predecessors, in scarlet
cloaks, curled wigs, cocked hats, and bearing gold-headed canes."
—Strang's *Glasgow and its Clubs*.

† Inkle manufacture was introduced in 1732 by Mr. Alexander
Harvey, who brought over from Haarlem two looms and a Dutch
workman.

‡ Messrs. Ingram started the first calico print-field at Pollock-
shaws about 1742.

6

well acquainted with him twenty years afterwards, when Drs. Smith and Wight were members of the club, and was made sensible that too much could not be said of his accurate and extensive knowledge, of his agreeable manners, and colloquial eloquence. Dr. Smith acknowledged his obligations to this gentleman's information, when he was collecting materials for his *Wealth of Nations* ; and the junior merchants who have flourished since his time, and extended their commerce far beyond what was then dreamt of, confess, with respectful remembrance, that it was Andrew Cochrane who first opened and enlarged their views.*

It was not long before I was well established in close intimacy with many of my fellow-students, and soon felt the superiority of an education in the College of Edinburgh ; not in point of knowledge, or acquirements in the languages or sciences, but in knowledge of the world, and a certain manner and address that can only be attained in the capital. It must be confessed that at this time they were far behind in Glasgow, not only in their manner of living, but in those accomplishments and that taste that belong to people of opulence, much more to persons of education. There were only a few families of ancient citizens who pretended to be gentlemen ; and a few others, who were recent settlers there, who had obtained wealth and con-

* For information regarding Cochrane, Simson, and the other Glasgow celebrities mentioned in this chapter, the reader is referred to *Glasgow and its Clubs*, by Dr. Strang, and to the *Cochrane Correspondence*, printed in 1836 for the Maitland Club.

sideration in trade. The rest were shopkeepers and mechanics, or successful pedlars, who occupied large warerooms full of manufactures of all sorts, to furnish a cargo to Virginia. It was usual for the sons of merchants to attend the College for one or two years, and a few of them completed their academical education. In this respect the females were still worse off, for at that period there was neither a teacher of French nor of music in the town. The consequence of this was twofold; first, the young ladies were entirely without accomplishments, and in general had nothing to recommend them but good looks and fine clothes, for their manners were ungainly. Secondly, the few who were distinguished drew all the young men of sense and taste about them; for, being void of frivolous accomplishments, which in some respects make all women equal, they trusted only to superior understanding and wit, to natural elegance and unaffected manners.

There never was but one concert during the two winters I was at Glasgow, and that was given by Walter Scott, Esq. of Harden, who was himself an eminent performer on the violin; and his band of assistants consisted of two dancing-school fiddlers and the town-waits.

The manner of living, too, at this time, was but coarse and vulgar. Very few of the wealthiest gave dinners to anybody but English riders, or their own relations at Christmas holidays. There were not half-a-dozen families in town who had men-servants;

some of those were kept by the professors who had boarders. There were neither post-chaises nor hackney-coaches in the town, and only three or four sedan-chairs for carrying midwives about in the night, and old ladies to church, or to the dancing assemblies once a-fortnight.

The principal merchants, fatigued with the morning's business, took an early dinner with their families at home, and then resorted to the coffeehouse or tavern to read the newspapers, which they generally did in companies of four or five in separate rooms, over a bottle of claret or a bowl of punch. But they never stayed supper, but always went home by nine o'clock, without company or further amusement. At last an arch fellow from Dublin, a Mr. Cockaine, came to be master of the chief coffeehouse, who seduced them gradually to stay supper by placing a few nice cold things at first on the table, as relishers to the wine, till he gradually led them on to bespeak fine hot suppers, and to remain till midnight.

There was an order of women at that time in Glasgow, who, being either young widows not wealthy, or young women unprovided for, were set up in small grocery-shops in various parts of the town, and generally were protected and countenanced by some creditable merchant. In their back shops much time and money were consumed ; for it being customary then to drink drams and white wine in the forenoon, the tipplers resorted much to those shops, where there were bedrooms ; and the patron, with his friends, frequently passed the evening there also, as taverns were not frequented by persons who affected characters of strict decency.

I was admitted a member of two clubs, one entirely literary, which was held in the porter's lodge at the College, and where we criticised books and wrote abridgements of them, with critical essays ; and to this society we submitted the discourses which we were to deliver in the Divinity Hall in our turns, when we were appointed by the professor. The other club met in Mr. Dugald's tavern near the Cross, weekly, and admitted a mixture of young gentlemen, who were not intended for the study of theology. There met there John Bradefoot, afterwards minister of Dunsire ; James Leslie, of Kilmarnock ; John Robertson, of Dunblane ; James Hamilton, of Paisley; and Robert Lawson, of London Wall. There also came some young merchants, such as Robin Bogle, my relation ; James and George Anderson, William Sellar and Robin Craig. Here we drank a little punch after our beefsteaks and pancakes, and the expense never exceeded 1s. 6d., seldom 1s.

Our conversation was almost entirely literary ; and we were of such good fame, that some ministers of the neighbourhood, when occasionally in Glasgow, frequented our club. Hyndman had been twice introduced by members ; and being at that time passing his trials as a probationer before that presbytery in which his native town of Greenock lay, he had become well acquainted with Mr. Robert Paton, minis-

ter of Renfrew, who, though a man well accomplished
and of liberal sentiments, was too much a man of
worth and principle not to be offended by licentious
manners in students of divinity.   Hyndman, by way
of gaining favour with this man, took occasion to hint
to him to advise his nephew, Robert Lawson, not to
frequent our club, as it admitted and encouraged conversation not suitable to the profession we were to
follow.   He mentioned two instances, one of which
Lawson said was false, and the other disguised by ex-
aggeration.   Lawson, who was a lad of pure morals,
told me this ; and as the best antidote to this injuri-
ous impression, which had been made chiefly against
me, I begged him to let his uncle know that I would
accept of the invitation he had given through him, to
pass a night or two with him at Renfrew.   We accordingly went next Saturday, and met with a gracious
reception, and stayed all next day and heard him
preach, at which he was thought to excel (though he
was almost the only person who read in those days,
in which he truly excelled) ; and being a very handsome man, his delivery much enhanced the value of
his composition.   We heard him read another sermon
at night in his study, with much satisfaction, as he
told us it was one of his best, and was a good model ;
to this we respectfully assented, and the good man
was pleased.   When we took leave on Monday morning, he politely requested another visit, and said to
me, with a smile, he was now fortified against tale-
bearers.   These societies contributed much to our

improvement ; and as moderation and early hours were inviolable rules of both institutions, they served to open and enlarge our minds.

Towards the end of the session, however, I was introduced to a club which gave me much more satisfaction—I mean that of Mr. Robert Simson,* the celebrated Professor of Mathematics. Mr. Robert Dick, Professor of Natural Philosophy, an old friend of my father's, one evening after I had dined with him, said he was going to Mr. Robert's club, and if I had a mind, he would take me there and introduce me. I readily accepted the honour. I had been introduced to Mr. Robert before in the College court, for he was extremely courteous, and showed civility to every student who fell in his way. Though I was not attending any of his classes, having attended M'Laurin in Edinburgh for three sessions, he received me with great kindness ; and I had the good fortune to please him so much, that he asked me to be a member of his Friday's club,† which I readily agreed to. Mr. Simson, though a great humorist, who had a very particular way of living, was well-bred and complaisant,

* Dr. Robert Simson was born in 1689 at Kirktonhall, Ayrshire, and was elected to the chair of Mathematics in Glasgow University in 1711. He died in 1768.

† Some ten years later than the date of Dr. Carlyle's visit to the Friday Club, Professor Simson founded the Anderston Club at an hostelry in the village of that name kept by " ane God-fearing host—John Sharpe." Among the members of this club were Adam Smith, Professor Leechman, Professor Dick, Robert Bogle, David Hume, and other of Carlyle's friends.—Strang's *Glasgow and its Clubs*.

was a comely man, of a good size, and had a very prepossessing countenance. He lived entirely at the small tavern opposite the College gate, kept by a Mrs. Millar. He breakfasted, dined, and supped there, and almost never accepted of any invitations to dinner, and paid no visits, but to illustrious or learned strangers, who wished to see the University ; on such occasions he was always the cicerone. He showed the curiosities of the College, which consisted of a few manuscripts and a large collection of Roman antiquities, from Severus' Wall or Graham's Dyke, in the neighbourhood, with a display of much knowledge and taste. He was particularly averse to the company of ladies, and, except one day in the year, when he drank tea at Principal Campbell's, and conversed with gaiety and ease with his daughter Mally, who was always his first toast, he was never in company with them. It was said to have been otherwise with him in his youth, and that he had been much attached to one lady, to whom he had made proposals, but on her refusing him he became disgusted with the sex. The lady was dead before I became acquainted with the family, but her husband I knew, and must confess that in her choice the lady had preferred a satyr to Hyperion.

Mr. Simson almost never left the bounds of the College, having a large garden to walk in, unless it was on Saturday, when, with two chosen companions, he always walked into the country, but no farther than the village of Anderston, one mile off, where he had a dinner bespoke, and where he always treated the company, not only when he had no other than his two humble attendants, but when he casually added one or two more, which happened twice to myself. If any of the club met him on Saturday night at his hotel, he took it very kind, for he was in good spirits, though fatigued with the company of his satellites, and revived on the sight of a fresh companion or two for the evening. He was of a mild temper and an engaging demeanour, and was master of all knowledge, even of theology, which he told us he had learned by being one year amanuensis to his uncle, the Professor of Divinity.* His knowledge he delivered in an easy colloquial style, with the simplicity of a child, and without the least symptom of self-sufficiency or arrogance.

His club at that time consisted chiefly of Hercules Lindsay, Teacher of Law, who was talkative and assuming; of James Moore, Professor of Greek on the death of Mr. Dunlop,† a very lively and witty man, and a famous Grecian,‡ but a more famous punster; Mr. Dick, Professor of Natural Philosophy, a very

---

* Professor John Simson. See p. 105.

† Mr. Dunlop had the power of " giving to his pupils a taste and stimulus for the work of the class, vital enough to impel them to prosecute the study from a love of it in after life."— Stewart's *Glasgow University, Old and New*.

‡ " When interpreting Homer to his class, he [Dr. Moor] never looked at the book, and from numerous references which he made to parallel passages in his favourite author, it appeared that he could repeat most accurately the whole *Iliad* or *Odyssey*." —Bower's *History of Edinburgh University*.

worthy man, and of an agreeable temper; and Mr.
James Purdie, the rector of the grammar-school,* who
had not much to recommend him but his being an
adept in grammar.   Having been asked to see a
famous comet that appeared this winter or the following, through Professor Dick's telescope, which was the
best in the College at that time, when Mr. Purdie
retired from taking his view of it, he turned to Mr.
Simson, and said, " Mr. Robert, I believe it is *hic* or
hæc cometa, a comet." To settle the gender of the
Latin was all he thought of this great and uncommon
phenomenon of nature.

Mr. Simson's most constant attendant, however,
and greatest favourite, was his own scholar, Mr.
Mathew Stewart, afterwards Professor of Mathematics in the College of Edinburgh, much celebrated
for his profound knowledge in that science.   During
the course of summer he was ordained minister of
Roseneath, but resided during the winter in Glasgow
College.   He was of an amiable disposition and of
a most ingenuous mind, and was highly valued in
the society of Glasgow University; but when he
was preferred to a chair in Edinburgh, being of
diminutive stature and of an ordinary appearance,
and having withal an embarrassed elocution, he was
not able to bring himself into good company; and
being left out of the society of those who should

* The Grammar School stood in Greyfriars' Wynd, formerly
Grammar School Wynd, on the west side of the High Street.
It was built in 1601 and abandoned in 1782 for a new building in
George Street.

have seen through the shell, and put a due value on the kernel, he fell into company of an inferior sort, and adopted their habits with too great facility.*

With this club, and an accidental stranger at times, the great Mr. Robert Simson relaxed his mind every evening from the severe studies of the day ; for though there was properly but one club night in the week, yet, as he never failed to be there, some one or two commonly attended him, or at least one of the two minions whom he could command at any time, as he paid their reckoning.

The fame of Mr. Hutcheson had filled the College with students of philosophy, and Leechman's high character brought all the students of divinity from the western provinces, as Hutcheson attracted the Irish.   There were sundry young gentlemen from Ireland, with their tutors, one of whom was Archibald M'Laine, pastor at the Hague, the celebrated translator of Mosheim's *Ecclesiastical History* (who had himself been bred at Glasgow College).   With him I became better acquainted next session, and I have often regretted since that it has never been my lot to meet him during the many times I have been for months in London, as his enlightened mind, engaging

* Writing of Professor Stewart after he became professor at Edinburgh, the Rev. Dr. Somerville says : " He was of a disposition so bashful and sensitive that the slightest irregularity or approach to rudeness in the behaviour of the students disconcerted him.   The misconduct of any of these boys—for such most of his pupils were—instead of meeting with a reproof from the professor, made him blush like a child."—*Memoirs of My Life and Times.*

manners, and animated conversation gave reason to
hope for excellent fruit when he arrived at maturity.
There were of young men of fashion attending the
College, Walter Lord Blantyre,* who died young ;
Sir Thomas Kennedy, and his brother David, afterwards Lord Cassilis ; † Walter Scott of Harden ; James
Murray of Broughton ; and Dunbar Hamilton, afterwards Earl of Selkirk. The education of this last
gentleman had been marred at an English academy
in Yorkshire. When his father, the Hon. Basil Hamilton, died, he came to Glasgow, but finding that he
was so ill founded in Latin as to be unfit to attend a
public class, he had resolution enough, at the age
of fifteen, to pass seven or eight hours a-day with
Purdie the grammarian for the greater part of two
years, when, having acquired Latin, he took James
Moore, the Greek scholar, for his private tutor,
fitted up rooms for himself in the College, and lived
there with Moore in the most retired manner, visiting
nobody but Miss M. Campbell, and letting nobody
in to him but Lord Blantyre and myself, as I was his
distant relation. In this manner he lived for ten years,
hardly leaving the College for a few weeks in summer,
till he had acquired the ancient tongues in perfection,
and was master of ancient philosophy : the effect of

* Walter, eighth Lord Blantyre. He had a reputation as a
scholar, and " has the sweetest temper in the world, and to all
appearance will be a very great honour to his country." He,
however, died in 1751 at the age of twenty-five.

† David, tenth Earl of Cassillis. Passed Advocate in 1752,
and succeeded his brother Sir Thomas in 1776.

which was, that with much rectitude and good intention, and some talent, he came into the world more fit to be a Professor than an Earl.

There was one advantage I derived from my Edinburgh education, which set me up a little in the eyes of my equals, though I soon tired of the employment. Professor Leechman devoted one evening every week from five to eight to conversation with his students, who assembled on Fridays about six or seven together, and were first received in the Professor's own library. But Dr. Leechman was not able to carry on common conversation, and when he spoke at all, it was a short lecture. This was therefore a very dull meeting, and everybody longed to be called in to tea with Mrs. Leechman, whose talent being different from that of her husband, she was able to maintain a continued conversation on plays, novels, poetry, and the fashions. The rest of the lads being for the most part raw and awkward, after trying it once in their turns, they became silent, and the dialogue rested between the lady and me. When she observed this, she requested me to attend as her assistant every night. I did so for a little while, but it became too intolerable not to be soon given up.

What Dr. Leechman wanted in the talent for conversation was fully compensated by his ability as a Professor, for in the chair he shone with great lustre. It was owing to Hutcheson and him that a new school was formed in the western provinces of Scotland, where the clergy till that period were narrow and bigoted, and had never ventured to range in their mind beyond the bounds of strict orthodoxy. For though neither of these professors taught any heresy, yet they opened and enlarged the minds of the students, which soon gave them a turn for free inquiry; the result of which was, candour and liberality of sentiment. From experience, this freedom of thought was not found so dangerous as might at first be apprehended; for though the daring youth made excursions into the unbounded regions of metaphysical perplexity, yet all the judicious soon returned to the lower sphere of long-established truths, which they found not only more subservient to the good order of society, but necessary to fix their own minds in some degree of stability.

Hutcheson was a great admirer of Shaftesbury, and adopted much of his writings into his lectures; and, to recommend him more to his students, was at great pains in private to prove that the noble moralist was no enemy to the Christian religion; but that all appearances of that kind, which are very numerous in his works, flowed only from an excess of generous indignation against the fanatics of Charles I.'s reign. Leechman and he both were supposed to lean to Socinianism. Men of sense, however, soon perceived that it was an arduous task to defend Christianity on that ground, and were glad to adopt more common and vulgar principles, which were well compacted together in a uniform system, which it was not easy to demolish.

Leechman's manner of teaching theology was excellent, and I found my sphere of knowledge in that science greatly enlarged, though I had attended the Professor in Edinburgh pretty closely for two or three years ; but he copied the Dutch divines, and, had he lived, would have taken twenty years to have gone through the system which Dr. Leechman accomplished in two years, besides giving us admirable lectures on the Gospels, on the proofs of Christianity, and the art of composition. If there was any defect, it was in the small number of exercises prescribed to the students, for one discourse in a session was by no means sufficient to produce a habit of composition : our literary clubs, in some degree, supplied that defect.

I had been called home to Prestonpans in January to see my brother James, who was then dying of a consumption ; he was in his nineteenth year, and died in March. He had been sent to London several years before to be bred to business, but an accident threw him into bad health, and he had been at home for two years or more. He was not a lad of parts, but remarkably handsome and agreeable. I found him perfectly reconciled to a premature death.

I had left my original companions at Edinburgh, who had every kind of merit to create attachment ; but I found a few in Glasgow University who in some degree supplied their places, who were worthy and able young men, and afterwards filled their ranks in society with credit, though they had neither the

strength nor the polish of the Blairs, and Robertsons,
and Fergusons, and Homes. Near the end of the
session I made an acquaintance with a young gentleman, which next year grew into the strictest friendship. This was William Sellar, then an apprentice
in his third or fourth year with the Oswalds, at that
time among the most eminent merchants in Glasgow.
He was the son of a Writer to the Signet in Edinburgh,
had been two or three years at the College there, was
handsome and well-bred, and of very agreeable
manners. Though not learned, he had a philosophical
and observing mind, and was shrewd in discerning
characters. This young man, my junior by a year or
two, attached himself to me on our first acquaintance,
and I soon repaid him with my affection, for I found
that the qualities of his heart were not inferior to those
of his understanding. He was daily conversant with
the principal merchants, as I was with the students
and members of the University, on whom our observations were a great source of instructive entertainment. He had the celebrated Jenny Fall * (afterwards Lady Anstruther), a coquette and a beauty, for
months together in the house with him ; and as his
person and manner drew the marked attention of the
ladies, he derived considerable improvement from
the constant intercourse with this young lady and
her companions, for she was lively and clever, no
less than beautiful. He had also the benefit of Mr.

* " Jenny Fall " was the daughter of James Fall of Dunbar,
and married Sir John Anstruther, the second baronet in 1750.

Richard Oswald's* conversation, a man afterwards so
much celebrated as to be employed by Government in
settling the peace of Paris in 1788.   This gentleman
was much confined to the house by sore eyes, and yet
was able to pass his time almost entirely in reading,
and becoming a very learned and intelligent merchant;
and having acquired some thousand pounds by being
prize agent to his cousins, whose privateer had taken
a prize worth £15,000, he a few years after this period
established himself in London, and acquired a great
fortune, which, having no children of his own, he left
to the grandson of his brother, a respectable clergyman of the Church of Scotland ; and thus founded
that family of Oswalds, who continue to flourish in
the shire of Ayr.

I lived this winter in the same house with Dr.
Robert Hamilton, Professor of Anatomy, an ingenious
and well-bred man ; but with him I had little intercourse, except at breakfast now and then, for he
always dined abroad.   He had a younger brother, a
student of divinity, afterwards his father's successor
at Bothwell, who was vain and showy, but who exposed himself very much through a desire of distinction.   He was a relation of Mrs. Leechman's, and it
had been hinted to him that the Professor expected a
remarkable discourse from him.   He accordingly delivered one which gave universal satisfaction, and was

* Richard Oswald, second son of Rev. George Oswald of Dunnet,
Caithness.   He acquired the estate of Auchencruive in Ayrshire
in 1755.   The date of the peace of Paris was 1782.   Richard
Oswald died in 1784.

7

much extolled by the Professor.   But, very unfortunately for Hamilton, half-a-dozen of students, in going
down a street, resorted to a bookseller's shop, where
one of them, taking a volume from a shelf, was struck,
on opening the book, to find the first sermon from the
text he had just heard preached upon.   He read on,
and found it was verbatim from beginning to end
what he had heard in the hall.   He showed it to his
companions, who laughed heartily, and spread the
story all over the town before night—not soon enough
to prevent the vainglorious orator from circulating
two fine copies of it, one among the ladies in the
College, and another in the town.   What aggravated
the folly and imprudence of this young man was, that
he was by no means deficient in parts, of which he
gave us sundry specimens.   His cousin and name-
sake, James Hamilton, afterwards minister of Paisley,
was much ashamed of him, and being a much more
sterling man, was able to keep down his vanity ever
after.   He had submitted his manuscript to the club,
and two or three criticisms had been made on it, but
he would alter nothing.   After Dr. Robert Hamilton's
death, which was premature, a younger brother succeeded him in the anatomical chair, who was very able.
He dying young also, his son was advanced, who was
said to have surpassed all his predecessors in ability.
They were descended from the family of Hamiltons of
Preston, a very ancient branch of Duke Hamilton's
family.

Dr. Johnstone, who was said to be very able, was

at this time Professor of Medicine, but he was very old, and died this year ; and was succeeded by Dr. William Cullen, who had been settled at Hamilton. In those days there were but few students of physic in Glasgow University. Dr. Cullen, and his successor Dr. Black, with the younger Hamiltons, brought the school of medicine more into repute there.

In the month of March or April this year, having gone down with a merchant to visit New Port-Glasgow, as our dinner was preparing at the inn, we were alarmed with the howling and weeping of half-a-dozen of women in the kitchen, which was so loud and lasting that I went to see what was the matter, when, after some time, I learnt from the calmest among them that a pedlar had left a copy of Peden's *Prophecies* that morning, which having read part of, they found that he had predicted woes of every kind to the people of Scotland; and in particular that Clyde would run with blood in the year 1744, which now being some months advanced, they believed that their destruction was at hand. I was puzzled how to pacify them, but calling for the book, I found that the passage which had terrified them was contained in the forty-fourth paragraph, without any allusion whatever to the year ; and by this means I quieted their lamentations. Had the intended expedition of Mareschal Saxe been carried into execution in that year, as was intended, their fears might have been realised.

Though the theological lectures closed in the beginning of May, on account of some accidental circum-

stances, I did not get to my father's till the middle of
that month. My father's wish was, that I should pass
through my trials to be admitted a probationer in
summer 1745, and leave nothing undone but the finishing forms, when I returned in 1746 from a foreign
Protestant university, where I was bound to go by the
terms of the exhibition I held. I was therefore to
spend a part of this summer, 1744, in visiting the
clergy of the presbytery of Haddington, as the forms
required that I should perform that duty before I was
admitted to trials.

I made my tour accordingly early in summer, and
shall give a short specimen of my reception and the
characters I met with. I first passed a day at Aberlady, where Mr. Andrew Dickson was then minister,
the father of Adam Dickson, the author of many
excellent works on agriculture. Mr. Dickson was a
well-bred formal old man, and was reckoned a good
preacher, though lame enough in the article of knowledge, or indeed in discernment. Among the first
questions he put to me was, " Had I read the famous
pamphlet, *Christianity not founded on Argument?*" I
answered that I had. He replied that certainly that
elaborate work was the ablest defence of our holy
religion that had been published in our times ; and
that the author of it, who was unknown to him, deserved the highest praise. I looked surprised, and
was going to make him an answer according to my
opinion, which was that it was the shrewdest attack
that ever had been made on Christianity. But his

son observed me, and broke in by saying that he had had some disputes with his father on the subject, but now yielded, and had come in to his opinion : I only subjoined, that whoever saw it in that light must subscribe to its superiority. The old gentleman was pleased, and went on descanting on the great merit of this new proof of revealed religion, which was quite unanswerable. Having settled that point, there was no danger of my differing from him in any other of his notions.

Next day I proceeded to Dirleton, the neighbouring parish, where Mr. James Glen was the incumbent. This was a man of middle age, fat and unwieldy, good-natured and open-hearted, very social, though quick-tempered and jealous. He was a great master of the Deistical controversy, had read all the books, and never stopped, for it was his first topic with me, till he completely refuted *Christianity not founded on Argument*, which he said was truly very insidious. There was not much time, however, this day for theology, as it happened to be his *cherry feast*. There being many fine trees of that fruit in his garden, when they were fully ripe it was his custom to invite some of his neighbours and their families to pass the day with him and his daughters, and the only son then at home, Mr. Alexander Glen, who was a student, and two years my junior. We were a very large company, among whom were Congalton of that Ilk, a very singular gentleman, of very good parts, and extremely promising when he passed advocate, but

who had become a drunken laird, though the brilliancy
of his wit frequently broke through the cloud.   There
were likewise four Miss Hepburns of Beanston, who
were young, handsome, and gay.   The old people dispersed not long after dinner, and went their several
ways ; Congalton and his swaggering blades went to
the village changehouse, and remained there all night.
There not being lodging in the house for us all, the
young men remained as late as they could in the parlour, and then had mattresses brought in to sleep a
while upon.

When I wished to depart next day with the rest of
the company, the old man protested against that, for
we had not yet sufficiently settled the Deistical controversy, and the foundations of moral sentiment.   I
consented, and as his daughters had detained two
Misses Hepburns, I passed the day very well between
disputing with my landlord and walking about and
philandering with the ladies.   When I came to leave
him after breakfast the next day, it was with the
greatest difficulty he would part with me, and not till
after he had taken my solemn promise to come soon
back, as I was the only friend he had left in the world.
I at last escaped, after he had shed a flood of tears.
I was uneasy, and asked afterwards if he was not a
very solitary man : " No," they said, " but he was of
a jealous temper, and thought he was hated if he was
not resorted to more than was possible."

The next clergyman, Mr. George Murray of North
Berwick, was in appearance quite the opposite of Mr.

Glen, for he was a dry, withered stick, and as cold and
repulsive in his manner as the other was kind and inviting ; but he was not the less to be depended on for
that, for he was very worthy and sensible, though, at
the age of fifty, as torpid in mind, as in body. His
wife, however, of the name of Reid, the former minister's daughter, by whose interest he got the church,
was as swift to speak as he was slow ; and as he never
interrupted her, she kept up the conversation, such as
it was, without ceasing, except that her household
affairs took her sometimes out of the room, when he
began some metaphysical argument, but dropped it
the moment she appeared, for he said *Anny* did not
like those subjects. Worn out, however, with the
fatigue of the cherry feast, I longed to be in bed, and
took the first opportunity of a cessation in Anny's
clapper to request to be shown to my room ; this was
complied with about eleven ; but the worthy man accompanied me, and being at last safe and at liberty,
he began a conversation on liberty and necessity, and
the foundation of morals, and the Deistical controversy, that lasted till two in the morning. I got away
time enough next day to reach Haddington before
dinner, having passed by Athelstaneford, where the
minister, Mr. Robert Blair, author of *The Grave*, was
said to be dying slowly ; or, at any rate, was so austere
and void of urbanity as to make him quite disagreeable to young people. His wife, who was in every respect the opposite (a sister of Sheriff Law), was frank
and open, and uncommonly handsome; yet, even with

her allurements and his acknowledged ability, his house was unfrequented. I passed on to Haddington, and dined with Mr. Edward Stedman, a man of first-rate sense and ability, and a leader of the presbytery. We called on his father-in-law, Mr. Patrick Wilkie, who had as little desire to examine young men as he had capacity to judge of their proficiency, so that I had only to pay my compliments and pass an hour or two with Stedman, whom I knew well before, and who, with the sombre constrained air of a Jesuit or an old Covenanter, had an enlightened and ardent mind, and comprehended all things human and divine. From him I went early in the evening to Mr. Barclay's at Moreham, a good sensible man, but with not many words or topics of conversation, for he was a great mathematician : with the help of his wife and daughter, however, we made shift to spend the evening, and retired at an early hour.

I passed on next forenoon to Garvald, where his son-in-law, Mr. Archibald Blair, brother of Mr. Robert, lived. He seemed as torpid as George Murray, and not more enlightened than Patrick Wilkie. He conversed none. As we walked out before dinner to see the views, which were not remarkable, I thought I might try to examine him, and put a question to him as we entered the churchyard, which he answered when we got to the far end of the glebe. His wife, however, made it well up. This, with other instances, convinced me that it would have been better if the wives had preached, and the husbands spun.

From hence I went to the next manse, which was Yester, where I had been very frequently before with John Witherspoon, afterwards the celebrated doctor.* The father, who had very few topics to examine on, as the depth of his reading was in the sermons of the French Calvinist ministers, which he preached daily, was, besides, too lazy to engage in anything so arduous as the examination of a student—how to eat and drink and sleep being his sole care, though he was not without parts, if the soul had not been buried under a mountain of flesh. The next I went to was old Lundie of Saltoun, a pious and primitive old man, very respectful in his manners, and very kind. He had been bred an old Scotch Episcopalian, and was averse to the Confession of Faith : the presbytery showed lenity towards him, so he did not sign it to his dying day, for which reason he never could be a member of Assembly.

The last I went to on this tour was Mathew Simson, of Pencaitland, a brother of Professor Simson's, who had been suspended for heresy, and an uncle of the celebrated Dr. Robert Simson, both of Glasgow. Their father was Mr. Patrick Simson, of Renfrew, who had been tutor to some of the family of Argyle. Mr. Mathew was an old man, but very different in his manner from Mr. Lundie, for he was frank and open and familiar, as much as the other was reserved and dignified. He was an excellent examinator, for he answered all his own questions, and concluded all with

* See above, p. 72.

a receipt for making sermons, which he said would
serve as a general rule, and answer well, be the text
what it would.   This was to begin first with an account of the fall of man, and the depravity of human
nature; then a statement of the means of our recovery
by the grace of our Lord Jesus Christ; and, thirdly,
an application consisting of observations, or uses, or
reflections, or practical references tending to make us
good men.   For my patient hearing, he made me a
present of a pen-case of his own turning, and added,
if I would come and stay a week with him he would
teach me to turn, and converse over the system with
me, for he saw I was tolerably well founded, as my
father was an able Calvinist.   He said he would order
his son Patrick, who was a more powerful master of
the turning-loom than he was, to turn me a nice snuff-
box or egg-cup, which I pleased.   But Pat was lazy,
and liked better to go about with the gun, from which
he did not restrain him, as he not only furnished his
sisters with plenty of partridges and hares, but likewise gratified the Lady Pencaitland with many.   Thus
ended my preparatory trial by visiting the clergy,
for with the two or three nearer home I was well acquainted.

Early in November this year, 1744, I returned to
Glasgow.   As it was a hard frost, I chose to walk, and
went the first day to my friend Mr. Hew Horn's * at
Foxhall, near Kirkliston.   He had been married for

* Hew Horn Dalrymple, second son of Lord Drummore.   He
died in 1746.   See p. 60.

a year or two to Miss Inglis, a daughter of Sir John Inglis, a handsome, agreeable woman. I perceived that he was much changed, and thought him in a very dangerous way. He was, however, very cheerful and pleasant, and sat up with me till eleven o'clock. I breakfasted with him next morning, and then took my leave, with a foreboding that I should see him no more, which was verified, for he gave way not many months afterwards. In him I lost a most valuable friend. I walked to Whitburn at an early hour, but could venture no further, as there was no tolerable lodging-house within my reach. There was then not even a cottage nearer than the Kirk of Shotts, and Whitburn itself was a solitary house in a desolate country.

Next morning the frost was gone, and such a deluge of rain and tempest of wind took possession of the atmosphere, as put an end to all travelling. This was on Thursday morning; and the wet thaw and bad weather continuing, I was obliged to remain there for several days, for there was in those days neither coach nor chaise on the road, and not even a saddle-horse to be had. At last, on Sunday morning, being the fourth day, an open chaise returning from Edinburgh to Glasgow took me in, and conveyed me safe. I had passed my time more tolerably than I expected; for though the landlord was ignorant and stupid, his wife was a sensible woman, and in her youth had been celebrated in a song under the name of the " Bonny Lass of Livingstone." They had five children, but no books but the Bible and Sir Richard Blackmore's epic poem of " Prince Arthur," which the landlord brought me in one day by the name of a song-book, which he said would divert me ; and so it did, for I had not met with it before. The walls and windows were all scrawled with poetry ; and I amused myself not a little in composing a satire on my predecessors, which I also inscribed on the wall, to the great delight of my landlady, who showed it for many years afterwards with vanity to her travellers. When I came to pay my reckoning, to my astonishment she only charged me 3s. 6d. for lodging and board for four days. I had presented the little girls with ribbons I bought from a wandering pedlar who had taken shelter from the storm. But my whole expense, maid-servant and all, was only 5s. ; such was the rate of travelling in those days.

I had my lodging this session in a college-room, which I had furnished for the session at a moderate rent. I had never been without a cough in the former winter, when I lodged in a warm house in King Street, opposite to what was the butchers' market in those days ; but such was the difference between the air of the College and the lower streets of Glasgow, that in my new apartment, though only bare walls, and twenty feet by seventeen, I never had cold or cough all the winter. John Donaldson, a college servant, lighted my fire and made my bed ; and a maid from the landlady who furnished the room, came once a fortnight with clean linens. There were two English students of the-ology who lived on the floor below, and nobody above me. I again attended the lectures of Professors Leechman and Hutcheson, with much satisfaction and improvement.

Young Sellar, whom I mentioned before, became my most intimate friend; he came to me whenever he was at leisure, and we passed our time very agreeably together. He enlarged my circle of acquaintance by introducing me to the ladies whom he visited; and I introduced him to my two intimates, Miss Campbell and Mrs. D.,* who, he admitted, were superior to any of his former acquaintance. In an excursion with him to Hamilton the year before, he had made me acquainted with Dr. Cullen, and now that he was come to Glasgow, I improved that acquaintance. I became intimate with Dr. M'Lean, whom I mentioned before, and on his suggestion we prepared to act the tragedy of *Cato* to a select company in the College. Our parts were allotted, and we rehearsed it well, though we never acted it before an audience. M'Lean and I allotted the parts: I was to be Cato; he was Marcus; our friend Sellar, Juba; a Mr. Lesly was to do Lucius; an English student of the name of Seddon was to be Styphax; and Robin Bogle, Sempronius. Miss Campbell was our Marcia, and Miss Wood, Lucia; I have forgot our Portius. We rehearsed it twice, but never acted it. Though we never acted our play, we attained one of our chief purposes, which was, to become more intimate with the ladies. Lord Selkirk

* This lady may be the same mentioned at foot of p. 79, who, the author says, was of the Limekiln family.

would not join us, though he took much pleasure in instructing Miss Campbell.

In our literary club this session we took to reviewing books as a proper exercise. Mr. Thom, who was afterwards minister of Govan, a learned man, of a very particular but ingenious turn of mind, though much senior to any of us, was one of our members, and had great sway among us. He had quarrelled with Hutcheson; and having heard me say that Hutcheson's book on the *Passions* was not intelligible, he assigned it to me, that I might understand it better. I accordingly reviewed it in a few pages, and took much pains to unravel certain intricacies both of thought and expression that had run through it : this I did with much freedom, though not without respect to the author. This essay pleased my friends ; and one of them, by Thom's instigation, carried a copy of it to Hutcheson. He glanced it over and returned it, saying that the young gentleman might be in the right, but that he had long ago made up his mind on those subjects, and could not now take the trouble to revise them.

Not long after this, I had certain proof of the gentleness and candour of this eminent Professor ; for when I delivered a discourse in the Divinity Hall, it happened to please the Professor (Leechman) so much, that he gave it very liberal praise, both in public and private ; insomuch that it was borrowed by one of his minions, and handed about the College with so much approbation that Mr. Hutcheson wished to see it.

When he had read it, he returned it with unqualified applause, though it contained some things which a jealous mind might have interpreted as an attack on his favourite doctrine of a moral sense. His civility was now accompanied with some degree of confidence.

I preserved my intimacy with my friends of last winter, and added a few more families to my acquaintance, which made the time pass very agreeably. I had been introduced to Mr. Purdie, the rector of the school, who had, at North Berwick, taught many of my young friends in the Lothians, and particularly the whole name of Dalrymple. He had half-a-dozen or eight boarders, for whom his daughters kept a very good table, insomuch that I was often invited to dinner, and became intimate in the family. The eldest daughter, who was a sensible, prudent woman, and mistress of the house, being about forty, sent for me one Saturday morning in haste ; and when I arrived, she took me into a room apart from her sisters, who were girls under twenty ; and there, with many tears, informed me that her father, having been much intoxicated on the Friday or Saturday before, had never since been sober ; that he had not attended the school all the week, and that he now was firmly determined to resign his office, as he was sensible he could not abstain from dram-drinking. She added that he had not saved much money, having been held down by some idle and wasteful sons, and that they could ill afford to want the emoluments of his office. She concluded by telling me that she had previously informed her father that she was going to send for me, and impart his secret to me for advice. To this he had not objected, and when I was carried to his room he received me with open arms, told me his dismal case with tears and lamentations, and his firm resolution to resign, as he was sensible he could not reform, and could no longer be of use. He concluded by asking for a dram, which was the second he had called for before nine o'clock. I laughed and rallied, and was serious and grave with him by turns, and used every argument I could to break him off his habit, but to no purpose; for he answered all my arguments by the impossibility of his ever reforming, and consequently of ever appearing again in the world. He concluded with "Nelly, give me a dram," which she durst not refuse, otherwise he would have fired the house. To have time to think and consult about him, I went from him to the breakfast parlour. When I was leaving him, he prayed me to return as soon as possible, as he could not bear his own thoughts alone.

When at breakfast, I thought of an expedient which I imagined I could depend upon for him, if it took effect. I communicated my plan to his daughter, and she was pleased. When I went to him again, I told him I was truly sorry I could not pass that day with him, as I was obliged to go to Stirling, by my father's orders, upon business, and that I had made choice of that day, as I could return without missing more than one day of the College. I added that I had never been

there, and had not been able to find a companion, for
which I was sorry. "Nelly," said he, with great quickness, "do you think I could sit on a horse? if I could,
I would go with him and show him the way." I
cajoled him on this, and so did his daughter; and, in
short, after an early dinner while the horses and a
servant were preparing, we set out for Stirling about
one o'clock, I having taken his word before his daughter, that in all things he would comply with my will,
otherwise I would certainly return.

I had much difficulty to get him to pass the little
village public-houses which were in our way, without
calling for drams. He made this attempt half-a-dozen
times in the first stage, but I would not consent, and
besides promised him he should have as much wine as
he pleased. With much difficulty I got him to Kilsyth,
where we stopped to feed our horses, and where we
drank a bottle of claret. In short, I got him to Stirling before it was quite dark, in the second week of
April, old style: he ate a hearty supper, and we had
another bottle of claret, and he confessed he never
slept sound but that night, since he was taken ill. In
short, we remained at Stirling all Sunday, attended
church, and had our dinner and claret, and our walk
on the Castle-hill in the evening. I brought him to
his own house on Monday by five o'clock. The man's
habit was broken; he was again of a sound mind, and
he attended his school on Tuesday in perfect health.
As many of the Professors were Purdie's friends, this
successful act of kindness to him raised me in their

8

esteem, and atoned for many levities with which I had been taxed.

He lived many years after this, but did not leave his family independent. One of his daughters was married creditably in Edinburgh : the two eldest came to live there after his death, but were in indigence.   In the year 1778 I happened to be for a few weeks at Buxton, where I met with Sir William Gordon, K.B., who had been a boarder at Purdie's for two or three years before 1745, and who was at Leyden with me in the end of that year.   Riding out with him one day, he happened to ask me in what state Purdie's family was left ?   I told him what I knew, and added that they had a kind remembrance of him, for that not many months after he had left them, I heard Nelly say, with tears in her eyes, upon an insult having been offered them by some of their neighbours, that they durst not have done so if Willy Gordon had been in the house.   He answered that the father had very often licked him, but he had no resentment, as it was for his advantage, and that the daughters were good girls.   He concluded by offering me a sum of money.   I thought it better to accept of an annual pension of £10, which he remitted to them by me for several years.

My friendship with Mrs. D.* and her brother never impaired, though, having a more extended acquaintance than I had the preceding year, I was frequently engaged when they wished to have me with them.

I became acquainted with Mr. Wood's family, where

* See p. 109.

there were three or four very agreeable daughters, besides the Governor of the Isle of Man, and Andrew the
clergyman, who died rector of Gateshead, by Newcastle, in the year 1772, of a fever which he contracted
by exerting himself with the utmost humanity to save
his parishioners on the fatal night when the bridge of
Newcastle fell.   Here it was that I met with Colonel
Robert Hepburn of Keith for the first time since we
had been at the same class together in the year 1736.
We left Mr. Wood's early in an evening after drinking
tea, retired to Cockaine's tavern, and did not part till
near five in the morning.   Most unfortunately for me,
I had made an appointment with Mr. James Hogg,
a probationer, and tutor to the four sons of Sir John
Douglas of Kelhead, to ride ten or twelve miles with
them on their way to Annandale ; and I had hardly
become warm in bed when rap-rap he came to my
door, and insisted on my getting up and fulfilling my
promise.   Never in my life had I such reluctance to
fulfil any promise, for Hepburn had proposed to make
rack punch our beverage after supper, which I had
never tasted before, and which had given me the first
headache I had almost ever felt.   There was no help
for it.   It was a fine morning in the second week of
May; we breakfasted at Hamilton, and I rode six miles
farther with them and returned.

James Hogg was a man of a good heart and uncommon generosity.   Sir John's affairs were completely deranged, and he could raise no money to carry on the
education of his boys.   Hogg had a little patrimony

of his own, nearly £200 : rather than his pupils should suffer, two of them were fit for college, he came to Glasgow with all the four, and with a trusty old woman of a servant : he kept a small house for them in King Street, and being an excellent economist, fed them well at the least possible expense. I frequently dined with him and them, and was astonished at his good management. This he continued all the next year also, when Sir John was sent to the Tower of London for rebellious practices. This debt, together with arrears of wages, was not paid till many years afterwards, when Hogg was minister of Linlithgow, where he died by a fall from a horse in spring 1770. Had his understanding been as strong as his heart was generous, he would have been a first-rate character.

In that week, or that immediately following, Will Sellar and I, and Robin Bogle of Shettleston, went on a party with ladies, two Miss Woods and Peggy Douglas of Mains, a celebrated wit and a beauty, even then in the wane. When we came to Hamilton, she prayed us to send a messenger a few miles to bring to us a clergyman of a neighbouring parish, a Mr. Thomas Clelland. He came to us when we were viewing the romantic gardens of Barncluch, which lie between Hamilton and the Dog Kennel.

Thomas Clelland was a good-looking little man, but his hair was becoming grey, which no sooner Margaret observed, than she rallied him pretty roughly (which was her way) on his being an old fusty bachelor, and on his increasing marks of age since she had seen him, not more than a year before. After bearing patiently all the efforts of her wit, " Margaret," says he, " you know that I am master of the parish register where your age is recorded, and that I know when you must be with justice called an old maid, in spite of your juvenile airs." "What care I, Tom?" said she ; "for I have for some time renounced your worthless sex : I have sworn to be Duchess of Douglas, or never to mount a marriage-bed." This happened in May 1745. She made her purpose good. When she made this pre- diction she was about thirty. It was fulfilled a few years after.*

I had an opportunity of seeing the temper and spirit of the clergy in the neighbourhood of Glasgow a second time this year, by means of a trial of a clergyman in the county of Ayr for certain alleged crimes, which came by appeal before the Synod of Glasgow. The person tried was a very sensible man, of much wit and humour, who had made a butt of a neighbouring clergyman, who was weak, and at the same time good- natured, and had all the qualities of a butt. He was found out, however, to be a man full of deep resent- ment, and so malicious as to turn frolic into crime. After many very late sederunts of the Synod, and at last a hearing of the General Assembly, the affair was

* Margaret, daughter of James Douglas of Mains, was married in 1758 to Archibald, first and last Duke of Douglas. She died in 1774, leaving a traditional reputation for much freedom of speech and action.—J. H. B.
" An old lady," wrote Dr. Johnson, " who talks broad Scotch, with a paralytic voice, and is scarce understood by her own countrymen."

dismissed.   The gentleman was settled in the parish
to which he was presented, and many years afterwards
died minister of Glasgow, where his good name had
been so much traduced, much regretted ;—a caution
to young men of wit and humour to beware of fools as
much as knaves.

I was detained later at Glasgow than I would have
chosen, that I might obtain my credentials from the
University, as by the tenor of the Act of Bursary I
was obliged on this third year to repair to some foreign
Protestant university.   I had taken my degree of A.M.
at Edinburgh, and had only to get here my certificate
of attendance for two years, and my Latin letter recommending me to foreign academies.   I must acknowledge that I had profited much by two years' study at
Glasgow in two important branches—viz., moral philosophy and theology; along with which last I received
very excellent instructions on composition, for Leechman was not only fervent in spirit when he lectured,
but ornamented all his discourses with a taste derived
from his knowledge of belles-lettres.

In the months of June and July 1745, I went
through most of my trials in the presbytery of Haddington, as my father was resolved I should be ready
to take out my licence within a month after my return
from abroad.   In the month of August I went to Dumfriesshire, to pass a few weeks there, and to take leave
of my friends. About the end of that month I received
orders from my father to repair to Drumlanrig Castle,
to meet his friend Dr. John Sinclair, M.D., who was to

be some days there on his way from Moffat to Dumfries, and after that to return home as soon as I could, as he expected to be home about the 18th of next month with my mother from Langton, near Dunse, where they were drinking goats' whey.

I accordingly met Dr. Sinclair at Drumlanrig, where I had been frequently before with my friend James Ferguson of Craigdarroch, who was then acting commissioner for his Grace the Duke of Queensberry. He had been bred to the law, but relinquished the bar for this employment, which seated him within a few miles of his own estate, which needed improvement. His first lady was a sister of Sir Henry Nisbet's, who died young; his second was her cousin, a daughter of the Hon. Baron Dalrymple. Dr. Sinclair had been my father's classfellow, and had a great regard for him; he was an elegant scholar, and remarkable for his perfect knowledge of the Latin tongue, which in those days was much cultivated in Scotland. The professors of medicine then taught in Latin, and Dr. Sinclair was one of that first set who raised the fame of the school of medicine in Edinburgh above that of any other in Europe. He and Dr. John Clerk, the great practising physician, had found Moffat waters agree with themselves, and frequented it every season in their turns for a month or six weeks, and by that means drew many of their patients there, which made it be more frequented than it has been of late years, when there is much better accommodation.

I had promised Mr. R. Bogle and his sister to pass

a few days with them at Moffat, on the road to which
I passed one day with my friend William Cunningham,
minister of Durisdeer, the Duke of Queensberry's
parish church. He was knowing and accomplished,
and pleasing and elegant in his manners, beyond most
of the Scottish clergymen of that day. The Duchess
of Queensberry* (Lady K. Hyde) had discovered his
merit on her visit to Scotland, and had him constantly
with her, so that he was called the Duchess's Walking-
staff. From his house I crossed to Moffat, about fifteen miles off, but did not reach it that night on account
of a thunder-storm which had made the waters impas-
sable, so that I was obliged to lodge in what they call a
shieling, where I was used with great hospitality and
uncommon politeness by a young farmer and his sister,
who were then residing there, attending the milking of
the ewes, the business of that season in a sheep country.

When I got to Moffat, I found my expecting friends
still there, though the news had arrived that the
Chevalier Prince Charles had landed in the north with
a small train, had been joined by many of the clans,
and might be expected to break down into the low
country, unless Sir John Cope, who was then on his
march north, should meet with them and disperse
them. I remained only a few days at Moffat, as the
news became more important and alarming every

* This lady and her husband were the patrons of Gay, the poet,
and brought him to Edinburgh where he resided with them at
Queensberry House, Canongate. He became an intimate friend
of Allan Ramsay and constantly frequented his shop at the eastern
end of the Luckenbooths.

day; and, taking leave of my friends, I got home to
Prestonpans on the evening of the 12th of September.
My father, etc., were not returned, but I was perfectly
informed of the state of public affairs by many persons in the place, who told me that Prince Charles
had evaded Sir John Cope, who found himself obliged
to march on to Inverness, not venturing to attack the
Highlanders on the hill of Corry-arrock, and was then
proceeding to Aberdeen, where transports were sent
to bring his army by sea to the Firth.   I was also informed that as the Highlanders were making hasty
marches, the city of Edinburgh was putting itself in
some state of defence, so as to be able to resist the
rebels in case of an attack before Sir John Cope arrived.

On this news I repaired to Edinburgh the next day,
which was the 13th, and, meeting many of my companions, found that they were enlisting themselves in
a corps of four hundred Volunteers, which had been
embodied the day before, and were thought necessary
for the defence of the city.   Messrs. William Robertson, John Home, William M'Ghie, Hugh Bannatyne,
William Cleghorn, William Wilkie, George Logan, and
many others, had enlisted into the first or College Company, as it was called, which was to be commanded
by Provost Drummond, who was expected to return
that day from London, where he had been for some
time.   On the 14th I joined that company, and had
arms put into my hands, and attended a drill-sergeant
that afternoon and the next day to learn the manual
exercise, which I had formerly been taught by my

father, who had himself been a Volunteer in the end of Queen Anne's reign, when there was an alarm about the Pretender, but were obliged to hold their meetings in malt-barns in the night, and by candle-light.

The city was in great ferment and bustle at this time; for besides the two parties of Whigs and Jacobites—of which a well-informed citizen told me there were two-thirds of the men in the city of the first description, or friends to Government; and of the second, or enemies to Government, two-thirds of the ladies,—besides this division, there was another between those who were keen for preparing with zeal and activity to defend the city, and those who were averse to that measure, which were Provost Stuart and all his friends; and this appeared so plainly from the Provost's conduct and manner at the time, that there was not a Whig in town who did not suspect that he favoured the Pretender's cause; and however cautiously he acted in his capacity of chief magistrate, there were not a few who suspected that his backwardness and coldness in the measure of arming the people, was part of a plan to admit the Pretender into the city.

It was very true that a half-armed regiment of new raised men, with four hundred Volunteers from the city, and two hundred from other places, might not be thought sufficient for the defence of the city, had it been seriously besieged ; yet, considering that the Highlanders were not more than 1800, and the half of them only armed—that they were averse to approach walls, and afraid of cannon—I am persuaded that, had the dragoons proved firm and resolute, instead of running away to Dunbar to meet Sir John Cope, it was more than two to one that the rebels had never approached the city till they had defeated Cope, which, in that case, they would probably have attempted. Farther, I am of opinion, that if that part of the Town Council who were Whigs had found good ground to have put Stuart under arrest, the city would have held out.

In this opinion of Stuart I was confirmed, when in London, the following month of April. I happened to be in the British or Forrest's Coffeehouse, I forget which, in the afternoon of the day when the news of the victory at Culloden arrived. I was sitting at a table with Dr. Smollett* and Bob Smith (the Duke of Roxburgh's Smith), when John Stuart, the son of the Provost, who was then confined in the Tower, after turning pale and murmuring many curses, left the room in a rage, and slapped the door behind him with much violence. I said to my two companions, that lad Stuart is either a madman or a fool to discover himself in this manner, when his father is in the Tower on suspicion. Smith, who knew him best, acquiesced in my opinion, and added, that he had never seen him so much beside himself.

For a few days past M'Laurin the professor had been busy on the walls on the south side of the town, endeavouring to make them more defensible, and had even erected some small cannon near to Potterrow

* Tobias Smollett, author of *Humphrey Clinker*, etc.

Port, which I saw. I visited my old master when he was busy, who seemed to have no doubt that he could make the walls defensible against a sudden attack, but complained of want of service, and at the same time encouraged me and my companions to be diligent in learning the use of arms. We were busy all Saturday, when there arrived in town Bruce of Kennett, with a considerable number of Volunteers, above 100 from his country, and Sir Robert Dickson with 130 or 140 from Musselburgh and the parish of Inveresk; this increased the strength and added to the courage of the loyal inhabitants.

On Sunday morning the 15th, however, news had arrived in town that the rebel army had been at Linlithgow the night before, and were on full march towards Edinburgh. This altered the face of affairs, and made thinking people fear that they might be in possession of Edinburgh before Cope arrived. The Volunteers rendezvoused in the College Yards before ten o'clock, to the number of about 400. Captain Drummond appeared at ten, and, walking up in front of the right of his company, where I stood with all my companions of the corps, he addressed us in a speech of some length, the purport of which was, that it had been agreed by the General, and the Officers of the Crown, that the military force should oppose the rebels on their march to Edinburgh, consisting of the Town Guard, that part of the new regiment who had got arms, with the Volunteers from the country. What he had to propose to us was, that we should join this force, and expose our lives in defence of the capital of Scotland, and the security of our country's laws and liberties. He added that, as there was a necessity for leaving some men in arms for the defence of the city, that any persons choosing the one service rather than the other would bring no imputation of blame, but that he hoped his company would distinguish themselves by their zeal and spirit on this occasion. This was answered by an unanimous shout of applause.

We were marched immediately up to the Lawnmarket, where we halted till the other companies should follow. They were late in making their appearance, and some of their officers, coming up to us while in the street, told us that most of the privates were unwilling to march. During this halt, Hamilton's dragoons, who had been at Leith, marched past our corps, on their route to join Gardiner's regiment, who were at the Colt Bridge. We cheered them, in passing, with a huzzah; and the spectators began to think at last, that some serious fighting was likely to ensue, though before this moment many of them had laughed at and ridiculed the Volunteers. A striking example of this we had in our company, for a Mr. Hawthorn, a son of Bailie Hawthorn, who had laughed at his companions among the Volunteers, seeing us pass through the Luckenbooths in good order, and with apparent military ardour, ran immediately upstairs to his father's house, and, fetching his fowling-piece and his small sword, joined us before we left the Lawnmarket.

While we remained there, which was great part of an hour, the mob in the street and the ladies in the windows treated us very variously, many with lamentation, and even with tears, and some with apparent scorn and derision.   In one house on the south side of the street there was a row of windows, full of ladies, who appeared to enjoy our march to danger with much levity and mirth.   Some of our warm Volunteers observed them, and threatened to fire into the windows if they were not instantly let down, which was immediately complied with.   In marching down the Bow, a narrow winding street, the scene was different, for all the spectators were in tears, and uttering loud lamentations ; insomuch that Mr. Kinloch, a probationer, the son of Mr. Kinloch, one of the High Church ministers, who was in the second rank just behind Hew Ballantine, said to him in a melancholy tone, " Mr. Hew, Mr. Hew, does not this remind you of a passage in Livy, when the Gens Fabii marched out of Rome to prevent the Gauls entering the city, and the whole matrons and virgins of Rome were wringing their hands, and loudly lamenting the certain danger to which that generous tribe was going to be exposed ? "   "Hold your tongue," says Ballantine, " otherwise I shall complain to the officer, for you'll discourage the men."   " You must recollect the end, Mr. Hew, *omnes ad unum perieri.*"   This occasioned a hearty laugh among those who heard it, which being over, Ballantine half whispered Kinloch, " Robin, if you are afraid, you had better steal off when you can find an opportunity ; I shall

not tell that you are gone till we are too far off to recover you." *

We halted in the Grassmarket, near the West Port,
that the other bodies who were to join us might come.
On our march, even our company had lost part of their
number, and none of the other Volunteers had come
up. The day being advanced to between twelve and
one o'clock, the brewers who lived in that end of the
street brought out bread and cheese, and strong ale and
brandy, as a refreshment for us, in the belief that we
needed it, in marching on such an enterprise. While
we remained in this position, my younger brother William, then near fifteen, as promising a young man as
ever was born, of a fine genius, and an excellent scholar,
though he had been kept back with very bad health,
came up to me. He had walked into town that morning in his anxiety about me, and learning that I was
with the company on our march to fight the rebels, he
had run down with great anxiety from the house where
I lodged, to learn how things really stood. He was
melancholy and much alarmed. I withdrew with him
to the head of a neighbouring close, and endeavoured
to abate his fears, by assuring him that our march was

---

* Sir Walter Scott tells another tale of one of these volunteers,
"a very worthy man, a writing master by occupation, who had
ensconced his bosom beneath a professional cuirass, consisting
of two quires of long foolscap writing paper, and doubtful that
even this defence might be unable to protect his valiant heart
from claymores, amongst which its impulses might carry him, had
written on the outside, in his best flourish, ' This is the body of
I—— M——, pray give it Christian burial,' "—*Miscellanies*, vol.
xix.

only a feint to keep back the Highlanders, and that we should in a little while be ordered back to our field for exercise in the College. His anxiety began to abate, when, thinking that, whatever should happen, it would be better for me to trust him with a Portugal piece of thirty-six shillings and three guineas that I had in my pocket, I delivered them over to him. On this he burst into tears, and said I surely did not think as I said, but believed I was going out to danger, otherwise I would not so readily part with my money. I comforted him the best way I could, and took back the greater part of the money, assuring him that I did not believe yet that we would be sent out, or if we were, I thought we would be in such force that the rebels would not face us. The young man was comforted, and I gave him a rendez-vous for nine at night.

While we were waiting for an additional force, a body of the clergy (the forenoon service being but ill attended on account of the ringing of the fire bell, which is the great alarm in Edinburgh), who were the two Wisharts, Wallace, Glen, Logan, etc., came to us. Dr. William Wishart, Principal of the College, was their prolocutor, and called upon us in a most pathetic speech to desist from this rash enterprise, which he said was exposing the flower of the youth of Edinburgh, and the hope of the next generation, to the danger of being cut off, or made prisoners and maltreated, without any just or adequate object; that our number added so very little to the force that was intended against the rebels, that withdrawing us would make little difference, while our loss would be irreparable, and that at any rate a body of men in arms was necessary to keep the city quiet during the absence of the armed force, and therefore he prayed and besought the Volunteers and their officers to give up all thoughts of leaving the city defenceless, to be a prey to the seditious.

This discourse, and others similar to it, had an effect upon many of us, though youthful ardour made us reluctant to abandon the prospect of showing our prowess. Two or three of the warmest of our youths remonstrated against those unreasonable speeches, and seemed eager for the fight. From that moment I saw the impropriety of sending us out, but till the order was recalled, it was our duty to remain in readiness to obey. We remained for near an hour longer, and were joined by another body of Volunteers, and part of the new regiment that was raising. Not long after came an order for the Volunteers to march back to the College Yards, when Provost Drummond, who had been absent, returned and put himself at our head, and marched us back. In the mean time the other force that had been collected, with ninety men of the Town Guard, etc., etc., marched out to the Colt Bridge, and joined the dragoons, who were watching the approach of the enemy. Some of the Volunteers imagined that this manœuvre about the Volunteers was entirely Drummond's, and that he had no mind to face the rebels, though he had made a parade of courage and zeal, to make himself popular. But this was not the man's character—want of personal courage was not

9

his defect. It was civil courage in which he failed; for all his life he had a great deference to his superiors. But I then thought as I do now, that his offer to carry out the Volunteers was owing to his zeal and prowess —for personally he was a gallant Highlander; but on better considering the matter, after hearing the remonstrance of the clergy, he did not think that he could well be answerable for exposing so many young men of condition to certain danger and uncertain victory.

When we were dismissed from the College Yards, we were ordered to rendezvous there again in the evening, as night guards were to be posted round the whole city. Twelve or thirteen of the most intimate friends went to a late dinner to a Mrs. Turnbull's, then next house to the Tron Church. Many things were talked of with great freedom, for the company were William M'Ghie, William Cleghorn, William Robertson, John Home, Hugh Ballantine, and I. The other names I have forgot. Sundry proposals were made, one of which was that we should march off with our arms into England, and raise a volunteering spirit; or at any rate that we should join Sir John Cope's army, and try to get as many as possible to follow us. As I had been separated from my companions for two years, by my attendance at Glasgow, I had less confidence to speak my mind, especially as some of my warm associates thought everybody cowardly, or a secret Jacobite, who did not agree with them. However, perceiving that some of the company did not agree with the chief speakers, I ventured to state, that before we resolved to march off with our arms, we should take care to have a sufficient number of followers ; for even if it were a lawful act to march off with our arms without orders, we would appear ridiculous and contemptible if there were no more of us than the present company, and I guessed we could not reckon on three or four more.   This brought out M'Ghie and Hew Ballantine, who were considered the steadiest men amongst us. This occasioned a warm altercation, for Cleghorn and Home, in those days, were very fiery.   At last, however, it was settled that we should try, in the course of the next day, to find if we could prevail on any considerable number to follow us, and if not, that we should carry our arms to the Castle, that they might not fall into the enemies' hands, and then make the best of our way separately to Sir John Cope's army, and offer our service.

When the night-watch was set, all the company I have now mentioned were appointed to guard the Trinity Hospital, in Leith Wynd, which was one of the weakest parts of the city.   There twelve of us were placed under the command of Lieutenant Alexander Scott, a young man of spirit, a merchant in the city, and not two or three years senior to the eldest of us. Here we had nothing to do all night but make responses every half hour, as the " All's well " came round from the other guards that were posted at certain distances, so that a stranger who was approaching the city would have thought it was going to be gallantly defended.

But we knew the contrary; for, as Provost Stuart and all his friends had been against making any preparation for defence, when they yielded to the zeal of their opponents, they hung a dead weight on every measure. This we were all sensible of, and had now no doubt that they wished the city to fall into the Pretender's hands, however carefully they might hide their intentions.* At one o'clock, the Lord Provost and his guard visited all the posts, and found us at Trinity Hospital very alert. When he was gone, " Did you not see," said John Home to me, " how pale the traitor looked, when he found us so vigilant?" " No," I replied, " I thought he looked and behaved perfectly well, and it was the light from the lantern that made him appear pale." When we were relieved in the morning, I went to my lodging, and tried to get a few hours' sleep; but though the house was down a close, the noise was so great, and my spirits so much agitated, that I got none.

At noon on the 16th, when I went to the streets, I heard that General Fowlks had arrived from London early, and, by order of General Guest, had taken command of the 2nd Regiment of Dragoons, who, having retired the night before from Corstorphine, where they left only a guard, had marched with them to the Colt Bridge, a mile nearer than Corstorphine, and were

---

* " Mr. Thomas Williamson, son of the Rev. David Williamson, minister of St. Cuthbert's Church, was then Town Clerk of Edinburgh.   He absolutely refused to give up the keys of the City, even to the Lord Provost. When commanded to do so he implored permission to escape over the walls in order that he might not share in the general disgrace of the City."—*Woodhouselee MSS.*

joined by the same body of foot that had been with them on the 15th. The rebels, however, were slowly approaching, and there was no news of Sir John Cope's arrival with the army from Aberdeen ; and the general opinion was, that the town would certainly be given up. The most zealous Whigs came now to think this necessary, as they plainly thought they saw Provost Stuart and his friends, so far from co-operating with their zeal, retarded every measure.

But the fate of the city was decided early in the afternoon, when the two regiments of dragoons were seen about four o'clock on their march from the Colt Bridge to Leith, by the long dykes, as then called; now George Street in the New Town. Then the clamour arose, that it would be madness to think of defending the town, as the dragoons had fled. The alarm bell was rung—a meeting of the inhabitants with the magistrates was convened, first in the Goldsmith's Hall, and when the crowd increased, in the New Church aisle. The four companies of Volunteers rendezvoused in the Lawnmarket, and, growing impatient, sent two of their lieutenants to the Provost for orders, for the captains had been sent for to the meeting. They soon returned without any orders, and said all was clamour and discordance. While they were absent, two Volunteers in the rear rank (Boyle and Weir), just behind, quarrelled, when debating whether or not the city should be surrounded, and were going to attack one another, one with his musket and bayonet, and the other with his small sword, having flung down his musket. They were soon separated without any harm, and placed asunder from each other.   At this time, a man on horseback, whom nobody knew, came up from the Bow, and, riding at a quick pace along the line of Volunteers, called out that the Highlanders were at hand, and that they were 16,000 strong.   This fellow did not stop to be examined, but rode off at the gallop. About this time, a letter had come, directed to the Provost, summoning the town to surrender, and alarming them with the consequence in case any opposition was made.

The Provost made a scrupulous feint about reading the letter, but this point was soon carried, and all idea of defence was abandoned. Soon after, Captain Drummond joined us in the Lawnmarket, with another captain or two. He sent to General Guest, after conversing a little with the lieutenant, to acquaint him that the Volunteers were coming to the Castle to deliver their arms.   The messenger soon returned, and we marched up, glad to deliver them, lest they should have fallen into the hands of the enemy, which the delay of orders seemed to favour, though not a little ashamed and afflicted at our inglorious campaign.

We endeavoured to engage as many as we could to meet us at Haddington, and there deliberate what was to be done, as we conjectured that, now that the town of Edinburgh had surrendered, Sir John Cope would not land nearer than Dunbar.   Upon being asked by two of my friends what I was to do—viz., William Robertson and William Cleghorn—I told them that I meant to go that night to my father's, at Prestonpans, where, if they would join me next day, by that time events might take place that would fix our resolution. Our ardour for arms and the field was not abated.

As it was now the dusk of the evening, I went to a house near the Nether Bow Port, where I had appointed my brother to meet me, that we might walk home together.   Having foreseen the events that took place, as the rebels were so near the town, I wished to take the road as soon as possible, but on attempting to get out of the gate, in the inside of which several loaded carts or waggons were standing, I found the gates locked, and the keys lodged with the Provost.   The carts were said to contain the baggage of Sir John Cope's army, etc., and each party interpreted the shutting of the gates according to their own fancy—one side thinking this was a manœuvre to prevent their reaching Sir John; and the other, to hinder them from falling into the hands of the enemy.   Be that as it may, it was half-past eight o'clock before the gate was opened, when I heard the baggage was ordered back to the Castle.   At a later hour they were sent to Dunbar.

My brother and I set out immediately, and after passing through the crowd at the head of the Canongate, who were pressing both ways to get out and in, we went through the Abbey, by St. Ann's Yards and the Duke's Walk, to Jock's Lodge, meeting hardly a mortal the whole way.   When we came down near the sands, I chose that way rather than the road through the whins, as there was no moonlight, and the whins were dark and solitary, but the sands always lightsome when the sea is in ebb, which was then the case. We walked slowly, as I had been fatigued, and my brother not strong; and, having met no mortal but one man on horseback as we entered the sands, riding at a brisk trot, who hailed us, we arrived at the west end of Preston-pans, having shunned Musselburgh by passing on the north side, without meeting or being overtaken by anybody. When we came to the gate of Lucky Vint's Courtyard, a tavern or inn then much frequented, I was astonished to meet with the utmost alarm and confusion —the officers of the dragoons calling for their horses in the greatest hurry. On stepping into the Court, Lord Drummore, the judge, saw me (his house being near, he had come down to sup with the officers). He immediately made up to me, and hastily inquired "Whence I had come?" "From Edinburgh direct." "Had the town surrendered?" "No! but it was expected to fall into the hands of the rebels early to-morrow." "Were there any Highlanders on their march this way?" "Not a soul;" I could answer for it, as I had left Edinburgh past eight o'clock, and had walked out deliberately, and seen not a creature but the horseman in the sands.

He turned to the officers, and repeated my intelligence, and asserted that it must be a false alarm, as he could depend on me. But this had no effect, for they believed the Highlanders were at hand. It was in vain to tell them that they had neither wings nor horses, nor were invisible—away they went, as fast as they could, to their respective corps, who, on marching from Leith, where they thought themselves not safe, had halted in an open field, above the west end of Preston-pans, between Prestongrange and the enclosures of Mr. Nisbet, lying west from the village of Preston. On inquiring what was become of Gardiner, Drummore told me, that being quite worn out on their arrival on that ground, he had begged to go to his own house, within half a mile, where he had been since eight o'clock, and where he had locked himself in, and could not be awaked till four in the morning, his usual hour. I went through the town to my father's, and before I got there I heard the dragoons marching in confusion, so strong was their panic, on the road that leads by the back of the gardens to Port Seaton, Aberlady, and North Berwick, all the way by the shore. My father and mother were not yet come home.

Before six on Tuesday morning, the 17th, Mr. James Hay, a gentleman in the town, who was afterwards a lieutenant in the Edinburgh Regiment, came to my bed-side, and eagerly inquired what I thought was to be done, as the dragoons, in marching along in their confusion, had strewed the road eastward with accoutrements of every kind—pistols, swords, skullcaps, etc. I said that people should be employed immediately to gather them up, and send them after, which was done, and amounted to what filled a close cart and a couple of creels on horse-back. By this time it was reported that the transports with Cope were seen off Dunbar. But it was not this news, for it was not then come, that made the dragoons scamper from their ground on the preceding night. It

was an unlucky dragoon, who, slipping a little aside
for a pea-sheaf to his horse, for there were some on the
ground not led off, fell into a coal-pit, not filled up, when
his side-arms and accoutrements made such a noise,
as alarmed a body of men, who, for two days, had been
completely panic-struck.

About mid-day, I grew anxious for the arrival of my
two companions, Cleghorn and Robertson. I, therefore,
walked out on the road to Edinburgh, when on going as
far as where the turnpike is now, below Drummore, I
met with Robertson on horseback, who told me that a
little way behind him was Cleghorn and a cousin of his
own, a Mr. Fraser of the Excise, who wished to accompany us to Sir John Cope's camp, for it was now known
that he was to land that day at Dunbar, and the city of
Edinburgh had been surrendered early that morning to
the Highland army.

We waited till our companions came up, and walked
together to my father's house, where I had ordered some
dinner to be prepared for them by two o'clock.   They
were urgent to have it sooner, as they wished to begin
our journey towards Dunbar as long before sunset as
they could.

As we were finishing a small bowl of punch that I had
made for them after dinner, James Hay, the gentleman
I mentioned before, paid us a visit, and immediately
after the ordinary civilities, said earnestly that he had
a small favour to ask of us, which was that we would be
so good as accept of a small collation which his sister and
he had provided at their house—that of Charles Sheriff,

the most eminent merchant in the place, who had died not long before, and left a widow and four daughters with this gentleman, their uncle, to manage their affairs. We declined accepting this invitation, for fear of being too late. He continued strongly to solicit our company, adding that he would detain us a very short while, as he had only four bottles of burgundy, which if we did not accept of, he would be obliged to give to the Highlanders. The name of burgundy, which some of us had never tasted, disposed us to listen to terms, and we immediately adjourned to Mrs. Sheriff's, not an hundred yards distant. We found very good apples and pears and biscuit set out for us, and after one bottle of claret to wash away the taste of the whisky punch, we fell to the burgundy, which we thought excellent; and in little more than an hour we were ready to take the road, it being then not long after five o'clock. Robertson mounted his horse, and left us to go round by his house at Gladsmuir to get a little money, as he had not wherewithal to defray his expenses, and mentioned an hour when he promised to meet us at Bangley Braefoot, Maggie Johnstone's, a public-house on the road leading to Dunbar, by Garlton Hills, a mile to the north of Haddington. There were no horses here for me, for though my father kept two, he had them both at the Goat Whey quarters.

When we came within sight of the door of this house, we saw Robertson dismounting from his horse: we got some beer or porter to refresh us after our walk, and having broken off in the middle of a keen dispute be-

tween Cleghorn and a recruiting sergeant, whether the
musket and bayonet, or broadsword and target, were
the best weapons, we proceeded on our journey, still a
little doubtful if it was true that Sir John Cope had arrived.   We proceeded slowly, for it was dark, till we
came to Linton Bridge.   Robertson, with his usual prudence, proposed to stay all night, it being ten o'clock,
and still double beds for us all.   Cleghorn's ardour and
mine resisted this proposal; and getting a loan of
Robertson's horse, we proceeded on to the camp at
Dunbar, that we might be more certain of Sir John's
arrival.   At Belton Inn, within a mile of the camp, we
were certified of it, and might then have turned in, but
we obstinately persisted in our plan, fancying that we
should find friends among the officers to receive us into
their tents.   When we arrived at the camp we were not
allowed admittance, and the officer on the picket, whom
Cleghorn knew, assured us that there was not an inch of
room for us or our horse, either in camp or at Dunbar,
and advised us to return.   Being at last persuaded that
Cope was landed, and that we had played the fool, we
first attempted Belton Inn, but it was choked full by
that time, as we were convinced by eight or ten foot-
men lounging in the kitchen on tables and chairs.   We
tried the inn at Linton with the same success.   At last
we were obliged to knock up the minister, Mat. Reid, at
two in the morning, who, taking us for marauders from
the camp, kept us an hour at the door.   We were hardly
well asleep, when, about six, Robertson came to demand
his horse, quite stout and well refreshed, as well as his

cousin Fraser, while we were jaded and undone; such is the difference between wisdom and folly.

After breakfasting, however, at the inn, we set out again for Dunbar, in sanguine hopes that we should soon return with the army, and give a good account of Sir John Cope. On our way, we visited the camp, which lay a mile west of Dunbar. As soon as I arrived at the town, I inquired for Colonel Gardiner, and went and visited him at Mr. Pyot's the minister of the town, where he lodged. He received me with kindness, and invited me to dine with him at two o'clock; and to come to him a little before the hour. I went to him at half-past one, and he took me to walk in the garden. He looked pale and dejected, which I attributed to his bad health and the fatigue he had lately undergone. I began to ask him if he was not now quite satisfied with the junction of the foot with the dragoons, and confident that they would give account of the rebels. He answered dejectedly that he hoped it might be so, but —and then made a long pause. I said, that to be sure they had made a very hasty retreat; " a foul flight," said he, " Sandie and they have not recovered from their panic; and I'll tell you in confidence that I have not above ten men in my regiment whom I am certain will follow me. But we must give them battle now, and God's will be done ! "

We were called to dinner, where there was nobody but the family and Cornet Kerr, a kinsman of the colonel. He assumed an air of gaiety at dinner, and inquiring of me the adventures of the night, rallied me as a raw soldier in not taking up with the first good quarters I could get ; and when the approaching event was mentioned, spoke of victory as a thing certain, "if God were on our side." We sat very short time after dinner. The Colonel went to look after his regiment, and prepare them for to-morrow's march, and I to look out for my companions ; on finding them, it was agreed to return back to Linton, as between the dragoons and the concourse of strangers, there was not a bed to be had. We returned accordingly to Linton, and made good our quarters at the minister's, where we remained till the army passed in the morning on their route to Haddington. John Home had arrived at Dunbar on Wednesday, and said he had numbered the Highlanders, and thought there were about 1900, but that they were ill armed, though that defect was now supplied at Edinburgh. There were many of the volunteers all night at Linton, whom we saw in the morning, and with whom we appointed to meet in an inn at Haddington.

As the army passed about eleven or twelve, we joined them and marched along with them ; they took the hill road by Charteris Dykes ; and when we were about Beanston, I was accosted by Major Bowles, whom I knew, and who, desirous of some conversation with me, made his servant dismount and give me his horse, which I gladly accepted of, being a good deal worn out with the fatigue of the preceding day. The major was completely ignorant of the state of the country and of the character of the Highlanders. I found him perfectly ignorant and credulous, and in the power of every person with whom he conversed. I was not acquainted with the discipline of armies; but it appeared to me to be very imprudent to allow all the common people to converse with the soldiers on their march as they pleased, by which means their panic was kept up, and perhaps their principles corrupted. Many people in East Lothian at that time were Jacobites, and they were most forward to mix with the soldiers. The commons in general, as well as two-thirds of the gentry at that period, had no aversion to the family of Stuart; and could their religion have been secured, would have been very glad to see them on the throne again.

Cope's small army sat down for the afternoon and night in an open field on the west side of Haddington. The Volunteers, to the number of twenty-five, assembled at the principal inn, where also sundry officers of dragoons and those on the staff came for their dinner. While our dinner was preparing, an alarm was beat in the camp, which occasioned a great hurry-scurry in the courtyard with the officers taking their horses, which some of them did with no small reluctance, either through love of their dinner or aversion to the enemy. I saw Colonel Gardiner passing very slowly, and ran to him to ask what was the matter. He said it could be nothing but a false alarm, and would soon be over. The army, however, was drawn out immediately, and it was found to be a false alarm. The Honourable Francis Charteris*had been married the day before, at Preston-

---

* Afterwards, seventh Earl of Wemyss.

hall, to Lady Frances Gordon, the Duchess of Gordon's daughter, who was supposed to favour the Pretender, though she had a large pension from Government. How that might be nobody knew, but it was alleged that the alarm followed their coach, as they passed to their house at New Amisfield.

After dinner, Captain Drummond came to us at the inn, to whom we unanimously gave a commission to apply to the general for arms to us, and to appoint us a station in the line, as we had not only our captain, but one of our lieutenants with us. Drummond left us to make this application, but was very long in returning, and the answer he brought was not so agreeable. It was, that the General did not think we could be so serviceable by taking arms, as we might be in taking posthorses through the night, and reconnoitring the roads leading from the enemy towards our army, and bringing an account of what movements there were. This was agreed to after some hesitation, and sixteen of us were selected to go out, two and two—one set at eight in the evening, and another at twelve. Four of these were thought useless, as there were only three roads that could be reconnoitred. I was of the first set, being chosen by Mr. William M'Ghie as his companion, and we chose the road by the sea-coast, through Longniddry, Port Seaton, and Prestonpans, as that with which I was best acquainted. We set out not long after eight o'clock, and found everything perfectly quiet as we expected. At Prestonpans we called at my father's, and found that they had returned home on Wednesday; and having requested them to wait supper till our return, we rode on to Westpans, in the county of Midlothian, near Musselburgh; and still meeting with nothing on which to report, we returned to supper at my father's. While we were there, an application was made to us by Bailie Hepburn, the baron bailie or magistrate of the place, against a young gentleman, a student of medicine, as he said, who had appeared in arms in the town, and pretended that he wished to be conducted to Cope's army. We went down from the manse to a public-house, where this gentleman was confined. At the first glance, M'Ghie knew him to be a student, though not personally acquainted with him, and got him relieved immediately, and brought him up to supper. M'Ghie took all the pains he could to persuade this gentleman, whose name was Myrie, to attach himself to the Volunteers, and not to join the army; but he would not be persuaded, and actually joined one of the regiments on their march next morning, and was sadly wounded at the battle.

Francis Garden, afterwards Lord Gardenstone, and Robert Cunningham, afterwards the General in Ireland, followed Mr. M'Ghie and me, and were taken prisoners, and not very well used. They had gone as far as Crystall's Inn, west of Musselburgh, and had sat with a window open after daylight at a regale of white wine and oysters, when they were observed by one of the Prince's Life Guards who was riding past, not in uniform, but armed with pistols; they took to their horses, when he, pretending to take them for rebels, they

10

avowed they were King's men, and were taken to the camp at Duddingston.*

When M'Ghie and I returned to Haddington about one o'clock, all the beds were taken up, and we had to sleep in the kitchen on benches and chairs. To our regret we found that several Volunteers had single beds to themselves, a part of which we might have occupied. Sir John Cope and his army marched in the morning, I think, not till nine o'clock, and to my great surprise, instead of keeping the post-road through Tranent Muir, which was high ground and commanded the country south for several miles, as it did that to the north for two or three miles towards the sea, they turned to the right by Elvingston and the village of Trabroun, till they past Longniddry on the north, and St. Germains on the south, when, on entering the defile made by the enclosures there, they halted for near an hour, and then marched into the open field of two miles in length and one and a half in breadth, extending from Seaton to Preston, and from Tranent Meadow to the sea. I understood afterwards that the General's intention was (if he had any will of his own) to occupy the field lying between Walliford, Smeaton, and Inveresk, where he would have had the river Esk running through, deep banks in front, and the towns of Dalkeith and Musselburgh at hand to supply him with provisions. In this camp he could not have been surprised; and in marching to this ground the road through Tranent was not more distant by 100

* Scott in his review of Home's Works records this incident in ludicrous light.—*Miscellanies*, vol. xix.

yards than that by Seaton.   But they were too late in marching; for when they came to St. Germains, their scouts, who were chiefly Lords Home and Loudon, brought them intelligence that the rebel army were on their march, on which, after an hour's halt, when, by turning to the left, they might have reached the high ground at Tranent before the rebels, they marched on to that plain before described, now called the field of battle. This field was entirely clear of the crop, the last sheaves having been carried in the night before ; and neither cottage, tree, or bush were in its whole extent, except one solitary thorn bush which grew on the march between Seaton and Preston fields, around and near to which lay the greatest number of slain, and which re- mains there to this day,* though the fields have been long since completely enclosed.

The army marched straight to the west end of this field till they came near the walls of the enclosures of Preston, which reached from the road leading from the village of Preston north to Tranent meadow and Bank- town, down almost half-way to Prestonpans, to which town, from this enclosure, there was no interruption ; and the whole projections of those enclosures into the plain to the east were not above 300 yards. That part of it which belonged to Preston estate was divided into three shots, as they were called, or rigg lengths, the under shot, the middle, and the upper. A cart road for

---

* About half a mile east of Prestonpans Railway Station, a thorn tree, growing in a field a few yards north of the main road to Long- niddry, is still pointed out as marking the site of the battle.

carrying out dung divided the two first, which lay gently
sloping to the sea, from which it was separated by garden walls, and a large enclosure for a rabbit warren. The
upper shot was divided from the middle one by a foot-
path, and lay almost level, sloping almost impercept-
ibly to Tranent Meadow. This was properly the field of
battle, which on account of the slope was not seen fully
from the lower fields or the town. Near to those walls
on the east the army formed their first line of battle
fronting west. They were hardly formed, when the
rebel army appeared on the high ground at Birsley,
south-west of our army about a mile. On sight of them
our army shouted. They drew nearer Tranent, and our
army shifted a little eastward to front them. All this
took place by one o'clock.

Colonel Gardiner having informed the General and
his staff that I was at hand to execute anything in my
power for the good of the service, there was sent to me
a message to inquire if I could provide a proper person
to venture up to the Highland army, to make his observations, and particularly to notice if they had any
cannon, or if they were breaking ground anywhere.
With some difficulty I prevailed on my father's church-
officer, a fine stout man, to make this expedition, which
he did immediately. A little further on in the afternoon the same aide-de-camp, an uncle of Sir Ralph Aber-
crombie's, came to request me to keep a look-out from
the top of the steeple, and observe if at any time any
detachment from the main army was sent westwards.
In the mean time the Highlanders lay with their right

close to Tranent, and had detached some companies down to the churchyard, which was close by a waggon-way which led directly down to our army, and crossed the road leading between Preston and Seaton, where Cope's six or seven pieces of cannon were placed, not above a third of a mile distant from the church.   As the Highlanders appeared north of the church in the churchyard, which was higher than the waggon-way, the cannon were fired, and dislodged them from thence. Not long after this, about four in the afternoon, the rebels made a movement to the westward of Birsley, where they had first appeared, and our army took their first position. Soon after this I observed from the steeple a large detachment of Highlanders, about 300 or 400, lodge themselves in what was called the Thorny Loan, which led from the west end of Preston to the village of Dolphingston to the south-west. I mounted my horse to make this known to the General, and met the aide-de-camp riding briskly down the field, and told him what I had seen. I immediately returned to my station in the steeple. As twilight approached, I observed that detachment withdrawn, and was going up the field to tell this when my doughty arrived, who was going to tell me his story how numerous and fierce the Highlanders were —how keen for the fight—and how they would make but a breakfast of our men. I made him go with me to the General to tell his own story. In the mean time I visited Colonel Gardiner for a third time that day on his post, and found him grave, but serene and resigned; and he concluded by praying God to bless me, and that he could not wish for a better night to lie on the field; and then called for his cloak and other conveniences for lying down, as he said they would be awaked early enough in the morning, as he thought, by the countenance of the enemy, for they had now shifted their position to a sloping field east from the church, and were very near our army, with little more than the morass between. Coming down the field I asked my messenger if they had not paid him for his danger. Not a farthing had they given him, which being of a piece with the rest of the General's conduct raised no sanguine hopes for to-morrow. I gave the poor fellow half-a-crown, which was half my substance, having delivered the gold to my father the night before.

When I returned to my father's house, I found it crowded with strangers, some of them Volunteers, and some Merse clergymen, particularly Monteith and Laurie, and Pat Simson. They were very noisy and boastful of their achievements, one of them having the dragoon's broadsword who had fallen into the coal-pit, and the other the musket he had taken from a Highland soldier between the armies. Simson, who was cousin to Adam Drummond of Meginch, captain and paymaster in Lee's regiment, had a pair of saddle-bags intrusted to him, containing 400 guineas, which Patrick not imprudently gave to my father to keep all night for him, out of any danger of being plundered. Perceiving that there would be no room for me, without incommoding the strangers, I stole away to a neighbouring widow gentlewoman's, where I bespoke a bed, and returned

to supper at my father's.   But no sooner had I cut up
the cold surloin which my mother had provided, than
I fell fast asleep, having been much worn out with all
the fatigues of the preceding week.   I retired directly.

I directed the maid to awake me the moment the
battle began, and fell into a profound sleep in an in-
stant.   I had no need to be awaked, though the maid
was punctual, for I heard the first cannon that was
fired, and started to my clothes ; which, as I neither
buckled nor gartered, were on in a moment, and immediately went to my father's, not a hundred yards off.
All the strangers were gone, and my father had been
up before daylight, and had resorted to the steeple.
While I was conversing with my mother, he returned
to the house, and assured me of what I had guessed
before, that we were completely defeated.   I ran into
the garden where there was a mount in the south-east
corner, from which one could see the fields almost to
the verge of that part where the battle was fought.
Even at that time, which could hardly be more than
ten or fifteen minutes after firing the first cannon,* the
whole prospect was filled with runaways, and Highlanders pursuing them.   Many had their coats turned
as prisoners, but were still trying to reach the town in
hopes of escaping.   The pursuing Highlanders, when
they could not overtake, fired at them, and I saw two
fall in the glebe.   By-and-by a Highland officer whom

---

* " This battle . . . was fought on (Saturday) 21st of September
1745, and was ended just as the sun gott up : it did not last full
a quarter of an hour."—Lord Elcho's *Journal*.

I knew to be Lord Elcho passed with his train, and had an air of savage ferocity that disgusted and alarmed. He inquired fiercely of me where a public-house was to be found ; I answered him very meekly, not doubting but that, if I had displeased him with my tone, his reply would have been with a pistol bullet.

The crowd of wounded and dying now approached with all their followers, but their groans and agonies were nothing compared with the howlings, and cries, and lamentations of the women, which suppressed manhood and created despondency. Not long after the Duke of Perth appeared with his train, who asked me, in a very different tone, the way to Collector Cheap's, to which house he had ordered our wounded officers. Knowing the family were from home, I answered the questions of victorious clemency with more assurance of personal safety, than I had done to unappeased fury. I directed him the way to the house, which was hard by that where I had slept.

The rebel army had before day marched in three divisions, one of which went straight down the waggon-way to attack our cannon, the other two crossed the Morass near Seaton House; one of which marched north towards Port Seaton, where the field is broadest, to attack our rear, but overmarched themselves, and fell in with a few companies that were guarding the baggage in a small enclosure near Cockenzie, and took the whole. The main body marched west through the plains, and just at the break of day attacked our army. After firing once, they run on with their broadswords, and our people fled. The dragoons attempted to charge, under Colonel Whitney, who was wounded, but wheeled immediately, and rode off through the defile between Preston and Bankton, to Dolphingston, half a mile off. Colonel Gardiner, with his division, attempted to charge, but was only followed by eleven men, as he had foretold, Cornet Kerr being one. He continued fighting, and had received several wounds, and was at last brought down by the stroke of a broadsword over the head.* He was carried to the minister's house at Tranent, where he lived till next forenoon. His own house, which was nearer, was made an hospital for the Highlanders, no person of our army being carried there but the Master of Torphichen, who was so badly wounded that he could be sent to no greater distance. Some of the dragoons fled as far as Edinburgh, and one stood all day at the Castlegate, as General Guest would not allow him to be taken in. A considerable body of dragoons met at Dolphingston immediately after the rout, little more than half a mile from the field, where Cope joined them; and where it was said Lord Drummore offered to conduct them back, with assurance of victory when the Highlanders were busy with the booty. But they could not be prevailed on by his eloquence no more than by the youthful ardour of Earls Home and Loudon. After a short halt, they marched over Falside Hill to Lauder. Sir Peter Halket, a captain in Lee's regiment, acted a distin-

---

* "Poor Collenell Gardiner, one of the best men and experienced officers, was lost. It is said he was against the General's disposition, but the good man was in so bad a state of nealth he could not have lived long."—*Woodhouselee MSS.*

guished part on this occasion; for after the rout he kept his company together; and getting behind a ditch in Tranent Meadow, he kept firing away on the rebels till they were glad to let him surrender on terms.

In the mean time my father became very uneasy lest I should be ill treated by the rebels, as they would discover that I had been a Volunteer in Edinburgh; he therefore ordered the horses to be saddled, and telling me that the sea was out, and that we could escape by the shore without being seen, we mounted, taking a short leave of my mother and the young ones, and took the way he had pointed out. We escaped without interruption till we came to Portseton harbour, a mile off, where we were obliged to turn up on the land, when my father observing a small party of Highlanders, who were pursuing two or three carts with baggage that were attempting to escape, and coming up with the foremost driver, who would not stop when called to, they shot him on the spot. This daunted my father, who turned immediately, and took the way we came. We were back again soon after, when, taking off my boots and putting on shoes, I had the appearance of a person who had not been abroad. I then proposed to go to Collector Cheap's house, where I understood there were twenty-three wounded officers, to offer my assistance to the surgeons, Cunningham and Trotter, the first of whom I knew. They were surgeons of the dragoons, and had surrendered that they might attend the officers. When I went in, I told Cunningham (afterwards the most eminent surgeon in Dublin) that I had come to offer them my services, as, though no surgeon, I had better hands than a common servant. They were obliged to me; but the only service I could do to them was to try to find one of their medicine-chests among the baggage, as they could do nothing for want of instruments. I readily undertook this task, provided they would furnish me with a guard. This they hoped they could do; and knocking at the door of an inner room, a Highland officer appeared, whom they called Captain Stewart. He was good-looking, grave, and of polished manners. He answered that he would soon find a proper conductor for me, and despatched a servant with a message. In the mean time I observed a very handsome young officer lying in an easy-chair in a faint, and seemingly dying. They led me to a chest of drawers, where there lay a piece of his skull, about two fingers' breadth and an inch and a half long. I said, "This gentleman must die." "No," said Cunningham, "the brain is not affected, nor any vital part: he has youth and a fine constitution on his side; and could I but get my instruments, there would be no fear of him." This man was Captain Blake. Captain Stewart's messenger arrived with a fine, brisk, little, well-dressed Highlander, armed cap-a-pie with pistol, and dirk, and broadsword. Captain Stewart gave him his orders, and we set off immediately.

Never did any young man more perfectly display the boastful temper of a raw soldier, new to conflict and victory, than this Highland warrior. He said he had that morning been armour-bearer to the Duke of Perth, whose valour was as conspicuous as his clemency; that now there was no doubt of their final success, as the Almighty had blessed them with this almost bloodless victory on their part ; that He had made the sun to shine upon them uninterruptedly since their first setting out; that no brawling woman had cursed, nor even a dog had barked at them ; that not a cloud had interposed between them and the blessings of Heaven, and that this happy morning——here he was interrupted in his harangue by observing in the street a couple of grooms leading four fine blood-horses. He drew a pistol from his belt, and darted at the foremost in a moment. "Who are you, sir ? and where are you going ? and whom are you seeking ? " It was answered with an uncovered head and a dastardly tone, " I am Sir John Cope's coachman, and I am seeking my master." " You'll not find him here, sir, but you and your man and your horses are my prisoners. Go directly to the Collector's house, and put up your horses in the stable, and wait till I return from a piece of public service. Do this directly, as you regard your lives." They instantly obeyed. A few paces further on he met an officer's servant with two handsome geldings and a large and full clothes-bag. Similar questions and answers were made, and we found them all in the place to which they were ordered, on our return.

It was not long before we arrived at Cockenzie, where, under the protection of my guard, I had an opportunity of seeing this victorious army. In general they were of low stature and dirty, and of a contemptible appearance. The officers with whom I mixed were gentleman-like, and very civil to me, as I was on an errand of humanity. I was conducted to Lochiel, who was polished and gentle, and who ordered a soldier to make all the inquiry he could about the medicine-chests of the dragoons. After an hour's search, we returned without finding any of them, nor were they ever afterwards recovered. This view I had of the rebel army confirmed me in the prepossession that nothing but the weakest and most unaccountable bad conduct on our part could have possibly given them the victory. God forbid that Britain should ever again be in danger of being overrun by such a despicable enemy, for, at the best, the Highlanders were at that time but a raw militia, who were not cowards.

On our return from looking for the medicine-chests, we saw walking on the sea-shore, at the east end of Prestonpans, all the officers who were taken prisoners. I then saw human nature in its most abject form, for almost every aspect bore in it shame, and dejection, and despair. They were deeply mortified with what had happened, and timidly anxious about the future, for they were doubtful whether they were to be treated as prisoners of war or as rebels. I ventured to speak to one of them, who was nearest me, a Major Severn ; for Major Bowles, my acquaintance, was much wounded, and at the Collector's. He answered some questions I put to him with civility, and I told him what errand I had been on, and with what humanity I had seen the wounded officers treated, and ventured to assert that the prisoners would be well used. The confidence with which I spoke seemed to raise his spirits, which I completed by saying that nothing could have been expected but what had happened, when the foot were so shamefully deserted by the dragoons.

Before we got back to the Collector's house, the wounded officers were all dressed; Captain Blake's head was trepanned, and he was laid in bed, for they had got instruments from a surgeon who lived in the town, of whom I had told Cunningham ; and they were ordered up to Bankton, Colonel Gardiner's house, where the wounded Highlanders were, and also the Honourable Mr. Sandilands. Two captains of ours had been killed outright besides Gardiner—viz., Captain Stewart of Physgill, whose wife was my relation, and who has a monument for him erected in the churchyard of Prestonpans by his father-in-law, Patrick Heron of Heron, Esq.; the other was Captain Brymer of Edrom, in the Merse.

While we were breakfasting at my father's, some young friends of mine called, among whom was James Dunlop, junr., of Garnkirk, my particular acquaintance at Glasgow. He and his companions had ridden through the field of battle, and being well acquainted with the Highland chiefs, assured us there was no danger, as they were civil to everybody. My father, who was impatient till he saw me safe, listened to this, and immediately ordered the horses. We rode through the field of battle where the dead bodies still lay, between eleven and twelve o'clock, mostly stript. There were about two hundred, we thought. There were only slight guards and a few straggling boys. We rode along the field to

Seaton, and met no interruption till we came close to the village, when four Highlanders darted out of it, and cried in a wild tone, presenting their pieces, "Fourich, fourich!" (*i.e.* Stop, stop!) By advice of our Glasgow friends we stopped, and gave them shillings a-piece, with which they were heartily contented. We parted with our friends and rode on, and got to Mr. Hamilton's, minister of Bolton, a solitary place at a distance from any road, by two o'clock, and remained there all day. My father, having time to recollect himself, fell into a new anxiety, for he then called to mind that, besides sundry watches and purses which he had taken to keep, he also had Pat. Simson's four hundred guineas. After many proposals and projects, and among the rest my earnest desire to return alone, it was at last agreed to write a letter in Latin to John Ritchie the schoolmaster, afterwards minister of Abercorn, and instruct him how to go at night and secrete the watches and purses if still there, and bury the saddle-bags in the garden. Ritchie was also requested to come to us next day.

My father and Mr. Hamilton carried on the work of that day, Sunday, with zeal, and not only prayed fervently for the King, but warned the people against being seduced by appearances to believe that the Lord was with the rebels, and that their cause would in the end be prosperous. But no sooner had we dined than my father grew impatient to see my mother and the children, Ritchie having written by the messenger that all was quiet. He wanted to go alone, but that I could not allow. We set out in due time, and arrived before it was dark, and found the family quite well, and my mother in good spirits. She was naturally strong-minded, and void of imaginary fears; but she had received comfort from the attention paid to her, for Captain Stewart, by the Duke of Perth's order, as he said, gave one of his ensigns, a Mr. Brydone, a particular charge of our family, and ordered him to call upon her at least twice a-day.

We soon began to think of my father's charge of watches and money; and when it was dark enough I went into the garden to look for the place where Ritchie had buried the saddle-bags. This was no difficult search, for he had written us that they were below a particular pear-tree. To be sure, he had buried the treasure, but he had left the leather belts by which they were fixed fully above ground, so that if the Highlanders had been of a curious or prowling disposition, they must have discovered this important sum.

Soon after this Ritchie arrived. He had set out for Bolton early in the afternoon; but taking a different road, that was nearer for people on foot, he did not meet us, and had returned immediately. On setting out, not twenty yards from the manse of Prestonpans, he was stopped by a single Highlander, who took from him all the money that he had, which was six shillings; but as he spared his watch, he was contented. Not long after came in my mother's guard, Ensign Brydone, a well-looking, sweet-tempered young man, about twenty years of age. He was Captain Stewart's ensign. Finding all the family assembled again, he resisted my mother's faint invitation to supper. She replied that as he was her guard, she hoped he would come as often as he could. He promised to breakfast with us next morning. He came at the hour appointed, nine o'clock. My mother's custom was to mask the tea before morning prayer, which she did; and soon after my father came into the room he called the servants to prayers. We knelt down, when Brydone turning awkwardly, his broad sword swept off the table a china plate with a roll of butter on it. Prayer being ended, the good lady did not forget her plate, but, taking it up whole, she said, smiling, and with a curtsey, " Captain Brydone, this is a good omen, and I trust our cause will be as safe in the end from your army as my plate has been from the sweep of your sword." The young man bowed, and sat down to breakfast and ate heartily ; but I afterwards thought that the bad success of his sword and my mother's application had made him thoughtful, as Highlanders are very superstitious.

During the rest of the week, while I remained at home, finding him very ignorant of history and without political principles, unless it was a blind attachment to the chief, I thought I convinced him, in the many walks I had with him, that his cause would in the end be unsuccessful. I learned afterwards, that though he marched with them to England, he retired before the battle of Falkirk, and appeared no more. He was a miller's son near Drummond Castle.

On Tuesday, and not sooner, came many young surgeons from Edinburgh to dress the wounded soldiers, most of whom lay on straw in the schoolroom. As

11

almost all their wounds were with the broadsword, they
had suffered little. The surgeons returned to Edinburgh
in the evening, and came back again for three days. As
one of them was Colin Simson, a brother of Patrick's,
the clergyman at Fala, and apprentice to Adam Drummond their uncle, we trusted him and his companions
with the four hundred guineas, which at different times
they carried in their pockets and delivered safe to Captain Adam Drummond of Megginch, then a prisoner
in Queensberry House in the Canongate.

I remained at home all this week, about the end of
which my friend William Sellar came from Edinburgh
to see me, and pressed me much to come to Edinburgh
and stay with him at his father's house. Having
several things to purchase to prepare for my voyage to
Holland, I went to town on the following Monday, and
remained with him till Thursday. Besides his father
and sisters, there lodged in the house Mr. Smith; and
there came also to supper every night his son, afterwards Mr. Seton of Touch, having married the heiress
of that name. As Prince Charles had issued a procla-
mation allowing all the Volunteers of Edinburgh three
weeks, during which they might pay their court to him
at the Abbey, and receive a free pardon, I went twice
down to the Abbey Court with my friend about twelve
o'clock, to wait till the Prince should come out of the
Palace and mount his horse to ride to the east side of
Arthur Seat to visit his army. I had the good fortune
to see him both days, one of which I was close by him
when he walked through the guard. He was a good-

looking man, of about five feet ten inches; his hair was dark red, and his eyes black. His features were regular, his visage long, much sunburnt and freckled, and his countenance thoughtful and melancholy. He mounted his horse and rode off through St. Ann's Yards and the Duke's Walk to his army. There was no crowd after him—about three or four hundred each day. By that time curiosity had been satisfied.

In the house where I lived they were all Jacobites, and I heard much of their conversation. When young Sellar and I retired from them at night, he agreed with me that they had less ground for being so sanguine and upish than they imagined. The court at the Abbey was dull and sombre—the Prince was melancholy; he seemed to have no confidence in anybody, not even in the ladies, who were much his friends; far less had he the spirit to venture to the High Church of Edinburgh and take the sacrament, as his great-uncle Charles II. had done the Covenant, which would have secured him the low-country commons, as he already had the Highlanders by attachment. He was thought to have loitered too long at Edinburgh, and, without doubt, had he marched immediately to Newcastle, he might have distressed the city of London not a little. But besides that his army wanted clothing and necessaries, the victory at Preston put an end to his authority. He had not a mind fit for command at any time, far less to rule the Highland chiefs in prosperity.

I returned to Prestonpans on Thursday, and as I was to set out for Newcastle on Monday to take shipping for Holland, I sent to Captain Blake, who was recovering well, to tell him that if he had any letters for Berwick, I would take charge of them. He prayed me to call on him immediately. He said he was quite well, and complained of nothing but the pain of a little cut he had got on one of his fingers. He said he would trouble me with a letter to a friend at Berwick, and that it would be ready on Saturday at four o'clock, when he begged I would call on him. I went at the hour, and found him dressed and looking well, with a small table and a bottle and glasses before him. "What!" says I; "Captain Blake, are you allowed to drink wine?" "Yes," said he, "and as I expected you, I postponed my few glasses till I should drink to your good journey." To be sure, we drank out the bottle of claret; and when I sent to inquire for him on Sunday, he said he had slept better than ever. I never saw this man more; but I heard he had sold out of the army, and was married. In spring 1800, when the King was very ill, and in danger, I observed in the papers that he had left a written message, mentioning the wounds he had received at the battle of Preston. On seeing this, I wrote to him as the only living witness who could attest the truth of his note left at St. James's. I had a letter from him dated the 1st of March that year, written in high spirits, and inviting me to Great George Street, Westminster, where he hoped we would uncork a bottle with more pleasure than we had done in 1745, but to come soon, for he was verging on eighty-one. He died this spring, 1802.

CHAPTER IV

ON Monday morning, the 9th of October, old style, my
father and I set out for Newcastle on horseback, where
we arrived on Wednesday to dinner. Having secured
my passage on board a small vessel going to Rotterdam,
that was to sail whenever there was a convoy, we rode
to Sunderland to visit some emigrants whom we understood were there, and found old George Buchan and
his brother-in-law, Mr. William Grant, afterwards Lord
Advocate, and Lord Prestongrange. We dined with
them, and were told that Lord Drummore and many
others of our friends had taken up their residence at
Bishop Auckland, where they wished to have been had
there been room. Next day my father and the servant
set out on their journey home, and I having been acquainted with some of the Common Council of Newcastle, was invited to dine with the mayor at one of
their guild dinners. A Mr. Fenwick, I think, was mayor
that year. I was seated at the end of one of the long
tables in the same room, next Mr. John Simpson, afterwards Alderman Simpson, sheriff of Newcastle for that

year. As I was fresh from Scotland, I had to answer all the questions that were put to me concerning the affairs of that country, and I saw my intelligence punctually detailed in the *Newcastle Journal* next morning. Of that company there was one gentleman, a wine merchant, who was alive in the year 1797 or 1798; when happening to dine with the mayor, the subject was talked of, and he recollected it perfectly.

At the inn where I slept I met with my companion Bob Cunningham, who had been a Volunteer in Edinburgh, and with Francis Garden, who had been taken prisoner by the rebels, as narrated in Home's *History*.* He and I supped together one of the nights. He was studying law; but his father being an officer, and at that time Lieutenant of Stirling Castle, he had a military turn, which was heightened by the short campaign he had made. He resented the bad usage his father's nephew, Murray of Broughton, the Pretender's Secretary, had given him during the day he was a captive, and was determined to become a volunteer in some regiment till the rebellion was suppressed; but expressed a strong abhorrence at the subordination in the army, and the mortifications to which it exposed a man. I argued that he ought either to return immediately to his studies, or fix on the army for his profession, and

---

* The incident is mentioned above, p. 145. Francis Garden was raised to the bench in 1764, when he took the title of Lord Gardenstone: he was author of miscellanies in prose and verse, and travelling memorandums. The immediately following sentences might seem to refer to him, but they are intended to refer to Cunningham. —J. H. B.

stated the difference between modern armies and those
of Greece and Rome, with which his imagination was
fired, where a man could be a leading citizen and a great
general at the same time. He debated on this point till
two in the morning, and though he did not confess he
was convinced, he went into the army immediately,
and rose till he became a general of horse in Ireland.
He was, at the time I met him, very handsome, and
had an enlightened and ardent mind. He went to
Durham next morning, and I never saw him more.

On the Tuesday I was summoned to go down to
Shields, as the sloop had fallen down there, and was
to sail immediately with the London convoy. I went
down accordingly, and had to live for six days with the
rude and ignorant masters of colliers. There was one
army surgeon of the name of Allan, a Stirling man, who
had taken his passage, and had some conversation. At
last, on Monday the 14th of October, I went on board
the *Blagdon* of Newcastle, Tim Whinny, master, who
boasted that his vessel had ridden out the great storm
of January 29, 1739, at the back of Inchkeith. She was
loaded with kits of butter and glass bottles. I was the
only passenger. There was, besides the master, a mate,
an old sailor, and two boys. As we let the great ships
go out before us, it was night almost before we got
over the bar.

Next day, the weather being calm and moderate, we
had an agreeable sail along the coast of Yorkshire ;
in the evening, however, the gale rose, separated the
fleet of about eighty sail, and drove us off shore. We

passed a dreary night with sickness, and not without fear, for the idle boys had mislaid things, and it was two hours before the hatches could be closed. The gale abated in the morning, and about mid-day we made for the coast again, but did not come in with the land till two o'clock, when we descried the Norfolk coast, and saw many ships making for Yarmouth. About ten at night we came up with them, and found them to be part of the fleet with which we had sailed from Shields. Next day, Friday the 18th, we came into Yarmouth Roads, when the master and I went ashore in the boat. The master was as much a stranger there as I was, for though he had been often in the roads, he had never gone ashore. This town is handsome, and lies in a singular situation. It stands on a flat plain, about a quarter of a mile from the sea. It is an oblong square, about a mile in length, and a third part as broad. The whole length is intersected by three streets, which are rather too narrow. That nearest is well built, and lands on the market-place to the north, which is very spacious, and remarkably well provided with every kind of vivres for the pot and the spit.

The market-women are clean beyond example, and the butchers themselves dressed with great neatness indeed. In short, there was nothing to offend the eye or any of the senses in Yarmouth market. Very genteel-looking women were providing for their families. But the quay which is on the west side of the town, and lies parallel to the beach, is the most remarkable thing about the town, though there is a fine old Gothic church in the market-place, with a very lofty steeple, the spire of which is crooked, and likewise a fine modern chapel-of-ease in the street leading to it. The quay is a mile long, and is formed by a river, the mouth of which, above a mile distant at the village of Gorleston, forms the harbour. The largest colliers can deliver their goods at the quay, and the street behind it has only one row of the handsomest houses in the town. As the master and I knew nobody, we went into the house of a Robin Sad, at the sign of the Three Kings, who, standing at his own door near the south end of the quay, had such an inviting aspect and manner that I could not resist him. His house was perhaps not second-best, but it was cleanly, and I stayed two nights with him. He entertained me much, for he had been several years a mate in the Mediterranean in his youth, and was vain and boastful, and presumptuous and ignorant, to my great delight.

In the evening two men had come into the house and drank a pot or two of ale. He said they were custom-house officers, and was ill-pleased, as they did not use to frequent his house, but they had come into the common room on hearing of my being in the house ; and though they sat at a distance from the fireplace, where the landlord and I were, they could hear our conversation. Next morning, after nine, they came again, and with many apologies, addressing themselves to me, said they had orders from the Commissioners to inquire my name and designation, as they under-

stood I was going beyond sea to Holland. I had no
scruple in writing it down to them. They returned in
half an hour and told me that they were ordered to
carry me before the Lord Mayor. I went accordingly
down to Justice Hall, where I waited a little while in
an ante-chamber, and overheard my landlord Sad
under examination. He was very high and resentful
in his answers, and had a tone of contempt for men
who, he said, were unfit to rule, as they did not know
the value of any coins but those of England. He
answered with a still more saucy pride, when they
asked him what expense I made, and in the end told
them exultingly that I had ordered him to buy the best
goose in the market for to-morrow's dinner. I was
called in and examined. The Mayor was an old grey-
headed man, of a mild address. He had been a common
fisher, and had become very rich, though he could not
write, but signed his name with a stamp. After my
examination, under which I had nothing to conceal,
they told me, as I was going abroad, they were obliged
to tender me the oaths or detain me. I objected to
that, as they had no ground of suspicion, and offered
to show them my diploma as Master of Arts of the
University of Edinburgh, and a Latin letter from the
University of Glasgow to any Foreign University where
I might happen to go. They declined looking at them,
and insisted on my taking the oaths, which, accordingly were administered, and I was dismissed. I did
not know that the *habeas corpus* was not then suspended, and that if they had detained me I could have

recovered large expenses from them. I amused myself in town till the master came on shore, when, after dinner, we walked down to Gorleston, the harbour at the mouth of the river, where we heard of three vessels which were to sail without convoy, on Monday, with the ebb tide.

I stayed this night with landlord Sad, and invited the master to dine with us next day, being Sunday, when we were to have our fine goose roasted. I went in the morning to their fine chapel, which was paneled with mahogany, and saw a very populous audience. The service and the sermon were but so so. Tim Whinny came in good time, and we were on board by four o'clock, and fell down opposite the harbour of Gorleston. As the three colliers which were to venture over to Holland without convoy were bound for a different port from Helvoet, which was our object, our master spent all the morning of Monday making inquiry for any ship that was going where we were bound, and ranged the coast down as far as Lowestoff for this purpose, but was disappointed. This made us so late of sailing, that the three ships which took through the gat or opening between sand-banks, were almost out of sight before we ventured to sail. Tim's caution was increased by his having his whole property on board, which he often mentioned. At last, after a solemn council on the quarter-deck, where I gave my voice strongly for our immediate departure, we followed the track of the three ships, the last of which was still in sight; and having a fine night, with a fair breeze of wind, we came within sight of land at ten o'clock next day. The shore is so flat, and the country so level, that one sees nothing on approaching it but tops of steeples and masts of ships. Early in the afternoon I got on shore at Helvoet, on the island of Voorn, and put up at an English house, where one Fell was the landlord.

There I saw the first specimen of Dutch cleanliness, so little to be expected in a small seaport. As I wished to be as soon as I could at Rotterdam, I quitted my friend Tim Whinny to come up at his leisure, and went on board the Rotterdam schuyt at nine in the morning, and arrived there in a few hours. The beauty of this town, and of the river Maas that flows by it and forms its harbour, is well known. The sight of the Boompjes, and of the canals that carry shipping through the whole town, surprised and pleased me much. I had been directed to put up at Caters, an English house, where I took up my lodgings accordingly, and adhered to it in the two or three trips I made afterwards to this city, and found it an exceeding good house, where the expense was moderate, and everything good. In the afternoon I inquired for Mr. Robert Herries, on whom I had my credit, and found his house on the Scotch Dyke, after passing in the doit-boat over the canal that separates it from the end of the Boompjes.

From Mr. Herries I met with a very kind reception. He was a handsome young man, of a good family in Annandale, who had not succeeded in business at Dumfries, and had been sent over by my uncle Provost George Bell, of that town, as their agent and factor—as at that time they dealt pretty deep in the tobacco trade. He had immediately assimilated to the manners of the Dutch, and was much respected among them. He lived in a very good house, with a Mr. Robertson and his wife from Aberdeen—very sensible, good sort of people. They took very much to me, and insisted on my dining with them every day. Next door to them lived a Mr. Livingston, from Aberdeen also, who was thought to be rich. His wife was the daughter of Mr. Kennedy, one of the ministers of the Scotch Church. She was a very handsome and agreeable woman; and neither of the ladies having children, they had little care, and lived a very sociable and pleasant life, especially my landlady, whose attractions consisted chiefly in good sense and good temper. Our neighbour being young and gay as well as handsome, had not quite so much liberty. Mr. Herries and his friends advised me to remain some days with them, because, our king's birthday having happened lately, the British students were to have a grand entertainment, and it was better for me to escape the expense that might be incurred by going there too soon. Besides, I had to equip myself in clothes, and with a sword and other necessaries, with which I could be better and cheaper supplied at Rotterdam than at Leyden. I took their advice, and they were so obliging as to have new company for me every day, among whom were Mess. Kennedy, and Ainslie his colleague; the first was popular, and pompous, and political, and an Irishman. The second was a plain, sensible Scotchman, less sought after, but more respectable than his colleague. During my stay at

Rotterdam I was informed of everything, and saw everything that was new or curious.

Travelling in Holland by means of the canals is easy and commodious; and though the country is so flat that one can see to no distance, yet the banks of the canals, especially as you approach the cities, are so much adorned with pleasure-houses and flower-gardens as to furnish a constant succession, not of the grand and sublime or magnificent works of nature, but of a profusion of the rich and gaudy effects of opulence without taste. When I arrived at Leyden, which was in a few hours, I found my lodgings ready, having had a correspondence from Rotterdam with Thomas Dickson, M.D., afterwards my brother-in-law. They were in the house of a Madame Vandertasse, on the Long Bridge. There were in her house besides, Mr. Dickson, Dr. John Gregory, Mr. Nicholas Monckly, and a Mr. Skirrat, a student of law. Vandertasse's was an established lodging-house, her father and mother having carried on that business, so that we lived very well there at a moderate rate—that is, sixteen stivers for dinner, two for coffee, six for supper and for breakfast. She was a lively little Frenchwoman, about thirty-six, had been tolerably well-looking, and was plump and in good condition. As she had only one maid-servant, and five gentlemen to provide for, she led an active and laborious life; insomuch that she had but little time for her toilet, except in the article of the coif, which no Frenchwoman omits. But on Sundays, when she had leisure to dress herself for the French Church, either in the morning or evening, then who but Mademoiselle Vandertasse! She spoke English perfectly well, as the guests of the house had been mostly British.

As I had come last, I had the worst bed-chamber. Besides board, we paid pretty high for our rooms, and dearest of all for fuel, which was chiefly peat. We had very good small claret at a shilling a bottle, giving her the benefit of our exemption from town duty for sixty stoups of wine for every student. Our house was in high repute for the best coffee, so that our friends were pleased when they were invited to partake with us of that delicious beverage. We had no company to dinner; but in the evenings about a dozen of us met at one another's rooms in turn three times a week, and drank coffee, and smoked tobacco, and chatted about politics, and drank claret, and supped on bukkam (Dutch red-herrings), and eggs, and salad, and never sat later than twelve o'clock —at Mr. Gowan's, the clergyman, never later than ten, unless when we deceived him by making such a noise when the hour was ringing as prevented his hearing it.

Though I had not been acquainted with John Gregory formerly, which was owing to my two winters' residence at Glasgow when he was in Edinburgh, yet, as he knew most of my friends there, we soon became intimate together, and generally passed two hours every forenoon in walking. His friend Monckly being very fat, and a bad walker, could not follow us. There were at this time about twenty-two British students at Leyden, of whom, besides the five at our house already named, were the Honourable Charles Townshend, afterwards a distinguished statesman and husband to Lady Dalkeith, the mother of the Duke of Buccleuch; Mr. James Johnstone, junior, of Westerhall; Dr. Anthony Askew; John Campbell, junior, of Stonefield; his tutor Mr. Morton, afterwards a professor at St. Andrews; John Wilkes,* his companion Mr. Bland, and their tutor Mr. Lyson; Mr. Freeman from Jamaica; Mr. Doddeswell,† afterwards Chancellor of the Exchequer; Mr. Wetherell from the West Indies; Dr. Charles Congalton, to this day physician in Edinburgh; an Irish gentleman, Keefe, I think, in his house; Willie Gordon, afterwards K.B., with four or five more, whose names I have forgot, and who did not associate with my friends.

On the first Sunday evening I was in Leyden, I walked round the Cingle-a fine walk on the outside of the Rhine, which formed the wet ditch of the town—with John Gregory, who introduced me to the British students as we met them, not without giving me a short character of them, which I found in general a very just outline. When we came to John Wilkes, whose ugly countenance in early youth was very striking, I asked earnestly who he was. His answer was, that he was the son of a London distiller or brewer, who wanted to be a fine gentleman and man of taste, which he could never be, for God and nature had been against him. I came to know Wilkes very well afterwards, and found him to be a sprightly entertaining fellow-too much so for his years, as he was

* The famous Radical M.P.

† Of Mr. Doddeswell, Burke wrote: "There never was a soul so remote as his from duplicity, or fear, so perfectly free from any rapacious unevenness of temper which embitters friendships and perplexes business."

but eighteen; for even then he showed something of daring profligacy, for which he was afterwards notorious. Though he was fond of learning, and passionately desirous of being thought something extraordinary, he was unlucky in having an old ignorant pedant of a dissenting parson for his tutor. This man, a Mr. Leeson or Lyson, had been singled out by the father as the best tutor in the world for his most promising son, because, at the age of threescore, after studying controversy for more than thirty years, he told his congregation that he was going to leave them, and would tell them the reason next Sunday; when, being fully convened, he told them that, with much anxiety and care, he had examined the Arian controversy, and was now convinced that the creed he had read to them as his creed was false, and that he had now adopted that of the Arians, and was to bid them farewell. The people were shocked with this creed, and not so sorry as they would otherwise have been to part with him, for he was a good-natured well-meaning man. His chief object seemed to be to make Wilkes an Arian also, and he teased him so much about it that he was obliged to declare that he did not believe the Bible at all, which produced a quarrel between them, and Wilkes, for refuge, went frequently to Utrecht, where he met with Immateriality Baxter, as he was called, who then attended Lord Blantyre and Mr. Hay of Drummellier, as he had formerly done Lord John Gray.

This gentleman was more to Wilkes's taste than his own tutor; for though he was a profound philosopher and a hard student, he was at the same time a man of

the world, and of such pleasing conversation as attracted
the young.   Baxter was so much pleased with Wilkes
that he dedicated one of his pieces to him.   He died in
1750, which fact leads me to correct an error in the account of Baxter's life, in which he is much praised for
his keeping well with Wilkes, though he had given so
much umbrage to the Scotch.   But this is a gross mistake, for the people of that nation were always Wilkes's
favourites till 1763, thirteen years after Baxter's death,
when he became a violent party-writer, and wished to
raise his fame and fortune on the ruin of Lord Bute.*

Wilkes was very fond of shining in conversation very
prematurely, for at that time he had but little knowledge except what he derived from Baxter in his frequent
visits to Utrecht.   In the art of shining, however, he
was much outdone by Charles Townshend, who was not
above a year older, and had still less furniture in his
head ; but then his person and manners were more engaging.   He had more wit and humour, and a turn for
mimicry; and, above all, had the talent of translating

* The friendship here alluded to is interesting, as affording
evidence that Wilkes had been able to attach to himself at least
one virtuous and enlightened friend.   Baxter afterwards wrote to
him thus: "We talked much on this, you may rèmember, in the
capuchin's garden at Spa.   I have finished the *Prima Cura*; it
is in the dialogue way, and design to inscribe it to my dear John
Wilkes, whom, under a borrowed name, I have made one of the
interlocutors.   If you are against this whim (which a passionate
love for you has made me conceive), I will drop it."—Wilkes's
Correspondence, i. 15.   Wilkes does not appear to have been
against this whim.   The *Appendix to the First Part of the Inquiry
into the Nature of the Human Soul*, appeared in 1750, within a few
months after this letter was written.   Its author did not live to
see it printed, but it contains the dedication.—J. H. B.

other men's thoughts, which they had produced in the simple style of conversation, into the most charming language, which not only took the ear but elevated the thoughts. No person I ever knew nearly equalled Charles Townshend in this talent, but Dr. Robertson, who, though he had a very great fund of knowledge and thought of his own, was yet so passionately fond of shining, that he seized what was nearest at hand—the conversation of his friends of that morning or the day before*—and embellished it with such rich language, that they hardly knew it again themselves, insomuch that he was the greatest plagiary in conversation that ever I knew. It is to this, probably, that his biographer alludes (his strong itch for shining) when he confesses he liked his conversation best when he had not an audience.†

Gregory's chum, Dr. Monckly, had this talent too, and exercised it so as to bring on him the highest ridicule. He was in reality an ignorant vain blockhead, who had the most passionate desire of shining, which Gregory was entirely above. His usual method was to get Gregory

---

* Lord Cockburn's sketch of Dr. Robertson in his later years (*Memorials of his Life and Times*) notices this strong characteristic of the Principal.

† In allusion evidently to the following passage in Dugald Stewart's account of the life and writings of Robertson.—J. H. B. "In the company of strangers he increased his exertions to amuse and inform; and the splendid variety of his conversation was commonly the chief circumstance on which they dwelt in enumerating his talents; and yet I must acknowledge, for my own part, that much as I always admired his powers, when they were thus called forth, I enjoyed his society less than when I saw him in the circle of his intimates, or in the bosom of his family."

into his room, either before or after breakfast, when he
settled with him what were to be the leading topics of
the day, especially at our coffee-parties and our club
suppers, for we soon broke him of his attempt to shine at
dinner. Having thus settled everything with Gregory,
and heard his opinion, he let him go a-walking with me,
and jotted down the topics and arguments he had heard.
The very prospect of the glory he was to earn in the
evening made him contented and happy all day.
Gregory kept his secret as I did, who was generally
let into it in our walk, and prayed not to contradict
the fat man, which I seldom did when he was not too
provoking. Unfortunately, one night Gregory took it
into his head to contradict him when he was haran-
guing very pompously on tragedy or comedy, or some
subject of criticism. The poor man looked as if he
had been shot, and after recovering himself, said with
a ghastly smile, " Surely this was not always your
opinion." Gregory persisted, and after saying that
criticism was a subject on which he thought it lawful
to change, he entirely refuted the poor undone doctor :
not another word did he utter the whole evening. He
had his coffee in his room next morning, and sent for
Gregory before we left the parlour. I waited for an
hour, when at last he joined me, and told me he had
been rated at no allowance by the fat man; and when
he defended himself by saying that he had gone far
beyond the bounds prescribed, the poor soul fell into
tears, and said he was undone, as he had lost the only
friend he had in the world. It cost Gregory some time

to comfort him and to exhort him, by exacting from him some deference to himself at our future parties (for the blockhead till then had never so much as said what is your opinion on this subject, Dr. Gregory). A new settlement was made between them, and we went on very well; for when some of the rest were debating *bonâ fide* with the absurd animal, I, who was in the secret, gave him line and encouragement till he had got far beyond his depth, while Gregory was sitting silent in a corner, and never interposed till he was in danger of being drowned in the mud. This may seem a cruel amusement, but I forgave Gregory, for there was no living with Monckly without it.

We passed our time in general very agreeably, and very profitably too; for the conversations at our evening meetings of young men of good knowledge, intended for different professions, could not fail to be instructive, much more so than the lectures, which, except two, that of civil law and that of chemistry, were very dull. I asked Gregory why he did not attend the lectures, which he answered by asking in his turn why I did not attend the divinity professors (for there was no less than four of them). Having heard all they could say in a much better form at home, we went but rarely, and for form's sake only, to hear the Dutchmen. At this time we were in great anxiety about the Rebellion, and were frequently three or four weeks without getting a packet from England; insomuch that Gregory and I agreed to make a trip to Rotterdam to learn if they had heard anything by fishing-boats. We went one day

and returned the next, without learning anything. We
dined with my agreeable friends on the Scotch Dyke,
Herries and Robertson. In returning in the schuyt,
I said to Gregory that he would be laughed at for
having gone so far and having brought back no news,
but if he would support me I would frame a gazette.
He promised, and I immediately wrote a few paragraphs, which I said I had copied from Allan the
banker's private letter he had got by a fishing-boat.
This was to impose on Dr. Askew, for Allan was his
banker. I took care also to make Admiral Townshend take two ships of the line at Newfoundland, for
he was Charles Townshend's uncle, and so on with the
rest of our friends. On our arrival they all assembled
at our lodging, and our news passed current for all that
day. At night we disclosed our fabrication, being unable to hold out any longer. On another occasion I
went down with Dr. Askew, who, as a learned man of
twenty-eight, had come over to Leyden to collate
manuscripts of Æschylus for a new edition. His father
had given him £10,000 in the stocks, so that he was a
man of importance. Askew's errand at this time was
to cheat his banker Allan, as he said he would draw on
him for £100, which he did not want, because Exchange
was at that time against Holland. In vain did I try to
persuade him that the banker would take care not to
lose by him. But he persisted, such being the skill in
business of this eminent Grecian. He had some drollery,
but neither much sense nor useful learning. He was much
alarmed when the Highlanders got as far as Derby, and

believed that London would be taken and the bank ruined. I endeavoured in vain to raise his spirits; at last I told him that personally I did not much care, for I had nothing to lose, and would not return to Britain under a bad Government. You are the very man I want, says he, for I have £400 or £500 worth of books, and some name as a Greek scholar. We'll begin bookselling, and you shall be my partner and auctioneer, This was soon settled, and as soon forgot when the rebels marched back from Derby. When Gregory and I were alarmed at some of the expensive suppers some of our friends gave from the taverns, we went to Askew, whose turn was next, and easily persuaded him to limit his suppers to eggs and bukkam and salad, which he accordingly gave us next night, which, with tobacco of 40 stivers a lb. and very good claret, pleased us all. After this no more fine suppers were presented, and Gowans, the old minister of the Scottish Church,* ventured to be of our number, and was very pleasant.

I went twice to the Hague, which was then a very delightful place. Here I met with my kinsman, Willie Jardine, now Sir William, who was a cornet in the Prince of Orange's Horse Guards, and then a very handsome genteel fellow, for as odd as he has turned out since. Though I had no introduction to anybody there, and no acquaintance but the two students who accompanied me the first time, I thought it a delightful

---

* The Rev. Mr. Gowans was minister of the Scots Kirk at Leyden from 1716 till 1753.

place. A ball that was given about this time by the Imperial Ambassador, on the Empress's birthday, was fatal to one of our students—a very genteel, agreeable rake, as ever I saw, from the West Indies. At a preceding dancing assembly he had been taken out by a Princess of Waldeck, and had acquitted himself so well that she procured him an invitation to the birthday ball, and engaged him to dance with her. He had run himself out a good deal before; and a fine suit of white and silver, which cost £60, completed his distress, and he was obliged to retire without showing it to us more than once. There was another West Indian there, a Mr. Freeman, a man of fortune, sedate and sensible. He was very handsome and well-made. Having been three years in Leyden, he was the best skater there. There was an East India captain resident in that city, whom the Dutch set up as a rival to Freeman, and they frequently appeared on the Rhine together. The Dutchman was tall and jolly, but very active withal. The ladies, however, gave the palm to Freeman, who was so handsome, and having a figure much like Garrick, all his motions were perfectly genteel. This gentleman, after we left Leyden, made the tour of Italy, Sicily, and Greece, with Willie Gordon and Doddeswell; the former of whom told me long afterwards that he had died soon after he returned to Jamaica, which was Gordon's own native country, though his parents were Scotch, and cousins of Gordon of Hawhead, in Aberdeenshire. He was too young and too dissipated to attend our evening meetings;

neither did Charles Congalton, who was one of the best
young men I have ever known. His pretence was that
he could not leave his Irish chum of the name of Keefe;
but the truth was, that having been bred a Jacobite, and
having many friends and relations in the Rebellion, he
did not like to keep company with those who were warm
friends of Government. Dickson and he were my companions on a tour to Amsterdam, where we stayed only
three days, and were much pleased with the magnifi-
cence, wealth, and trade of that city. Dickson was a
very honest fellow, but rather dull, and a hard student.
As I commonly sat up an hour after the rest had gone
to their rooms, chatting or reading French with Mademoiselle, and as Dickson's apartment was next the
parlour, he complained much of the noise we made,
laughing and talking, because it disturbed him, who
was a midnight student. He broke in upon us with
impertinent curiosity, but I drove him to his bed, and
by sitting up an hour longer that night, and making
more noise than usual, we reduced him to patience
and close quarters ever after, and we made less noise.
I mentioned somewhere that Mademoiselle had paid
for her English, which was true, for she had an affair
with a Scotch gentleman ten or twelve years before,
and had followed him to Leith on pretence of a
promise, of which, however, she made nothing but a
piece of money.

At Christmas time, three or four of us passed three
days at Rotterdam, where my friends were very agreeable to my companions. Young Kennedy, whom we

had known at Amsterdam, was visiting his father at this time, as well as young Ainslie, the other minister's son, which improved our parties. Mrs. Kennedy, the mother, was ill of a consumption, and British physicians being in great credit there, Monckly, who was called Doctor, though he had not taken his degree, being always more forward than anybody in showing himself off, was pitched upon by Mr. Kennedy to visit his wife. Gregory, who was really a physician, and had acquired both knowledge and skill by having been an apprentice in his brother's shop at Aberdeen, and visited the patients with him, was kept in the background; but he was anxiously consulted by Monckly twice a-day, and taught him his lesson, which he repeated very exactly, for I heard him two or three times, being a familiar in the house, while the good Doctor was unconscious that I knew of his secret oracle. For all this, Monckly was only ridiculous on account of his childish vanity, and his love of showing himself off. He was, in reality, a very good-natured and obliging man, of much benevolence as well as courtesy. He practised afterwards in London with credit, for they cured him of his affectation at Batson's. He died not many years after.

At this time five or six of us made an agreeable journey on skates, to see the painted glass in the church at Tergou. It was distant twelve miles. We left Rotterdam at ten o'clock, saw the church, and dined, and returned to Rotterdam between five and six in the evening. It was moonlight, and a gentle breeze on our back, so that we returned in an hour and a quarter.

Gregory, though a far abler man than Monckly, and not less a man of learning for his age than of taste, in the most important qualities was not superior to Monckly. When he was afterwards tried by the ardent spirits of Edinburgh and the prying eyes of rivalship, he did not escape without the imputation of being cold, selfish, and cunning. His pretensions to be more religious than others of his profession, and his constant eulogies on the female sex as at least equal, if not superior, to the male, were supposed to be lures of reputation, or professional arts to get into business. When those objections were made to him at Edinburgh, I was able to take off the edge from them, by assuring people that his notions and modes of talking were not newly adopted for a purpose, for that when at Leyden, at the age of twenty-one or twenty-two, he was equally incessant and warm on those topics, though he had not a female to flatter, nor ever went to church but when I dragged him to please old Gowans. Having found Aberdeen too narrow a circle for him, he tried London for a twelve-month without success—for being ungainly in his person and manner, and no lucky accident having befallen him, he could not make his way suddenly in a situation where external graces and address go much further than profound learning or professional skill. Dr. Gregory, however, was not without address, for he was much a master of conversation on all subjects, and without gross flattery obtained even more than a favourable hearing to himself ; for never contradicting you at first, but rather assenting or yielding, as it were, to your knowledge and taste, he very often brought you round to think as he did, and to consider him a superior man. In all *my* dealings with him—for he was my family physician—I found him friendly, affectionate, and generous.

An unlucky accident happened about the end of January, which disturbed the harmony of our society, and introduced uneasiness and suspicion among us. At an evening meeting, where I happened not to be, Charles Townshend, who had a great deal of wit which he was fond to show, even sometimes at the expense of his friends, though in reality one of the best-natured of men, took it in his head to make a butt of James Johnstone, afterwards Sir James of Westerhall.* Not contented with the smartness of his raillery, lest it should be obscure, he frequently accompanied it with that motion of the tongue in the cheek which explains and aggravates everything. He continued during the evening to make game of James, who, slow of apprehension and unsuspicious, had taken all in good part. Some one of the company, however, who had felt Charles's smartness, which he did not choose to resent, had gone in the morning to Johnstone and opened his eyes on Townshend's behaviour over-night.

Johnstone, though not apt to take offence, was

* Brother of Sir William Johnstone Pulteney, by whom he was succeeded in the baronetcy of Westerhall.

prompt enough in his resentment when taken, and immediately resolved to put Charles's courage to the test. I was sent for next forenoon by twelve o'clock to Charles's lodgings, who looked pale and undone, more than I had ever seen him. He was liable at that time to convulsion fits, which seldom failed to attack him after a late supper. I asked him what was the matter with him ; he answered, that he had been late up, and had been ill. He next asked me if I had ever observed him use James Johnstone with ill-natured raillery or sarcasm in company, or ridicule him behind his back. I answered him that I had never perceived anything between them but that playsome kind of raillery so frequent among good friends and companions, and that when Johnstone was absent I had never heard him ridicule him but for trifles, in spite of which I conceived he had a respect for him. Upon this he showed me a letter from Johnstone, taxing him with having often treated him with contempt in company, and particularly for his behaviour the night before, which having been made to advert to by a friend who was sharper-sighted than him, had brought sundry things to his recollection, which, though he did not mind at the time, were fully explained to him by his behaviour to him the night before. The letter concluded with a challenge. " And what answer are you to make to this ? " said I. " Not fight, to be sure," said he, " for I have no quarrel with Johnstone, who is the best-natured man in the world." " If you can make

it up, and keep it secret, it may do, otherwise you'll
be dishonoured by the transaction." I added, "Find
out the malicious scoundrel if you can who has acted
like a vile informer, and take vengeance on him." He
seemed quite irresolute, and I left him with this
advice, either to make it up, or put it over as soon as
possible. He made it up, to be sure, but it was in a
manner that hurt him, for Johnstone and he went
round all the lodgings in Leyden, and inquired of
everybody if any of them had ever heard or seen him
ridicule Johnstone. Everybody said no to this, and
he and Johnstone became the greater friends. But it
did him more harm than it would or ought to have
done at his raw age, if he had not afterwards betrayed
want of firmness of character. This was a pity, for
he had unbounded capacity and application, and was
good-tempered and affectionate.

This accident in some measure broke the bond of
our society, but it was of little importance to us,
who meant to leave Leyden very soon. Gregory and
I had agreed to go to London together, and when
Monckly heard of this resolution, he determined to
accompany us. His monitor had advised him to take
his degree in Leyden, but the honest man did not
choose to stand the examination ; and he knew that
by paying a little more he could get his diploma sent
after him. Dickson remained to take his degree, as
he regarded the additional guineas much more than
he feared the examination. Gregory, with a degree
of malice due to the fat man for his vanity and pre-

sumption, pressed him very much to abide the trial, and blazoned to him the inglorious retreat he was about to make ; but it would not do, as Gregory knew perfectly beforehand.

About the end of February or the beginning of March we set out on our return to Britain ; when, passing two days very agreeably with our friends at Rotterdam, we fell down to Helvoet, and took our passage on board the packet, which was to sail for Harwich next morning. On the journey and voyage Monckly assumed his proper station, which was that of treasurer and director ; and, to say the truth, he did it well ; for except in one instance, he managed our affairs with a decent economy, no less than with the generosity that became his assumed office. The exception to this was his allowing himself to be imposed upon by the landlord of the inn at Helvoet, in laying in sea-stores for our voyage, for he said he had known packets on the sea for a week by calms, etc. The director elect, therefore, laid in a cold ham and a couple of fowls, with a sirloin of beef, nine bottles of wine and three of brandy, none of all which we were able to taste except the brandy.

We sailed from Helvoet at eight in the morning, and having a fine brisk gale, quite fair, we arrived on the coast of England by eight in the evening; though, having made the land too far to the northward, it was near twelve before we got down to Harwich. We had beds in the cabin, and were all so heartily sea-sick that we were hardly able to lift up our heads the whole day, far less to partake of any of our sea-stores, except a little brandy to settle our stomachs.

We had one cabin passenger, who was afterwards much celebrated. When we were on the quarter-deck in the morning, we observed three foreigners, of different ages, who had under their care a young person of about sixteen, very handsome indeed, whom we took for a Hanoverian baron coming to Britain to pay his court at St. James's. The gale freshened so soon that we had not an opportunity of conversing with those foreigners, when we were obliged to take to our beds in the cabin. The young person was the only one of the strangers who had a berth there, because, as we supposed, it occasioned an additional freight. My bed was directly opposite to that of the stranger, but we were so sick that there was no conversation among us till the young foreigner became very frightened in spite of the sickness, and called out to me in French, if we were not in danger. The voice betrayed her sex at once, no less than her fears. I consoled her as well as I could, and soon brought her above the fear of danger. This beautiful person was Violetti the dancer,* who was engaged to the opera in the Haymarket. This we were made certain of by the man, who called himself her father, waiting on us next day at Harwich, requesting our countenance to his daughter on her first appearance,

* " She surprised her audience at her first appearance on the stage ; for at her beginning to caper she showed a neat pair of black velvet breeches, with roll'd stockings ; but finding they were unusual in England she changed them the next time for a pair of white drawers."—Lord Stafford in *Cathcart Collection*.

and on her benefit. I accordingly was at the opera the first night she appeared, where she was the first dancer, and maintained her ground till Garrick married her.

We had so much trouble about our baggage that we did not get from Harwich till one o'clock, and I was obliged to leave Leeson's picture, which I had undertaken to carry to London for John Wilkes. We passed the night at Colchester, where the foreigners were likely to be roughly treated, as the servants at the inn took offence at the young woman in men's clothes, as one room was only bespoke for all the four. We interposed, however, when Monckly's authority, backed by us, prevented their being insulted. They travelled in a separate coach from us, but we made the young lady dine with us next day, which secured her good treatment. We were so late in getting to London that we remained all night together in an inn in Friday Street, and separated next day, with a promise of seeing one another often ; yet so great is the city of London, and so busy is everybody kept there, that, intimate as we had been, it was three weeks or a month before we met again. We had not yet found out the British Coffeehouse, where so many of our countrymen assembled daily.*

I got a coach, and went to New Bond Street to my cousin, Captain Lyon's, who had been married for

---

* This noted coffeehouse was so much patronised by Scotsmen that Horace Walpole notes, when the Duke of Bedford wished to secure support to a motion in the House of Lords, he wrote to sixteen Scottish peers placing the letters under one cover addressed to the British Coffeehouse.

13

a few years to Lady Catherine Brydges, a daughter of
the Marquess of Carnarvon, and grandchild of the
Duke of Chandos. Lyon's mother was an acquaintance of the Marchioness, the young lady's mother of
the Dysart family. The Marchioness had fallen in
love with Lyon, who was one of the handsomest men
in London, but he escaped by marrying the daughter,
who, though not handsome, was young and alluring,
and had the prospect of a great fortune, as she had
only one sister, who was deformed. Here I renewed
my acquaintance with my aunt Lyon, who was still
a fine woman. Her elder sister, Mrs. Paterson, the
widow of a Captain Paterson of the Bannockburn
family, a very plain-looking sensible woman, kept
house with her, while the son and his family lived in
the next house, which belonged to Mrs. Lyon. Lady
Catherine had by this time two girls, three and four
years of age, as beautiful children as ever were seen.
They had bespoke for me a small lodging in Little
Maddon Street, within sight of the back of their
house. Lyon was a cheerful fine fellow as ever was
born, who had just returned with his troop of the
Horse-Guards from Flanders, where he and they had
been for two campaigns under the Duke of Cumberland. With them and their friends I passed part of
my time ; but having found some of my old friends
lounging about the British and Forrest's Coffeehouses,
in Cockspur Street, Charing Cross—viz. John Blair,
afterwards a prebendary of Westminster, Robert
Smith, afterwards distinguished by the appellation of

the Duke of Roxburgh's Smith, who introduced me
to Dr. Smollett, with whom he was intimate, and
Charles Congalton arriving in a few weeks from Leyden, who was a stranger as well as myself in London
—I was at no loss how to pass my time agreeably,
when Lyon and his family were engaged in their own
circle.*

By Lyon, however, I was introduced to some
families of condition, and was carried to court of an
evening, for George II. at that time had evening
drawing-rooms, where his Majesty and Princess
Amelia, who had been a lovely woman, played at
cards, and the courtiers sauntered for an hour or two.
This was a very insipid amusement. I went with
Lyon also and his lady to a ridotta at the Haymarket,
a ball where there were not fewer than fifteen hundred
people, and which Robert Keith, the ambassador,
told me, in the entry, was a strong proof of the greatness and opulence of London, for he had stood in the
entry, he said, and had seen all the ladies come in,
and was certain that not one-half of them were of the
Court end of the town, for he knew every one of *them*.
Lady Catherine Lyon, whom I squired that night, and
with whom I danced, introduced me to many of her
acquaintances, and among the rest to Lady Dalkeith

* Of John Blair, the chronologist, some notices will be found
in the *History of Hinckley* (of which he was vicar) by Nichols, in
the sixth volume of the *Topographia Britannica*. Robert Smith
is probably the same who succeeded Bentley as Master of Trinity
College, Cambridge. He was very eminent in optics and mathematics, but scarcely anything is now known of him beyond a
scanty notice in Hutton's *Mathematical Dictionary*.—J. H. B.

and her sisters, the daughters of John, Duke of Argyle, who, she said, were her cousins. The Countess was then with child of Henry, Duke of Buccleuch,* who was born on the 14th of September thereafter, who was my much-respected patron and highly-honoured friend.

Captain Lyon introduced me to his friends, the officers of the Horse-Guards, with whom I lived a good deal. The troop he belonged to, which, I think, was Lord Tyrawley's,† was one of the two which had been abroad in Flanders, between whom and those at home there was a strong emulation who should entertain most expensively when on guard. Their parties were generally in the evening, when they had the most expensive suppers that could be got from a tavern—amongst other things champagne and ice-creams, both which were new to me, and the last then rare in London. I had many very agreeable parties with those officers, who were all men of the world, and some of them of erudition and understanding. One I must particularly mention was Captain Elliot, afterwards Lord Heathfield,‡ the celebrated defender of Gibraltar. A parcel of us happened to meet in the Park in a fine evening in April, who, on asking each other how they were engaged, seven or eight of us agreed to sup at the Cardigan at Charing Cross, among

* Henry, third Duke of Buccleuch and fifth Duke of Queensberry. He succeeded his grandfather in 1751.

† James, Lord Tyrawley, became Ambassador at Lisbon, Governor of Port Mahon and Gibraltar, and colonel of a regiment of Horse-Guards.

‡ Second son of Sir Gilbert Elliot, third baronet of Stobs, Roxburghshire.

whom Elliot was one. Lyon and I undertook to go directly to the house and bespeak a room, and were soon joined by our company and two or three more of their friends, whom they had met in their walk. We passed the evening very pleasantly, and when the bill was called for, a Mr. Philips, who was in the chair, and who, by the death of a relation that morning, had succeeded to an estate of £1000 a-year, wished to pay the whole reckoning, which he said was a trifle. This was resisted. He then said he would play odds or evens with all the company in their turns, whether he or they should pay. This was agreed to, and he contrived to lose to everybody except Captain Elliot, who said he never played for his reckoning. I observed on this afterwards to Lyon that this appeared particular, and that Elliot, though by his conversation a very sensible man, yet did not yield to the humour of the company, which was to gratify Philips. He answered me, that though Captain Elliot was somewhat singular and austere in his manners, yet he was a very worthy and able officer, for whom he had great esteem. This trait of singularity occurred to me when he became so distinguished an officer, whom I should rather have noted as sour and untractable.

John Blair had passed his trials as a preacher in Scotland, but having a few hundred pounds of patrimony, chose to pay a visit to London, where he loitered till he spent it all. After some time he thought of completing and publishing his Chronological Tables, the plan of which had been given him by Dr. Hugh Blair, the celebrated preacher. He became acquainted with the Bishop of Lincoln, with whom he was soon a favourite, and having been ordained by him, was presented to the living of Burton Cogles, in his diocese. He was afterwards teacher of mathematics to the Duke of York, the King's brother, and was by his interest preferred to be a prebendary of Westminster. He was a lively agreeable fellow, and one of the most friendly men in the world. Smith had been abroad with the young Laird of M'Leod of that period, and was called home with his pupil when the Rebellion began. He had been ill rewarded, and was on his shifts in London. He was a man of superior understanding, and of a most gentlemanly address. With Smollett he was very intimate. We four, with one or two more, frequently resorted to a small tavern in the corner of Cockspur Street at the Golden Ball, where we had a frugal supper and a little punch, as the finances of none of the company were in very good order. But we had rich enough conversation on literary subjects, which was enlivened by Smollett's agreeable stories, which he told with peculiar grace.

Soon after our acquaintance, Smollett showed me his tragedy of *James I. of Scotland*, which he never could bring on the stage. For this the managers could not be blamed, though it soured him against them, and he appealed to the public by printing it; but the public seemed to take part with the managers.

I was in the coffeehouse with Smollett when the news of the battle of Culloden arrived, and when

London all over was in a perfect uproar of joy. It
was then that Jack Stuart, the son of the Provost,*
behaved in the manner I before mentioned. About
9 o'clock I wished to go home to Lyon's, in New Bond
Street, as I had promised to sup with him that night,
it being the anniversary of his marriage night, or the
birthday of one of his children. I asked Smollett if
he was ready to go, as he lived at Mayfair ; he said
he was, and would conduct me. The mob were so
riotous, and the squibs so numerous and incessant
that we were glad to go into a narrow entry to put our
wigs in our pockets, and to take our swords from our
belts and walk with them in our hands, as everybody
then wore swords ; and, after cautioning me against
speaking a word, lest the mob should discover my
country and become insolent, " for John Bull," says
he, " is as haughty and valiant to-night as he was
abject and cowardly on the Black Wednesday when
the Highlanders were at Derby." After we got to
the head of the Haymarket through incessant fire,
the Doctor led me by narrow lanes, where we met nobody but a few boys at a pitiful bonfire, who very
civilly asked us for sixpence, which I gave them. I
saw not Smollett again for some time after, when he
showed Smith and me the manuscript of his *Tears of
Scotland*, which was published not long after, and had
such a run of approbation. Smollett, though a Tory,
was not a Jacobite, but he had the feelings of a Scotch

---

* Lord Provost of Edinburgh when Prince Charlie took possession of the city.

gentleman on the reported cruelties that were said to
be exercised after the battle of Culloden.

My cousin Lyon was an Englishman born, though
of Scottish parents, and an officer in the Guards, and
perfectly loyal, and yet even he did not seem to rejoice
so cordially at the victory as I expected. " What's the
matter?" says I; "has your Strathmore blood got up,
that you are not pleased with the quelling of the Rebellion ? " "God knows," said he, " I heartily rejoice
that it is quelled; but I'm sorry that it has been accomplished by the Duke of C——, for if he was before
the most insolent of all commanders, what will he be
now ? " I afterwards found that this sentiment prevailed more than I had imagined; and yet, though no
general, he had certainly more parts and talents than
any of the family.

I was witness to a scene in the British Coffeehouse,
which was afterwards explained to me. Captain
David Cheap, who was on Anson's voyage, and had
been wrecked on the coast of Chili, and was detained
there for some time by the Spaniards, had arrived in
London, and frequented this coffeehouse. Being a
man of sense and knowledge, he was employed by
Lord Anson to look out for a proper person to write
his voyage, the chaplain, whose journal furnished the
chief materials, being unequal to the task. Captain
Cheap had a predilection for his countrymen, and
having heard of Guthrie, the writer of the *Westminster Journal*, etc., he had come down to the coffeehouse that evening to inquire about him, and, if he

was pleased with what he heard, would have him introduced. Not long after Cheap had sat down and called for coffee, Guthrie arrived, dressed in laced clothes, and talking loud to everybody, and soon fell a-wrangling with a gentleman about tragedy and comedy and the unities, etc., and laid down the law of the drama in a peremptory manner, supporting his arguments with cursing and swearing. I saw he [Cheap] was astonished, when rising and going to the bar, he asked who this was, and finding it was Guthrie, whom he had come down to inquire about, he paid his coffee and slunk off in silence. I knew him well afterwards, and asked him one day if he remembered the incident. He told me that it was true that he came there with the design of talking with Guthrie, on the subject of the voyage, but was so much disgusted with his vapouring manner that he thought no more of him.*

* Of William Guthrie, whose name is on the title-pages of many voluminous works, one of which, the *Geographical Grammar*, had great celebrity and a vast circulation, various notices will be found in D'Israeli's *Calamities of Authors* and Boswell's *Johnson*. The account of Anson's voyage, so well esteemed in its own day, and so well worth reading in the present, both from the interesting character of the events and the admirable way in which they are told, professes to have been compiled from Anson's own papers by Richard Walter, surgeon of the *Centurion*, one of the vessels in the expedition. It is believed, however, that the work was edited, if not almost rewritten, by Benjamin Robins, the mathematician. William Davis, in his *Olio, or Bibliographical and Literary Anecdotes and Memoranda*, says: "Walter's manuscript, which was at first intended to have been printed, being little more than a transcript from the ship's journals, Mr. Robins was recommended as a proper person to revise it; and it was then determined that the whole should be written by him, the transcripts of the journals serving as materials only; and that, with the Introduction and many dis-

I met Captain Cheap in Scotland two years after this, when he came to visit his relations. I met him often at his half-brother's, George Cheap, Collector of Customs, at Prestonpans, and in summer at goat-whey quarters, where I lived with him for three weeks, and became very confidential with him. He had a sound and sagacious understanding and an intrepid mind, and had great injustice done to him in Byron's Narrative, which Major Hamilton,* who was one of the unfortunate people in the *Wager*, told me was in many things false or exaggerated.† One instance I remember, which is this, that Cheap was so selfish that he had concealed four pounds of seal in the lining of his coat to abstract from the company for his own use. He, no doubt, had the piece of seal, and Captain Hamilton saw him secrete it ; but when they had got clear of a cazique, who plundered them of all he could,

sertations in the body of the book, of which not the least hint had been given by Walter, he extended the account, in his own peculiar style and manner, to nearly twice its original size." Davis prints a letter from Lord Anson, tending to confirm his statement.— J. H. B.

* Of the 8th Dragoons, from which he retired in 1762. He built a house at Musselburgh which he called Olivebank, the site of which is now occupied by the North British Railway.

† The book here referred to, written by the poet's grandfather, and cited in *Don Juan* as "My grandad's Narrative," was very popular. Its title is "The Narrative of the Honourable John Byron (commander in a late expedition round the world); containing an account of the great distresses suffered by himself and his companions on the coast of Patagonia, from the year 1740 till their arrival in England in 1746; with a description of St. Jago de Chili, and the manners and customs of the inhabitants. Also a relation of the loss of the *Wager* man-of-war, one of Lord Anson's squadron," 1768.—J. H. B.

the captain producing his seal, said to his companions, " That devil wanted to reduce me to his own terms by famine, but I outplotted him ; for with this piece of seal we could have held out twenty-four hours longer." Another trait of his character Captain Hamilton told me, which was,—that when they arrived in Chili, to the number of eleven, who had adhered to Cheap, and who were truly, for hunger and nakedness, worse than the lowest beggars, and were delighted with the arrival of a Spanish officer from the governor, who presented Cheap with a petition, which he said he behoved to sign, otherwise they could not be taken under the protection of the Spanish governor ; Cheap, having glanced this paper with his eye, and throwing it indignantly on the ground, said sternly to the officer that he would not sign such a paper, for the officers of the King of England could die of hunger, but they disdained to beg. Hamilton and Byron and all the people fell into despair, for they believed that the captain was gone mad, and that they were all undone. But it had a quite contrary effect, for the officer now treated him with unbounded respect, and, going hastily to the governor, returned immediately with a blank sheet of paper, and desired Captain Cheap to dictate or write his request in his own way.

Hamilton added that Byron and he being then very young, about sixteen or seventeen, they frequently thought they were ruined by the captain's behaviour, which was often mysterious, and always arrogant and high ; but that yet in the sequel they found that he had always acted under the guidance of a sagacious foresight. This was marking him as a character truly fit for command, which was the conclusion I drew from my intercourse with him in Scotland. On my inquiring at Hamilton what had made Byron so severe, he said he believed it was that the captain one day had called him "puppy" when he was petulant, and feeling himself in the wrong, he endeavoured to make up with Byron by greater civility, which the other rejecting, Cheap kept him at a greater distance. He entirely cleared Cheap from any blame for shooting Cozens, into which he was led by unavoidable circumstances, and which completely re-established his authority.

As I had seen the Chevalier Prince Charles frequently in Scotland, I was appealed to if a print that was selling in all the shops was not like him. My answer was, that it had not the least resemblance. Having been taken one night, however, to a meeting of the Royal Society by Microscope Baker, there was introduced a Hanoverian baron, whose likeness was so strong to the print which passed for the young Pretender, that I had no doubt that, he being a stranger, the printsellers had got him sketched out, that they might make something of it before his vera effigies could be had. Experiments in electricity were then but new in England, and I saw them well exhibited at Baker's, whose wife, by the by, was a daughter of the celebrated Daniel Defoe.

I dined frequently with a club of officers, mostly Scotch, at a coffeehouse at Church Court in the Strand, where Charles Congalton lodged, and who introduced me to the club, many of whom were old acquaintances, such as Captain Henry Fletcher, Boyd Porterfield, and sundry more who had been spared at the fatal battle of Fontenoy. We had an excellent dinner at 10d.— I thought as good as those in Holland at a guilder. The company, however, were so much pleased that they voluntarily raised it to 1s. 6d., and they were right, for as they generally went to the play at six o'clock, the advance of the ordinary left them at liberty to forsake the bottle early.

The theatres were not very attractive this season, as Garrick had gone over to Dublin ; there still remained, however, what was enough for a stranger— Mrs. Pritchard, and Mrs. Clive, and Macklin, who were all excellent in their way. But I had seen Hughes and Mrs. Hamilton in Edinburgh, and whether or not it might be owing to the force of first impressions, I then thought that they were not surpassed by those I saw in London.

Of the literary people I met with at this time in London, I must not forget Thomson the poet and Dr. Armstrong.* Dickson had come to London from Leyden with his degree of M.D., and had been introduced

* Armstrong belonged to Castleton, Roxburghshire. He was a poet and essayist as well as a physician, in which profession he attributed *his limited success to the fact that* " he could neither tell a heap of lies in his own praise wherever he went ; nor intrigue with nurses, much less assimilate with the various knots of pert insipid, lively stupid, well-bred impertinent, good-humoured malicious, obliging deceitful, waspy drivelling gossips ; nor enter into juntos with people who were not to his liking."—Armstrong's *Medical Essays.*

to Armstrong, who was his countryman.   A party was
formed at the Ducie Tavern at Temple Bar, where the
company were Armstrong, Dickson, and Andrew
Millar, with Murdoch his friend.*   Thomson came at
last, and disappointed me both by his appearance and
conversation.   Armstrong bore him down, having got
into his sarcastical vein by the wine he had drunk
before Thomson joined us.

At that particular time strangers were excluded from
the House of Commons, and I had not then a strong
curiosity for that kind of entertainment.   I saw all
the sights as usual for strangers in London, and having
procured a small pamphlet which described the public
buildings with taste and discernment, I visited them
with that in my hand.   On Sundays I went with Lyon
and his family to St. George's Church in Hanover
Square.   Sometimes I went to St. James's Church to
hear Dr. Secker,† who was the rector of that parish
and a fine preacher.   I was twice at the opera, which
seemed so very far from real life and so unnatural that
I was pleased with nothing but the dancing, which
was exquisite, especially that of Violetti.

* As to Dickson, see further on, p. 215.   The Reverend Patrick
Murdoch was the author of several scientific works, and of memoirs
of M'Laurin the mathematician and Thomson the poet, to whom
he is said to have sat for the portrait of the " little, fat, round,
oily man of God " in the *Castle of Indolence*, who " had a roguish
twinkle in his eye, and shone all glittering with ungodly dew."
—J. H. B.

† Dr. Secker became Archbishop of Canterbury and baptized
George IV.   " As he began life a dissenter," writes Mrs. Montague,
"anxious churchwomen thought that the Archbishop's christening
George, Prince of Wales, would not make a Christian of him.   And
it cannot be said that it did."—Doran's *Lady of the Last Century*.

CHAPTER V

1746–1748   AGE, 24–26

VAUXHALL furnished early in May a fine entertainment, but I was now urged by my father to return home ; and accordingly Charles Congalton and I left London about the middle of May on horseback, and, having Windsor and Oxford to see, we took the west road, and were delighted with the beauty of the country. At Windsor, which charmed us, we met with some old acquaintances—Dr. Francis Home and Dr. Adam Austin, who were then surgeons of dragoons, and who, when afterwards settled at Edinburgh as physicians, became eminent in their line. At Oxford we knew nobody but Dr. John Smith, M.D., who was a Glasgow exhibitioner, and then taught mathematics with success in Oxford. He was a good kind of man, and became an eminent practitioner. He went about with us, and showed us all the colleges, with which we were really astonished. We took the road by Warwick, and were much pleased with that town and Lord Brooks' castle. When we came to Lichfield, we met, as we expected, with John Dickson of Kilbucho, M.P., who accompanied us during the rest of our journey, till we arrived in Scotland.

As three make a better travelling party than two, society was improved by this junction ; for though Kilbucho was a singular man, he knew the country, which he had often travelled ; and his absurdities, which were innocent, amused us.   As well as he knew the country, however, when we came to the river Esk, and to the usual place of passing it—for there was then no bridge opposite Gretna Green—although he had insisted on our dismissing the guide we had brought from some distance to show us the road, yet nothing could persuade him, nor even his servant, to venture into that ford which he professed he knew so well.   The tide was not up, but the river was a little swollen.   Congalton and I became impatient of his obstinate cowardice, and, thinking we observed the footstep of a horse on the opposite side (what we thought a horse's footstep turned out a piece of sea-ware which the tide had left), we ventured in together and got safe through, while the gallant knight of the shire for the county of Peebles,with his squire, stood on the bank till he saw us safe through.   This disgusted us not a little, but as I was to part with him at Gretna, and go round by Annan and Dumfries to visit my friends, I had only half an hour more of his company, which I passed in deriding his cowardice. Congalton, anxious to get soon to Edinburgh, accompanied him by the Moffat road.   But strange to tell of a Scotch laird, when they came to the Crook Inn, within a few miles of Kilbucho, which lies about half a mile off the road as it approaches Broughton, he wished Congalton a good-evening without having the hospitality to ask him to lodge a night with him, or even to breakfast as he passed next morning. I was happy to find afterwards that all the Tweeddale lairds were not like this savage.

I passed only two days at Dumfries and Tinwald, at which last place my old grandfather, who was then seventy-two, was rejoiced to see me, and not a little proud to find that his arguments had prevailed, and had sufficient force to prevent my deviating into any other profession than the clerical. When I returned to my father's house, I found all the family in good health except my brother William, who was then in his sixteenth year, and had all the appearance of going into a decline. My favourite sister Catherine had fallen a prey to the same disease in February. I had described to Gregory when at Leyden the state of her health, and the qualities of mind and temper that had attached me to her so strongly. He said that I would never see her again, for those exquisite qualities were generally attached to such a frail texture of body as promised but short duration. William was as remarkable in one sex as she was in the other ; an excellent capacity for languages and sciences, a kind and generous temper, a magnanimous soul, and that superior leading mind that made him be always looked up to by his companions; with a beautiful countenance and a seemingly well-formed body, which were

14

not proof against the slow but certain progress of that insidious disease. He lived to November 1747, and then, to my infinite regret, gave way to fate.

I had only one sermon to deliver before the Presbytery of Haddington to become a preacher, which was over in June. My first appearances were attended to with much expectation ; and I had the satisfaction to find that the first sermon I ever preached, not on trials, which was on the fast day before the sacrament at Tranent, had met with universal approbation. The genteel people of Prestonpans parish were all there; and one young lady, to whom I had been long attached, not having been able to conceal her admiration of my oratory, I inwardly applauded my own resolution of adhering to the promise I had made my family to persevere in the clerical profession.

I revisited Dumfries and Tinwald again to preach two Sundays for my grandfather, who gave me his warmest approbation. One Mr. William Stewart, an old clergyman, who heard me on a week-day at Dumfries, gave me more self-confidence, for he was a good judge, without partiality. I returned home, and continued composing a sermon now and then, which I first preached for my father, and then in the neighbourhood.

Our society was still pretty good ; for though Hew Horn * was no more, Mr. Keith had left us, and Cheap's eldest son, Alexander, had been killed at the battle of Fontenoy,—Mr. William Grant, then Lord

* Hew Horn Dalrymple.   See p. 60,

Advocate, had bought Prestongrange, and resided much there : Lord Drummore, too, was still in the parish, and with both of them I was in good habits. Hew Bannatine had been ordained minister of Ormiston, who was a first-rate man for sound understanding and classical learning ; Robertson was at Gladsmuir ; and in January 1747 John Home was settled at Athelstaneford; so that I had neighbours and companions of the first rank in point of mind and erudition.

In harvest this year I was presented by John Hay, Esq. of Spot, to the church of Cockburnspath. As my father and grandfather were always against resisting Providence, I was obliged to accept of it. It was an obscure distant place, without amenity, comfort, or society, where if I had been settled, I would have more probably fallen into idleness and dissipation than a course of study ; for preferment is so difficult to be obtained in our Church, and so trifling when you have obtained it, that it requires great energy of mind not to fall asleep when you are fixed in a country charge. From this I was relieved, by great good-luck. There was a Mr. Andrew Gray, afterwards minister of Abernethy, who was a very great friend of my father's. He had been preaching one Sunday in the beginning of 1747 for Fred. Carmichael, minister of Inveresk, and stayed with him all night: from him he had drawn the secret that President Forbes, who lived in his parish,* had

* Lord President Forbes had the liferent of Stoneyhill from the famous Colonel Charteris, in recognition of the successful issue

secured for him a church that was recently vacant in
Edinburgh. Gray, who was very friendly and ardent,
and knew my father's connections, urged him without
loss of time to apply for Inveresk. By this time I
had preached thrice at Cockburnspath, and was very
acceptable to the people. My father was unwilling to
take any step about a church that would not even be
vacant for a year to come; but Gray was very
urgent, and backed all his other arguments with my
father with the idea that his not doing his utmost
would be peevishly rejecting the gift of Providence
when within his reach. My father at last mounted
his horse, for that he would have done had the distance been but half a mile, and away he went, and
found Lord Drummore on the point of going to Edinburgh for the week. My father opened his budget,
which he received most cordially, and told him there
was great probability of success, for that he was well
enough to write both to the Duke of Buccleuch * the
patron, and to the Duke of Queensberry, his brother-
in-law. Besides that, Provost Bell of Dumfries had
everything to say with the Duke of Queensberry. In
a few posts there were favourable answers from both
the dukes, and a promise of Inveresk.

Lord Drummore was a true friend of my father, and
had in summer 1746 recommended me to Lord Stair
for one of his churches that was about to be vacant by

of a criminal charge brought against the Colonel in which Forbes,
then Lord Advocate, defended him.

* Francis, second Duke of Buccleuch, who died in 1751.

the translation of the minister ; and I preached a day
at Kirkliston before his lady with that view.   But the
translation did not take place at that time.   Mr. Hay
had presented me to Cockburnspath, and on that I
would have been settled.   The Crown, soon after I
gave it up, commenced a prosecution against Mr. Hay,
and were found to have the right.   Mr. John Hay of
Spot was a very good man, though not of remarkable
talents : he died unmarried, and the estate went to his
brother William.   My father had been their tutor in the
year 1714–15, and they retained the greatest regard
for him.

In the preceding winter I had preached three times
at Cockburnspath, and was so acceptable to the people
that I should have an unanimous call, which was on
the point of being moderated when the promise of
Inveresk was obtained.   My father wished me to let
my settlement go on, but I resisted that, as I thought
it was tampering with people to enter into so close a
relation with them that was so soon to be dissolved.
The puzzle was how to get off from the Presbytery
of Dunbar, who were desirous of having me among
them ; but I soon solved the difficulty by saying to
Lord Drummore and my father that nothing could
be so easy ; for as I had accepted of the presentation
by a letter of acceptance, I had nothing to do but to
withdraw that acceptance ; this I accordingly did in
January or February 1747.   At this period it was
that John Home was settled in Athelstaneford, which
he obtained by the interest of Alexander Home, Esq. of

Eccles, afterwards Solicitor-General, with Sir Francis Kinloch, who was his uncle. He was still alive as well as his lady, but his son David, who was the year before married to Harriet Cockburn, the sister of Sir Alexander, was living in the house of Gilmerton, which, as it had been always hospitable, was rendered more agreeable by the young people; for the husband was shrewd and sensible, and his wife beautiful, lively, and agreeable, and was aspiring at some knowledge and taste in belles-lettres. This house, for that reason, became a great resort for John Home and his friends of the clergy.

This summer, 1747, passed as usual in visiting Dumfriesshire, where I had many friends and relations; where, in addition to the rest, I became well acquainted with Mr. William Cunningham, at that time minister of Durrisdeer, and one of the most accomplished and agreeable of our order. When the Duchess of Queensberry was at Drumlanrig, where she was at least one summer after he was minister, she soon discovered his superior merit, and made him her daily companion, insomuch that the servants and country people called him her Grace's walking-staff. My cousin, William Wight, afterwards professor at Glasgow, was a great favourite of this gentleman, and used to live much with him in summer during the vacation of the College of Edinburgh, and was very much improved by his instructive conversation.

My sister Margaret, who had been brought up at Dumfries by her aunt Bell, who had no children, was now past fifteen, and already disclosed all that beauty of person, sweetness of temper and disposition, and that superiority of talents which made her afterwards be so much admired, and gave her a sway in the politics of the town which was surprising in so young a female. Her uncle, George Bell, was the political leader, who was governed by his wife—who was swayed by her neice and Frank Paton, Surveyor of the Customs, who was a very able man, and who, with my sister, were the secret springs of all the provost's conduct.

Dr. Thomas Dickson, who was his nephew, by his solicitation, after trying London for nine years, was prevailed on by his uncle, the provost, to come down to Dumfries in 1755, to try his fortune as a practitioner of physic ; but Dr. Even Gilchrist was too well established, and the field too narrow, for him to do anything ; so at the end of a year he returned to London again, where he did better. During that year, however, he did what was not very agreeable to me. He gained my sister's affections, and a promise of marriage, though in point of mind there was a very great inequality ; but he had been the only young man in the town whose conversation was enlightened enough for her superior understanding, and she had been pestered by the courtship of several vulgar and illiterate blockheads, to be clear of whom she engaged herself, though that engagement could not be fulfilled for four years or more, when their uncle the provost was dead, and Dickson in better circumstances.

I had, for three weeks this summer, been at the goat-whey with Mrs. Cheap's family, at a place called Duchery, at the head of the Forth, where I met Captain David Cheap, above mentioned. There was also the magnet which drew me after her, with unseen though irresistible power,—the star that swayed and guided all my actions ; and there I hoped that, by acquiring the esteem of the uncle, I had the better chance of obtaining my object. In the first I succeeded, but in the last I finally failed, though I did not desist from the persistence for several years after. In the end of this year my brother William died, at the age of seventeen, who, in spite of his long bad health, was likely to have acquired as much learning and science as, with his good sense, would have made him a distinguished member of society. He was much regretted by all his companions, who loved him to excess. His own chief regret was, that he was not to live to see me minister of Inveresk, the prospect of which settlement so near my father had given him much satisfaction.

When Mr. Frederick Carmichael was translated to Edinburgh, and the time drew near when I was to be presented to Inveresk, there arose much murmuring in the parish against me, as too young, too full of levity, and too much addicted to the company of my superiors, to be fit for so important a charge, together with many doubts about my having the grace of God, an occult quality which the people cannot define, but surely is in full opposition to the defects they saw in me.* A part of my early history was on this occasion of more effect than can be conceived. There was one Ann Hall, a sempstress, who had lived close by the manse of Prestonpans when I was a boy. She was by this time married at Dalkeith, and a Seceder of the strictest sect, and a great leader among her own people. As many people from Inveresk parish frequented her shop at Dalkeith on market-days, the conversation naturally fell on the subject of who was to be their minister. By this time I had been presented, but they said it would be uphill work, for an opposition was rising against so young a man, to whom they had many faults, and that they expected to be able to prevent the settlement. " Your opposition will be altogether in vain," says Mrs. Ann, " for I know that it is foreordained that he shall be your minister. He foretold it himself when he was but six years of age ; and you know that ' out of the mouths of babes and sucklings,' " etc. The case was, that soon after I had read the Bible to the old wives in the churchyard, as I mentioned (p. 4), I was diverting myself on Mrs. Ann's stairhead, as was often the case. She came to the door, and, stroking my head and caressing me, she called me a fine boy, and hoped to live to see me my father's successor. " No, no," says I (I suppose, alarmed at the thoughts of my father dying so soon), " I'll never be minister of *that* church ;

* In his *Recollections*, he adds to this catalogue of objections —" I danced frequently in a manner prohibited by the laws of the Church ; that I wore my hat agee ; and had been seen galloping through the Links one day between one and two o'clock."

but yonder's my church," pointing to the steeple of Inveresk, which was distinctly seen from the stair-head. She held up her hands with wonder, and stored it up in her heart; and telling this simple story twenty times every market-day to Musselburgh people for several months, it made such an impression that the opposition died away. The reign of enthusiasm was so recent, that such anecdotes still made an impression on the populace.

After all the forms were gone through, and about a year had elapsed after the translation of Mr. Frederick Carmichael to Edinburgh, I was ordained minister of Inveresk, on the 2nd of August, O.S., 1748, by Mr. Robert Paton, minister of Lasswade (as honest and gentlemanly a person as any of his cloth), with the almost universal goodwill of the parish. The only person of consideration who was not present at the ordination was Sir James Dalrymple * of Newhailes, who had taken umbrage at his being refused the presentation, when he had applied for it to Gersham Carmichael, the brother of Frederick. He and his family, however, attended the church on the first Sunday after the ordination, when he came round and welcomed me to the parish, and invited me to dine with him the next day, which I did, and continued ever after in perfect friendship with him till his death in 1751.

Sir James Dalrymple was the son of Sir David, who had been King's Advocate from 1709 to 1720, and was

---

* Second baronet of Hailes, Haddingtonshire, and Newhailes, Midlothian.   M.P. for the former county 1722–1734.

the youngest, and, as was said, the ablest, of all the sons of the first Lord Stair. He had loaded himself with debt in the South Sea, but his son Sir James was Auditor of the Exchequer, which enabled him to keep up the rank of his family. He was hospitable and gentlemanly, and very charitable. He died in 1751 of a lingering disorder (an anasarca), and wished me to be often with him when he was ill; and though he never wished me to pray with him when we were left alone, always gave the conversation a serious turn, and talked like a man who knew he was dying. His lady (Lady Christian Hamilton, a sister of the celebrated Lord Binning, who died before him) had warned me against speaking to him about death, "for Jamie," she said, "was timid;" so I allowed him always to lead the conversation. One day we were talking of the deistical controversy, and of the progress of deism, when he told me that he knew Collins, the author of one of the shrewdest books against revealed religion. He said he was one of the best men he ever had known, and practised every Christian virtue without believing in the Gospel; and added, that though he had swam ashore on a plank—for he was sure he must be in heaven— yet it was not for other people to throw themselves into the sea at a venture. This proved him to be a sincere though liberal-minded Christian. I was sorry for his death, for he was respected in the parish, and had treated me with much kindness.

There was a Mr. James Graham, advocate, living here at this time, a man of distinguished parts and

great business.   He was raised to the bench in 1749,
and died in 1751.   He had one daughter, Mrs. Baron
Mure.   He was an open friendly man, and gave me
every sort of countenance both as his minister and
friend, and was a man of great public spirit.   He
was liable in a great degree to a nervous disorder,
which oppressed him with low spirits : he knew when
he was going to fall ill, and as it sometimes confined
him for three months, he sent back his fees to the agents,
who all of them waited till he recovered, and applied
to him again.   He was Dougalstone's brother, and a
very powerful barrister.*

Lord Elchies, a senior Judge, lived at Carberry, in
the parish, and was in all respects a most regular and
exemplary parishioner.†   His lady, who was a sister
of Sir Robert Dickson's, was dead, and his family consisted of three sons and three or four daughters, unmarried, for some of the elder daughters were married.
He came every Sunday with all his family to church,
and remained to the afternoon service.   As he lived in
the House of Carberry, he had the aisle in the church
which belonged to that estate, where there was a very
good room, where he retired to a cold collation,‡ and

* Dougalston was the name of the family estate, inherited by the
elder brother. The Judge took the title of Lord Easdale.—J. H. B.

† Patrick Grant, Lord Elchies, well known to lawyers by his
Collection of Reports of the Decisions of the Court of Session
from 1733 to 1754, arranged in alphabetical order, according to
the matter of the legal principle involved in each case.   See
TYTLER'S *Life of Kames*, i. 39.—J. H. B.

‡ A " cold collation " in the laird's room at church was a
common practice in the eighteenth century.   It was the only

took Sir Robert Dickson and me always with him when I did not preach in the afternoon. He was an eminent Judge, and had great knowledge of the law ; but though he was held to be a severe character, I found him a man agreeable and good-tempered in society. He attended as an elder at the time that the sacrament of the Lord's Supper was administered, and followed one practice, in which he was singular. It is the custom for elders to serve tables in sets and by turns, that all may serve and none be fatigued. When it was his turn to retire to his seat, he entered it, as it was close by the communion-table, but never sat down till the elements were removed, which could not be less than an hour and a half. I mentioned this singularity to him one day, wishing to have it explained, when he said that he thought it irreverent for any one who ministered at the table to sit down while the sacred symbols were present. He removed to the House of Inch, nearer Edinburgh (when an owner came to live at Carberry, about the year 1752), and died of a fever in 1754, being one of nine Judges who died in the course of two years, or a little more. His eldest son was Mr. Baron Grant ; his second, Robert, captain of a fifty-gun ship, died young ; Andrew, the third, survived his brothers, and died, as the Baron did, in Granada.

Sir Robert Dickson of Carberry, Bart., was great-grandson of Dr. David Dickson, a celebrated professor

apartment in which there was a fireplace.—Graham's *Social Life in the Eighteenth Century*.

of divinity in Edinburgh, who was one of the committee who attended the Scotch army in England, in Charles I.'s time, and got his share of the sum that was paid for delivering the King to the English army. His having acquired an estate in those days does not imply that he had acquired much money, for land was very cheap in those days. There was annexed to the estate the lordship of Inveresk, now in the Duke of Buccleuch, with the patronage of the parish.

This Sir Robert, being a weak vain man, had got through his whole fortune. The estate was sold, and he now lived in a house in Inveresk, opposite to Mr. Colt's, called Rosebank, built near a hundred years before by Sir Thomas Young, Knight. Sir Robert Dickson's lady was a daughter of Douglas of Dornoch, a worthy and patient woman, who thought it her duty not only to bear, but palliate the weaknesses and faults of her husband. They had one son, Robert, who was in the same classes at the College with me, and was very promising. He went young to the East Indies to try to mend their broken fortunes, and died in a few years. There were three or four daughters. Sir Robert had obtained an office in the Customs or Excise of about £130, on which, by the good management of his wife and daughters, he in those days lived very decently, and was respected by the common people, as he had been once at the head of the parish. He loved twopenny and low company, which contributed to his popularity, together with his being mild and silent even in his cups.

Colin Campbell, Esq., who had been Collector at Prestonpans, and was promoted to the Board of Customs in 1738, lived now at Pinkie House, and had several sons and daughters, my early companions.

There lived at that time, in the corner of Pinkie House, by himself, Archibald Robertson, commonly called the Gospel, uncle to the celebrated Dr. Robertson—a very singular character, who made great part of our amusement at Pinkie House, as he came through a passage from his own apartment every night to supper, and dined there likewise, as often as he pleased, for which he paid them a cart of coals in the week, as he took charge of Pinkie coal, which his brother-in-law, William Adam, architect, and he, had a lease of. He was a rigid Presbyterian, and a severe old bachelor, whose humours diverted us much. He was at first very fond of me, because he said I had common sense, but he doubted I had but little of the grace of God in me ; and when Dr. George Kay, one of his great friends, posed him on that notion, he could not explain what he meant, but answered that I was too good company to have any deep tincture of religion. Kay then asked if he thought he had any grace, as he had seen him much amused and pleased when he sang, which was more than I could do. He replied, that his singing, though so excellent, did not much raise him in his opinion.

There was likewise living at Inveresk, John Murray, Esq., Clerk of Session, of the Ochtertyre family, who, having been a rake and spendthrift, had married Lucky Thom, a celebrated tavern-keeper, to clear £4000 of debt that he had contracted to her.* She was dead, but there was a fine girl of a daughter, who kept house for her father. There was very good company, especially of the Jacobite party, came about the house, where I was very often.

There was likewise Mr. Oliver Colt, who resided in the family house in Inveresk, who, in two or three years afterwards, by the death of an uncle and brother, had come to a large fortune. He was descended of those clergymen of the parish,† the first of whom was ordained in 1609, whose father, I have heard, was a professor at St. Andrews.

Oliver was a man of mean appearance and habits, and had passed much of his time with the magistrates and burghers of Musselburgh, and, having humour, was a great master of their vulgar wit. When he grew rich, he was deserted by his old friends, and had not manners to draw better company about him, insomuch that, having been con-

* Lest the reader should doubt the printer's accuracy, it is deemed prudent to state that £4000 is the actual amount stated in the author's MS.

† The first clergyman in Inveresk of that name was Adam Coult or Colt. He took his degree at St. Andrews in 1585 and became a regent of Edinburgh University the following year. He was minister of Inveresk for forty-two years and was succeeded by his son Oliver who held the charge for twenty-eight years. Oliver's eldest son, Robert, became Dean of the Faculty of Advocates and Solicitor-General for Scotland, and was knighted by Charles II. He was succeeded by his son Adam, also an advocate and Dean of Faculty, whose son Oliver is referred to by Dr. Carlyle.

fined for a good while to his house by illness, though not keeping his room, when an old lady, a Mrs. Carse, went in to ask for him, he complained bitterly that it was the forty-third day that he had been confined, and no neighbour had ever come near him. He married afterwards a lady of quality, and had enough of company. His son Robert, who died in 1798, was one of the best and worthiest men that ever the parish bred in my time, and I was much afflicted with his early death.

The magistrates and town-council were at this time less respectable than they had been ; for the Whigs, in 1745, had turned out the Jacobites, who were more gentlemanlike than their successors, and were overlooked by Government, as Musselburgh was only a burgh of regality, dependent on the Duke of Buccleuch. The new magistrates were of very low manners and habits, but good Whigs and Presbyterians. All of the burghers, except two of the old magistrates, Smart and Vernon, still preserved the old custom at their family feasts of making the company pay for their drink. There were few or no shops in the town, and but one in each of the streets of Musselburgh and Fisherrow, where even a pound of sugar could be bought, and that always one penny per pound dearer than at Edinburgh ; so that they had very little sale at a time when a woman would have run to Edinburgh with her basket, and brought half a hundredweight for a groat, which did not rise to above sixpence till after the year 1760.

15

There were no lodging-houses at this time in the town, and as it was a dragoon quarter, where generally two troops lay, the officers were obliged to accept their billets in burghers' houses. The only lodging I remember was in a by-street, between Musselburgh and New-bigging, where the late General George Ward and his chum lodged for a year, and where a corporal and his wife would not think themselves well accommodated now. As in those days the dragoons generally stayed two years in Scotland, and did not always change quarters at the end of a year, I became intimate with Ward, then a lieutenant, a sensible man and a good scholar, and pleasant company, though he stuttered.

I have not yet mentioned the two most able inhabitants here at this time, who were Alexander Wood, surgeon, and Commissioner Cardonnel. Sandie Wood was very young, not above twenty-one or twenty-two; but there being an opening here by means of the illness of the senior practitioner, Wood was invited out by a few of the principal people, and got immediately into some business. His father, an opulent farmer in the neighbourhood of Edinburgh,* had bound him an apprentice to his brother, a surgeon well employed by people of inferior rank, and surgeon to the poorhouse, then recently erected. Sandie

* His father was the youngest son of Mr. Wood of Warriston Midlothian. "Wood's Farm" extended over the northern slope of the new town from Queen Street to Canonmills and the farm house stood at the western extremity near what is now Wemyss Place. Chambers says:—" Game used to be plentiful upon these grounds—in particular partridges and hares."

Wood was a handsome stout fellow, with fine black eyes, and altogether of an agreeable and engaging appearance. He was perfectly illiterate in everything that did not belong to his own profession, in which even he was by no means a great student. Some scrapes he got into with women drove him from this place in two or three years for his good. One gentlewoman he got with child, and did not marry. When he got over this difficulty, another fell with child to him, whom he married. She died of her child ; and Sanders was soon after called to a berth in Edinburgh, on the death of his uncle.

Sanders supplied his want of learning with good sense, and a mind as decisive as his eye was quick. He knew the symptoms of diseases with a glance, and having no superfluous talk about politics or news— for books very few of the profession knew anything about—he wasted no time in idle talk, like many of his brethren, but passed on through steep and narrow lanes, and upright stairs of six or seven stories high, by which means he got soon into good business, and at last, his hands being as good as his eyes, on the death of George Lauder he became the greatest and most successful operator for the stone, and for all other difficult cases. His manners were careless and unpolished, and his roughness often offended ; but it was soon discovered that, in spite of his usual demeanour, he was remarkably tender-hearted, and never slighted any case where there was the least danger. I found him always a very honest, friendly, and kind physician.   He is doing business yet in his seventy-fourth year, and although his faculties are impaired, and his operations long over, he gives satisfaction to his patients.   He has always been convivial, belongs to many clubs, and sings a good song

The other person was Mansfelt Cardonnel, Esq. Commissioner of the Customs.   His father, Adam de Cardonnel (for they were French Protestants by descent), had been secretary to the Duke of Schomberg,* who was killed at the battle of the Boyne, at the age of eighty.   He had been affronted the day before by King William not having intrusted him as usual with his plan of the battle, as Adam de Cardonnel told his son.   Another brother, James, was secretary to the Duke of Marlborough, and had made a large fortune.   His daughter and heiress was Lady Talbot mother of Lord Dynevor.   My friend's mother was a natural daughter of the Duke of Monmouth ; and as he was by some other line related to Waller the poet he used to boast of his being descended from the Usurper as well as the royal line.   He was not a man of much depth of genius, but he had a right sound

* There appears to be some confusion in Dr. Carlyle's narrative of the Cardonnel family.   Adam de Cardonnel was secretary to the Duke of Marlborough, and on the Duke's recommendation became Secretary at War.   He acquired considerable wealth not entirely, it was alleged, by legitimate means.   He had an only daughter Mary, who was his heir, and at the age of fifteen became the wife of William, first Earl of Talbot and first Baron Dynevor Their daughter Cecil succeeded to the barony as Baroness Dynevor on the death of her father, and her son became the second Lord Dynevor.

understanding, and was a man of great honour and
integrity, and the most agreeable companion that
ever was. He excelled in story-telling, like his great-
grandfather, Charles II., but he seldom or ever repeated them, and indeed had such a collection as
served to season every conversation. He was very
fond of my companions, particularly of John Home,
who was very often with me. On a very limited income he lived very hospitably ; he had many children,
but only one son, a doctor, remained. The son is
now Adam de Cardonnel Lawson of Chirton, close by
Shields, a fine estate that was left him by a Mr. Hilton
Lawson, a cousin of his mother's, whose name was
Hilton, of the Hilton Castle family, near Sunderland.*

There was another gentleman, whom I must mention, who then lived at Loretto, a Mr. Hew Forbes, a
Principal Clerk of Session. He was a nephew of the
celebrated President Duncan Forbes, and had, at the
request of his uncle, purchased Loretto from John

* There is an " Adam de Cardonnel " known as the author of a
work on the Scottish Coinage, and of *Picturesque Antiquities of
Scotland,* containing etchings of many of the ruined ecclesiastical
and baronial buildings of Scotland. The editor has often endeavoured, without success, to find out who it was that took so
much interest in these architectural relics, and made so meritorious
an effort to represent them in his sketches. From his peculiar
name there can be little doubt that he was a member of the family
referred to by the author.—J. H. B.

The " Adam de Cardonnel " referred to in the footnote is the
same person mentioned by Dr. Carlyle as assuming the name of
Lawson on succeeding to the Chirton Estate. He was the first
curator of the Society of Antiquaries of Scotland (1782–1784).
He was of great assistance to Grose and accompanied him on
several expeditions. He left Scotland about 1798.

Steel, a minion of the President's, who had been a singer in the concert, but had lost his voice, and was patronised by his lordship, and had for some years kept a celebrated tavern in that house.*   Hew Forbes was the second of three brothers, whom I have seen together, and, to my taste, had more wit and was more agreeable than either of them.   Arthur, the eldest, laird of Pittencrieff and a colonel in the Dutch service, was a man of infinite humour, which consisted much in his instantaneous and lively invention of fictions and tales to illustrate or ridicule the conversation that was going on ; and as his tales were inoffensive, though totally void of truth, they afforded great amusement to every company.   The third brother, John, was the gentleman who retrieved our affairs in North America, after Braddock's defeat. He was an accomplished, agreeable gentleman, but there appeared to me to be more effort and less naïveté in his conversation than in that of Hew, whose humour was genuine and natural.

With so many resident families of distinction, my situation was envied as superior to most clergymen for good company and agreeable society ; and so it was at that period preferable to what it has often been since, when the number of genteel families was doubled or tripled, as they have long been.   But though I lived very well with the upper families, and could occasionally consort with the burgesses, some of whom, though

* In the novel "St. Johnstoun," dealing with the time of James IV., Loretto is referred to as a well-known hostelry.

unpolished, were sensible people; yet my chief society
was with John Home, and Robertson, and Bannatine,
and George Logan, who were clergymen about my own
age, and very accomplished.

In the month of October this year I had a very
agreeable jaunt to Dumfriesshire to attend the marriage of my cousin, Jean Wight, with John Hamilton, the minister of Bolton.   She was very handsome,
sprightly, and agreeable—about twenty; he a sensible,
knowing man. . . .* John Home was his "best man;"
I was the lady's attendant of the same occupation, according to the fashion of the times. We set out together
on horseback, but so contrived it that we had very little
of the bridegroom; for being in a greater haste to get
to his journey's end than we were, he was always at
the baiting-place an hour before us, where, after our
meal, we lingered as long after he had departed. Our
grandfather Robison wished to solemnise this first marriage of any of his grandchildren at his own house at
Tinwald, which, though an ordinary manse, had thirty
people to sleep in it for two or three nights.   John
Home and I had been one day in Dumfries with the
bridegroom, where we met with George Bannatine,
our friend Hew's brother, at that time minister of
Craigie.   As he was an old schoolfellow of Hamilton's,
we easily induced him to ask him to the marriage;

* The rest of his character is scored out, so as to be totally
illegible; and in the handwriting in which the original MS. is
altered throughout, the sentence stands, " He was not less than
thirty-five; and though a sensible, knowing man, was in other
respects seemingly unsuitable for so young and so lively a woman."

and George, having a great deal of Falstaffian humour, helped much to enliven the company. Home and he and I, with Willie Wight, the bride's brother, then a fine lad of eighteen, had to ride four miles into Dumfries to our lodgings at Provost Bell's, another uncle of mine, after supper, where Bannatine's vein of humour kept us in perpetual laughter.

I shall take this opportunity of correcting a mistake into which the English authors have fallen, in which they are supported by many of the Scotch writers, particularly by those of the *Mirror*,—which is, that the people of Scotland have no humour. That this is a gross mistake, could be proved by innumerable songs, ballads, and stories that are prevalent in the south of Scotland, and by every person old enough to remember the times when the Scottish dialect was spoken in purity in the low country, and who have been at all conversant with the common people. Since we began to affect speaking a foreign language, which the English dialect is to us, humour, it must be confessed, is less apparent in conversation. The ground of this pretension in the English to the mono-poly of humour is their confounding two characters together that are quite different—the humorist and the man of humour. The humorist prevails more in England than in any country, because liberty has long been universal there, and wealth very general, which I hold to be the father and mother of the humorist. This mistake has been confirmed by the abject humour of the Scotch, who, till of late years, allowed John Bull, out of flattery, to possess every quality to which he pretended.

John Home was an admirable companion, and most acceptable to all strangers who were not offended with the levities of a young clergyman, for he was very handsome and had a fine person, about 5 feet 10½ inches, and an agreeable catching address; he had not much wit, and still less humour, but he had so much sprightliness and vivacity, and such an expression of benevolence in his manner, and such an unceasing flattery of those he liked (and he never kept company with anybody else)—the kind commendations of a lover, not the adulation of a sycophant— that he was truly irresistible, and his entry to a company was like opening a window and letting the sun into a dark room.

After passing eight days at Dumfries, with such a variety of amusement as would fill half a volume of a novel, we returned with our young couple home to East Lothian, and passed two or three days with them at their residence.

There was an assistant preacher at Inveresk when I was ordained, whose name was George Anderson, the son of a clergyman in Fife, and, by his mother, grandson of a Professor Campbell of Edinburgh,* who made a figure in the divinity chair towards the end of the seventeenth century. His aunt was the mother of Dr. John Gregory of Edinburgh; but he had not

* Professor George Campbell, minister of Dumfries, appointed to the Chair of Divinity in Edinburgh University in 1690.

partaken of the smallest spark of genius from either of the families. He was good-natured and laborious in the parish, however, and likely to fall into the snare of such kind of people, by partaking of their morning hospitality—viz. a dram, very usual in those days. He was reckoned an excellent preacher by the common people, because he got a sermon faithfully by heart (his father's, I suppose), and delivered it with a loudness and impetuosity surpassing any schoolboy, without making a halt or stop from beginning to end. This galloping sort of preaching pleased the lairds as well as the people, for Sir David Kinloch was much taken with him, and he would have been popular in all respects had not his conversation and conduct betrayed his folly. With a very small income, he ventured [to marry] a handsome sempstress, Peggy Derquier, the daughter of a Swiss ensign, who had got into the British army. They had children, and a very slender subsistence, not above £40 per annum, so that I was obliged to look about for some better berth for them. At last, in 1751, a place cast up in South Carolina, to which he and his family were with difficulty sent out, as a sum of money had to be borrowed to fit out him and his wife and two children for the voyage. I was one of his securities for the money, and lost nothing but the interest of £50 for two years. His wife was mettlesome, and paid up the money the year after he died, which was not above two years ; for poor George, being a guzzling fellow, could not remain long enough from

Charlestown, near which his meeting-house was, till he recovered his strength after a severe fever : the rum-punch got the better of him, and he relapsed and died. His widow, being still handsome and broody, married well next time, and got her children well provided for.

In a ludicrous poem which John Home wrote on the march of his Volunteers to the battle of Falkirk, he gives Anderson his character under the nickname of Lungs—for the wags called him Carlyle's Lungs on account of his loud preaching—of which I remember one line,—

"And if you did not beat him, Lungs was pleased."

Like other gluttons, Lungs was a coward, and the first man at Leith after the battle—for he was a Volunteer in the company of which Home was a lieutenant—and showed his activity chiefly in providing the company with victuals and drink, in begging of which he had no shame.

CHAPTER VI

IN winter 1748 I remained much at home in my own parish, performing my duties, and becoming acquainted with my flock. The Cheaps took a house in Edinburgh this winter to entertain Captain Cheap, who, being a man past fifty, and a good deal worn out, his very sensible niece thought he would never marry, and therefore brought her young female companions about to amuse him. Among the rest she had much with her the Widow Brown, Anny Clerk that was, whose husband, Major Brown [was killed at the battle of Falkirk*]. She was a handsome, lively coquette as ever was, being of a gay temper and a slight understanding. My sagacious friend had taken her measures ill indeed, for, as she told me afterwards, she never dreamt that her grave respectable uncle would be catched with a woman of Mrs. Brown's description. But he was so captivated at the very first glance that he very soon proposed marriage; and having executed his design, and taken

* Left blank by Carlyle, and filled up in another hand.

the House of Preston for next summer, they came and lived there for several months, where I saw them frequently, and was asked to marry a niece of hers with a gentleman at Dunbar, which I accordingly did. They went to Bath and London, where his niece joined him in 1749.

It was in the General Assembly of this year that some zealous west-country clergymen formed the plan of applying to Parliament for a general augmentation of stipends, by raising the minimum from 800 merks to 10 chalders of grain, or its value in money. The clergy having shown great loyalty and zeal during the Rebellion in 1745, which was acknowledged by Government, they presumed that they would obtain favour on this occasion; but they had not consulted the landed interest, nor even taken the leaders among the Whigs along with them, which was the cause of their miscarriage. The committee appointed by this Assembly to prepare the form of their application, brought it into next Assembly, and by a very great majority agreed to send commissioners to London the session thereafter to prosecute their claim, which, when it failed, raised some ill-humour, for they had been very sanguine. Dr. Patrick Cuming,* who was then the leader of the Moderate party, lent his whole aid to this scheme, and was one of the commissioners. This gave him still a greater lead among the clergy.

---

* Minister of Edinburgh and Professor of Church History in Edinburgh University. He had the unusual honour of being three times elected Moderator of the General Assembly.

The same thing happened to Lord Drummore, the judge, who espoused their cause warmly. On the other hand, Principal Wishart and his brother George followed Dundas of Arniston, the first President of that name, and lost their popularity. Of the two brothers William and George Wishart, sons of Principal Wishart, William the eldest, and Principal of the University of Edinburgh, was the most learned and ingenuous, but he had been for seventeen years a dissenting minister in London, and returned with dissenting principles. He had said some things rashly while the augmentation scheme was going on, which betrayed contempt of the clergy ; and as he was rich, and had the expectation of still more—being the heir of his two uncles, Admiral and General Wisharts, of Queen Anne's reign—his sayings gave still greater offence. George, the younger brother, was milder and more temperate, and was a more acceptable preacher than his brother,* though inferior to him in genius; but his understanding was sound, and his benevolence unbounded, so that he had many friends. When his brother, who misled him about ecclesiastical affairs, died in 1754, he came back to the Moderate party, and was much respected among us.

About this period it was that John Home and I, being left alone with Dr. Patrick Cuming after a synod supper, he pressed us to stay with him a little

---

* He was minister of the Tron Church, Principal Clerk of Assembly, and one of the Deans of the Chapel Royal. He died in 1795 at the age of eighty-three.

longer, and during an hour or two's conversation, being desirous to please us, who, he thought, would be of some consequence in church courts, he threw out all his lures to gain us to be his implicit followers; but he failed in his purpose, having gone too far in his animosity to George Wishart—for we gave up the Principal. We said to each other when we parted that we would support him when he acted right, but would never be intimate with him as a friend.

It was the custom at this time for the patrons of parishes, when they had litigations about settlements, which sometimes lasted for years, to open public-houses to entertain the members of Assembly, which was a very gross and offensive abuse. The Duke of Douglas had a cause of this kind, which lasted for three Assemblies, on which occasion it was that his commissioner, White of Stockbridge, opened a daily table for a score of people, which vied with the Lord Commissioner's for dinners, and surpassed it far in wine. White, who was a low man, was delighted with the respect which these dinners procured him. After the case was finished, Stockbridge kept up his table while he lived, for the honour of the family, where I have often dined, after his Grace's suit was at an end. There was another of the same kind that lasted longer, the case of St. Ninian's, of which Sir Hew Paterson was patron.*

John Home, and Robertson, and Logan, and I,

* The settlement of Mr. Thomson at St. Ninian's occupied the General Assembly from 1767 to 1776.

entered into a resolution to dine with none of them while their suits were in dependence. This resolution we kept inviolably when we were members, and we were followed by many of our friends. Dr. Patrick Cuming did not like this resolution of ours, as it showed us to be a little untractable ; but it added to our importance ; and after that no man, not even Lord Drummore, to whom I was so much obliged, and who was a keen party man, ever solicited my vote in any judicial case.

The Lord President Dundas, who led the opposition to the scheme of augmentation, was accounted the first lawyer this country ever had bred. He was a man of a high and ardent mind, a most persuasive speaker, and to me, who met him but seldom in private, one of the ablest men I had ever seen. He declined soon after this, and was for two or three years laid aside from business before his death.

Hew, Earl of Marchmont, appeared in this Assembly, who had been very ignorantly extolled by Pope, whose hemistichs stamped characters in those days.*

---

* ———" Lo, th' Ægerian grot,
Where nobly pensive St. John sat and thought,
Where British sighs from dying Wyndham stole,
And the bright flame was shot through Marchmont's soul."

The passage cited farther on (p. 152) is from the inverted characters in the epilogue to the " Satires " :—

"Cobham's a coward, Polwarth is a slave,
And Littleton a dark designing knave."

About Lord Polwarth, afterwards Earl of Marchmont, and other members of his family, abundant information will be found in

In winter 1749 it was that John Home went to London with his tragedy of *Agis,* to try to bring it on the stage, in which he failed ; which was the cause of his turning his thoughts on the tragedy of *Douglas* after his return. He had a recommendation to Mr. Lyttleton, afterwards Lord Lyttleton,* whom he could not so much as prevail with to read his tragedy; and his brother, afterwards a bishop, would not so much as look at it, as he said he had turned his thoughts to natural history. Home was enraged, but not discouraged. I had given him a letter to Smollett, with whom he contracted a sincere friendship, and he consoled himself for the neglect he met with by the warm approbation of the Doctor, and of John Blair and his friend Barrow, an English physician, who had escaped with him from the Castle of Doune, and who made him acquainted with Collins the poet, with whom he grew very intimate. He extended not his acquaintance much further at this time, except to a Governor Melville, a native of Dunbar, of whom he was fond ; and passed a good deal of time with Captain Cheap's family, which was then in London.

I had several letters from him at that time which displayed the character he always maintained, which was a thorough contempt of his non-approvers, and a blind admiration of those who approved of his works,

---

A Selection from the Papers of the Earls of Marchmont, 3 vols., 1831.—J. H. B.

  * First Baron known as " the good Lord Lyttleton."

and gave him a good reception, whom he attached still more to him by the most caressing manners, and the sincere and fervent flattery of a lover. In all the periods of his long life his opinions of men and things were merely prejudices.

It was in the year 1750, I think, that he gave his manse (for he boarded himself in a house in the village) to Mr. Hepburn of Keith, and his family—a gentleman of pristine faith and romantic valour, who had been in both the Rebellions, in 1715 and '45 ; and had there been a third, as was projected at this time, would have joined it also. Add to this, that Mr. Hepburn was an accomplished gentleman, and of a simple and winning elocution, who said nothing in vain. His wife, and his daughters by a former lady, resembled him in his simplicity of mind, but propagated his doctrines with more openness and ardour, and a higher admiration of implicit loyalty and romantic heroism. It was the seductive conversation of this family that gradually softened and cooled Mr. Home's aversion to the Pretender and to Jacobites (for he had been a very warm Whig in the time of the Rebellion), and prepared him for the life he afterwards led.

Mr. Home, in his *History of the Rebellion*, has praised this gentleman for an act of gallant behaviour in becoming Gentleman-Usher to Prince Charles, by ushering him into the Abbey with his sword drawn. This has been on false information ; for his son, Colonel Riccart Hepburn, denied to me the possibility of it, his father being a person of invincible modesty, and void of all ostentation. The Colonel added, that it was his father's fortune to be praised for qualities he did not possess—for learning, for instance, of which he had no great tincture, but in mathematics—while his prime quality was omitted, which was the most equal and placid temper with which ever mortal was endowed ; for in his whole life he was never once out of temper, nor did ever a muscle of his face alter on any occurrence. One instance he told of a serving-boy having raised much disturbance one day in the kitchen or hall. When his father rose to see what was the matter, he found the boy had wantonly run a spit through the cat, which lay sprawling. He said not a word, but took the boy by the shoulder, led him out of the house door, and locked it after him, and returned in silence to play out his game of chess with his daughter.

It was from his having heard Mrs. Janet Denoon,* Mr. Hepburn's sister-in-law, sing the old ballad of " Gil Morrice," that he [Home] first took his idea of the tragedy of *Douglas*, which, five years afterwards, he carried to London, for he was but an idle composer, to offer it for the stage, but with the same bad

* " Miss Jenny was humpbacked and breasted but sang with much taste, was clever at composing music and counted a great nib." Charles Kirkpatrick Sharpe in Wilson's *Reminiscences of Old Edinburgh*. She was the niece of Christian Bruce, wife of Colonel James Riccart Hepburn of Keith. Christian Bruce and her sister-in-law, Lady Bruce of Kinross, and Jenny Denoon were, according to C. K. Sharpe, the joint composers of the poetical skit entitled "The Ridotto at Holyrood House."

success as formerly. The length of time he took, however, tended to bring it to perfection ; for want of success, added to his natural openness, made him communicate his compositions to his friends, whereof there were some of the soundest judgment, and of the most exquisite taste. Of the first sort there were Drs. Blair and Robertson, and Mr. Hew Bannatine ; and of the second, Patrick Lord Elibank, the Hepburn family, and some young ladies with whom he and I had become intimate—viz., Miss Hepburn of Monkriggs, Lord Milton's niece ; Miss Eliza Fletcher, afterwards Mrs. Wedderburn, his youngest daughter ; and Miss Campbell of Carrick, at that time their great friend. As Home himself wrote a hand that was hardly legible, and at that time could ill afford to hire an amanuensis, I copied *Douglas* several times over for him—which, by means of the corrections of all the friends I have mentioned, and the fine and decisive criticisms of the late Sir Gilbert Elliot, had attained to the perfection with which it was acted ; for at this time Home was tractable, and listened to our remarks.

It was at this period that George Logan, the son of a minister in Edinburgh of note, was presented to the church of Ormiston, vacant by the translation of Mr. Hew Bannatine to Dirleton. Logan was a man of parts and genius, and of a particular turn to mathematical and metaphysical studies, but he was of an indolent and dilatory disposition. When he passed trials before the Presbytery of Dalkeith, he met with unexpected opposition. When he came to the last of his discourses, which was the popular sermon, from Heb. ii. 10 was appointed to him. He came home with me, and inquiring if my popular sermon, when I was licensed by the Presbytery of Haddington, was not on the same text, which was the case, he pressed me to lend it to him, as it would save him much trouble, to which I with reluctance consented. He copied it almost verbatim, and delivered it at our next meeting.* Being averse to Logan, many of them thought there was heresy in it, and insisted on an inquiry, and that a copy should be deposited with the Clerk. This inquiry went on for several meetings, till at last Logan, being impatient, as he had a young lady engaged to marry him, took the first opportunity of appealing to the Synod. After several consultations with our ablest divines, who were Drs. Wishart and Wallace, with Professor Goldie, and Messrs. Dalgleish of Linlithgow, Nassmith of Dalmeny, and Stedman of Haddington, it was agreed that Logan's sermon was perfectly orthodox, and that the Presbytery in their zeal had run into heretical opinions, insomuch that those friends were clear in their judgment that the panel should be

* *Popular Sermon.* The sermon preached to the people of the parish by a presentee, as distinguished from the other trials of his fitness, which take place in the presence of the Presbytery. The Logan here mentioned is not the poet ; and it is perhaps still more necessary to distinguish him from a contemporary, George Logan, also a clergyman of the Church of Scotland, and eminent in his day for a long and bitter political controversy with Ruddiman the grammarian. The affair of the censured sermon is mentioned in Mackenzie's *Account of Home*, p. 12.—J. H. B.

assoilzied and the Presbytery taken to task. But the motive I have already mentioned induced young Logan to be desirous of making matters up without irritating the Presbytery, and therefore it was agreed that he should make a slight apology to the Presbytery, and that they should be ordained to proceed in the settlement. Yet, in spite of this sacrifice to peace, the zealots of the Presbytery still endeavoured to delay the settlement by embarrassing him on what is called the *extempore* trials; but as he was an able and a learned young man, he baffled them all in an examination of three hours, four or five times longer than usual, when he answered all their questions, and refuted all their cavils in such a masterly manner, as turned the chase in the opinion of the bystanders, and made the Presbytery appear to be heretical, instead of the person accused.

Among the accusers of Logan, the most violent were Plenderleath of Dalkeith, Primrose at Crichton, Smith at Cranston, Watson at Newbottle, and Walker at Temple. The first had been a minion of Dr. George Wishart's, and set out as one of the most moral preachers at the very top of the Moderate interest, giving offence by his quotations from Shaftesbury; but being very weak, both in body and mind, he thought to compensate for his disability by affecting a change of sentiment, and coming over to the popular side, both in his sermons and his votes in the courts. He was truly but a poor soul, and might have been pardoned, but for his hypocrisy. Primrose was a shallow pedant, who was puffed up by the flattery of his brethren to think himself an eminent scholar because he was pretty well acquainted with the system, and a person of a high independent mind because he was rich and could speak impertinently to his heritors, and build a manse of an uncommon size and pay for the overplus. He had a fluent elocution in the dialect of Morayshire, embellished with English of his own invention ; but with all this he had no common sense. Smith was a sly northern, seemingly very temperate, but a great counsellor of his neighbour and countryman Primrose. Watson was a dark inquisitor, of some parts. Walker was a rank enthusiast, with nothing but heat without light. John Bonar at Cockpen, though of the High party, was a man of sense—an excellent preacher ; he was temperate in his opposition. Robin Paton, though gentlemanly, was feeble in church courts. His father was just dead, so that I had no zealous supporter but Rab Simson and David Gilchrist at Newton. On those inferior characters I need not dwell.

Logan was settled at Ormiston and married, not three years after which he died of a high brain fever. John Home and I felt our loss. A strong proof of our opinion of his ability was, that a very short time before his death we had prevailed with him to make David Hume's philosophical works his particular study, and to refute the dangerous parts of them—a task for which we thought him fully equal. This was sixteen or eighteen years before Beattie thought of

it.   Dr. Wight and I saw him [Beattie] frequently at
Aberdeen in 1765 or 1766, when he opened his design
to us, from which we endeavoured to dissuade him,
having then a settled opinion that such metaphysical
essays and treatises—as they were seldom read, certainly never understood, but by the few whose minds
were nearly on a level with the author—had best be
left without the celebrity of an answer.   It was on
occasion of this trial of Logan that we first took
umbrage at Robert Dundas, junior, of Arniston, then
Solicitor-General, who could easily have drawn off
the Presbytery of Dalkeith from their illiberal pursuit,
and was applied to for that purpose by some friends,
who were refused.   His father, the President, was by
this time laid aside.

It was in the year 1751 or 1752, I think, that a few of
us of the Moderate party were for two or three days
united in a case that came before the Synod of
Lothian in May, with Dr. Alexander Webster, the
leader of the high-flying party.   Webster, with a few
more of his brethren, whereof Drs. Jardine and
Wallace were two, had objected to Mr. John Johnstone, a new chaplain of the castle, being admitted to
a seat in the Presbytery of Edinburgh.   They were
defeated in the Presbytery by a great majority, on
which they appealed to the Synod, when a few of us,
taking part with the minority, had an opportunity
of seeing Webster very closely.

Our conclusions on this acquaintance were (and
we never altered them), that though he was a clever

fellow, an excellent and ready speaker, fertile in expedients, and prompt in execution, yet he had by no means a leading or decisive mind, and consequently was unfit to be the head of a party. He had no scruples ; for, with a little temporary heating, he seemed to be entirely without principle. There was at this time a Mr. John Hepburn, minister in the Old Greyfriars, who, though he never appeared to take any share in ecclesiastical affairs but by his vote, was in secret Webster's counsellor and director, so that while he lived, Webster did well as the ostensible head of his party. Mr. Hepburn was grandfather of the present Earl of Hyndford, and the son of a celebrated mountaineer in Galloway, the Rev. Mr. John Hepburn, in Queen Anne's time.* But when he [Hepburn] died not long after, he [Webster] fell into the hands of Dr. Jardine, who managed him with great dexterity, for he allowed him to adhere to his party, but restrained him from going too far. As Jardine was son-in-law to Provost Drummond, with whom Webster wished to be well, Jardine, who had much sagacity, with great versatility of genius, and a talent for the management of men, had not such a difficult task as one would have imagined. Webster had published a satirical sermon against Sir Robert Walpole, for which he had been taken to task in the General Assembly by the Earl of Islay, by this time

* The term " mountaineer " is a metonymy for hillman or Covenanter. Daniel Carmichael of Mauldsley, whose son Andrew became sixth Earl of Hyndford, married in 1742 Emilia, daughter of the Rev. John Hepburn.—*Wood's Peerage*, i. 759.—J. H. B.

Duke of Argyle, and of great political power in Scotland. Webster, in case of accidents, wished to have a friendly mediator between him and the Duke. This is the true key to all his political disingenuity.

Webster had justly obtained much respect amongst the clergy, and all ranks, indeed, for having established the Widows' Fund ; for though Dr. Wallace, who was an able mathematician, had made the calculations, Webster had the merit of carrying the scheme into execution. Having married a lady of fashion,* who had a fortune of £4000 (an estate in those days), he kept better company than most of the clergy. His appearance of great strictness in religion, to which he was bred under his father, who was a very popular minister of the Tolbooth Church, not acting in restraint of his convivial humour, he was held to be excellent company, even by those of dissolute manners ; while, being a five-bottle man, he could lay them all under the table.† This had [brought]

---

* Miss Mary Erskine. It is told of Dr. Webster that while minister of Culross, where Miss Erskine resided, he was employed to plead the cause of a gentleman who had himself hitherto done so in vain to the lady. The outcome of young Webster's eloquence was a hint that if he had been pleading for himself he would have had more success. On his appointment to the Tolbooth Church, Edinburgh, he married Miss Erskine.

† An acquaintance overtaking the Doctor on his way home in early morning and showing signs of conviviality, saluted him with "Eh, doctor, what would the auld wives o' the Tolbooth say if they saw ye noo ? " " Tut man," was the retort, " they wouldna believe their een." In this connection a good story is told of Dr. Carlyle himself. The late Dr. Lindsay Alexander, of St. Augustine's Church, Edinburgh, recalled hearing, when a

on him the nickname of Dr. Bonum Magnum in the time of faction; but never being indecently the worse of liquor, and a love of claret to any degree not being reckoned in those days a sin in Scotland, all his excesses were pardoned.*

When it was discovered that Jardine led him, his party became jealous; and it was no wonder, for he used to undermine them by his speeches, and vote with them to save appearances. But the truly upright and honourable men among them, such as Drs. Erskine and Hunter, etc., could not think of parting with his abilities, which, both in the pulpit and the Assembly, gave some lustre to their party. He could pass at once from the most unbounded jollity to the most fervent devotion; yet I believe that his hypocrisy was no more than habit grounded merely on temper, and that his aptness to pray was as easy and natural to him as to drink a convivial glass. His familiar saying, however, that it was his lot to drink with gentlemen and to vote with fools, made too full

child, one of the servants at Pinkieburn tell of Carlyle dining there, and following him with admiring gaze as he left the house on his way home. "There he gaed, dacent man, as steady as a wall, after his ain share o' five bottles o' port."

* Dr. Alexander Webster and Dr. Robert Wallace were both men of much celebrity in their day as clergymen of the Church of Scotland. Of Webster's very peculiar characteristics there is perhaps a fuller account in this work than anywhere else. Wallace, who was a man of less notable peculiarities, wrote several books, the most remarkable of which is *A Dissertation on the Numbers of Mankind in Ancient and Modern Times*, which, along with Hume's Essay on the populousness of ancient nations, contributed some ideas subsequently brought to bear on the great discussion on population inaugurated by Malthus.—J. H. B.

a discovery of the laxity of his mind. Indeed, he lived too long to preserve any respect ; for in his latter years his sole object seemed to be where to find means of inebriety, which he at last too often effected, for his constitution having lost its vigour, he was sent home almost every evening like other drunkards who could not boast of strength. Besides the £4000 he got with his lady, he spent £6000 more, which was left him by Miss Hunter, one of his pious disciples, which legacy did not raise his character. In aid of his fortune, when it was nearly drained, he was appointed Collector of the Widows' Fund when a Mr. Stewart died, who was the first, and likewise obtained one of the deaneries from the Crown. When the New Town of Edinburgh came to be planned out, he was employed by the magistrates, which gratified his two strongest desires—his love of business and of conviviality, in both of which he excelled. The business was all done in the tavern, where there was a daily dinner, which cost the town in the course of the year £500, the whole of an additional revenue which had been discovered a little while before by Buchan, the Town's Chamberlain.* He had done many private and public injuries to me in spite of the support I and my friends had given him in his cause before the Synod in May 1752, for which I did not

---

* " I have heard Dr. Webster himself say, that by his advice the Town Council had adopted the measure of appointing a Chamberlain to be constantly and entirely trusted with the business of the revenue instead of a Treasurer annually elected."—Somerville's *Memoirs of my Life and Times*.

spare him when I had an opportunity, by treating him with that rough raillery which the fashion of the times authorised, which he bore with inimitable patience; and when I rose into some consideration, he rather courted than shunned my company, with the perfect knowledge of what I thought of him.

As John Home and I had made speeches in his support at the Synod, he thought he could do no less than invite us to dinner on the day after : we went accordingly, and were well enough received by him, while his lady treated us not only with neglect, but even with rudeness; while she caressed with the utmost kindness Adams of Falkirk, the very person who, by disobeying the Assembly and escaping unhurt in 1751, drew the thunder of the Church on Gillespie the following year.

Another instance of Webster's hostility to me happened some time afterwards. His colleague, Mr. William Gusthart, who was a very old man, and lived for many summers in my parish, and at last the whole year round, engaged me to preach for him in the Tolbooth Church one Sunday afternoon. I was averse to this service, as I knew I would not be acceptable in that congregation. But being urged by the old man and his family, I agreed, and went to town, and preached to a very thin audience. I was afterwards certainly informed that Webster had sent round to many of his principal families, warning them that I was to do duty for his colleague, and hoping that they would not give countenance to a person who had attended the theatre. This, I think, was in 1759, two years after I had foiled the High party in the General Assembly. This I considered as most malicious ; and with this I frequently taxed him in very plain terms indeed. There were a few of us who, besides the levity of youth and the natural freedom of our manners, had an express design to throw contempt on that vile species of hypocrisy which magnified an indecorum into a crime, and gave an air of false sanctimony and Jesuitism to the greatset part of the clergy, and was thereby pernicious to rational religion. In this plan we succeeded, for in the midst of our freedom having preserved respect and obtained a leading in the Church, we freed the clergy from many unreasonable and hypocritical restraints.

I have dwelt longer on Dr. Webster than on any other person, because such characters are extremely pernicious, as they hold up an example to unprincipled youth how far they may play fast and loose with professed principles without being entirely undone ; and how far they may proceed in dissipation of manner without entirely forfeiting the public good opinion. But let the young clergy observe, that very few indeed are capable of exhibiting for their protection such useful talents, or of displaying such agreeable manners as Dr. Webster did in compensation for his faults.

In 1751 the schoolmaster of Musselburgh died, a

Mr. Munro, who had only seven scholars and one boarder, he and his wife had become so unpopular. As the magistrates of Musselburgh came in place of the heritors as patrons of the school, by a transaction with them about the mortcloths, the emoluments of which the heritors gave up on the town's agreeing to pay the salary, I took the opportunity that this gave me as joint patron to persuade them, as their school had fallen so low, to fill it up by a comparative trial before a committee of Presbytery, with Sir David Dalrymple * and Dr. Blair as assessors, when a Mr. Jeffry, from the Merse, showed so much superiority that he was unanimously elected. He soon raised the school to some eminence, and got about twenty-five or thirty boarders the second year. When he died, eight or ten years afterwards, his daughters, by my advice, took up the first female boarding-school that ever was there, which has been kept up with success ever since ; and such has been the encouragement that two others have been well supported also. On Jeffry's death, John Murray succeeded him, who did well also. When he grew old, I got him to resign on a pension, and had John Taylor to succeed him, who has surpassed them all, having got as far as seventy boarders, his wife being the best qualified of any person I ever knew in her station.

It was in this year, 1751, the foundation was laid

---

* Third baronet of Hailes, who was raised to the Bench in 1766 and took the title of Lord Hailes.   He was the author of *Annals of Scotland*, and many other works.

for the restoration of the discipline of the Church the next year, in which Dr. Robertson, John Home and I had such an active hand. Mr. Adams, at Falkirk, had disobeyed a sentence of the General Assembly, appointing the Presbytery of Linlithgow to settle Mr. Watson, minister of the parish of Torphichen, to which he had been presented, and for which, after trial, he was found fully qualified. Mr. Adams had been appointed *nominatim* by the Act of Assembly to preside at this ordination. This was the second year this presbytery had disobeyed, because there was an opposition in the parish. This had happened before, and the plea of conscience had always brought off the disobedient. The Assembly had fallen on a wretched expedient to settle presentees who were in this state. They appointed a committee of their number, who had no scruple to obey the sentence of the Supreme Court, to go to the parish on a certain day and ordain the presentee. This had been done in several instances with the very worst effect ; for the presbyteries having preserved their own popularity by their resistance, they had no interest in reconciling the minds of the people to their new pastor; and accordingly, for most part, cherished their prejudices, and left the unfortunate young man to fight his way without help in the best manner he could. This was a great abuse, and was likely to destroy the subordination of church courts, which of old had been the great boast of our Presbyterian form of government, and had been very complete and perfect in early times. The departure from that strictness of discipline, and the adoption of expedients in judicial cases, was of very recent growth, and was chiefly owing to the struggle against patronages after their restoration in the 10th of Queen Anne; so that the Assembly had only to recur to her first principles and practice to restore her lost authority. So far was it from being true that Dr. Robertson was the inventor of this system, as was afterwards believed, and as the strain of Dugald Stewart's *Life of Robertson* has a tendency to support.

The rise of the attempt to revive the ancient discipline in this Assembly was as follows :—Some friends and companions having been well informed that a great majority of the General Assembly 1751 were certainly to let Mr. Adams of Falkirk, the disobedient brother, escape with a very slight censure, a select company of fifteen were called together in a tavern, a night or two before the case was to be debated in the Assembly, to consult what was to be done. There met accordingly in the tavern the Right Honourable the Lord Provost Drummond; the Honourable William Master of Ross; Mr. Gilbert Elliot, junior of Minto; Mr. Andrew Pringle, advocate; Messrs. Jardine, Blair, Robertson, John Home, Adam Dickson of Dunse, George Logan of Ormiston, Alexander Carlyle of Inveresk, and as many more as made fifteen, two of whom—viz. Logan and Carlyle —were not members of Assembly. The business was talked over, and having the advice of those two able

17

lawyers, Messrs. Elliot and Pringle, we were confirmed in our opinion that it was necessary to use every means in our power to restore the authority of the Church, otherwise her government would be degraded, and everything depending on her authority would fall into confusion ; and though success was not expected at this Assembly, as we knew that the judges, and many other respectable elders, besides the opposite party of the clergy, were resolved to let Mr. Adams and the disobedient Presbytery of Linlithgow escape with a very slight censure (an admonition only), yet we believed that, by keeping the object in view, good sense would prevail at last, and order be restored. We did not propose deposition, but only suspension for six months, which, we thought, was meeting the opposite party half-way. John Home agreed to make the motion, and Robertson to second him. Neither of them had ever spoken in the Assembly till then, and it was till that period unusual for young men to begin a debate. They plucked up spirit, however, and performed their promise, and were ably supported by Messrs. Pringle and Elliot, and one or two more of those who had engaged with them. When they came to vote, however, two of the eighteen lost heart, and could not vote in opposition to all the great men in the Assembly. Those two were Messrs. John Jardine and Hew Blair, who soon repented of their cowardice, and joined heartily in the dissent from a sentence of the Commission in March 1752, which brought on the deposition of

Gillespie, and re-established the authority of the Church. Adam Dickson of Dunse, who had been ill treated by John Home's friends in that Presbytery when he was presentee to that parish, was the first who voted on our side. Home made a spirited oration, though not a business speech, which talent he never attained. Robertson followed him, and not only gained the attention of the Assembly, but drew the praise of the best judges, particularly of the Lord President Dundas,* who I overheard say that Robertson was an admirable speaker, and would soon become a leader in the church courts.

Although the associated members lost the question by a very great majority, yet the speeches made on that occasion had thoroughly convinced many of the senior members, who, though they persisted in their purpose of screening Adams, yet laid to heart what they heard, and were prepared to follow a very different course with the next offender. Adams' own speech, and those of his apologists, had an equal effect with those on the other side in bringing about this revolution on the minds of sensible men, for the plea of conscience was their only ground, which the more it was urged appeared the more absurd when applied to the conduct of subordinate judicatories in an Established Church.

This occasional union of some of the young clergymen with the young lawyers and other elders of rank had another happy effect, for it made them well ac-

* First Lord President Dundas.

quainted with each other. Besides casual meetings,
they had two nights set apart during every Assembly,
when Messrs. Ross, Elliot, and Pringle, with additional young elders as they came up, supped together,
and conferred about the business with their friends
of the Assembly 1752, and whoever they thought
were fit associates. Thus was anticipated what took
place on a larger scale, a few years afterwards, by
the institution of the Select Society. Till this period
the clergy of Scotland, from the Revolution downwards, had in general been little thought of, and
seldom admitted into liberal society, one cause of
which was, that in those days a clergyman was thought
profane who affected the manners of gentlemen, or
was much seen in their company. The sudden call
for young men to fill up vacancies at the Revolution,
obliged the Church to take their entrants from the
lower ranks, who had but a mean education. It
must be observed, too, that when Presbytery was
re-established in Scotland at the Revolution, after the
reign of Episcopacy for twenty-nine years, more than
two-thirds of the people of the country, and most
part of the gentry, were Episcopals; the restoration
of Presbytery by King William being chiefly owing
to the Duke of Argyle, Marchmont, Stair, and other
leading nobles who had suffered under Charles and
James, and who had promoted the Revolution with
all their interest and power.

As it was about this period that the General
Assembly became a theatre for young lawyers to

display their eloquence and exercise their talents, I shall mention the impression which some of them made on me in my early days. The Lord President Arniston—the father of a second President of the same name, Robert Dundas, and of Lord Viscount Melville, by different wives—had been King's Advocate in the year 1720, which he had lost in 1725, by his opposition to Sir Robert Walpole and Lord Islay. He was one of the ablest lawyers this country ever produced, and a man of a high independent spirit. His appearance was against him, for he was ill-looking, with a large nose and small ferret eyes, round shoulders, a harsh croaking voice, and altogether unprepossessing ; yet by the time he had uttered three sentences, he raised attention, and went on with a torrent of good sense and clear reasoning that made one totally forget the first impression. At this Assembly he did not speak, and soon after fell into a debility of mind and body, which continued to 1753, when he died. I never happened to be in company with this Lord President but once, which was at a meeting of Presbytery for dividing the church of Newbottle. The Presbytery and the heritors who attended were quite puzzled how to proceed in the business, and Arniston, who was an heritor, was late in coming. But he had no sooner appeared than he undid all that we had been trying to do, and having put the meeting on a right plan, extricated and settled the business in a short time. To the superiority of his mind he added experience in that sort of business.

There was a dinner provided for us in the Marquis [of Lothian's] house, where Sandy M'Millan, W.S.,* presided in the absence of the Marquis, when I was quite delighted with the President's brilliant parts and fine convivial spirit. I was earnestly invited to go to him at Arniston, where I should probably have been very often, had not this happened a very short while, not above a month or two, before he fell into debility of mind, and was shut up. Hew Dalrymple, Lord Drummore, who was much inferior to him in talents, was a very popular speaker, though neither an orator nor an acute reasoner. He was the lay leader of the Moderate party ; and Arniston was inclined to favour the other side, though he could not follow them in their settled opposition to the law of patronage. Drummore devoted himself during the Assembly to the company of the clergy, and had always two or three elders who followed him to the tavern, such as Sir James Colquhoun, Colin Campbell Commissioner of Customs, etc. Drummore's speaking was not distinguished for anything but ease and popularity, and he was so deservedly a favourite with the clergy, that, taking up the common sense of the business, or judging from what he heard in conversation the day before, when dining with the clergy of his own side, he usually made a speech in every cause, which generally seemed to sway the Assembly, though there was not much argument. He used to

* Alexander M'Millan of Dunmore, was Deputy-Keeper of the Signet 1726–1742 and 1746–1770.

nod to Arniston with an air of triumph (for they were relations, and very good friends), as much as to say, " Take you that, Robin."

I heard Lord Islay once speak in the Assembly, which was to correct the petulance of Alexander Webster, which he did with dignity and force, but was in the wrong to commit himself with a light horseman who had nothing to lose. I heard Lord Marchmont likewise speak on the motion for an augmentation, which he did with much elegance and a flowery elocution, but entirely without sense or propriety, insomuch that he by his speech forfeited the good opinion of the clergy, who had been prepossessed in his favour by Pope's panegyrical line " Polwarth is a slave." Pope, according to his manner, intended this as a panegyric on his patriotism and independence ; but this was the voice of party, for Marchmont was in reality as much a slave of the Court as any man of his time.

Mr. Gilbert Elliot showed himself in the Assembly equal to the station to which he afterwards attained as a statesman, when Sir Gilbert, by his superior manner of speaking. But Andrew Pringle, Solicitor-General, and afterwards Lord Aylmer [Alemoor], excelled all the laymen of that period for genuine argument and eloquence ; * and when on the bench, he delivered his opinion with more dignity, clearness,

* " He was one of the few eloquent judges who appeared not to contend for victory but for justice."—Ramsay's *Scotland and Scotsmen*.

and precision than any judge I ever heard either in
Scotland or England. It was a great loss to this
country that he did not live to fill the President's
chair, and indeed had not health to go through the
labour of it, otherwise it was believed that he would
have set an example of elegance and dignity in our
law proceedings that could not easily have been forgotten. In those respects the bench has been very
unlucky, for however great lawyers or impartial
judges the succeeding Presidents may have been, in
the qualities I have mentioned they have all been
inferior even to the first President Arniston, who
could not be called an elegant speaker, with all his
other great qualities. In those days there were very
few good speakers among the clergy, as no young
men almost ever ventured to speak but when at the
bar till after 1752. The custom invariably was for
the Moderator to call for the opinion of two or three
of the old men at the green table who were nearest
him, and after them one or two of the judges, or the
King's Advocate and Solicitor, who were generally all
of a side, and were very seldom opposed or answered
but by James Lindsay and one or two of his followers.
With respect to Lindsay, I have to add that he was a
fine brisk gentlemanlike man, who had a good manner of speaking, but, being very unlearned, could only
pursue a single track. He set out on the popular
side in opposition to patronage, but many of his
private friends being on the other side, and Church
preferment running chiefly in that direction, he came

for two or three years over to them ; but on Drysdale's getting the deanery during the Marquis of Rockingham's administration, he took pet and returned to his old party. The ground of his patriotism was thus unveiled, and he was no longer of any consequence, though he thought he could sway the burgh of Lochmaben, where he was minister at that time. He was a very pleasant companion, but jealous and difficult, and too severe a rallier.

The clergyman of this period who far outshone the rest in eloquence was Principal Tullidelph of St. Andrews. He had fallen into bad health or low spirits before my time, and seldom appeared in the Assembly ; but when he did, he far excelled every other speaker. I am not certain if even Lord Chatham in his glory had more dignity of manner or more command of his audience than he had. I am certain he had not so much argument, nor such a convincing force of reasoning. Tullidelph was tall and thin like Pitt, with a manly and interesting aspect ; and rising slowly, and beginning in a very low tone, he soon swelled into an irresistible torrent of eloquence and, in my opinion, was the most powerful speaker ever I heard. And yet this great man was overcome and humbled by the buffoonery of a man much his inferior in everything but learning. This was John Chalmers, minister of Elie.* Tullidelph soon gained the leading of his university, the Presbytery of St. Andrews, and

* The grand-uncle of Dr. Thomas Chalmers. See Hanna's *Memoirs*, i. 2.

the Synod of Fife ; but being of a haughty and over-bearing disposition (like Chatham), he soon disgusted his colleagues both in the University and Presbytery, of which the younger brethren made a cabal against him, in which Chalmers was the principal agent. Though he was far behind Tullidelph in eloquence, he was superior to him in some things, especially in ancient learning. But his chief mode of attack was by a species of buffoonery, which totally unhinged the Principal, who was very proud, and indignant of opposition. Chalmers watched his arguments, and by turning them all into ridicule, and showing that they proved the very reverse of what he intended, he put Tullidelph in such a rage as totally disabled him,* and made him in a short time absent himself both from Presbytery and Synod. He at last became hypochondriac, sat up all night writing a dull commentary on the Gospels, and lay in bed all day.

After this period, however, when the young clergy distinguished themselves—and particularly after the Assembly 1753, when, Alexander Webster being Moderator, he on the very first question dropped the old mode of calling upon the senior members—the young clergy began to feel their own importance in debate, and have ever since continued to distinguish themselves, and have swayed the decision of the Assembly

* " The impetuosity of his temper, which could ill brook contradiction or reproof, betrayed him sometimes into fits of passion, which were neither seemly nor wise in one who sought to be at the head of a great party."—Ramsay's *Scotland and Scotsmen.*

so that the supreme ecclesiastical court has long been a school of eloquence for the clergy, as well as a theatre for the lawyers to display their talents.

It was in the Assembly 1752 that the authority of the Church was restored by the deposition of Gillespie. Robertson and John Home, having been dissenters, with some others, from a sentence of the Commission in March that year in the affair of the settlement of Inverkeithing, similar to that of Torphichen in 1751, had entered a complaint against the Commission, which gave them an opportunity of appearing and pleading at the bar of the Assembly, which they did with spirit and eloquence. The minds of the leaders of the Assembly having been now totally changed, a vigorous measure was adopted by a great majority. The Presbytery of Dunfermline were brought before the Assembly, and peremptorily ordered to admit the candidate three days after, and report to the Assembly on the following Friday. They disobeyed, and Mr. Gillespie was deposed.* I was for the first time a member, with my friend and co-presbyter George Logan. It was thought proper that, on the first day's debate, the speaking should be left to the senior clergy and the lay members. But when, at a general meeting of the party after Gillespie was deposed, it was moved that it would be proper to propose next day that the Assembly should proceed

* Rev. Thomas Gillespie, minister of Carnock. He formed the body known as the Relief Presbytery, which was founded at Colinsburgh, Fife, in 1761.

to depose one or two more of the offending brethren, Mr. Alexander Gordon of Kintore, and George Logan and I, were pointed out as proper persons to make and second the motion. I accordingly began, and was seconded by Gordon in very vigorous speeches, which occasioned a great alarm on the other side, as if we were determined to get rid of the whole Presbytery; but this was only *in terrorem*, for by concert one of our senior brethren, with much commendation of the two young men, calmly proposed that the Assembly for this time should rest contented with what they had done, and wait the effects of the example that had been set. After some debate this was carried. Logan not having done his part, I asked him why he had been silent ; he answered that Gordon and I had spoken in such a superior manner that he thought he would appear inferior, and had not the courage to rise. As it was the first time I had ever opened my mouth in the Assembly—for I was not a member till that year —I was encouraged to go on by that reply from my friend. At the same time, I must observe that many a time, as in this case, the better man is dazzled and silenced for life, perhaps, by the more forward temper and brilliant appearances of his companions. My admiration of Robertson and Home, with whom I was daily versant at that time, and who communicated their writings to me, made me imagine that I was incapable of writing anything but sermons, insomuch that till the year 1751 I wrote nothing else except some juvenile poems. Dr. Patrick

Cuming * was at this time at the head of the Moderate interest ; and had his temper been equal to his talents, might have kept it long ; for he had both learning and sagacity, and very agreeable conversation, with a constitution able to bear the conviviality of the times.†

* Dr. Patrick Cumming, minister of St. Giles, and Professor of Church History in the University of Edinburgh, appears to have been to the Government of Walpole that guide in ecclesiastical politics and distribution of patronage which Carstairs was under William III.—Burton's *Life of Lovat.*

† For further information on the ecclesiastical affairs of the time discussed in this chapter, the reader is referred to *Annals of the General Assembly of the Church of Scotland from* 1739 *to* 1766, known as "Morren's Annals," and to *The Church History of Scotland,* by the Rev. John Cunningham, minister of Crieff, 1859. —J. H. B.

CHAPTER VII

1753-1756

It was this year [1753] that the 1st Regiment of
dragoons lay at Musselburgh, with some of the officers of which I was very intimate, particularly with
Charles Lyon, the surgeon, who was a very sensible,
handsome, and agreeable young man. He afterwards became an officer, and rose to the rank of a
lieutenant-general. He was at York when Captain
Burton and Wind fought a duel, in which the first
was run through the lungs, and recovered. Lyon
wrote to me twice a week, as I had a great regard for
Burton, and had foretold the duel. He was afterwards well known by the name of General Philipson.
The celebrated Major Johnstone, so much admired
for his beauty and for his many duels, was of this regiment, and one of the best-natured men in the intercourse of friends that ever I met with. George II.
had put a cross at his name on his behaving very
insolently at one of the theatres to a country gentleman, and afterwards wounding him in a duel. In
George III.'s time John Home got the star taken off,

and he was promoted. He was of the family of Hilton, which is descended from that of Westerhall ; and Hew Bannatine had been his travelling tutor when abroad.

The parish of Inveresk this year lost a very agreeable member ; for the estate of Carberry being sold to a Mr. Fullerton, who came to live at it, Lord Elchies left the place and went to Inch, where he died soon after. His place was in some respects filled by his son, Mr. John Grant, afterwards Baron Grant,* who bought Castle Steads. Mr. Grant was a good worthy man of considerable parts, but of a weak, whimsical mind. He was at this time chief commissioner for the Duke of Buccleuch, and much improved the family gallery in the church, where he attended regularly. He married Miss Fletcher, the eldest daughter of Lord Milton, who received the marriage company at Carberry. I was frequently asked to dine while she stayed there, and by that means became well acquainted with the Fletchers, whom I had not visited before, for their house was not in my parish, and I was not forward in pushing myself into acquaintance elsewhere without some proper introduction. From this period I became intimate with that family, of which Lord Milton himself and his youngest daughter Betty, afterwards Mrs. Wedderburn of Gosford, were my much valued friends. Lord Milton was nephew of the famous patriot, Andrew Fletcher of Saltoun, and the successor to his

* Eldest son of Patrick Grant, Lord Elchies. See p. 220.

estate.   He had been Lord Justice-Clerk and political
manager of this country under Lord Islay ; and now
that his lordship had been Duke of Argyle since 1744,
when his brother John died, their influence was completely established.   The Duke had early made choice
of Fletcher for his coadjutor, and had proved his
sagacity by making so good a choice ; * for Lord
Milton was a man of great ability in business, a man
of good sense, and of excellent talents for managing
men ; and though his conversation was on a limited
scale, because his knowledge was very much so, yet
being possessed of indefeasible power at that time in
Scotland, and keeping an excellent table, his defects
were overlooked, and he was held to be as agreeable
as he was able.†

His talents had been illustrated by the incapacity
of the Tweeddale Ministry, who were in power during
the Rebellion, and who had been obliged to resort to
Milton for intelligence and advice.   When the Rebellion was suppressed, and the Duke of Argyle brought
again into power, he and Fletcher very wisely gained
the hearts of the Jacobites, who were still very
numerous, by adopting the most lenient measures,
and taking the distressed families under their protection, while the Squadrone party continued as violent

* " I have heard Sir Hugh Paterson say, who knew Saltoun
well, that he early predicted his nephew would turn out a *corrupt
fellow*, and a perfect courtier.   Saltoun, however, hated all kings
and Ministers of State."—Ramsay's *Scotland and Scotsmen*.

† Lord Milton built Milton House in the Canongate, Edinburgh,
which he occupied till his death in 1766.   He had the walls finely
decorated with landscapes by an Italian artist.

against them as ever. This made them almost universally successful in the parliamentary election which
followed the Rebellion, and established their power
till the death of the Duke, which happened in 1761.

His [Lord Milton's] youngest daughter, afterwards
Mrs. Wedderburn, was one of the first females in
point of understanding as well as heart that ever fell
in my way to be intimately acquainted with. As
there was much weakness and intrigue in the mother
and some other branches of the family, she had a
difficult part to act, but she performed it with much
address ; for while she preserved her father's predilection and confidence, she remained well with the
rest of the family. The eldest brother, Andrew, lived
for most part with the Duke of Argyle, at London, as
his private secretary, and was M.P. for East Lothian ;
and though not a man who produced himself in public
life, was sufficiently knowing and accomplished to be
a very amiable member of society. After the death
of the Duke of Argyle in 1761, and of his father in
1767, he lived for most part at his seat at Saltoun, in
East Lothian. He was succeeded as member of
Parliament for that county by Sir George Suttie, who
had been a lieutenant-colonel in the army, and who,
with many others, left the service in disgust with the
Duke of Cumberland, who, though he had always
been beat in Flanders, had disobliged sundry officers
of good promise. This Sir George, however, was
much overrated. He was held to be a great officer,
because he had a way of thinking of his own, and had

18

learned from his kinsman, Marshal Stair, to draw the plan of a campaign. He was held to be a great patriot, because he wore a coarse coat and unpowdered hair, while he was looking for a post with the utmost anxiety. He was reckoned a man of much sense because he said so himself, and had such an embarrassed stuttering elocution that one was not sure but it was true. He was understood to be a great improver of land, because he was always talking of farming, and had invented a cheap method of fencing his fields by combining a low stone wall and a hedge together, which, on experiment, did not answer. For all those qualities he got credit for some time ; but nobody ever mentioned the real strength of his character, which was that of an uncommonly kind and indulgent brother to a large family of brothers and sisters, whom he allowed, during his absence in a five years' war, to dilapidate his estate, and leave him less than half his income. Lord Stair had been caught by the boldness of his cousin in attempting to make the plan of a campaign, which had given the young man a false measure of his own ability.

For two summers, about this time, I went for some weeks to Dunse Well, which was in high vogue at this period, when I was often at Polwarth Manse, the dwelling of Mr. and Mrs. Home, the last of whom was aunt of Mary Roddam, the young lady whom I afterwards married, and who had lived there since the death of her father and mother in the years 1744 and 1745. John Home passed half his time in this house,

Mr. William Home, a brother of the Laird of Bassen-
dean, being his cousin, and Mrs. Home (Mary Roddam) a superior woman. By frequenting this house
I was introduced to the Earl of Marchmont, whose
seat was hard by. His second lady, who was young
and handsome, but a simple and quiet woman, and
three daughters he had by his former lady, were all
under due subjection, for his lordship kept a high
command at home. The daughters were all clever,
particularly Lady Margaret, and stood less in awe
than the Countess, who, had it not been for her only
child, Lord Polwarth, then an infant, would have led
but an uncomfortable life.* The family of Marchmont—which rose to the peerage at the Revolution,
and to the ascendant in the country, through the
weakness and Jacobitism of the more ancient Earls
of Home, from whom they were descended—to preserve their superiority, paid great court to the county,

* " Lord Marchmont has had the most extraordinary adventure
in the world. About three weeks ago he was at the play when
he espied in one of the boxes a fair virgin, whose looks, airs and
manners, had such a powerful and undisguised effect on him as
was visible by every bystander. . . . He soon was told that her
name was Crompton, a linen draper's daughter, that had been
bankrupt last year and had not been able to pay above five
shillings in the pound. The fair nymph herself was about
sixteen or seventeen, and, being supported by some relations,
appeared in every public place, and had fatigued every eye but
that of his Lordship, which being entirely employed in severer
studies, had never till that fatal moment opened upon her
charms. . . . He wrote next morning to her father desiring
to visit his daughter on honourable terms ; and in a few days
she will be the Countess of Marchmont."—David Hume to
Oswald of Dunnikier in Oswald's *Correspondence.*

and particularly to the clergy, because they were the only stanch friends to Government. Marchmont was lively and eloquent in conversation, with a tincture of classical learning, and some knowledge of the constitution, especially of the forms of the House of Peers ; but his wit appeared to me to be petulant, and his understanding shallow. His twin-brother, Hume Campbell,* then Lord-Register for Scotland, and one of the most eloquent lawyers in the House of Commons, seemed to me to be a man of sounder judgment than his brother ; his want of manhood, however, had been disclosed by his receiving an insult from William Pitt, the father, which he had probably been tempted to inflict on his having heard what had happened to him in Edinburgh in his youthful days.

In one of the summers in which I was in that part of the country, the Lord-Register gave a ball and supper in the town-hall of Greenlaw, which I mention because I had there an opportunity of conversing with Lady Murray and her friend Lady Hervey, who was understood to be one of the most accomplished and witty ladies in England. There were in this neighbourhood several very agreeable clergymen : Chatto was very acute and sensible—Ridpath judicious and learned—Dickson an able ecclesiastic, and master of agriculture.

* Alexander Hume Campbell, M.P. for Berwickshire from 1734 till his death, was, in 1756, appointed Lord Clerk Register for life. He died in 1760.

In one of those years it was, when Dunse Well was most frequented, that the Marchmont family for several weeks attended, and came to Dunse, and breakfasted at a small tavern by the bowling-green. We generally sat down twenty-four or twenty-five to breakfast in a very small room. Marchmont and his brother behaved with great courtesy, seldom sitting down, but aiding the servants. Francis Garden * was there, and increased the mirth of the company. Most of the company remained all the forenoon at the bowling-green, where we had very agreeable parties.

It was also in one of those years that Smollett visited Scotland for the first time, after having left Glasgow immediately after his education was finished, and his engaging as a surgeon's mate on board a man-of-war, which gave him an opportunity of witnessing the siege of Carthagena, which he has so minutely described in his *Roderick Random*. He came out to Musselburgh and passed a day and a night with me, and went to church and heard me preach. I introduced him to Cardonnel the Commissioner, with whom he supped, and they were much pleased with each other. Smollett has reversed this in his *Humphrey Clinker*, where he makes the Commissioner his old acquaintance.† He went next to Glasgow and that neighbourhood to visit his friends, and returned

* Lord Gardenstone.
† But on naming the far more distinguished men seen by him in the "hotbead of genius," Bramble says, "These acquaintances I owe to the friendship of Dr. Carlyle, who wants nothing but inclination to figure with the rest on paper."—J. H. B.

again to Edinburgh in October, when I had frequent meetings with him—one in particular, in a tavern, where there supped with him Commissioner Cardonnel, Mr. Hepburn of Keith, John Home, and one or two more. Hepburn was so much pleased with Cardonnel, that he said that if he went into rebellion again, it should be for the grandson of the Duke of Monmouth. Cardonnel and I went with Smollett to Sir David Kinloch's, and passed the day, when John Home and Logan and I conducted him to Dunbar, where we stayed together all night.

Smollett was a man of very agreeable conversation and of much genuine humour ; and, though not a profound scholar, possessed a philosophical mind, and was capable of making the soundest observations on human life, and of discerning the excellence or seeing the ridicule of every character he met with. Fielding only excelled him in giving a dramatic story to his novels, but, in my opinion, was inferior to him in the true comic vein. He was one of the many very pleasant men with whom it was my good fortune to be intimately acquainted. Mr. Cardonnel, whom I have mentioned, was another who excelled, like Smollett, in a great variety of pleasant stories. Sir Hew Dalrymple,* North Berwick, had as much conversation and wit as any man of his time, having been long an M.P. David Hume and Dr. John Jardine

---

* Second baronet of North Berwick and grandson of Sir Hew, Lord President of the Court of Session. He was M.P. for Haddingtonshire and King's Remembrancer for Scotland.

were likewise both admirable, and had the peculiar talent of rallying their companions on their good qualities. Dr. William Wight and Thomas Hepburn were also remarkable—the one for brilliancy, vivacity, and smartness ; the other for the shrewdness of his remarks and irresistible repartees. The Right Honourable Charles Townshend and Patrick Lord Elibank were likewise admirable ; for though the first was inferior in knowledge to the second, yet he had such flowing eloquence, so fine a voice, and such richness of expression, joined to brilliant wit and a fine vein of mimicry, as made him shine in every company. Elibank was more enlightened and more profound, and had a mind that embraced the greatest variety of topics, and produced the most original remarks. He was rather a humorist than a man of humour ; but that bias of his temper led him to defend paradoxes and uncommon opinions with a copiousness and ingenuity that was surprising. He had been a lieutenant-colonel in the army, and was at the siege of Carthagena, of which he left an elegant and Xenophon-like account (which I'm afraid is lost). He was a Jacobite, and a member of the famous Cocoa-tree Club,* and resigned his commission on some disgust. Soon after the Rebellion of 1745 he took up his residence in Scotland, and his seat being between

* The " Cocoa-tree " chocolate house famous in the reign of Queen Anne at the headquarters of the Tory party. It was removed from Pall Mall to St. James's Street, where in Walpole's time it was the rendezvous of the Jacobites and acquired a reputation for the high play carried on under its roof.

Dr. Robertson's church and John Home's, he became intimately acquainted with them, who cured him of his contempt for the Presbyterian clergy, made him change or soften down many of his original opinions, and prepared him for becoming a most agreeable member of the Literary Society of Edinburgh, among whom he lived during the remainder of his life admiring and admired. We used to say of Elibank, that were we to plead for our lives, he was the man with whom we would wish to converse for at least one whole day before we made our defence.

Dr. M'Cormick, who died Principal of St. Andrews, was rather a merry-andrew than a wit ; but he left as many good sayings behind him, which are remembered, as any man of his time. Andrew Gray,* minister of Abernethy, was a man of wit and humour, which had the greater effect that his person was diminutive, and his voice of the smallest treble.

Lindsay was a hussar in raillery, who had no mercy, and whose object was to display himself and to humble the man he played on. Monteath was more than his match, for he lay by, and took his opportunity of giving him such southboards as silenced him for the whole evening.† Happily for conversation, this horse-play raillery has been left off for more than thirty years among the clergy and other liberals. Drummore—of the class of lawyers who

* See page 211.

† Lindsay was minister of the parish of Kirkliston, and Monteath of the parish of Longformacus.—J. H. B.

got the epithet of Monk from Quin, at Bath, on account of his pleasing countenance and bland manners—was a first-rate at the science of defence in raillery : he was too good-natured to attack. He had the knack, not only of pleasing fools with themselves, but of making them tolerable to the company. There were two men, however, whose coming into a convivial company pleased more than anybody I ever knew : the one was Dr. George Kay, a minister of Edinburgh, who, to a charming vivacity when he was in good spirits, added the talent of ballad-singing better than anybody ever I knew ; the other was John Home.

I should not omit Lord Cullen here, though he was much my junior, who in his youth possessed the talent of mimicry beyond all mankind ; for his was not merely an exact imitation of voice and manner of speaking, but a perfect exhibition of every man's manner of thinking on every subject. I shall mention two or three instances, lest his wonderful powers should fall into oblivion.

When the Honourable James Stuart Wortley lived with Dr. Robertson, the Doctor had sometimes, though rarely, to remonstrate and admonish the young gentleman on some parts of his conduct. He came into the room between ten and eleven in the morning, when Mr. Stuart was still in bed, with the windows shut and the curtains drawn close, when he took the opportunity, in his mild and rational manner (for he could not chide), to give him a lecture on the manner of life he was leading. When he was done, "This is rather too much, my dear Doctor," said James; "for you told me all this not above an hour ago." The case was, that Cullen had been beforehand with the Doctor, and seizing the opportunity, read his friend such a lecture as he thought the Doctor might probably do that morning. It was so very like in thought and in words, that Stuart took it for a visitation from the Doctor.

I was witness to another exhibition similar to this. It was one day in the General Assembly 1765, when there happened to be a student of physic who was seized with a convulsion fit, which occasioned much commotion in the house, and drew a score of other English students around him. When the Assembly adjourned, about a dozen of us went to dine in the Poker club-room at Nicholson's, when Dr. Robertson came and told us he must dine with the Commissioner, but would join us soon. Immediately after we dined, somebody wished to hear from Cullen what Robertson would say about the incident that had taken place, which he did immediately, lest the Principal should come in. He had hardly finished when he arrived. After the company had drank his health, Jardine said slyly, " Principal, was it not a strange accident that happened to-day in the Assembly ? " Robertson's answer was exactly in the strain, and almost in the very words, of Cullen. This raised a very loud laugh in the company, when the Doctor, more ruffled than I ever almost saw him, said, with a severe look at Cullen, " I perceive some-body has been ploughing with my heifer before I came in."

On another occasion he was asked to exhibit, when he answered that his subjects were so much hackneyed that he could not go over them with spirit ; but if any of them would mention a new subject, he would try to please them. One of the company mentioned the wild beast in the Gevaudan, when, after laying his head on the table, not for more than two or three minutes, he lifted himself up and said, " Now I have it," and immediately gave us the thoughts of the Judges Auchinleck, Kames, and Monboddo, and Dr. Robertson, with a characteristical exactness of senti-ment, as well as words, tone, and manner, as aston-ished the company. This happened at Dr. Blair's, who then lived in James's Square.*

This was a very pleasing but dangerous talent, for it led to dissipation. When he had left off his usual mode of exhibition when called upon, yet he could not restrain himself from displaying in his common conversation, in which he intermingled specimens of his superlative art as the characters came in his way, which to me was much more agreeable than the pro-fessed exhibition. As he was more knowing and accomplished than almost any judge in his time,

---

* The sanguinary feats attributed to " the great beast of the Gevaudan " excited all Europe in 1764, and there was much astonishment when, being at last killed, it was found to be only a large wolf. Horace Walpole saw its carcass in the Queen's antechamber at Versailles.—J. H. B.

had all other qualities been of a piece, his company would very long have been courted. In giving some account of those very pleasant characters which it was my good fortune to know, I have anticipated several years ; for Mr. Robert Cullen, for instance, did not begin to be known till after 1760. But I shall now return to my narrative.

It was in the General Assembly 1753, as I have before mentioned, that Dr. Webster being Moderator, he put an end to the ancient mode of calling up Principals, and Professors, and Judges, etc., to give their opinion on cases which came before the Assembly, by declaring that he would call upon no person, but would expect that every member should freely deliver his opinion when he had any to offer. This brought on the junior members, and much animated and improved the debates. The old gentlemen at first were sulky and held their tongues, but in two or three days they found them again, lest they should lose their ascendant. I never afterwards saw the practice revived of calling upon members to speak, except once or twice when Principal Tullidelph attended, whom everybody wished to hear, but who would not rise without having that piece of respect paid to him.

At this Assembly it was that an attempt was made to have Gillespie, the deposed minister, restored ; but as he had not taken the proper steps to conciliate the Church, but, on the contrary, had continued to preach, and had set up a separate congregation, the application by his friends was refused by a great majority, and was never repeated.

At this time David Hume was living in Edinburgh and composing his *History of Great Britain*. He was a man of great knowledge, and of a social and benevolent temper, and truly the best-natured man in the world. He was branded with the title of Atheist, on account of the many attacks on revealed religion * that are to be found in his philosophical works, and in many places of his History—the last of which are still more objectionable than the first, which a friendly critic might call only sceptical. Apropos of this, when Mr. Robert Adam, the celebrated architect, and his brother, lived in Edinburgh with their mother, an aunt of Dr. Robertson's, and a very respectable woman, she said to her son, " I shall be glad to see any of your companions to dinner, but I hope you will never bring the Atheist here to disturb my peace." But Robert soon fell on a method to reconcile her to him, for he introduced him under another name, or concealed it carefully from her. When the company parted she said to her son, " I must confess that you bring very agreeable companions about you, but the large jolly man who sat

---

* " Dr. Jardine and Hume were attached friends, and though they might argue about the necessity of revealed religion, it was always in good humour. One night Hume, having declined to be lighted down the turnpike stair from his friend's lodging, fell in the darkness. Jardine rushed for a candle, and as he lifted the bulky body of his guest slyly said, ' Davie, I have often tell't ye that '' natural licht '' is no' sufficient.' "—Graham's *Men of Letters of the Eighteenth Century*.

next me is the most agreeable of them all." "This was the very Atheist," said he, "mother, that you was so much afraid of." "Well," says she, "you may bring him here as much as you please, for he's the most innocent, agreeable, facetious man I ever met with." This was truly the case with him ; for though he had much learning and a fine taste, and was professedly a sceptic, though by no means an atheist, he had the greatest simplicity of mind and manners with the utmost facility and benevolence of temper of any man I ever knew. His conversation was truly irresistible, for while it was enlightened, it was naïve almost to puerility.

I was one of those who never believed that David Hume's sceptical principles had laid fast hold on his mind, but thought that his books proceeded rather from affectation of superiority and pride of understanding and love of vainglory. I was confirmed in this opinion, after his death, by what the Honourable Patrick Boyle,* one of his most intimate friends, told me many years ago at my house in Musselburgh, where he used to come and dine the first Sunday of every General Assembly, after his brother, Lord Glasgow, ceased to be Lord High Commissioner. When we were talking of David, Mrs. Carlyle asked Mr. Boyle if he thought David Hume was as great an unbeliever as the world took him to be ? He answered, that the world judged from his books, as they

* The Hon. Patrick Boyle, second son of John, second Earl of Glasgow, was minister of Irvine, Ayrshire.

had a right to do ; but he thought otherwise, who had known him all his life, and mentioned the following incident : When David and he were both in London, at the period when David's mother died, Mr. Boyle, hearing of it, soon after went into his apartment—for they lodged in the same house—when he found him in the deepest affliction and in a flood of tears. After the usual topics of condolence, Mr. Boyle said to him, " My friend, you owe this uncommon grief to your having thrown off the principles of religion ; for if you had not, you would have been consoled by the firm belief that the good lady, who was not only the best of mothers, but the most pious of Christians, was now completely happy in the realms of the just." To which David replied, " Though I threw out my speculations to entertain and employ the learned and metaphysical world, yet in other things I do not think so differently from the rest of mankind as you may imagine." To this my wife was a witness. This conversation took place the year after David died, when Dr. Hill, who was to preach, had gone to a room to look over his notes.

At this period, when he first lived in Edinburgh, and was writing his *History of England*, his circumstances were narrow, and he accepted the office of Librarian to the Faculty of Advocates, worth £40 per annum. But it was not for the salary that he accepted this employment, but that he might have easy access to the books in that celebrated library ; for, to my certain knowledge, he gave every farthing

of the salary to families in distress. Of a piece with
this temper was his curiosity and credulity, which
were without bounds, a specimen of which shall be
afterwards given when I come down to Militia and
the Poker. His economy was strict, as he loved
independency ; and yet he was able at that time to
give suppers to his friends in his small lodging in the
Canongate. He took much to the company of the
younger clergy, not from a wish to bring them over
to his opinions, for he never attempted to overturn
any man's principles, but they best understood his
notions, and could furnish him with literary conversation. Robertson and John Home and Bannatine
and I lived all in the country, and came only periodically to the town. Blair and Jardine both lived in
it, and suppers being the only fashionable meal at
that time, we dined where we best could, and by
cadies assembled our friends to meet us in a tavern by
nine o'clock ; and a fine time it was when we could
collect David Hume, Adam Smith, Adam Ferguson,
Lord Elibank, and Drs. Blair and Jardine, on an
hour's warning. I remember one night that David
Hume, who, having dined abroad, came rather late to
us, and directly pulled a large key from his pocket,
which he laid on the table. This he said was given
him by his maid Peggy (much more like a man than
a woman) that she might not sit up for him, for she
said when the honest fellows came in from the
country, he never returned home till after one
o'clock. This intimacy of the young clergy with

David Hume enraged the zealots on the opposite
side, who little knew how impossible it was for him,
had he been willing, to shake their principles.

As Mr. Hume's circumstances improved he enlarged his mode of living, and instead of the roasted
hen and minced collops, and a bottle of punch, he
gave both elegant dinners and suppers, and the best
claret, and, which was best of all, he furnished the
entertainment with the most instructive and pleasing
conversation, for he assembled whosoever were most
knowing and agreeable among either the laity or
clergy. This he always did, but still more unsparingly when he became what he called rich. For
innocent mirth and agreeable raillery I never knew
his match. Jardine, who sometimes bore hard upon
him—for he had much drollery and wit, though but
little learning — never could overturn his temper.
Lord Elibank resembled David in his talent for collecting agreeable companions together, and had a
house in town for several winters chiefly for that
purpose.

David, who delighted in what the French call
plaisanterie, with the aid of Miss Nancy Ord, one of
the Chief Baron's daughters, contrived and executed
one that gave him very great delight. As the New
Town was making its progress westward, he built a
house in the south-west corner of St. Andrew Square.
The street leading south to Princes Street had not
yet got its name affixed, but they got a workman
early one morning to paint on the corner stone of

David's house " St. David's Street," where it remains to this day.*

He was at first quite delighted with Ossian's poems, and gloried in them ; but on going to London he went over to the other side, and loudly affirmed them to be inventions of Macpherson. I happened to say one day, when he was declaiming against Macpherson, that I had met with nobody of his opinion but William Caddel of Cockenzie, and President Dundas, which he took ill, and was some time of forgetting. This is one instance of what Smellie says of him, that though of the best temper in the world, yet he could be touched by opposition or rudeness. This was the only time I had ever observed David's temper change. I can call to mind an instance or two of his good-natured pleasantry. Being at Gilmerton, where David Hume was on a visit, Sir David Kinloch made him go to Athlestaneford Church, where I preached for John Home. When we met before dinner, " What did you mean," says he to me, " by treating John's congregation to-day with one of Cicero's academics ? I did not think that such heathen morality would have passed in East Lothian."

---

* Sir Daniel Wilson in his *Reminiscences of Old Edinburgh* gives another version of this story—or it may be the sequel to it. David Hume's housekeeper one morning noticed " St. David Street " painted on the corner of the building in which he lived. Taking this as an insult to her master, she rushed into his room exclaiming, " What d'ye think the ne'er-do-weels hae gane and painted on oor house front ? " When she had explained matters, the philosopher quietly replied, " Tut, Jenny ! is that all ? Many a better man than me has been called a saint."

On Monday, when we were assembling to breakfast, David retired to the end of the dining-room, when Sir David entered : " What are you doing there, Davy ? come to your breakfast." " Take away the enemy first," says David. The baronet, thinking it was the warm fire that kept David in the lower end of the room, rung the bell for a servant to carry some of it off. It was not the fire that scared David, but a large Bible that was left on a stand at the upper end of the room, a chapter of which had been read at the family prayers the night before, that good custom not being then out of use when clergymen were in the house. Add to this John Home saying to him at the Poker Club, when everybody wondered what could have made a clerk of Sir William Forbes run away with £900—" I know that very well," says John Home to David ; " for when he was taken, there was found in his pocket your *Philosophical Works* and Boston's *Fourfold State of Man.*"

David Hume, during all his life, had written the most pleasing and agreeable letters to his friends. I have preserved two of these. But I lately saw two of more early date in the hands of Mr. Sandiland Dysart, W.S., to his mother, who was a friend of David's and a very accomplished woman, one of them dated in 1751, on occasion of his brother Hume of Ninewell's marriage ; and the other in 1754, with a present of the first volume of his History, both of which are written in a vein of pleasantry and playfulness which nothing can exceed, and which makes me think that a collection of his letters would be a valuable present to the world, and present throughout a very pleasing picture of his mind.*

I have heard him say that Baron Montesquicu, when he asked him if he did not think that there would soon be a revolution in France favourable to liberty, answered, " No, for their noblesse had all become poltroons." He said that the club in Paris (Baron Holbach's) to which he belonged, were of opinion that Christianity would be abolished in Europe by the end of the eighteenth century ; and that they laughed at Andrew Stuart for making a battle in favour of a future state, and called him " L'ame Immortelle."

David Hume, like Smith, had no discernment at all of characters. The only two clergymen whose interests he espoused, and for one of whom he provided, were the two silliest fellows in the Church. With every opportunity, he was ridiculously shy of asking favours, on account of preserving his independence, which always appeared to me to be a very foolish kind of pride. His friend John Home, with not more benevolence, but with no scruples from a wish of independence, for which he was not born, availed himself of his influence and provided for hundreds, and yet he never asked anything for himself.

Adam Smith, though perhaps only second to David in learning and ingenuity, was far inferior to him in

* They will be found in *The Life and Correspondence of David Hume*, by John Hill Burton.

conversational talents. In that of public speaking
they were equal—David never tried it, and I never
heard Adam but once, which was at the first meeting
of the Select Society, when he opened up the design
of the meeting. His voice was harsh and enunciation
thick, approaching to stammering. His conversation was not colloquial, but like lecturing, in which
I have been told he was not deficient, especially when
he grew warm. He was the most absent man in
company that I ever saw, moving his lips, and
talking to himself, and smiling, in the midst of large
companies. If you awaked him from his reverie
and made him attend to the subject of conversation,
he immediately began a harangue, and never stopped
till he told you all he knew about it, with the utmost
philosophical ingenuity. He knew nothing of characters, and yet was ready to draw them on the slightest invitation. But when you checked him or doubted,
he retracted with the utmost ease, and contradicted
all he had been saying. His journey abroad with
the Duke of Buccleuch cured him in part of those
foibles ; but still he appeared very unfit for the intercourse of the world as a travelling tutor. But
the Duke was a character, both in point of heart and
understanding, to surmount all disadvantages—he
could learn nothing ill from a philosopher of the utmost probity and benevolence. If he [Smith] had
been more a man of address and of the world, he
might perhaps have given a ply to the Duke's fine
mind, which was much better when left to its own

energy. Charles Townshend had chosen Smith, not
for his fitness for the purpose, but for his own glory
in having sent an eminent Scottish philosopher to
travel with the Duke.

Smith had from the Duke a bond for a life annuity
of £300, till an office of equal value was obtained for
him in Britain. When the Duke got him appointed
a Commissioner of the Customs in Scotland, he went
out to Dalkeith with the bond in his pocket, and,
offering it to the Duke, told him that he thought himself bound in honour to surrender the bond, as his
Grace had now got him a place of £500. The Duke
answered that Mr. Smith seemed more careful of his
own honour than of his, which he found wounded by
the proposal. Thus acted that good Duke, who,
being entirely void of vanity, did not value himself
on splendid generosities. He had acted in much the
same manner to Dr. Hallam,* who had been his tutor
at Eton ; for when Mr. Townshend proposed giving
Hallam an annuity of £100 when the Duke was taken

* Dr. Hallam became Dean of Bristol and Canon of Windsor.
Ramsay of Ochtertyre tells the following story of him when as a
country lad he was a candidate for a scholarship on the Foundation
at Eton. He had gained the friendship of Sir David Dalrymple
(Lord Hailes), then an upper boy, and confided to him, after passing
his Latin and Greek classics, he knew nothing of Latin verse, which
would entitle him to a high place if successful. Young Dalrymple
" bade him throw the theme or exercise assigned over the window
in a quill and he should convey him the verses ere they were
wanted." Later the doorkeeper was instructed to carry a
pencase to the young examinee, who exhibited the theme and was
elected. Dr. Hallam confessed many years afterwards that,
next to the providence of God he owed all that he had to the
philanthropy of Sir David Dalrymple.

from him, " No," says he, " it is my desire that Hallam may have as much as Smith, it being a great mortification to him that he is not to travel with me."

Though Smith had some little jealousy in his temper, he had the most unbounded benevolence. His smile of approbation was truly captivating. His affectionate temper was proved by his dutiful attendance on his mother. One instance I remember which marked his character. John Home and he, travelling down from London together [in 1776], met David Hume going to Bath for the recovery of his health. He anxiously wished them both to return with him : John agreed, but Smith excused himself on account of the state of his mother's health, whom he needs must see. Smith's fine writing is chiefly displayed in his book on Moral Sentiment, which is the pleasantest and most eloquent book on the subject. His *Wealth of Nations*, from which he was judged to be an inventive genius of the first order, is tedious and full of repetition. His separate essays in the second volume have the air of being occasional pamphlets, without much force or determination. On political subjects his opinions were not very sound.

Dr. Adam Ferguson was a very different kind of man. He was the son of a Highland clergyman, who was much respected, and had good connections. He had the pride and high spirit of his countrymen. He was bred at St. Andrews University, and had gone early into the world ; for being a favourite of a

Duchess Dowager of Athole, and bred to the Church,
she had him appointed chaplain to the 42nd regiment, then commanded by Lord John Murray, her
son, when he was not more than twenty-two. The
Duchess had imposed a very difficult task upon him,
which was to be a kind of tutor or guardian to Lord
John ; that is to say, to gain his confidence and keep
him in peace with his officers, which it was difficult
to do. This, however, he actually accomplished,
by adding all the decorum belonging to the clerical
character to the manners of a gentleman ; the effect
of which was, that he was highly respected by all the
officers, and adored by his countrymen, the common
soldiers. He remained chaplain to this regiment,
and went about with them, till 1755, when they
went to America, on which occasion he resigned,
as it did not suit his views to attend them there.
He was a year or two with them in Ireland, and likewise attended them on the expedition to Brittany
under General Sinclair, where his friends David
Hume and Colonel Edmonstone also were. This
turned his mind to the study of war, which appears in
his *Roman History*, where many of the battles are
better described than by any historian but Polybius,
who was an eyewitness to so many.

He had the manners of a man of the world, and the
demeanour of a high-bred gentleman, insomuch that
his company was much sought after ; for though he
conversed with ease, it was with a dignified reserve.
If he had any fault in conversation, it was of a piece

with what I have said of his temper, for the elevation of his mind prompted him to such sudden transitions and dark allusions that it was not always easy to follow him, though he was a very good speaker. He had another talent, unknown to any but his intimates, which was a boundless vein of humour, which he indulged when there were none others present, and which flowed from his pen in every familiar letter he wrote. He had the faults, however, that belonged to that character, for he was apt to be jealous of his rivals, and indignant against assumed superiority. His wife used to say that it was very fortunate that I was so much in Edinburgh, as I was a great peacemaker among them. She did not perceive that her own husband was the most difficult of them all. But as they were all honourable men in the highest degree, John Home and I together kept them on very good terms : I mean by them, Smith and Ferguson and David Hume ; for Robertson was very good-natured, and soon disarmed the failing of Ferguson, of whom he was afraid. With respect to taste, we held David Hume and Adam Smith inferior to the rest, for they were both prejudiced in favour of the French tragedies, and did not sufficiently appreciate Shakespeare and Milton. Their taste was a rational act, rather than the instantaneous effect of fine feeling. David Hume said Ferguson had more genius than any of them, as he had made himself so much master of a difficult science—viz., Natural Philosophy, which he had never studied but when at college — in three months, so as to be able to teach it.

The time came when those who were overawed by Ferguson repaid him for his haughtiness ; for when his *Roman History* was published, at a period when he had lost his health, and had not been able to correct it diligently, by a certain propensity they had, unknown to themselves, acquired, to disparage everything that came from Ferguson, they did his book more hurt than they could have done by open criticism. It was provoking to hear those who were so ready to give loud praises to very shallow and imperfect English productions—to curry favour, as we supposed, with the booksellers and authors concerned—taking every opportunity to undermine the reputation of Ferguson's book. " It was not a Roman history," said they (which it did not say it was). " This delineation of the constitution of the republic is well sketched ; but for the rest, it is anything but history, and then it is so incorrect that it is a perfect shame." All his other books met with the same treatment, while, at the same time, there were a few of us who could not refrain from saying that Ferguson's was the best history of Rome ; that what he had omitted was fabulous or insignificant, and what he had wrote was more profound in research into characters, and gave a more just delineation of them than any book now extant. The same thing we said of his book on Moral Philosophy, which we held to be the book that did the most honour of any to the Scotch philosophers, because it gave the most perfect picture of moral virtues, with all their irresistible attractions. His book on Civil Society ought only to be considered as a college exercise, and yet there is in it a turn of thought and a species of eloquence peculiar to Ferguson. Smith had been weak enough to accuse him of having borrowed some of his inventions without owning them. This Ferguson denied, but owned he derived many notions from a French author, and that Smith had been there before him. David Hume did not live to see Ferguson's History, otherwise his candid praise would have prevented all the subtle remarks of the jealous or resentful.

With respect to Robertson and Blair, their lives and characters have been fully laid before the public—by Professor Dugald Stewart in a long life of Robertson, where, though the picture is rather in disjointed members, yet there is hardly anything omitted that tends to make a judicious reader master of the character. Dr. Blair's character is more obvious in a short but very elegant and true account of him, drawn up by Dr. Finlayson. John Hill is writing a more diffuse account of the latter, which may not be so like. To the character of Robertson I have only to add here, that though he was truly a very great master of conversation, and in general perfectly agreeable, yet he appeared sometimes so very fond of talking, even when showing-off was out of the question, and so much addicted to the translation of other people's thoughts, that he sometimes appeared tedious to his best friends.* Being on one occasion invited to dine with Patrick Robertson, his brother, I missed my friend, whom I had met there on all former occasions; " I have not invited him to-day," says Peter, " for I have a very good company, and he'll let nobody speak but himself." Once he was staying with me for a week, and I carried him to dine with our parish club, who were fully assembled to see and hear Dr. Robertson, but Dr. Finlay of Drummore took it in his head to come that day, where he had not been for a year before, who took the lead, being then rich and self-sufficient, though a great babbler, and entirely disappointed the company, and gave us all the headache. He [Robertson] was very much a master of conversation, and very desirous to lead it, and to make dissertations and raise theories that sometimes provoked the laugh against him. One instance of this was when he had gone a jaunt into England with some of Henry Dundas's (Lord Melville's) family. He [Dundas] and Mr. Baron Cockburn and Robert Sinclair were on horseback, and seeing a gallows on a neighbouring hillock, they rode round to have a nearer view of the felon on the gallows. When they met in the inn, Robertson immediately began a dissertation on the character of nations, and how much the English, like the Romans, were hardened by their cruel diversions of cock-fighting, bull-baiting, bruising, etc.; for had

* See above, p. 179.

they not observed three Englishmen on horseback do what no Scotchman or—— Here Dundas, having compassion, interrupted him, and said, " What ! did you not know, Principal, that it was Cockburn and Sinclair and me ? " * This put an end to theories, etc., for that day.   Robertson's translations and paraphrases on other people's thoughts were so beautiful and so harmless that I never saw anybody lay claim to their own ; but it was not so when he forgot himself so far as to think he had been present where he had not been, and done what he had not the least hand in—one very singular instance of which I remember.   Hugh Bannatine and some clergymen of Haddington Presbytery came to town in great haste, on their being threatened with having their goods distrained for payment of the window-tax.   One of them called on me as he passed ; but as I was abroad, he left a note (or told Mrs. C.), to come to them directly.   I rode instantly to town and met them, and it was agreed on to send immediately to the solicitor, James Montgomery.   A cady was despatched, but he could not be found, till I at last heard his voice as I passed the door of a neighbouring room. He came to us on being sent for, and he immediately granted the alarmed brethren a sist.   Not a week after, three or four of the same clergymen, dining at the Doctor's house where I was, the business was talked of, when he said, " Was not I very

* Baron Cockburn was the father of Lord Cockburn, author of *Memorials of his Time.*

fortunate in ferreting out the solicitor at Walker's, when no cady could find him ? " " No, no," says I, " Principal ; I had that good-luck, and you were not so much as at the meeting." We had sent to him, and he could not come. " Well, well," replied he, " I have heard so much about it that I thought I had been there." He was the best-tempered man in the world, and the young gentlemen who had lived for many years in his house declared they never saw him once ruffled. His table, which had always been hospitable, even when his income was small, became full and elegant when his situation was improved. As he loved a long repast, as he called it, he was as ready to give it at home as to receive it abroad. The softness of his temper, and his habits at the head of a party, led him to seem to promise what he was not able to perform, which weakness raised up to him some very inveterate enemies, while at the same time his true friends saw that those weaknesses were rather amiable than provoking. He was not so much beloved by women as by men, which we laughingly used to say was owing to their rivalship as talkers, but was much more owing to his having been very little in company with ladies in his youth. He was early married, though his wife (a very good one) was not his first choice, as Stewart in his Life would make us believe. Though not very complaisant to women, he was not beyond their regimen any more than Dr. George Wishart, for instances of both their frailties on that side could be quoted. 'Tis as well to mention them here. In the year '78, when Drs. Robertson and Drysdale had with much pains prepared an assembly to elect young Mr. Robertson * into the Procurator's chair, and to get Dr. Drysdale chosen Principal Clerk to the Assembly, as colleague and successor to Dr. George Wishart, it was necessary that Dr. Wishart should resign, in order to his being re-elected with Drysdale; but this, when first applied to, he positively refused to do, because he had given his word to Dr. Dick that he would give him a year's warning before he resigned. In spite of this declaration a siege was laid to the honest man by amazons. After several hearings, in which female eloquence was displayed in all its forms, and after many days, he yielded, as he said himself, to the earnest and violent solicitations of Dr. Drysdale's family. He never after had any intercourse with that family, nor saw them more. Mr. James Lindsay told me this anecdote.

Dr. Robertson's weakness was as follows : He had engaged heartily with me, when in 1788 I stood candidate for the clerkship, Dr. Drysdale having shown evident marks of decline. In the year 1787 I had a long evening's walk with the Procurator, when, after mentioning every candidate for that office we could think of, the Procurator at last said that nobody had such a good chance as myself. After a long discussion I yielded, and we in due form communicated this resolution to his father, who con-

* Son of Principal Robertson.

sented with all his heart, and gave us much advice and some aid. When the vacancy happened, in 1789, Robert Adam assisted his brother-in-law with all his interest, which was considerable. In the mean time the same influence was used with Dr. Robertson as had been with Dr. Wishart, in a still more formidable shape; for Mrs. Drysdale was his cousin-german, and threatened him with the eternal hate of all the family. He also yielded; and Robert Adam, when seriously pressed with a view to drop his canvass if Robertson advised to—" No," Robertson said, " go on "; as he thought he had the best chance. Robert Adam told this to Professor Ferguson when he solicited his vote.

Robertson's conversation was not always so prudent as his conduct, one instance of which was his always asserting that any minister of state who did not take care of himself when he had an opportunity was no very wise man. This maxim shocked most young people, who thought the Doctor's standard of public virtue was not very high. This manner of talking likewise seconded a notion that prevailed that he was a very selfish man. With all those defects, his domestic society was pleasing beyond measure; for his wife, though not a woman of parts, was well suited to him, who was more fitted to lead than to be led; and his sons and daughters led so happy a life that his guests, which we were often for a week together, met with nothing but welcome, and peace, and joy. This intercourse was not much diminished by his having not put any confidence in me when he left the business of the Church, further than saying that he intended to do it. Though he knew that I was much resorted to for advice when he retired, he never talked to me on the subject, at which I was somewhat indignant. His deviations in politics lessened the freedom of our conversation, though we still continued in good habits ; but ever after he left the leading in Church affairs, he appeared to me to have lost his spirits ; and still more, when the magistrates resorted to Dr. Blair, instead of him, for advice about their choice of professors and ministers. I had discovered his having sacrificed me to Mrs. Drysdale, in 1789, but was long acquainted with his weaknesses, and forgave him ; nor did I ever upbraid him with it but in general terms, such as that I had lost the clerkship by the keenness of my opponents and the coldness of my friends. I had such a conscious superiority over him in that affair that I did not choose to put an old friend to the trial of making his fault greater by a lame excuse.

Dr. Blair was a different kind of man from Robertson, and his character is very justly delineated by Dr. Finlayson, so far as he goes. Robertson was most sagacious, Blair was most naïf. Neither of them could be said to have either wit or humour. Of the latter Robertson had a small tincture—Blair had hardly a relish for it. Robertson had a bold and ambitious mind, and a strong desire to make himself considerable ; Blair was timid and unambitious, and

20

withheld himself from public business of every kind, and seemed to have no wish but to be admired as a preacher, particularly by the ladies. His conversation was so infantine that many people thought it impossible, at first sight, that he could be a man of sense or genius. He was as eager about a new paper to his wife's drawing-room, or his own new wig, as about a new tragedy or a new epic poem. Not long before his death I called upon him, when I found him restless and fidgety. " What is the matter with you to-day," says I, " my good friend—are you well ? " " Oh yes," says he, " but I must dress myself, for the Duchess of Leinster has ordered her granddaughters not to leave Scotland without seeing me."   " Go and dress yourself, Doctor, and I shall read this novel ; for I am resolved to see the Duchess of Leinster's granddaughters, for I knew their father and grand-father." This being settled, the young ladies, with their governess, arrived at one, and turned out poor little girls of twelve and thirteen, who could hardly be supposed to carry a well-turned compliment which the Doctor gave them in charge to their grand-mother.

Robertson had so great a desire to shine himself, that I hardly ever saw him patiently bear anybody else's showing-off but Dr. Johnson and Garrick. Blair, on the contrary, though capable of the most profound conversation, when circumstances led to it, had not the least desire to shine, but was delighted beyond measure to show other people in their best guise to his friends. " Did not I show you the lion well to-day ? " used he to say after the exhibition of a remarkable stranger. For a vain man, he was the least envious I ever knew. He had truly a pure mind, in which there was not the least malignity ; for though he was of a quick and lively temper, and apt to be warm and impatient about trifles, his wife, who was a superior woman, only laughed, and his friends joined her. Though Robertson was never ruffled, he had more animosity in his nature than Blair. They were both reckoned selfish by those who envied their prosperity, but on very unequal grounds ; for though Blair talked selfishly enough sometimes, yet he never failed in generous actions. In one respect they were quite alike. Having been bred at a time when the common people thought to play with cards or dice was a sin, and everybody thought it an indecorum in clergymen, they could neither of them play at golf or bowls, and far less at cards or backgammon, and on that account were very unhappy when from home in friends' houses in the country in rainy weather. As I had set the first example of playing at cards at home with unlocked doors, and so relieved the clergy from ridicule on that side, they both learned to play at whist after they were sixty. Robertson did very well—Blair never shone. He had his country quarters for two summers in my parish, where he and his wife were quite happy. We were much together. Mrs. C., who had wit and humour in a high degree, and an acuteness and extent of mind that made her fit to converse with philosophers, and indeed a great favourite with them all, gained much upon Blair ; and, as Mrs. B. alleged, could make him believe whatever she pleased. They took delight in raising the wonder of the sage Doctor. " Who told you that story, my dear Doctor ? " " No," says he, " don't *you* doubt it, for it was Mrs. C. who told me." On my laughing —" and so, so," said he, " I must hereafter make allowance for her imagination."

Blair had lain under obligation to Lord Leven's family for his first church, which he left within the year ; but though that connection was so soon dissolved, and though Blair took a side in Church politics wholly opposite to Lord Leven's, the Doctor always behaved to the family with great respect, and kept up a visiting correspondence with them all his life. Not so Robertson with the Arniston family, who had got him the church of Gladsmuir. The first President failed and died—not, however, till he had marked his approbation of Robertson—in 1753. His manner had not been pleasing to him, so that he was alienated till Harry grew up ; but him he deserted also, on the change in 1782, being dazzled with the prospect of his son's having charge of ecclesiastical affairs, as his cousin John Adam was to have of political, during Rockingham's new ministry. This threw a cloud on Robertson which was never dispelled. Blair had for a year been tutor to Simon Fraser, Lord Lovat's eldest son, whose steady friendship he preserved to the last, though the General was not remarkable for that amiable weakness ; witness the saying of a common soldier whom he had often promised to make a sergeant, but never performed, " Oh ! Simon, Simon, as long as you continue to live, Lord Lovat is not dead."

Five or six days before he [Blair] died, finding him well and in good spirits, I said to him, " Since you don't choose to dine abroad in this season (December), you may at least let a friend or two dine with you." " Well, well, come you and dine with me to-morrow," looking earnestly at Miss Hunter, his niece. " I am engaged to-morrow, but I can return at four to-day." He looked more earnestly at his niece. " What's to hinder him ? " said she, meaning to answer his look, which said, " Have you any dinner to-day, Betty ? " I returned, accordingly, at four, and never passed four hours more agreeably with him, nor had more enlightened conversation. Nay more, three days before his death he sent to John Home a part of his History, with two or three pages of criticism on that part of it that relates to Provost Drummond, in which he and I thought John egregiously wrong.

It was long before Blair's circumstances were full, yet he lived handsomely, and had literary strangers at his house, as well as many friends. A task imposed on both Robertson and Blair was reading manuscript prepared for the press, of which Blair had the greatest share of the poetry, and Robertson of the other writings, and they were both kind encouragers of young men of merit.

In John Home's younger days he had a good share of wit, much sprightliness and vivacity, so that he infused joy and a social exhilaration wherever he came. His address was cordial and benevolent, which inspired his companions with similar sentiments. Superior knowledge and learning, except in the department of poetry, he had not, but such was the charm of his fine spirits in those days, that when he left the room prematurely, which was but seldom the case, the company grew dull, and soon dissolved. As John all his life had a thorough contempt for such as neglected or disapproved of his poetry, he treated all who approved of his works with a partiality which more than approached to flattery. The effect of this temper was, that all his opinions of men and things were prejudices, which, though it did not disqualify him for writing admirable poetry, yet made him unfit for writing history or other prose works. He was in no respect a man of business, though he now and then spoke with some energy and success in the General Assembly ; but he had no turn for debate, which made me glad when he was disappointed in his wish of obtaining a seat in the House of Commons, which was owing to the good sense of Sir Gilbert Elliot and Sir William Pulteney.

This has been a long digression from my narration ; but having noted down one character, I thought it best to go on with a few more, lest I should forget some particulars which then occurred to me.

It was in the year 1754 that my cousin, Captain Lyon, died at London, of a high fever. His wife, Lady Catherine Brydges, had conducted herself so very loosely and ill, that it was suspected that she wished for his death; but it was a brain fever of which he died; and as his wife had sent for Dr. Monro, the physician employed about the insane, his mother, in the rage of her grief, alleged that his wife had occasioned his death. Her two children died not long after. Lady Catherine confirmed all her mother-in-law's suspicions by marrying a Mr. Stanhope, one of her many lovers. By this time a large fortune had fallen to her. She was truly a worthless woman, to my knowledge. Lyon and his children were buried in the Duke of Chandos's vault at Canons, by His Grace's order.

In this year, 1754, I remember nothing remarkable in the General Assembly. But this was the year in which the Select Society was established, which improved and gave a name to the *literati* of this country, then beginning to distinguish themselves. I gave an account of this institution, and a list of the members, to Dugald Stewart, which he inserted in his *Life of Robertson*. But that list did not contain the whole of the members; some had died before the list was printed, and some were admitted after it was printed. Of the first were Lord Dalmeny, the elder brother of the present Lord Rosebery, who was a man of letters and an amateur, and, though he did not speak himself, generally carried home six or eight of those who did to sup with him. There was also a Peter Duff, a writer to the signet, who was a shrewd, sensible fellow, and pretending to be unlearned, surprised us with his observations in strong Buchan.* The Duke of Hamilton of that period, a man of letters, could he have kept himself sober, was also a member, and spoke there one night. Lord Dalmeny died in 1755. Mr. Robert Alexander,† wine merchant, a very worthy man, but a bad speaker, entertained us all with warm suppers and excellent claret, as a recompense for the patient hearing of his ineffectual attempts, when I often thought he would have beat out his brains on account of their constipation. The conversation at those convivial meetings frequently improved the members more by free conversation than the speeches in the Society.‡ It was those meetings in particular that rubbed off all corners, as we call it, by collision, and made the *literati* of Edinburgh less captious and pedantic than they were elsewhere.

* Viz., with the accent peculiar to the district of Buchan, in Aberdeenshire.—J. H. B.

† Henry Mackenzie mentions a Mr. Alexander, a member of the Select Society, who having been much abroad modelled his suppers on those of Paris. They were frequented by all the literary and most of the fashionable persons of the time.

‡ The Select Society owed its existence chiefly to Allan Ramsay the painter. It met first in the Advocates' Library, when the membership was confined to thirty. Later, when its " select " character was departed from and the membership increased to three hundred, interest in the Society quickly declined.

The Earl of Hopetoun was Commissioner of the General Assembly. The Earl of Dumfries had wished for it ; but some of the ministers, thinking that it would be proper to disappoint him, by a little intrigue contrived to get the King to nominate Hopetoun, who accepted it for one year, and entertained his company in a sumptuous manner. At his table I saw the Duchess of Hamilton (Mary Gunning),* without doubt the most beautiful woman of her time.

In the end of summer, Lady Dalkeith, the Duke of Buccleuch's mother, who had been a widow since the year 1750, came to Dalkeith, and brought with her the Honourable Mr. Stuart M'Kenzie and his lady, the Countess's sister, and remained there for two months. They had public days twice in the week, and I frequently dined there. The Countess was well-bred and agreeable ; and, acting plays being the rage at the time among people of quality, she proposed to act a tragedy at Dalkeith House, viz. *The Fair Penitent*, in which her ladyship and Mr. M'Kenzie were to have principal parts. Mr. John Grant, advocate, then chief manager of the Duke of Buccleuch's estates, and living at Castlesteads, was to play the part of the father, and it was requested of me to assist him in preparing his part. I found him a stiff, bad reader, of affected English, which we call

* Elizabeth Gunning was Duchess of Hamilton, and afterwards Duchess of Argyle. She was the mother of two Dukes of Hamilton and two Dukes of Argyle. Mary (Maria) Gunning was Countess of Coventry.

napping, and tolerably obstinate. But luckily for both master and scholar, the humour was soon changed, by somebody representing to her ladyship that her acting plays would give offence. Mr. M'Kenzie was very agreeable, his vanity having carried him so far above his family pride as to make him wish to please his inferiors. I was simple enough then to think that my conversation and manners had not been disagreeable to him, so that when I was at London four years after, I attempted to avail myself of his acquaintance ; but it would not do, for I was chilled to death on my first approach, so that all my intimacy vanished in a few jokes, which sometimes he condescended to make when he met me on the streets, and which I received with the coldness they were entitled to.

By this time John Home had almost finished his tragedy of *Douglas* ; for on one of the days that I was at Dalkeith House I met Sir Gilbert Elliot, who, on my telling him that I had three acts of it written in my hand, came round with me to my house in Musselburgh, where I read them, to his great delight. This was in July or August 1754. I do not remember whether or not he saw the two last acts at this time. I should think not ; for I remember that I wrote three acts of it a good many months afterwards, to be sent up suddenly to Sir Gilbert, while a writer's clerk wrote out fair the other two acts.

In February of this year Home and I suffered severely by the death of friends. George Logan, minister of Ormiston, was seized with a brain fever, of which he died in a few days. I was sent for by his wife, and remained by his bedside from five in the afternoon till one in the morning, when he expired. He raved the whole time, except during the few minutes in which I prayed with him. I am not sure that he knew, for he soon relapsed into his ravings again, and never ceased till the great silencer came. I have given the character of his mind before (p. 244). The grief of his wife, who never could be comforted, though she lived to an advanced age, was a proof of his kind and affectionate temper. They had no children.

After my friend's death I had returned home on Sunday morning to do duty in Inveresk church, and in the evening about six, John Home, to whom I had sent an express, arrived from Polwarth. On hearing the bad news, he had almost fainted, and threw himself on the bed, and sobbed and wept. After a while I raised him, by asking if he could think of no misfortune greater than the death of Logan? He started up, and cried, " Is my brother David gone ? " I had received an express from his brother George, in Leith, that afternoon, to tell me of their brother David's death on the voyage. He was John's only uterine brother alive—had been at home the autumn before—and was truly a fine-spirited promising young man. He had gone out that fall first mate of an Indiaman. After another short paroxysm of grief—for his stock was almost spent before—he rose and took his supper, and, insist-

ing on my making a good bowl of punch, we talked
over the perfections of the deceased, went to bed and
slept sound. In the morning he was taken up with
the suit of mourning he was going to order, and for
which he went to Edinburgh on purpose. I mention
these circumstances to show that there are very
superior minds on which the loss of friends makes
very little impression. He was not likely to feel more
on any future occasion than on this ; for as people
grow older, not only experience hardens them to such
events, but, growing daily more selfish, they feel less
for other people.

In the month of February 1755, John Home's
tragedy of *Douglas* was completely prepared for the
stage, and had received all the corrections and im-
provements that it needed by many excellent critics,
who were Mr. Home's friends, whom I have mentioned before, and with whom he daily lived. [He
accordingly set out for London, and] were I to relate
all the circumstances, serious and ludicrous, which
attended the outset of this journey, I am persuaded
they would not be exceeded by any novelist who has
wrote since the days of the inimitable *Don Quixote*.
Six or seven Merse ministers—the half of whom had
slept at the manse of Polwarth, bad as it was, the
night before—set out for Woolerhaughhead in a
snowy morning in February. Before we had gone
far we discovered that our bard had no mode of
carrying his precious treasure, which we thought
enough of, but hardly foresaw that it was to be pro-

nounced a perfect tragedy by the best judges; for when David Hume gave it that praise, he spoke only the sentiment of the whole republic of belles-lettres. The tragedy in one pocket of his greatcoat, and his clean shirt and nightcap in the other, though they balanced each other, was thought an unsafe mode of conveyance; and our friend—who, like most of his brother poets, was unapt to foresee difficulties and provide against them—had neglected to buy a pair of leather bags as he passed through Haddington. We bethought us that possibly James Landreth, minister of Simprin, and clerk of the Synod, would be provided with such a convenience for the carriage of his Synod records; and having no wife, no *atra cura*, to resist our request, we unanimously turned aside half a mile to call at James's; and, concealing our intention at first, we easily persuaded the honest man to join us in this convoy to his friend Mr. Home, and then observing the danger the manuscript might run in a greatcoat-pocket on a journey of 400 miles, we inquired if he could lend Mr. Home his valise only as far as Wooler, where he would purchase a new pair for himself. This he very cheerfully granted. But while his pony was preparing, he had another trial to go through; for Cupples, who never had any money, though he was a bachelor too, and had twice the stipend of Landreth, took the latter into another room, where the conference lasted longer than we wished for, so that we had to bawl out for them to come away. We afterwards understood that Cup-

ples, having only four shillings, was pressing Landreth to lend him half-a-guinea, that he might be able
to defray the expense of the journey. Honest James,
who knew that John Home, if he did not return his
own valise, which was very improbable, would provide him in a better pair, had frankly agreed to the
first request ; but as he knew Cupples never paid
anything, he was very reluctant to part with his half-
guinea. However, having at last agreed, we at last
set out, and I think gallant troops, but so-and-so
accoutred, to make an inroad on the English border.
By good luck the river Tweed was not come down,
and we crossed it safely at the ford near Norham
Castle ; and, as the day mended, we got to Woolerhaughhead by four o'clock, where we got but an indifferent dinner, for it was but a miserable house in
those days ; but a happier or more jocose and merry
company could hardly be assembled.

John Home and I, who slept in one room, or perhaps in one bed, as was usual in those days, were disturbed by a noise in the night, which being in the
next room, where Laurie and Monteith were, we
found they had quarrelled and fought, and the former
had pushed the latter out of bed. After having acted
as mediators in this quarrel, we had sound sleep till
morning. Having breakfasted as well as the house
could afford, Cupples and I, who had agreed to go two
days' journey further with Mr. Home, set off south-
wards with him, and the rest returned by the way
they had come to Berwickshire again.

Mr. Home had by that time got a very fine galloway from his friend Robert Adam when he was setting out for Italy. John had called this horse Piercy, who, though only fourteen and a half hands high, was one of the best trotters ever seen, and having a good deal of blood in him, when he was well used, was indefatigable. He carried our bard for many years with much classical fame, and rose in reputation with his master, but at last made an inglorious end.* I had a fine galloway too, though not more than thirteen and a half hands, which, though much slower than Piercy, easily went at the rate of fifty miles a-day, on the turnpike road, without being at all tired.

* *Piercy's end.*—Robert Adam, on his setting out for London to go to Italy, and some of his brothers, with John, and Commissioner Cardonnel, had dined with me one day. Cardonnel, while their horses were getting ready, insisted on our going to his garden to drink a couple of bottles of some French white wine, which he said was as good as champagne. We went with him, but when we sat down in his arbour we missed Bob Adam. We soon finished our wine, which we drank out of rummers, and returned to the manse, where we found Robert galloping round the green on Piercy like a madman, which he repeated, after seeing us, for at least ten times. Home stopped him, and had some talk with him ; so the brothers at last went off quietly for Edinburgh, while Home remained to stay all night or go home. He told me what put Robert into such trim. He had been making love to my maid Jenny, who was a handsome lass, and had even gone the length of offering to carry her to London, and pension her there. All his offers were rejected, which had put him in a flurry. This happened in summer 1754. Many a time Piercy carried John to London, and once in six days. He sent him at last to Sir David Kinloch, that he might end his days in peace and ease in one of the parks of Gilmerton. Sir David tired of him in a few weeks, and sold him to an egg-carrier for twenty shillings !

Cupples and I attended Home as far as Ferryhill, about six miles, where, after remaining all night with him, we parted next morning, he for London, and we on our return home. Poor Home had no better success on this occasion than before, with still greater mortification; for Garrick, after reading the play, returned it with an opinion that it was totally unfit for the stage. On this occasion Home wrote a pathetic copy of verses, addressed to Shakespeare's image in Westminster Abbey.

Cupples and I had a diverting journey back; for as his money had failed, and I had not an overflow, we were obliged to feed our horses in Newcastle without dining, and to make the best of our way to Morpeth, where we got an excellent hot supper. Next day, staying too long in Alnwick to visit the castle, we lost our way in the night, and were in some hazard, and it was past twelve before we reached Berwick; but in those days nothing came wrong to us—youth and good spirits made us convert all maladventures into fun. The Virgin's Inn, as it was called, being at that time the best, and on the south side of the bridge, made us forget all our disasters.

It was in the time of the sitting of the General Assembly that Lord Drummore died, at the age of sixty-three. He had gone the Western Circuit; and by drying up an issue in his leg, being a corpulent man who needed such a drain, he contracted a gangrene, of which he died in a few weeks, very much regretted—more, indeed, than any man I ever knew.

His having got a legacy from *   the year
before, and built himself a comfortable house on his
small estate, where he only had a cottage before, and
where he had slept only two or three nights for his
illness, was a circumstance that made his family and
friends feel it the more.   He had been married to an
advocate's daughter of Aberdeenshire, of the name of
Horn, by whom a good estate came into his family.
By her he had five sons and three daughters.   Three
of the sons in succession inherited the name and estate
of Horn.

After Lord Drummore became a widower, he attached himself to a mistress, which, to do so openly as
he did, was at that time reckoned a great indecorum,
at least in one of his age and reverend office.   This
was all that could be laid to his charge, which, however, did not abate the universal concern of the city
and county when he was dying.   His cousin, Lord
Cathcart, was Commissioner that year for the first
time.   His eldest son at his death was Lieutenant-
General Horn Dalrymple ; his second, David Dalrymple, some time afterwards Lord Westhall ; his
youngest, Campbell, who was distinguished afterwards in the West Indies, and was a lieutenant-
colonel and Governor of Guadaloupe.

At my father's desire, who was minister of the
parish where Drummore resided, I wrote a character
of him, which he delivered from his pulpit the Sunday
after his funeral.   This was printed in the *Scots*

* Blank in MS.

Magazine for June 1755, and was commended by the publisher, and well received by the public. This was the first time I had seen my prose in print, and it gave me some confidence in my own talent.

In the year 1756 hostilities were begun between the French and British, after they had given us much provocation in America. Braddock, an officer of the Guards—very brave, though unfit for the business on which he was sent—having been defeated and slain at Fort Du Quesne (a misfortune afterwards repaired by General John Forbes), reprisals were made by the capture of French ships without a declaration of war. The French laid siege to Minorca, and Admiral Byng was sent with a fleet of thirteen ships of the line to throw in succours and raise the siege. The expectation of the country was raised very high on this occasion, and yet was disappointed.

Concerning this I remember a very singular anecdote. During the sitting of the General Assembly that year, by desire of James Lindsay, a company of seven or eight, all clergymen, supped at a punchhouse in the Bow, kept by an old servant of his, who had also been with George Wishart. In that time of sanguine hopes of a complete victory, and the total defeat of the French fleet, all the company expressed their full belief that the next post would bring us great news, except John Home alone, who persisted in saying that there would be no battle at all, or, at the best, if there was a battle, it would be a drawn one. John's obstinacy provoked the company, insomuch

that James Landreth, the person who had lent him
the valise the year before, offered to lay a half-crown
bowl of punch that the first mail from the Mediterranean would bring us news of a complete victory.
John took this bet ; and when he and I were walking
to our lodging together, I asked what in the world had
made him so positive. He answered that Byng was
a man who would shun fighting if it were possible ;
and that his ground of knowledge was from Admiral
Smith, who, a few years back, had commanded at
Leith, who lodged with his friend Mr. Walter Scott,
and who, when he was confined with the gout, used
to have him to come and chat with him, or play at
cards when he was able ; and that, talking of the
characters of different admirals, he had told him
that Byng, though a much-admired commander and
manœuvrer of a fleet, would shun fighting whenever
he could. The *Gazette* soon cleared up to us the
truth of this assertion, though the first accounts
made it be believed that the French were defeated.
A full confirmation of this anecdote I heard two years
afterwards.

It was during this Assembly that the Carriers' Inn,
in the lower end of the West Bow, got into some
credit, and was called the Diversorium. Thomas
Nicolson was the man's name, and his wife's Nelly
Douglas. They had been servants of Lord Elliock's,
and had taken up this small inn, in which there were
three rooms, and a stable below for six or eight
horses. Thomas was a confused, rattling, coarse

fellow; Nelly was a comely woman, a person of
good sense, and very worthy. Some of our companions frequented the house, and Home and I suspected it was the handsome landlady who had attracted their notice, but it was not so. Nelly was an
honest woman, but she had prompted her husband
to lend them two or three guineas on occasions, and
did not suddenly demand repayment. Home and I
followed Logan, James Craig, and William Gullen,
and were pleased with the house. He and I happening to dine with Dr. Robertson at his uncle's, who lived
in Pinkie House, a week before the General Assembly,
some of us proposed to order Thomas Nicolson to lay
in twelve dozen of the same claret, then 18s. per dozen,
from Mr. Scott, wine merchant at Leith—for in his
house we proposed to make our Assembly parties;
for, being out of the way, we proposed to have snug
parties of our own friends. This was accordingly executed, but we could not be concealed; for, as it hap-
pens in such cases, the out-of-the-way place and mean
house, and the attempt to be private, made it the
more frequented—and no wonder, when the company
consisted of Robertson, Home, Ferguson, Jardine, and
Wilkie, with the addition of David Hume and Lord
Elibank, the Master of Ross, and Sir Gilbert Elliot.

CHAPTER VIII

1756–1758 AGE, 34–36

IN October 1756, John Home had been taken by Lord
Milton's family to Inverary, to be introduced to the
Duke, who was much taken with his liveliness and
gentlemanlike manners. The Duke's good opinion
made Milton adhere more firmly to him, and assist in
bringing on his play in the end of that season.

It was in the end of this year, 1756, that *Douglas*
was first acted in Edinburgh. Mr. Home had been
unsuccessful in London the year before, but he was
well with Sir Gilbert Elliot, Mr. Oswald of Dunnikier,
and had the favour and friendship of Lord Milton and
all his family ; and it was at last agreed among them
that, since Garrick could not yet be prevailed on to
get *Douglas* acted, it should be brought on here ; for
if it succeeded in the Edinburgh theatre, then Garrick
could resist no longer.*

* The new play is thus modestly announced in the *Evening
Courant* of Saturday, 4th December 1756. "A new Tragedy
called *Douglas*, written by an ingenious gentleman of this
country, is now in rehearsal at the Theatre, and will be performed as speedily as possible. The expectations of the public

There happened to be a pretty good set of players ;
for Digges, whose relations had got him debarred from
the London theatres,* had come down here, and performed many principal parts with success.   He was a
very handsome young man at that time, with a
genteel address.   He had drunk tea at Mally Campbell's, in Glasgow College, when he was an ensign in
the year 1745.   I was there, and thought him very
agreeable.   He was, however, a great profligate and
spendthrift ;   and poltroon, I'm afraid, into the
bargain.   He had been on the stage for some time,
having been obliged to leave the army.   Mrs. Ward
turned out an exceeding good Lady Randolph ; Lowe
performed Glenalvon well ; Mr. Haymen the Old
Shepherd, and Digges himself young Douglas.   I
attended two rehearsals with our author, and Lord
Elibank, and Dr. Ferguson, and David Hume, and
was truly astonished at the readiness with which Mrs.
Ward conceived the Lady's character, and how
happily she delivered it.   To be near Digges's lodgings in the Canongate, where the first rehearsals were
performed, the gentlemen mentioned, with two or

from the performance are in proportion to the known talent and
ability of the author, whose modest merit would have suppressed
a Dramatick work which we think by the concurrent testimony of
many gentlemen of taste and literature will be an honour to the
country."

* " It has generally been considered that he was the natural
son of the Hon. Elizabeth West, who in 1724 married Thomas
Digges, Esq., of Chilham Castle, Kent.   But there are no grounds
for supposing that Digges was born out of wedlock.   The report
very likely arose from his mother's relatives not wishing to be
connected with an actor."—Dibdin's *History of Edinburgh Stage*.

three more, dined together at a tavern in the Abbey two or three times, where pork griskins being a favourite dish, this was called the Griskin Club, and excited much curiosity, as everything did in which certain people were concerned.

The play had unbounded success for a great many nights in Edinburgh, and was attended by all the literati and most of the judges, who, except one or two, had not been in use to attend the theatre. The town in general was in an uproar of exultation * that a Scotchman had written a tragedy of the first rate, and that its merit was first submitted to their judgment. There were a few opposers, however, among those who pretended to taste and literature, who endeavoured to cry down the performance in libellous pamphlets and ballads † (for they durst not attempt to oppose it in the theatre itself), and were openly countenanced by Robert Dundas of Arniston,‡ at that time Lord Advocate, and all his minions and expectants. The High-flying set were unanimous against it, as they thought it a sin for a clergyman to write

* " I have a perfect recollection of the strong sensation that *Douglas* excited among its [Edinburgh] inhabitants. The men talked of the rehearsals ; the ladies repeated what they had heard of the story. Some had procured as a great favour, copies of the most striking passages which they recited at the earnest request of the company. I was present at the representation ; the applause was enthusiastic, but a better criticism of its merits was the tears of the audience which the tender part of the drama drew forth unsparingly."—Mackenzie's *Life of Home*, vol. i.

† In *Notes and Queries*, 1866, will be found a reprint of one of the ballads—a parody on "Gil Morice."

‡ Afterwards second Lord President Dundas.

any play, let it be ever so moral in its tendency. Several ballads and pamphlets were published on our side in answer to the scurrilities against us, one of which was written by Adam Ferguson, and another by myself. Ferguson's was mild and temperate ; and, besides other arguments, supported the lawfulness and use of dramatic writing from the example of Scripture, which he exhibited in the story of Joseph and his brethren, as having truly the effect of a dramatic composition. This was much read among the grave and sober-minded, and converted some, and confirmed many in their belief of the usefulness of the stage. Mine was of such a different nature that many people read it at first as intended to *ridicule* the performance, and bring it into contempt, for it was entitled "An Argument to prove that the Tragedy of *Douglas* ought to be publicly burnt by the Hands of the Hangman." The zeal and violence of the Presbytery of Edinburgh, who had made enactments and declarations to be read in the pulpit, provoked me to write this pamphlet, which, in the ironical manner of Swift, contained a severe satire on all our opponents. This was so well concealed, however, that the pamphlet being published when I was at Dumfries, about the end of January, visiting Provost Bell, who was on his deathbed, some copies arrived there by the carriers, which being opened and read by my sister and aunt when I was abroad, they conceived it to be serious, and that the tragedy would be quite undone, till Mr. Stewart, the Comptroller of the Customs, who was a man of sense and reading, came in, and who soon undeceived them, and convinced them that *Douglas* was triumphant. This pamphlet had a great effect by elating our friends, and perhaps more in exasperating our enemies; which was by no means softened by Lord Elibank and David Hume, etc., running about and crying it up as the first performance the world had seen for half a century.

What I really valued myself most upon, however, was half a sheet, which I penned very suddenly. Digges rode out one forenoon to me, saying that he had come by Mr. Home's desire to inform me that all the town had seen the play, and that it would run no longer, unless some contrivance was fallen upon to make the lower orders of tradesmen and apprentices come to the playhouse. After hearing several ways of raising the curiosity of the lower orders, I desired him to take a walk for half an hour, and look at the view from Inveresk churchyard, which he did ; and, in the mean time, I drew up what I entitled " A full and true History of the Bloody Tragedy of *Douglas*, as it is now to be seen acting in the Theatre at the Canongate." This was cried about the streets next day, and filled the house for two nights more.

I had attended the playhouse, not on the first or second, but on the third night of the performance, being well aware that all the fanatics and some other enemies would be on the watch, and make all the advantage they possibly could against me. But six or seven friends of the author, clergymen from the

Merse, having attended, reproached me for my cowardice ; and above all, the author himself and some female friends of his having heated me by their upbraidings, I went on the third night, and having taken charge of the ladies, I drew on myself all the clamours of tongues and violence of prosecution which I afterwards underwent. I believe I have already mentioned that Dr. Patrick Cuming having become jealous of William Robertson and John Home and myself on account of our intimacy with Lord Milton, and observing his active zeal about the tragedy of *Douglas*, took it into his head that he could blow us up and destroy our popularity, and consequently disgust Lord Milton with us. Very warmly, with all the friends he could get to follow him—particularly Hyndman his second—he joined with Webster and his party in doing everything they could to depreciate the tragedy of *Douglas*, and disgrace all its partisans. With this view, besides the Act of the Presbytery of Edinburgh, which was read in all the churches, and that of the Presbytery of Glasgow, who followed them, they had decoyed Mr. Thomas Whyte, minister of Liberton, an honest but a quiet man, to submit to a six weeks' suspension for his having attended the tragedy of *Douglas*, which he had confessed he had done.* This they had contrived as an example for prosecuting me, and at least get-

---

* Whyte owed the mitigated sentence to his plea, that, though he attended, he concealed himself as well as he could to avoid giving offence.—J. H. B.

ting a similar sentence pronounced against me by the Presbytery of Dalkeith. On returning from Dumfries, in the second week of February 1757, I was surprised not only to find the amazing hue and cry that had been raised against *Douglas*, but all the train that had been laid against me, and a summons to attend the Presbytery, to answer for my conduct, on the 1st day of March.

On deliberating about this affair, with all the knowledge I had of the laws of the Church and the confidence I had in the goodwill of my parish, I took a firm resolution not to submit to what I saw the Presbytery intended, but to stand my ground on a firm opinion that my offence was not a foundation for a libel, but, if anything at all, a mere impropriety or offence against decorum, which ought to be done at privy censures by an admonition. This ground I took, and never departed from it ; but I, at the same time, resolved to mount my horse, and visit every member of Presbytery, especially my opponents, and, by a free confession, endeavour to bring them over to my opinion. They received me differently—some with a contemptible dissimulation, and others with a provoking reserve and haughtiness. I saw that they had the majority of the Presbytery on their side, and that the cabal was firm, and that no submission on my part would turn them aside from their purpose. This confirmed my resolution not to yield, but to run every risk rather than furnish an example of tame submission, not merely to a fanatical, but an illegal exertion of power, which would have stamped disgrace on the Church of Scotland, kept the younger clergy for half a century longer in the trammels of bigotry or hypocrisy, and debarred every generous spirit from entering into orders. The sequel of the story is pretty fully and correctly stated in the *Scots Magazine* for 1757, to which I shall only add a few particulars, which were less known.

Joseph M'Cormick, at this time tutor to young Mr. Hepburn of Clarkington, and afterwards Principal of St. Andrews United Colleges, had entered on trials before the Presbytery of Dalkeith, and had two or three times attended the tragedy of *Douglas*. This he told them himself, which threw them into a dilemma, out of which they did not know how to escape. To take no notice of his having attended the theatre, while they were prosecuting me, was a very glaring inconsistency. On the other hand, to send him out as a probationer, with the slur of an ecclesiastical censure on his character, was injustice to the young man, and might disoblige his friends. So reasoned the Jesuits of Dalkeith Presbytery. M'Cormick himself showed them the way out of this snare into which their zeal and hypocrisy had led them. After allowing them to flounce about in it for a quarter of an hour (as he told them afterwards with infinite humour), he represented that his pupil and he, having some time before gone into their lodgings for the remainder of the season, he would be much obliged to the Presbytery of Dalkeith if they would transfer him to the Presbytery of Edinburgh to take the remainder of his trials. With this proposal they very cheerfully closed, whilst M'Cormick inwardly laughed (for he was a laughing philosopher) at their profligate hypocrisy.

It is proper to mention here that during the course of this trial I received several anonymous letters from a person deservedly high in reputation in the Church for learning, and ability, and liberality of sentiment— the late Dr. Robert Wallace *—which supported me in my resolution, and gave me the soundest advice with respect to the management of my cause. I had received two of those letters before I knew from whence they came, when, on showing them to my father, he knew the hand, as the Doctor and he had been at college together. This circumstance prevented my father from wavering, to which he was liable, and even strengthened my own mind.

It is necessary, likewise, to advert here to the conduct of Robert Dundas of Arniston, at that time King's Advocate, as it accounts for that animosity which arose against him among my friends of the Moderate party, and the success of certain satirical ballads and pamphlets which were published some

---

* Before the production of *Douglas* upon the stage, the Edinburgh Presbytery was so zealous in its efforts to suppress the theatre "that the brethren resolved to prosecute the Actors upon the Vagrant Act at their own expense." Dr. Wallace, who had recently come to Edinburgh, opposed this resolution and pointed out that "a well regulated stage might be made a school of morals."

years after.   This was his decided opposition to the
tragedy of *Douglas*, which was perfectly known from
his own manner of talking—though more cautious
than that of his enemies, who opened loud upon
Home and his tragedy—and likewise from this circumstance, that Thomas Turnbull, his friend, who
took my side in the Presbytery, being influenced by
his brother-in-law, Dr. Wallace, was ever after out
of favour at Arniston ; and what was more, Dr. Wallace, who was of the Lord Advocate's political party,
incurred his displeasure so much, that, during the
remainder of his own life, George Wallace, advocate,
who was under the protection of the family of Arniston, was totally neglected.*   This piece of injustice
was not explained till after his death, when his son
Robert,† of the most amiable and liberal mind, gave
him [Wallace] a judge's place in the commissariat
of Edinburgh.   It was farther proved by the unsea-
sonable application of my friend, Mr. Baron Grant,
who was his political friend and companion, to allay
the heat of the Presbytery of Dalkeith, and induce
them to withdraw their prosecution, when a word
from him would have done.   This conduct of Dundas
might in part be imputed to his want of taste and
discernment in what related to the belles-lettres, and

* George Wallace, author of a folio volume—the first of an in-
definite series never completed—called *A System of the Prin-*
ciples of the Law of Scotland, and of a book on *The Nature and*
Descent of certain Peerages connected with the Kingdom of Scotland.
As to his father, see above, p. 251.—J. H. B.

† Afterwards Lord Chief-Baron Dundas of the Court of Exchequer.

to a certain violence of temper, which could endure no one that did not bend to him ; or to his jealousy of Sir G. Elliot and Andrew Pringle, who were our zealous friends ; or his hatred of Lord Milton, who so warmly patronised John Home. It was amusing to observe, during the course of the summer, when Wilkie's *Epigoniad* appeared, how loud the retainers of the house of Arniston were in its praise, saying they knew how to distinguish between good and bad poetry; and now they had got something to commend.

Cuming, Webster, and Hyndman, and a fiery man at Leith, whose name I forget, were the committee who drew up the libel. Webster, who had no bowels, and who could do mischief with the joy of an ape, suggested all the circumstances of aggravation, and was quite delighted when he got his colleagues of the committee to insert such circumstances as my eating and drinking with Sarah Ward, and taking my place in the playhouse by turning some gentlemen out of their seats, and committing a riot, etc.*

* " The libel " is the name of the document or writ by which, in Scotland, a clergyman, charged by an ecclesiastical court with an offence, is brought before his accusers for trial and judgment. The term is taken from the Roman *libelli accusatorii*. Of the libel against Carlyle, which is long, and well supplied with the usual technicalities, the following specimens will perhaps be considered sufficient : " On the eighth day of December, in the year seventeen hundred and fifty-six, or upon one or other of the days of November or October seventeen hundred and fifty-six, or upon one or other of the days of January seventeen hundred and fifty-seven years, he, the said Mr. Alexander Carlyle, did, without necessity, keep company, familiarly converse, and eat and drink with West Diggs (one of the actors on the unlicensed stage or theatre at the head of the Canongate of Edinburgh, commonly

At a very full meeting of my friends in Boyd's large room, in the Canongate, the night before the Synod met, I proposed Dr. Dick, who had recently been admitted a minister in Edinburgh, for the Moderator's chair. I had prepared my friends beforehand for this proposal, and was induced to do it for several reasons. One was to exclude Robertson, whose speaking would be of more consequence if not in the chair. Another was to show my friend Dick to the rest, and to make them confidential with him, and to fix so able an assistant in our party. He was accordingly elected without opposition, and performed his duty with the utmost spirit and manhood ; for, besides preserving general good order, he, with

called the Concert-hall), in the house of Henry Thomson, vintner in the Abbey, near to the Palace of Holyrood House, or in some other house or tavern within the city or suburbs of Edinburgh, or Canongate, or said Abbey, or Leith ; at least he, the said Mr. Alexander Carlyle, did, without necessity, at the time or times, place or places above libelled, converse in a familiar manner with the said West Diggs, or with Miss Sarah Ward, an actress on the said theatre, or with some other of the persons who are in the course of acting plays in the said theatre—persons that do not reside in his parish, and who, by their profession, and in the eye of the law, are of bad fame, and who cannot obtain from any minister a testimonial of their moral character . . . and he, the said Mr. Alexander Carlyle, did not only appear publicly in the said unlicensed theatre, but took possession of a box, or a place in one of the boxes, of the said house, in a disorderly way, and turned some gentlemen out of it in a forcible manner, and did there witness the acting or representation of the foresaid tragedy called *Douglas*, when acted for hire or reward, in which the name of God was profaned or taken in vain by mock prayers and tremendous oaths or expressions, such as—' by the blood of the cross,' and ' the wounds of Him who died for us on the accursed tree.' "—J. H. B.

uncommon decision and readiness, severely rebuked Hyndman when he was very offensive. The lachite of Hyndman's mind, which was well known to Dick and me, made him submit to this rebuke from the chair, though, in reality, he was not out of order. What a pity it was that Robertson afterwards lost this man in the manner I shall afterwards mention!

It was remarked that there were only three of a majority in the Synod for the sentence which my friends had advised, assisted by the very good sense of Professor Robert Hamilton,* and his intricate and embarrassed expression, which concealed while it palliated—and that two of those three were John Home, the author, and my father; but neither of their votes could have been rejected, and the moderator's casting-vote would have been with us.

My speech in my own defence in the Synod, which I drew up rather in the form of a remonstrance than an argument, leaving that to Robertson and my other friends, made a very good impression on the audience. John Dalrymple, junior of Cranstoun, was my advocate at the bar, and did justice to the cause he had voluntarily undertaken, which, while it served me effectually, gave him the first opportunity he had of displaying his talents before a popular assembly. Robertson's was a speech of great address, and had a good effect; but none was better than that of Andrew Pringle, Esq., the Solicitor, who, I think, was the most eloquent of all the Scottish bar in my time.

* Professor of Divinity 1754–1779, son of Principal Hamilton.

22

The Presbytery thought fit to appeal. When it came to the Assembly, the sentence of the Synod was ably defended, and as a proof that the heat and animosity raised against the tragedy of *Douglas* and its supporters was artificial and local, the sentence of the Synod was affirmed by 117 to 39. When it was over, Primrose, one of my warmest opposers, turned to me, and, shaking hands, " I wish you joy," said he, " of this sentence in your favour ; and if you hereafter choose to go to every play that is acted, I shall take no notice."

Next day, on a proposal which was seconded by George Dempster, my firm friend, the Assembly passed an Act declaratory, forbidding the clergy to countenance the theatre. But Primrose was in the right, for manners are stronger than laws ; and this Act, which was made on recent provocation, was the only Act of the Church of Scotland against the theatre —so was it totally neglected. Although the clergy in Edinburgh and its neighbourhood had abstained from the theatre because it gave offence, yet the more remote clergymen, when occasionally in town, had almost universally attended the playhouse ; and now that the subject had been solemnly discussed, and all men were convinced that the violent proceedings they had witnessed were the effects of bigotry or jealousy, mixed with party-spirit and cabal, the more distant clergy returned to their usual amusement in the theatre when occasionally in town. It is remarkable, that in the year 1784, when the great actress Mrs. Siddons first appeared in Edinburgh, during the sitting of the General Assembly, that court was obliged to fix all its important business for the alternate days when she did not act, as all the younger members, clergy as well as laity, took their stations in the theatre on those days by three in the afternoon. Drs. Robertson and Blair, though they both visited this great actress in private, often regretted to me that they had not seized the opportunity which was given them, by her superior talents and unexceptionable character, of going openly to the theatre, which would have put an end to all future animadversions on the subject. This conduct of theirs was keeping the reserve of their own imaginary importance to the last ; and their regretting it was very just, for by that time they got no credit for their abstinence, and the struggle between the liberal and the restrained and affected manners of the clergy had been long at an end, by my having finally stood my ground, and been so well supported by so great a majority in the Church.

Of the many exertions I and my friends have made for the credit and interest of the clergy of the Church of Scotland, there was none more meritorious or of better effects than this. The laws of the Church were sufficiently strict to prevent persons of conduct really criminal from entering into it ; and it was of great importance to discriminate the artificial virtues and vices, formed by ignorance and superstition, from those that are real, lest the continuance of such a bar should have given check to the rising liberality of the young scholars, and prevented those of better birth or more ingenious minds from entering into the profession.

One of the chief actors in this farce suffered most for the duplicity of his conduct, for he who was at the head of the Moderate party, through jealousy or bad temper, having with some of his friends headed the party against the tragedy of *Douglas*, his followers in the Highlands and remoter parts, of the Moderate party, were so much offended with his hypocritical conduct, as they called it, that they left him ever after, and joined with those whom he had taken so much pain to disgrace, whilst he and the other old leaders themselves united with their former opponents.*

Mr. Alexander Wedderburn, afterwards Lord Chancellor and Earl of Roslyn, not having come down time enough to speak or vote in the cause (by design or not is more than I know), but appearing on the day after, took an opportunity to give Peter Cuming a very complete dressing. Peter was chaplain to Lord Grange for some years before he was settled at Kirknewton, and after my father at Lochmaben, from whence he was brought to Edinburgh.

With respect to Webster, best known at that time by the designation of Dr. Bonum Magnum, his Proteus-like character seldom lost by any transaction, and in this case he was only acting his natural part,

* It was soon after this that the leadership of the Church passed from Cuming to Robertson.—J. H. B.

which was that of running down all indecencies in clergymen but those of the table, and doing mischief, like a monkey, for its own satisfaction.

One event was curious in the sequel. Mr. John Home, who was the author of the tragedy, and of all the mischief consequent upon it—while his Presbytery of Haddington had been from time to time obstructed in their designs by the good management of Stedman, Robertson, and Bannatine, and were now preparing in earnest to carry on a prosecution against him—on the 7th of June that year gave in a demission of his office, and withdrew from the Church, without the least animadversion on his conduct, which threw complete ridicule on the opposite party, and made the flame which had been raised against me, appear hypocritical and odious to the last degree.

Mr. Home, after the great success of his tragedy of *Douglas* in Edinburgh, went to London early in 1757, and had his tragedy acted in Covent Garden * (for Garrick, though now his friend, could not possibly let it be performed in his theatre after having pronounced it unfit for the stage), where it had great success. This tragedy still maintains its ground, has been more frequently acted, and is more popular, than any tragedy in the English language.

After John Home resigned his charge, he and Adam Ferguson retired to a lodging at Braid for three months to study, where they were very busy. During

* Covent Garden Theatre was at that time under the management of Rich.

that time, Mrs. Kinloch of Gilmerton was brought to
bed of her eighth child, and died immediately after.
This was a very great loss to her family of five sons
and three daughters, as her being withdrawn from
the care of their education accounts better for the
misconduct and misery of four of her sons, than the
general belief of the country that the house of Gilmerton could never thrive after the injustice done to
their eldest son by Sir Francis and his wife and their
son David, who was involved in their guilt, and was
made heir to the estate instead of his brother. These
superstitious notions, however ill founded, may sometimes, perhaps, check the doing of atrocious deeds.
But what shall we say when Sir Francis, who succeeded his father Sir David, survived him only a few
days, though he was the most able, the most ingenious, the most worthy and virtuous young man of the
whole county to which he belonged, and died by
fratricide—a crime rare everywhere, and almost unknown in this country.*   No greater misfortune can
befall any family, when children are in their infancy,
than the loss of a mother of good sense and dignity of
manners.

Home being very busy with some of his dramatic
works, and not having leisure to attend Sir David in
his affliction, which was sincere, applied to me to make
an excursion with him into the north of England for

* Sir Archibald Kinloch was brought to trial in 1795 for the
murder of his elder brother Sir Francis, whom he shot with a pistol
in the family mansion of Gilmerton. The verdict of the jury
sustained a plea of insanity. See *State Trials*, xxv. 891.

a week or two to amuse him.   I consented, and when
I went to Gilmerton by concert, I found that the
baronet had conjoined two other gentlemen to the
party—my friend Mr. Baron Grant, and Mr. Mont·
gomery, afterwards Chief-Baron and Sir James, who
was my friend ever after.   Those two gentlemen were
on horseback, and Sir David and I in his post-chaise,
a vehicle which had but recently been brought into
Scotland, as our turnpike roads were but in their infancy.   We went no farther than Sir John Hall's, at
Dunglass, the first day ; and as we pretended to be
inquiring into the state of husbandry, we made very
short journeys, turning aside to see anything curious
in the mode of improvement of land that fell in our
way, sometimes staying all night in inns, and sometimes in gentlemen's houses, as they fell in our way ;
for Sir David was well known to many of the North-
umbrians for his hospitality and skill in cattle.   We
went no farther than Newcastle and its environs, and
returned after a fortnight's very agreeable amusement.   On this expedition I made some very agreeable acquaintance, of which I afterwards availed
myself,—Ralph Carr, an eminent merchant, still alive
(August 1804), and his brother-in-law Mr. Withrington, styled " the honest attorney of the north," and
his son John, an accomplished young man, who died
a few years ago, and was the representative of the
ancient family of that name.

   Some time this summer, after a convivial meeting,
Dr. Wight and I were left alone for an hour or two

with Alexander Wedderburn, who opened himself to us as much as he was capable of doing to anybody, and the impression he left corresponded with the character he had among his intimates.

It was in the end of this year that I was introduced to Archibald, Duke of Argyle, who usually passed some days at Brunstane, Lord Milton's seat, as he went to Inverary and returned. It was on his way back to London that I was sent for one Sunday morning to come to Brunstane to dine that day with the Duke. That I could not do, as I had to do duty in my own church in the afternoon, and dinner in those days was at two o'clock. I went up in the evening, when the Duke was taking his nap as usual, in an elbow-chair, with a black silk cap over his eyes. There was no company but Lord and Lady Milton, Mr. Fletcher, and the young ladies, with William Alstone, who was a confidential and political secretary of Milton's.

After a little, I observed the Duke lift up his cap, and seeing a stranger in the room, he pulled it over his eyes again, and beckoned Miss Fletcher to him, who told him who I was. In a little while he got up, and advancing to me, and taking me by the hand, said he " was glad to see me, but that, between sleeping and waking, he had taken me for his cousin, the Earl of Home, who I still think you resemble ; but that could not be, for I know that he is at Gibraltar." When we returned to our seats, Mally Fletcher whispered me that *my bread was baken*, for that Lord Home was one of his greatest favourites. This I laughed at, for the old gentleman had said that as an apology for his having done what he might think not quite polite in calling Mally Fletcher to him, and not taking any notice of me for a minute or two afterwards. The good opinion of that family was enough to secure me a favourable reception at first, and I knew he would not like me worse for having stood a battle with, and beat, the Highflyers of our Church, whom he abhorred ; for he was not so accessible to Peter Cuming as Lord Milton was, whom he tried to persuade that his having joined the other party was out of tenderness to me, for it was the intention of the Highflyers to depose me if he had not moderated their counsels. But I had a friend behind the curtain in his daughter, Miss Betty, whom he used to take out in the coach with him alone, to settle his mind when he was in any doubt or perplexity ; for, like all other ministers, he was surrounded with intrigue and deceit. Ferguson was, besides, now come into favour with him, for his dignified and sententious manner of talking had pleased him no less than John Home's pleasantry and unveiled flattery. Milton had a mind sufficiently acute to comprehend Ferguson's profound speculations, though his own forte did not lie in any kind of philosophy, but the knowledge of men, and the management of them, while Ferguson was his admiring scholar in those articles. He had been much teased about the tragedy of *Douglas*, for

Cuming had still access to him at certain hours by the political back-door from Gray's Close, and had alarmed him much, especially immediately after the publication of my pamphlet, *An Argument, etc.*, which had irritated the wild brethren so much, said Peter, that he could not answer for what mischief might follow. When he had been by such means kept in a very frightful humour, he came up into the drawing-room, where David Hume was, with John and Ferguson and myself ; on David's saying something, with his usual good-humour, to smooth his wrinkly brow, Milton turned to him with great asperity, and said that he had better hold his peace on the subject, for it was owing to him, and keeping company with him, that such a clamour was raised. David made no reply, but soon after took his hat and cane, and left the room, never more to enter the house, which he never did, though much pains was taken afterwards, for Milton soon repented, and David would have returned, but Betty Fletcher opposed it, rather foregoing his company at their house than suffer him to degrade himself—such was the generous spirit of that young lady. Had it not been for Ferguson and her, John Home and I would have been expelled also.

Early in the year 1758 my favourite in the house of Brunstane changed her name, for on the 6th of February she was married to Captain John Wedderburn of Gosford, much to the satisfaction of Lord Milton and all her friends, as he was a man of superior

character, had then a good fortune and the prospect
of a better, which was fulfilled not long afterwards
when he succeeded to the title and estate of Pitferran
by the name of Sir John Halkett. As I was frequently at Brunstane about this time, I became the
confidant of both the parties, and the bride was
desirous to have me to tie the nuptial knot. But
this failed through Lord Milton's love of order, which
made him employ the parish minister, Bennet of
Duddingston. This she wrote me with much regret
on the morning of her marriage ; but added, that as
on that day she would become mistress of a house of
her own, she insisted that I should meet her there,
and receive her when she entered the house of Gosford.

About the end of February or beginning of
March this year, I went to London with my eldest
sister, Margaret, to get her married with Dr. Dickson, M.D.* It is to be noted that we could get no
four-wheeled chaise till we came to Durham, those
conveyances being then only in their infancy,—the
two-wheeled close chaise, which had been used for
some time, and was called an Italian chaise, having
been found very inconvenient. Turnpike roads were
only in their commencement in the north. Dr. Dickson, with a friend, met us at Stilton. We arrived
safe at my aunt Lyon's in New Bond Street, she being
then alive, as well as her sister, Mrs. Paterson. To
the proper celebration of the marriage there were
three things wanting—a licence, a parson, and a

* See above, p. 215.

best maid. In the last, the Honourable Miss Nelly Murray, Lord Elibank's sister, afterwards Lady Stewart, and still alive in September 1804, offered her services, which did us honour, and pleased my two aunts very much, especially Mrs. Lyon, whose head was constantly swimming with vanity, which even her uncommon misfortune, after having fulfilled the utmost wish of ambition, had not cured. A licence was easily bought at Doctors' Commons, and Dr. John Blair, afterwards a prebend of Westminster, my particular friend, was easily prevailed with to secure the use of a church and perform the ceremony. This business being put successfully over, and having seen my sister and her husband into lodgings in the city till their house was ready, I took up my abode at my aunts', and occasionally at John Home's lodging in South Audley Street, which he had taken to be near Lord Bute, who had become his great friend and patron, having introduced him to the Prince of Wales, who had settled on him a pension of £100 per annum.

CHAPTER IX

DR. ROBERTSON having come to London at this time
to offer his *History of Scotland* for sale, where he had
never been before, we went to see the lions together,
and had for the most part the same acquaintance.
Dr. William Pitcairn, a very respectable physician in
the city, and a great friend of Dr. Dickson's, was a
cousin of Dr. Robertson's, whose mother was a Pitcairn ; we became very intimate with him.   Drs.
Armstrong and Orme were also of their society.   Pitcairn was a very handsome man, a little turned of
fifty, of a very gentlemanly address.   When he
settled first in London he was patronised by an Alderman Behn, who, being a Jacobite, and not doubting
that Pitcairn was of the same side, as he had travelled
with Duke Hamilton, he set him up as a candidate
for Bartholomew's Hospital.   During the canvass the
Alderman came to the Doctor, and asked him with
impatient heat if it was true that he was the son of
a Presbyterian minister in Scotland,* which Pitcairn

* His father was the Rev. David Pitcairn, minister of Dysart.
A ward in St. Bartholomew's Hospital is named after Dr. Pitcairn.

not being able to deny, the other conjured him to conceal that circumstance like murder, otherwise it would
infallibly blow them up.   He was elected physician to
that hospital, and soon rose to great business in the
city.

Dr. Pitcairn was a bachelor, and lived handsomely,
but chiefly entertained young Scotch physicians who
had no establishment. Of those, Drs. Armstrong and
Dickson were much with him.   As our connections
drew Robertson and me frequently to the city before
my sister's house was ready, by earnest invitation we
both took up our lodging at his house. We never saw
our landlord in the morning, for he went to the hospital
before eight o'clock ; but his housekeeper had orders
to ask us at breakfast if we intended to dine there, and
to tell us when her master was expected.   The Doctor
always returned from his round of visits before three,
which was his hour of dinner, and quite happy if he
found us there. Exactly at five his chariot came to the
door to carry him out on his afternoon visits. We sat
as long as we liked at table, and drunk excellent claret.
He returned soon after eight o'clock ; if he found his
company still together, which was sometimes the case,
he was highly pleased.   He immediately entered into
our humour, ate a bit of cold meat, drank a little wine,
and went to bed before ten o'clock.   This was a very
uncommon strain of hospitality, which, I am glad to
record, on repeated trials, never was exhausted.   He
lived on in the same manner till 1782, when he was past
eighty; and when I was in London for the last time, he

was then perfectly entire, and made his morning tour on foot. I dined once with him at that period in his own house with a large company of ladies and gentlemen, and at Dr. Hamilton's, his cousin, of St. Martin's Church, on both of which occasions he was remarkably gay. He survived for a year or two longer. Dr. David Pitcairn, the son of his brother the major, who was killed early in the American rebellion, was heir both of his fortune and professional merit.

With Robertson and Home in London I passed the time very agreeably ; for though Home was now entirely at the command of Lord Bute, whose nod made him break every engagement—for it was not given above an hour or two before dinner—yet as he was sometimes at liberty when the noble lord was to dine abroad, like a horse loosened from his stake, he was more sportful than usual. We had Sir David Kinloch likewise, who had come to consult physicians, and Dr. Charles Congalton, who was his attendant. With them we met often at the British. Charles was my old companion, and a more naïf and ingenuous soul never was born. I said to him one day, " Charlie, how do you like the English, now that you have seen them twice for two or three months ? " " I cannot answer your question," replied he, " for I am not acquainted with any of them." "What ! not acquainted !" said I. " Yes," says he, " I have seen half-a-dozen of them calling on Sir David, but I never enter into conversation with the John Bulls, for, to tell you the truth, I don't yet well understand what they say."

The first William Pitt had at this time risen to the zenith of his glory, when Robertson and I, after frequent attempts to hear him speak, when there was nothing passing in the House that called him, we at last heard a debate on the Habeas Corpus Act, which Pitt had new modelled in order to throw a slur on Lord Mansfield, who had taken some liberties, it was alleged, with that law, which made him unpopular. We accordingly took our places in the gallery, and for the first three hours were much disposed to sleep by the dull tedious speeches of two or three lawyers, till at last the Attorney-General, afterwards Lord Camden, rose and spoke with clearness, argument, and eloquence. He was answered ably by Mr. Yorke, Solicitor-General. Dr. Hay, the King's Advocate in Doctors' Commons, spoke next, with a clearness, a force, and brevity, which pleased us much. At length Mr. Pitt rose, and with that commanding eloquence in which he excelled, he spoke for half an hour, with an overpowering force of persuasion more than the clear conviction of argument. He was opposed by several speakers, to none of whom he vouchsafed to make an answer, but to James Oswald of Dunnikier, who was a very able man, though not an eloquent speaker. With all our admiration of Pitt's eloquence, which was surely of the highest order, Robertson and I felt the same sentiment, which was the desire to resist a tyrant, who, like a domineering schoolmaster, kept his boys in order by raising their fears without wasting argument upon them. This haughty manner is necessary, perhaps, in every leader of the House of Commons ; for when he is civil and condescending, he soon loses his authority, and is trampledupon. Is this common to all political assemblies ? or is it only a part of the character of the English in all ordinary political affairs, till they are heated by faction or alarmed by danger, to yield to the statesman who is most assuming ? *

Sir Gilbert Elliot of Minto was at this time one of the Lords of the Admiralty, and we were frequently with him. He was a very accomplished and sensible man, and John Home had not found him a cold friend, as he was supposed to be, for by his means chiefly he had been put under the protection of Lord Bute, a favour which John did not coldly return ; for, on the accession of the Prince of Wales, Home, who was then in full confidence with his lordship, recommended the baronet most effectually to him,—a clear proof of which I saw in a letter from Lord Bute to Home.

Dr. John Blair, who, on account of a certain petulant and wrangling humour, was disliked by many people, particularly by Smollett, in spite of Bob Smith's intimacy with both, had been put about the Duke of York as his mathematical teacher, and was afterwards his secretary ; he also had been recommended to that situation by Sir Gilbert Elliot through Home, and was not ungrateful. Blair was

---

* *James Oswald.* See *Memorials of the Public Life and Character of the Right Hon. James Oswald*, 8vo, 1825.—J. H. B.

a good-natured pleasant fellow, and very agreeable to everybody who could bear his flippancy of speech. He was, indeed, one of the most friendly men in the world, as he showed in many instances, from purchasing a pair of shoes and stockings for any of his old companions, to providing them a settlement for life. He got to be a prebendary in Westminster by the interest of the Duke of York ; and, had his Royal Highness lived, would have been promoted to the bench of bishops. He was senior to J. Home and me, but we were well acquainted at college. He died of the influenza in 1782.*

John Douglas,† who has for some time been Bishop of Salisbury, and who is one of the most able and learned men on that bench, had at this time but small preferment. He had been tutor to Lord Pulteney, and was at this time secretary to Lord Bath, and lived with him, by which means he had acquired a very exact knowledge of the Court, as well as of both Houses of Parliament, and all their connections. I became acquainted with him at this time, and preserved my connection with him, which I valued much, by sundry meetings and frequent correspondence. He is still living, though two years older than me, and much weakened by the gout. His sister, Mrs. Anderson, who at this time kept the

* See above, p. 195.

† Son of a merchant of Pittenweem, Fifeshire, and grandson of the Episcopal Church clergyman who succeeded Bishop Burnet at Saltoun, East Lothian. John Douglas was educated at Dunbar and passed to Oxford where he was a contemporary of Adam Smith.

British Coffeehouse, was, like her brother, a person of superior character.*

Robertson had never seen Smollett, and was very desirous of his acquaintance. By this time the Doctor had retired to Chelsea, and came seldom to town. Home and I, however, found that he came once a-week to Forrest's Coffeehouse, and sometimes dined there ; so we managed an appointment with him on his day, when he agreed to dine with us. He was now become a great man, and being much of a humorist, was not to be put out of his way. Home and Robertson and Smith and I met him there, when he had several of his minions about him, to whom he prescribed tasks of translation, compilation, or abridgment, which, after he had seen, he recommended to the booksellers. We dined together, and Smollett was very brilliant. Having to stay all night, that we might spend the evening together, he only begged leave to withdraw for an hour, that he might give audience to his myrmidons ; we insisted that, if his business [permitted], it should be in the room where we sat. The Doctor agreed, and the authors were introduced, to the number of five, I think, most of whom were soon dismissed. He kept two, however, to supper, whispering to us that he believed they would amuse us, which they certainly did, for they were curious characters.

* In Wodrow's letters we read that the son of the Archbishop of St. Andrews (Bishop of Argyll and Glasgow), who died in 1704, was master of the Beau's Coffeehouse in Edinburgh.

We passed a very pleasant and joyful evening. When we broke up, Robertson expressed great surprise at the polished and agreeable manners and the great urbanity of his conversation. He had imagined that a man's manners must bear a likeness to his books, and as Smollett had described so well the characters of ruffians and profligates, that he must, of course, resemble them. This was not the first instance we had of the rawness, in respect of the world, that still blunted our sagacious friend's observations.

As Ferguson had one day in the week when he could be in town, we established a club at a coffee-house in Saville Row or Sackville Street, where we could meet him at dinner, which we did every Wednesday at three o'clock. There were J. Home, and Robertson, and Wedderburn, and Jack Dalrymple, and Bob Adam, Ferguson, and myself. Wedderburn brought with him an attorney of the name of Dagg, a little odd-looking silent fellow to be sure, whom none of us had ever seen before, and about whom Wedderburn had not condescended to explain himself. Somebody was appointed to talk to him, and to express the uneasiness of the club at his bringing an utter stranger among them. His answer was, that Dagg was a very important friend of his, who was extremely desirous to meet that company, and that he would answer for his silence and discretion. He added that he prayed the club to admit him, for he learned more from him of the forms of English law, in his walk from and re-

turn to the Temple, than he could do by a week's
reading.   This excuse was admitted, though some of
us thought it a lame one, and that it smelt of an
assumed superiority that we did not admit of.   As
Ferguson rode back to Harrow, we always parted
between five and six o'clock ; and it will hardly be
now believed that our reckoning never exceeded 5s.
a-piece.   We had a very good dinner, and plenty of
punch, etc., though no claret, for that sum.

Having met, we generally went that night to Drury
Lane Theatre, Garrick being in town.   I had frequent
opportunities of being in company with this celebrated actor, of whom Mr. Home was now in full
possession, though he had rejected his tragedy of
Douglas as totally unfit for the stage.   I am afraid it
was not his own more mature judgment that brought
him round, but his idolatry to the rising sun, for he
had observed what a hold Home had got of Lord Bute,
and, by his means, of the Prince of Wales.   As Garrick's vanity and interestedness had made him digest
the mortification of seeing *Douglas* already become
the most popular play on the stage, so John Home's
facility, and the hopes of getting him to play in his
future tragedies, made him forgive Garrick's former
want of taste and judgment, and they were now become the greatest friends in the world.   If anything
had been wanting to complete Garrick's conquest of
Home, it was making choice of him as his second in
a quarrel he had with Calcraft (for John was very
heroic), which never came to a duel, as well as several

other quarrels of the same kind, and with the same issue, in which John was chosen second.

Garrick, though not of an understanding of the first, nor of the highest cultivated mind, had great vivacity and quickness, and was very entertaining company. Though vanity was his prominent feature, and a troublesome and watchful jealousy the constant visible guard of his reputation to a ridiculous degree, yet his desire to oblige, his want of arrogance, and the delicacy of his mimicry, made him very agreeable. He had no affected reserve, but, on the least hint, would start up at any time and give the company one of his best speeches. As Garrick had been in Dublin when I was in London in 1746, I assiduously attended him at this time, and saw him in all his principal parts, both in tragedy and comedy. He used to say himself, that he was more at home in comedy than in tragedy, and I was of his opinion. I thought I could conceive something more perfect in tragedy, but in comedy he completely filled up my ideas of perfection. There may be a deception in this, for every well-educated person has formed to himself some idea of the characters, both in ancient and modern tragedy, and if the actor falls short of that, he is thought to be deficient in judgment : whereas comedy being an imitation of living manners, as they rise in succession among inferior orders of men, the spectator can have formed no rule or standard of judgment previous to the representation, but must accept of the picture the actor gives him, and must approve of it, if it is lively, though it should not be true.

Garrick was so friendly to John Home that he gave a dinner to his friends and companions at his house at Hampton, which he did but seldom. He had told us to bring golf clubs and balls that we might play at that game on Molesly Hurst. We accordingly set out in good time, six of us in a landau. As we passed through Kensington, the Coldstream regiment were changing guard, and, on seeing our clubs, they gave us three cheers in honour of a diversion peculiar to Scotland ; so much does the remembrance of one's native country dilate the heart, when one has been some time absent. The same sentiment made us open our purses, and give our countrymen wherewithal to drink the " Land o' Cakes." Garrick met us by the way, so impatient he seemed to be for his company. There were John Home, and Robertson, and Wedderburn,* and Robert and James Adam, and Colonel David Wedderburn,†who was killed when commander of the army in Bombay, in the year [1773]. He was held by his companions to be in every respect as clever and able a man as his elder brother the Chancellor, with a much more gay, popular, and social temper.

Immediately after we arrived, we crossed the river to the golfing-ground, which was very good. None of the company could play but John Home

---

* Afterwards Lord Loughborough, first Earl of Roslyn.
† Second son of Peter Wedderburn, Lord Chesterhall, and younger brother of Lord Chancellor Loughborough.

and myself, and Parson Black from Aberdeen, who, being chaplain to a regiment during some of the Duke of Cumberland's campaigns, had been pointed out to his Royal Highness as a proper person to teach him the game of chess : the Duke was such an apt scholar that he never lost a game after the first day ; and he recompensed Black for having beat him so cruelly, by procuring for him the living of Hampton, which is a good one.   We returned and dined sumptuously, Mrs. Garrick, the only lady, now grown fat, though still very lively, being a woman of uncommon good sense, and now mistress of English, was in all respects most agreeable company.*   She did not seem at all to recognise me, which was no wonder, at the end of twelve years, having thrown away my bag-wig and sword, and appearing in my own grisly hairs, and in parson's clothes ; nor was I likely to remind her of her former state.†

Garrick had built a handsome temple,‡ with a

* When a widow, Mrs. Garrick had twice the offer of marriage from Lord Monboddo during one of his lordship's periodical visits to London.—WALPOLE.

† See above, p. 192.

‡ " John and I are just going to Garrick's [at Hampton] with a grove of cypresses in our hands, like the Kentish men at the Conquest.   He has built a temple to his master Shakespeare and I am going to adorn the outside, since his modesty would not let me decorate it within, as I proposed, with these mottoes :—

> *Quod spiro et placeo—si placeo, tuum est.*
> That I spirit have and nature,
> That sense breathes in every feature,
> That I please, if please I do,—
> Shakespeare,—all I owe to you."—WALPOLE.

statue of Shakespeare in it, in his lower garden, on the banks of the Thames, which was separated from the upper one by a high-road, under which there was an archway which united the two gardens. Garrick, in compliment to Home, had ordered the wine to be carried to this temple, where we were to drink it under the shade of the copy of that statue to which Home had addressed his pathetic verses on the rejection of his play. The poet and the actor were equally gay, and well pleased with each other, on this occasion, with much respect on the one hand, and a total oblivion of animosity on the other; for vanity is a passion that is easy to be entreated, and unites freely with all the best affections. Having observed a green mount in the garden, opposite the archway, I said to our landlord, that while the servants were preparing the collation in the temple I would surprise him with a stroke at the golf, as I should drive a ball through his archway into the Thames once in three strokes. I had measured the distance with my eye in walking about the garden, and accordingly, at the second stroke, made the ball alight in the mouth of the gateway, and roll down the green slope into the river. This was so dexterous that he was quite surprised, and begged the club of me by which such a feat had been performed. We passed a very agreeable afternoon; and it is hard to say which were happier, the landlord and landlady, or the guests.

There was a club in London where Robertson and

I never failed to attend, as we were adopted members while we stayed in town. It was held once a week in the British Coffeehouse, at eight in the evening ; the members were Scotch physicians from the city and Court end of the town. Of the first set were Pitcairn, Armstrong, Orme, and Dickson ; of the second were William Hunter, Clephan, Mr Graham of Pall Mall, etc.—all of them very agreeable men ; Clephan especially was one of the most sensible, learned, and judicious men I ever knew—an admirable classical scholar and a fine historian. He often led the conversation, but it was with an air of modesty and deference to the company, which added to the weight of all he said. Hunter was gay and lively to the last degree, and often came in to us at nine o'clock fatigued and jaded. He had had no dinner, but supped on a couple of eggs, and drank his glass of claret ; for though we were a punch club, we allowed him a bottle of what he liked best. He repaid us with the brilliancy of his conversation. His toast was " May no English nobleman venture out of the world without a Scottish physician, as I am sure there are none who venture in." He was a famous lecturer on anatomy. Robertson and I expressed a wish to be admitted one day. He appointed us a day, and gave us one of the most elegant, clear, and brilliant lectures on the eye that any of us had ever heard. One instance I must set down of the fallacy of medical prediction—it was this : Dr. Hunter, by his attendance on Lady Esther Pitt, had frequent opportunities of seeing the great orator when he was ill of the gout, and thought so ill of his constitution that he said more than once to us, with deep regret, that he did not think the great man's life worth two years' purchase ; and yet Mr. Pitt lived for twenty years, for he did not give way to fate till 1778.

As soon as my sister got into her house in a court in Aldermansbury, Dr. Dickson and she gave a dinner to my friends, with two or three of his. There were Doctors Pitcairn, Armstrong, Smollett, and Orme, together with Dr. Robertson, John Blair, Home and myself. We passed an exceedingly pleasant day, although Smollett had given Armstrong a staggering blow at the beginning of dinner, by asking him some questions about his nose, which was still patched, on account of his having run it through the side-glass of his chariot when somebody came up to speak to him.   Armstrong was naturally glumpy, and this, I was afraid, would have silenced him all day, which it might, had not Smollett called him familiarly John soon after his joke on his nose ; but he knew that Smollett loved and respected him, and soon recovered his good-humour, and became brilliant.   My sister, who had one lady with her— one of Pitcairn's nieces, I believe—was happy and agreeable, and highly pleasing to her guests, who confessed they had seldom seen such a superior woman.

There was a friend of Dickson's, a Mr. Jackson, a Dumfries man and an Irish factor, as they are called, who was a great humorist, who, though he had no

carriage, kept six hunting-horses. This man offered
to mount us on his horses, and go with us to Windsor.
After a breakfast-dinner at his partner's, we set out
on the 16th day of April, the warmest that had been
that season. As the great road was very disagreeable, Jackson, who knew the environs of London
better than most people, as he belonged to a hunt,
took us through green lanes as soon as he could, and,
giving us a little wine and water when he pleased,
which was, he said, whenever he came to good port,
he landed us at Staines Bridge, in a very good inn
across the bridge. His servant, who rode an unruly
horse, had been thrown from him half an hour before
we reached Staines. He was very much hurt about
the head, and with difficulty we brought him along at
a slow pace. When we arrived, Jackson sent immediately for the nearest surgeon, who was a Mr. Green.
This man examined the servant, and found he was
not dangerously hurt, and Jackson invited him to
stay supper, which he did, and turned out a very
sensible conversible man. He spoke English so well
that we could not have detected him to be a Scotchman, far less an Aberdeensman, which he was ; but
he had gone very young into the navy as surgeon's-
mate, and had entirely lost his mother tongue—almost the only instance I ever knew of any one from
that shire. There was a poor Scotch Presbyterian,
who had a very small living ; Jackson had a small
present of two guineas to give him, for the humorist
was not ungenerous. He sent for him in the morn-

ing, and promised him a sermon in his meeting-house, for it was Sunday, and kept him to breakfast. I had been prepared to do this duty, for Jackson and I slept in the same room, and he had requested it as a favour, as he said the meeting and the audience were very poor indeed. I was dressed, and went down to breakfast, and was introduced to Mr. Coldstream. Soon afterwards came Robertson, undressed, and with his night-cap on, and, being introduced to Coldstream, took no further notice of him (not his usual manner), and breakfasted in silence. When the minister took his leave, he called Jackson aside, and said he hoped he remembered he never employed any of the people called Methodists. This was resolute in a man who had a wife and four children, and only £20 a-year, to a gentleman who had just made him a present of two guineas. Jackson assured him that none of us were Methodists, but that I was the person he had engaged to preach. I made Robertson's being taken for a Methodist a lasting joke against him.

We went to the meeting-house at the hour of eleven, the entry to which was over a pretty large dunghill. Although the congregation was reinforced by two officers of the Grey dragoons, and by a corporal and an officer's man, with Jackson's man with his head bound up, with the Doctor and Jackson and Coldstream and his wife, they amounted only to twenty-three. There were two brothers, Scotchmen, clothiers, who were there, who invited us to dinner. We repaired to them at one o'clock, and after walking round their garden, and being much delighted with two swans swimming in the Thames, whom they had attached to them by kindness, we sat down to an excellent citizen-like dinner, and drank some excellent port wine. Robertson and I bespoke a piece of parson's grey cloth of their making, which they sent to Scotland before us, and which turned out the best we ever had. We divided it among our friends. Before five o'clock we mounted our horses by order of our conductor, and rode to Windsor Forest, where, in spite of the warm weather before, we found the frost hard enough to bear our horses. We returned without going into Windsor. Next day we went there time enough to see the castle and all its curiosities, and to go down to Eton, after which we dined at an inn and rode back to Staines, making a circuit round the great park. Much to our satisfaction, we found Dr. Green waiting us, whom Jackson had appointed to meet us.

Jackson wished us to take a circuitous ride and see everything down the Thames to London ; but as we were engaged with a party of friends to dine at Billingsgate on fish of the season, we took leave of Mr. Jackson, and left him to come at his leisure, while we made the best of our way down the Thames, and halted only at Richmond, where Robertson had never been.

We arrived in time to meet our friends at the Gun, where Dr. Dickson had provided a choice dinner of all the varieties of fish then in season, at the moderate price of twenty-five shillings, one crown of which was paid for smelts. We were a company of fifteen or sixteen, whose names I can't exactly remember, but when I say that there were Sir David Kinloch, James Veitch (Lord Elliock), Sir Robert Keith, then only a captain in the Scotch Dutch, Robertson, Home, etc., I need not say that we were gay and jovial. An incident contributed not a little to our mirth. Charles Congalton, who happened to sit next to Sir David, our preses, it was observed, never filled above a thimbleful in his glass, when being asked the reason, he said he could not drink any of their London port, there was such a *drawing-togetherness* in it. " Ring the bell, Charlie," said our preses, " and we will learn if we can't get a bottle of claret for you." The bell was rung, the claret came, and was pronounced very good by the Baronet and his doctor. The whole company soon joined in that liquor, without which no Scotch gentleman in those days could be exhilarated. Bob Keith sung all his ludicrous songs, and repeated all his comic verses, and gave us a foretaste of that delightful company which he continued to be to the end of his days. His cousin, Charles Dalrymple, was only behind him in humorous description and naïve remark—as much only as he was in age and the habits of company. Our reckoning by this means, however, turned out, instead of five shillings and sixpence, as Dickson had supposed, to be three times that sum. The Baronet and Doctor were to set out in a few days to France, on their way to Barege.

I shall here mention an anecdote which struck me as a proof of the wonderful carelessness of physicians. Supping one night with Duncan Forbes, Sir David, Lord Elliock, and sundry physicians, while four of us were playing at whist, Lord Elliock took up a book, and after reading a while called out, " Sir David, here is your case, and a perfect cure for it, that I find in this book." He then read an account of the great effect of the waters of Barege, in the south of France, for such complaints as the Baronet laboured under. " Have you heard of this before, Sir David ? " " No, never," answered he. " Is it new to the Faculty ? " said he to Armstrong, who was sitting near him. " No," replied the crusty Doctor, " but we never thought of prescribing it, as we knew that he was such a coward that he would rather be damned by a fistula than cross the Channel in a packet-boat, especially in time of a French war." Sir David, having his pride irritated by this attack, did go to Barege and completed a cure which had been made by Dr. Ward.

As I had been introduced to the Duke of Argyle in the autumn before in Scotland, I went sometimes to his evening parties, which were very pleasant. He let in certain friends every night about seven o'clock, when, after tea and coffee, there were parties at sixpenny whist, his Grace never playing higher. About nine there was a sideboard of cold victuals and wine, to which everybody resorted in his turn. There was seldom or ever any drinking—never, indeed, but when some of his favourite young men came in, such as

Alexander Lord Eglinton, William Lord Home, etc., when the old gentleman would rouse himself and call for burgundy and champagne, and prolong the feast to a late hour. In general the company parted at eleven. There could not be a more rational way of passing the evening, for the Duke had a wide range of knowledge, and was very open and communicative.

The Right Honourable Charles Townshend, my old friend, had married Lady Dalkeith, the Duke of Buccleuch's mother. Home, who was become intimate with him, took me there one morning, after having told him I was in town, and intended to call. He received me with open arms, and was perfectly familiar, but not a hint of having seen me before. He held the same demeanour to Jack Campbell, Lord Stonefield, who had married one of Lord Bute's sisters ; and in spite of our intimacy afterwards in Scotland, he never made the most distant allusion to anything that had happened at Leyden. The Duke of Buccleuch, and his brother Campbell Scott, were in town for the Easter holidays. Mr. Scott was much handsomer and more forward than the Duke, who was at a table in the room where there were some books. The young Duke, then not twelve years of age, was turning over the leaves of a book. " Come along, Duke," says Charles—" I see what you would be at, silent as you are ; show the gentleman that dedication you are so fond of." The Duke slipt down the book on the table, and blushed to the eyes, retiring a step or two from it. I took up the book, and soon saw it was

24

Barclay the schoolmaster's Latin Grammar, which he had dedicated to his patron. " The Duke," says I, " need not be ashamed of this dedication, for the author of it is one of the best schoolmasters and grammarians of any in Scotland, and has brought the school at Dalkeith to its former name and lustre." This reassured the young man, and he smiled with some satisfaction. Little did I think at that time that I should live to see his grace the most respected and the most deservedly popular of any nobleman in Scotland. A few days after this we dined with Mr. Townshend and the Countess, and one or two gentlemen, but the boys had returned to school.

The clergy of Scotland, being under apprehensions that the window-tax would be extended to them, had given me in charge to state our case to some of the ministers, and try to make an impression in our favour. Sir Gilbert Elliot listened to me, and was friendly ; Marchmont pretended not to understand my statement, and was dry. But the only man who really understood the business, and seemed ready to enter into it with zeal was Jeremiah Dyson,* who, having been a Dissenter, and two years at the University

* Dyson, although left considerable wealth by his father, accepted a junior clerkship in the House of Commons, and when the principal clerkship became vacant, paid £6000 for the position. It was customary then for the principal to appoint a deputy and assistants and to recoup his payment from them. But Dyson condemned the practice and appointed his subordinates without exacting a fee. He resigned the clerkship and became a member of Parliament, occupying several positions under different governments.

of Edinburgh, and withal very acute, perfectly comprehended my argument, and was willing to assist in procuring an exemption. Without Robert Dundas, then Lord Advocate, nothing, however, could be done. I waited on him, and was received in his usual way, with frankness and familiarity enough ; but he did not think he could do anything, but deferred saying much about it till some future day when he would have some friends with me to dinner, and talk over the affair. This cold or rather haughty reception, added to some very slighting or calumnious sayings of his, both about Robertson and me, provoked us not a little, and revived the resentment we felt at his unhandsome behaviour about the tragedy of *Douglas*.

Our time drew near for returning, which we were to do on horseback, and with that we set about furnishing ourselves with horses. Home had his Piercy in town, and James Adam (who was to be our companion) had one also, so that Robertson and I only were to be provided, which we did without loss of time. We had some inclination to be introduced to Lord Bute, which John promised to do ; and for Robert Adam also, who could derive more benefit from it than any of us. Robert had been three years in Italy, and, with a first-rate genius for his profession, had seen and studied everything, and was in the highest esteem among foreign artists. From the time of his return—viz. in February or March 1758—may be dated a very remarkable improvement in building and furniture, and even stoneware, in London and

every part of England.*   As John put off the time of
our introduction to his great man, we yielded to a request of our friend Sir David Kinloch to accompany
him on a jaunt he wished to make to Portsmouth.
Home had signified his design to Lord Bute, who had
agreed to his absence for a few days ; and having
obtained a letter from Sir Gilbert Elliot, then a Lord
of the Admiralty, to Lieutenant Brett, clerk of the
cheque at Portsmouth, we set out, the Baronet and
his doctor in a chaise, and we three on horseback. As
it was towards the end of April, and the weather good,
we had a very agreeable journey. We were much
pleased with the diversified beauty of the country,
though not a little surprised with the great extent
of uncultivated heath which we went through. We
viewed with much pleasure and exultation the solid
foundation of the naval glory of Great Britain, in the
amazing extent and richness of the dockyards and
warehouses, etc., and in the grandeur of her fleet in
the harbour and in the Downs. It appeared a new
world to us, and our wonder had not ceased during all
the four days we remained there. We had good
mutton and good wine (claret) at the inn, and, above
all, an additional companion, Mr. Richard Oswald
(he who had so much hand in the peace of Paris long
after), who was a man of great knowledge and ready

* It is scarcely necessary to say that the two Adams, so often
referred to, were the architects of the many public and private
buildings, of some of which an account will be found in their work
called *The Works in Architecture of Robert and James Adam.*—
J. H. B.

conversation. There was a fine fleet of ten ships of the line in the Downs, with the *Royal George* at their head, all ready for sea, and one of our great objects was to get on board that ship, which was always kept in the highest order for the admittance of visitors. This short voyage was proposed every night, but was put off daily, as a landwind came on soon after breakfast. As we were only to stay one day longer, Congalton and I in despair went in the evening to Lieutenant Brett and stated our case to him. He said there was but one remedy, which was for him to ask Sir David and us all to breakfast next morning at eight ; that his dockyard sloop, in which he could sail to America, should be at hand and ready at nine, and that we might get to the *Royal George* not above three miles off, before the mackerel breeze sprung up.

This plan was accordingly put in execution, but it being half-past nine before we got on board, the breeze got up before we reached the fleet ; and the moment it arose, fear and sickness began to operate on our friends, their countenances grew pale, and the poet grew very vociferous for our immediate return. Our pilot, however, held on his course, and assured them that there was not the smallest danger, and that the moment they set their feet in the *Royal George*, their sickness would leave them. Congalton and I were quite disconcerted, and did not know what to do. Brett continued to assert that we might board with the greatest ease, and without the least danger ; but as we approached the ship their fears became so noisy and so unmanly that Brett yielded, and said it would be better to sail round the ship and return, lest the breeze should increase. Dr. Congalton and I were much disappointed, as this was probably the only opportunity we should have of seeing so fine a ship again.

We behoved to yield, however, and, what was remarkable, the moment we set our heads towards land their sickness entirely abated, and they got into spirits—Robertson was the only one of them who had thrown up his breakfast. When we arrived near the harbour, we overtook the *Ramilies*, a ninety-gun ship just entering the port. Mr. Brett proposed that we should go on board her, when we should see her rigging completely manned, a sight that in some degree would compensate our not seeing the *Royal George*. Our friends were delighted with this proposal, and John Home exulted provokingly on the superiority of the sight we were so fortunately going to have. We had no sooner set foot on the deck than an officer came up to us, bawling, " God preserve us ! what has brought the Presbytery of Edinburgh here ? for, damn me, if there is not Willy Robertson, Sandie Carlyle, and John Home come on board." This turned out to be a Lieutenant Neilson, a cousin of Robertson, who knew us all, who gave us a hearty welcome, and carried us to his cabin, and treated us to white wine and salt beef.

The remainder of this day we passed in seeing what we had omitted, particularly the Point after it was dark, or rather towards midnight—a scene of wonder, and even horror, to the civilised. Next day we took our departure, and sleeping a night by the way, as we had done going down, we arrived in London, and prepared in good earnest to set out on our journey north. The day was at last appointed for our being introduced to the great man, and we resolved among ourselves, that if he gave us an invitation to dine with him on an early day, we would stay for it, though contrary to our plan.

John Home's tragedy of *Agis* had been acted this season with tolerably good success, for it ran the nine nights, and the author made some hundreds by it. Garrick had acted the part of Lysander, as he did a year or two later that of Emilius in the *Siege of Aquileia*, which I think superior in merit to *Agis*. I had undertaken to review this play for the *British Magazine* (Smollett's), but had been indolent ; and it now cost me to sit up all night to write it, and I was obliged to give it to the press blotted and interlined, —but they are accustomed to decipher the most difficult hands.

The day came when we were presented to Lord Bute, but our reception was so dry and cold that when he asked when we were to go north, one of us said to-morrow. He received us booted and spurred, which in those days was a certain signal for going a-riding, and an apology for not desiring us to sit down. We very soon took our leave, and no sooner were we out of hearing, than Robert Adam, who was

with us, fell a-cursing and swearing. " What! had he
been presented to all the princes in Italy and France,
and most graciously received, to come and be treated
with such distance and pride by the youngest earl
but one in all Scotland ? "   They were better friends
afterwards, and Robert found him a kind patron,
when his professional merit was made known to him.
When I was riding with Home in Hyde Park a week
before, trying the horse I bought, we met his lordship,
to whom Home then introduced me, and we rode together for half an hour, when I had a very agreeable
chat with his lordship ; but he was a different man
when he received audience.   To dismiss the subject,
however, I believe he was a very worthy and virtuous
man—a man of taste, and a good belles-lettres scholar,
and that he trained up the prince in true patriotic
principles and a love of the constitution, though his
own mind was of the Tory cast, with a partiality to
the family of Stuart, of whom he believed he was
descended.   But he proved himself unfit for the
station he had assumed, being not versatile enough
for a prime minister ; and, though personally brave,
yet void of that political firmness which is necessary
to stand the storms of state. The nobility and gentry
of England had paid court to him with such abject
servility when the accession of his pupil drew near,
and immediately after it took place, that it was no
wonder he should behave to them with haughtiness
and disdain, and with a spirit of domination.   As
soon, however, as he was tried and known, and the

disappointed hopes of the courtiers had restored them to the exercise of their manhood, he showed a wavering and uncertain disposition, which discovered to them that he could be overthrown. The misfortune of great men in such circumstances is, that they have few or no personal friends on whose counsels they can rely. There were two such about him, who enjoyed his confidence and favour, Sir Harry Erskine * and John Home. The first, I believe, was a truly honest man, but his views were not extensive nor his talents great ; the second had better talents, but they were not at all adapted to business. Besides ambition and pride to a high degree, Lord Bute had an insatiable vanity, which nothing could allay but Home's incessant flattery, which being ardent and sincere, and blind and incessant, like that of a passionate lover, pleased the jealous and supercilious mind of the Thane. He knew John to be a man of honour and his friend, and though his discernment pointed out the excess of John's praises, yet his ardour and sincerity made it all take place on a temper and character made

* The second son of Sir John Erskine of Alva, who succeeded to the baronetcy on the death of his elder brother Sir Charles. Sir Harry was Deputy Quartermaster-General of the Forces under his uncle General St. Clair. After his military service he devoted himself to politics and literature. Because of his adhesion to the Leicester House party he was dismissed the service by George II., but restored by George III., who gave him the command of the Royal Scots. He married Miss Wedderburn (see p. 425), sister of Lord Chancellor Loughborough (Earl of Roslyn), and their eldest son subsequently succeeded to the Earldom and property. Sir Harry has been credited with the authorship of '' In the Garb of Old Gaul," but this is disputed.

accessible by vanity. With respect to John himself, his mind and manners had always been the same. He flattered Lord Milton, and even Adam Ferguson and me, as much as he did Lord Bute in the zenith of his power. What demonstrates the artlessness and purity of John's mind was, that he never asked anything for himself, though he had the undisputed ear of the Prime Minister. Even those who envied John for the place of favour he held, exclaimed against the chief for doing so little for the man of his right hand ; and John might have starved on a scanty pension (for he was required to be in attendance in London for more than half the year), had not Ferguson and I taken advantage of a vacancy of an office in Scotland, and pressed Lord Milton to procure the Lord Conservator's place for him, which more than doubled his income.* But though Home was careless of himself, he was warm and active at all times for the interest of his friends, and served a greater number of people effectually than it had been in the power of any private man to do before, some few of whom proved themselves not worthy of his friendship.

We now were to leave London, and make all suitable preparations ; and finding that there was a horse at Donaldson's, at the Orange Tree Inn, which the owner wished to have down to Edinburgh, we undertook to take him with us, and hired a man to ride him and carry our baggage. As there were

---

* The then sinecure office of Conservator of Scots Privileges at Campvere.—J. H. B.

four of us, we found one servant too few, to our great inconveniency. As the Adams were a wonderfully loving family, and their youngest brother James was going down with us, the rest of the sisters and brothers would accompany us as far as Uxbridge (a very needless ceremony, some of us thought); but since we were to be so numerous my sister thought of joining the party. We passed a very cheerful evening in spite of the melancholy parting we had in view. We parted, however, next morning, and we made the best of our way to Oxford, halting for an hour at Bulstrode, a seat of the Duke of Portland's, where we viewed the park, the house, and the chapel, which pleased us much, especially the last, which was ornamented in true taste as a place of worship. The chapel, which is still met with in many noblemen's houses in England, was a mark of the residence of a great family, which was striking and agreeable. It was here that we discovered the truth of what I had often heard, that most of the head-gardeners of English noblemen were Scotch, for on observing to this man that his pease seemed late on the 4th of May, not being then fully in bloom, and that I was certain there were sundry places which I knew in Scotland where they were further advanced, he answered that he was bred in a place that I perhaps did not know that answered this description. This was Newhaills, in my own parish of Inveresk. This man, whose name I have forgot, if it was not Robertson, was not only gardener but land-steward, and had the charge of the whole park and of the estate around it ;—such advantage was there in having been taught writing, arithmetic, and the mensuration of land, the rudiments of which were taught in many of the country schools of Scotland. This man gave us a note to the gardener at Blenheim, who, he told us, was our countryman, and would furnish us with notes to the head-gardeners all the way down.

We arrived at Oxford before dinner, and put up at the Angel Inn. Robertson and Adam, who had never been there before, had everything to see ; Home and I had been there before. John Douglas, who knew we were coming, was passing trials for his degree of D.D., and that very day was in the act of one of his wall-lectures, as they are called, for there is no audience. At that university, it seems, the trial is strict when one takes a Master's or Bachelor's, but slack when you come to the Doctor's Degree ; and *vice versa* at Cambridge. However that be, we found Douglas sitting in a pulpit, in one of their chapels, with not a soul to hear him but three old beggar-women, who came to try if they might get some charity. On seeing us four enter the chapel, he talked to us and wished us away, otherwise he would be obliged to lecture. We would not go away, we answered, as we wished a specimen of Oxford learning ; on which he read two or three verses out of the Greek Testament, and began to expound it in Latin.

We listened for five minutes, and then, telling where we were to dine, we left him to walk about. Douglas came to dinner ; and in the evening Messrs. Foster and Vivian, of Baliol College, came to us to ask us to a collation, to be given us by that society next day. They were well-informed and liberal-minded men, but from them and their conversation we learned that this was far from applying to the generality of the university. We stayed all next day, and passed a very agreeable evening at Baliol College, where several more Fellows were assembled.

Next morning we set out early for Woodstock, where we breakfasted, and went to see Blenheim, a most magnificent park indeed. We narrowly inspected the house and chapel, which, though much cried down by the Tory wits of Queen Anne's reign, appeared to us very magnificent, and worthy of the donors and of the occasion on which it was given. Our companion, James Adam, had seen all the splendid palaces of Italy, and though he did not say that Sir John Vanburgh's design was faultless, yet he said it ill deserved the aspersions laid upon it, for he had seen few palaces where there was more movement, as he called it, than in Blenheim. The extent of the park and the beauty of the water (now a sea almost, as I am told) struck us very much.

From Blenheim we made the best of our way to Warwick, where, as we had been much heated, and were very dusty, we threw off our boots, and washed and dressed ourselves before we walked out. John

Home would not put on his boots again; but in clean stockings and shoes, when he was looking at himself in the glass, and prancing about the room in a truly poetical style, he turned short upon the boot-catch who had brought in our clean boots, and finding the fellow staring at him with seeming admiration, " And am not I a pretty fellow ? " said John. " Ay," says he, " sir," with half a smile. " And who do you take me for ? " said John. " If you binna Jamy Dunlop the Scotch pedlar, I dinna ken wha ye are ; but your ways are very like his." This reply confounded our friend not a little, and he looked still more foolish than Robertson, when Jackson told at Staines that the Dissenting minister took him for a Methodist.

Warwick we found to be a very pleasant old town, finely situated, with a handsome old church. The Castle of Warwick, the seat of the earl of that name, with the park, was truly magnificent, and the priory on the way to it, the seat of Mr. Wise, not unworthy of being viewed. We dined here, and were rather late in getting to Birmingham, where a servant of Mr. Garbett's lay in wait for us at the inn, and conducted us to his house, without letting us enter it. This man, of singular worth and very uncommon ability, with whom Robertson and I were intimately acquainted in Scotland, had anxiously wished us to come his way, with which we complied, not merely to see the wonders of the place, but to gratify him. Six or seven years before this, Dr. Roebuck and he had established a vitriol work at Prestonpans, which succeeded well, and the profits of which encouraged them to undertake the grand ironworks at Carron, which had commenced not long before. Garbett, who was a man of sense and judgment, was much against that great undertaking, as, independent of the profits of the vitriol works, they had not £3000 of stock between them. But the ardent mind of Roebuck carried Garbett away, and he yielded—giving up to his superior genius for great undertakings the dictates of prudence and his own sober judgment. Roebuck, having been bred in the medical school of Edinburgh, had science, and particularly the skill of applying chemistry to the useful arts.

Ironworks were but recent in Scotland, and Roebuck had visited them all, and every station where they could be erected, and had found that Carron was by far the best, which, if they did not occupy immediately, some other company would, and they must remain in the background for ever. This idea dazzled and overpowered the judicious mind of Garbett, which had been contented with the limited project of availing themselves of the populations of Musselburgh and Fisherrow, and with the aid of Lord Milton, to whom I had introduced him, to begin an ironwork on a small scale on the Magdalene Burn, and introducing the manufactures of Birmingham at Fisherrow. This was highly gratifying to Milton, who would have lent his credit, and given the labours of his then active mind, to bring it to perfection.

Samuel Garbett was truly a very extraordinary man. He had been an ordinary worker in brass at Birmingham, and had no education farther than writing and accounts ; but he was a man of great acuteness of genius and extent of understanding. He had been at first distinguished from the common workmen by inventing some stamp for shortening labour. He was soon taken notice of by a Mr. Hollis, a great merchant in London, who employed him as his agent for purchasing Birmingham goods. This brought him into notice and rank among his townsmen ; and the more he was known, the more he was esteemed. Let me observe once for all, that I have known no person but one more of such strong and lively feelings, of such a fair, candid, and honourable heart, and of such quick and ardent conceptions, who still retained the power of cool and deliberate judgment before execution. I had been much in his way when he came first to Prestonpans about the year '51 or '52, and had distinguished him and attracted his notice. He knew all the wise methods of managing men, and was sensible that he could not expect to have the most faithful workmen unless he consulted the minister. To obtain this aid he paid all due respect to my father, and, though of the Church of England, regularly attended the church, and indeed made himself agreeable to the whole parish, high and low. Roebuck, though a scholar and of an inventive genius, was vain and inconstant, and an endless projector, so that the real executive and managing power lay in Garbett.

He received us with open hospitality, and we were soon convinced we were welcome by the cordiality of his wife and daughter (afterwards Mrs. Gascoign), who lodged the whole company but me, who, being their oldest acquaintance, they took the liberty to send to a friend's house. Hitherto they had lived in a very moderate style, but for his Scotch friends Garbett had provided very good claret, and for the time we stayed his table was excellent, though at that time they had only one maid and a blind lad as servants. This last was a wonder, for he did all the work of a man, and even brewed the ale, (but) that of serving at table ; and for this, Garbett [provided] according to the custom of the place, where no man was then ashamed of frugality. He made Patrick Downy, who was then an apprentice, stand at our backs. Patrick afterwards married the maid, who was the mistress's cousin ; was sent down to Prestonpans as an overseer, and was at last taken in as a partner : such was the primitive state of Birmingham and other manufacturing towns, and such encouragement did they then give to industry. *Sed tandem luxuria incubuit.* Few men have I ever known who united together more of the prime qualities of head and heart.

We passed the next day after our arrival in visiting the manufactures at Birmingham, though it was with difficulty I could persuade our poet to stay, by suggesting to him how uncivil his sudden departure would appear to our kind landlord. I got him, however, to go through the tedious detail, till at last

25

he said " that it seemed there as if God had created man only for making buttons." Next morning, after breakfast, Home set out for Admiral Smith's, his old friend, who, being a natural son of Sir Thomas Lyttleton, had built himself a good house in the village close by Hagley, the seat of Lord Lyttleton. We who were left, passed the day in seeing what remained unseen at Birmingham, particularly the Baskerville press, and Baskerville himself, who was a great curiosity. His house was a quarter of a mile from the town, and, in its way, handsome and elegant. What struck us most was his first kitchen, which was most completely furnished with everything that could be wanted, kept as clean and bright as if it had come straight from the shop, for it was used, and the fineness of the kitchen was a great point in the family ; for they received their company, and there were we entertained with coffee and chocolate. Baskerville was on hands with his folio Bible at this time, and Garbett insisted on being allowed to subscribe for Home and Robertson. Home's absence afflicted him, for he had seen and heard of the tragedy of *Douglas*. Robertson hitherto had no name, and the printer said bluntly that he would rather have one subscription to his work of a man like Mr. Home, than an hundred ordinary men. He dined with us that day, and acquitted himself so well that Robertson pronounced him a man of genius, while James Adam and I thought him but a prating pedant.

On agreement with John Home, we set out for Lord

Lyttleton's, and were to take the Leasowes, Shenstone's place, in our way.   Shenstone's was three or
four miles short of Lyttleton's.   We called in there on
our way, and walked over all the grounds, which were
finely laid out, and which it is needless to describe.
The want of water was obvious, but the ornaments
and mottoes, and names of the groves, were appro-
priate.   Garbett was with us, and we had [seen] most
of the place before Shenstone was dressed, who was
going to dine with Admiral Smith.   We left one or
two of the principal walks for him to show us.   At
the end of a high walk, from whence we saw far into
Gloster and Shrop shires, I met with what struck me
most,—that was an emaciated pale young woman,
evidently in the last stage of a consumption.   She
had a most interesting appearance, with a little girl
of nine or ten years old, who had led her there.   Shenstone went up and stood for some time conversing
with her, till we went to the end of the walk and returned : on some of us taking an interest in her appearance, he said she was a very sickly neighbour,
to whom he had lent a key to his walks, as she delighted in them, though now not able to use it much.
The most beautiful inscription he afterwards wrote
to the memory of Maria Dolman put me in mind of
this young woman ; but, if I remember right, she was
not the person.   It is to me the most elegant and
interesting of all Shenstone's works.

We set all out for Admiral Smith's, and had Mr.
Shenstone to ride with us.   His appearance surprised

me, for he was a large heavy fat man, dressed in white clothes and silver lace, with his grey hairs tied behind and much powdered, which, added to his shyness and reserve, was not at first prepossessing. His reserve and melancholy (for I could not call it pride) abated as we rode along, and by the time we left him at the Admiral's, he became good company,—Garbett, who knew him well, having whispered him, that though we had no great name, he would find us not common men.

Lord Lyttleton's we found superior to the description we had heard of it, and the day being favourable, the prospect from the high ground, of more than thirty miles of cultivated country, ending in the celebrated hill, the Wrekin, delighted us much. On our return to the inn, where we expected but an ordinary repast, we found a pressing invitation from the Admiral to dine with him, which we could not resist. Though a good deal disabled with the gout, he was kind and hospitable, and received Garbett, who was backward to go, very civilly. We intended to have rode back to Birmingham in the evening, but in the afternoon there came on such a dreadful storm of thunder, accompanied with incessant rain, as made the Admiral insist on our lodging all night with him. With this we complied ; but as he had no more than three spare beds, James Adam and Garbett were to go to the inn. Finding an interval of fair weather by eight o'clock, they rode to Birmingham, as Garbett was obliged to be home.

After supper, the Admiral made us a spacious bowl of punch with his own hand, a composition on which he piqued himself not a little, and for which John Home extolled him to the skies. This nectar circulated fast, and with the usual effect of opening the hearts of the company, and making them speak out. It was on this occasion that Home said to the Admiral, that, knowing what he knew by conversing with him at Leith, he was very much surprised when he recommended Byng to mercy.* " You should have known, John, that I could never all my life bear the idea of being accessory to blood, and therefore I joined in this recommendation, though I knew that by doing so I should run the risk of never more being employed." This was a full confirmation of what John Home had said at the time of the sea-fight (p. 323). This fine punch even unlocked Shenstone's breast, who had hitherto been shy and reserved ; for besides mixing freely in the conversation, he told Home apart, that it was not so agreeable as he thought to live in the neighbourhood and intimacy of Lord Lyttleton, for he had defects which the benevolence of his general manners concealed, which made him often wish that he had lived at an hundred miles' distance. When Home told me this, I very easily conceived that the pride of a patron, joined to the jealousy of a rival poet, must often produce effects that might prove intolerable. We returned

* Admiral Smith, as senior flag officer, was President of the Court-Martial of Byng at Portsmouth.

to Birmingham next morning, and, with the most
affectionate sense of the kindness of our landlord
and his family, we set out on our journey north
next morning. I have forgot to mention that we
supped the last night with Dr. Roebuck, who,
though a very clever and ingenious man, was far
behind our friend in some of the most respectable
qualities.

We kept on through a middle road by Lichfield
and Burton-on-Trent, where we could get no drinkable ale, though we threw ourselves there on purpose;
and next day, dining at Matlock, we were delighted
with the fine ride we had through a vale similar but
of more amenity than any we had seen in the
highlands. We took the bath, too, which pleased
and refreshed us much, for the day was sultry.
We went at night to Endsor Inn, opposite Chats-
worth, the Duke of Devonshire's fine house, which
we visited in the morning, with much admiration
both of the structure, ornaments, and situation. We
ascended a wild moor, and got to Sheffield to dinner,
where, as we declined visiting a brother of Dr. Roebuck's, on whom Garbett had given us a note of
credit, we sent his letter to him and went on. Next
day we saw Rockingham or Wentworth Castle in our
way, and became satisfied with sights, so that we
turned no more off our road till we came to Ripon,
where we could not resist the desire of visiting
Studley Park, then a great object of curiosity to
all people from our country, as it was then the near-

est fine place. Alnwick Castle had not then been repaired or beautified. After we had left Sheffield, where we might have got money, we discovered that we were like to run short, for Dr. Robertson, unlike his usual prudence, had only but two guineas in his pocket, trusting to the full purse of his cousin, James Adam, who had taken no more than he computed would pay the fourth part of our expense. Home and I had done the same. I was treasurer, and at Leeds, I believe, I demanded a contribution, when it was found that, by Robertson's deficiency and our purchasing some goods at Birmingham with the common stock, I was sensible we would run out before we came to Newcastle. This led us to inferior inns, which cost us as dear for much inferior entertainment. We held out till we passed Durham, which we did by keeping to the west of that city, and saving two miles, having made our meal at [   ], which Home knew to be a good house. From thence we might have got early into Newcastle, had we not been seduced by a horse-race we met with near Chester-le-Street. This we could not resist, as some of us had never seen John Bull at his favourite amusement. There was a great crowd, and the Mrs. and Misses Bull made a favourite part of the scene, their equipages being single and double horses, sometimes triple, and many of them ill mounted, and yet all of them with a keenness, eagerness, violence of motion and loudness of vociferation, that appeared like madness to us, for we thought

them in extreme danger by their crossing and just-
ling in all directions at the full gallop, and yet none
of them fell. Having tired our horses with this
diversion, we were obliged to halt at an inn to give
them a little corn, for we had been four hours on
horseback, and we had nine miles to Newcastle.
Besides corn to five horses and a bottle of porter to
our man Anthony, I had just two shillings remaining ;
but I could only spare one of them, for we had turn-
pikes to pay, and so called for a pint of port, which,
mixed with a quart of water, made a good drink
for each of us. Our horses and their riders being
both jaded, it was ten o'clock before we arrived at
Newcastle ; there we got an excellent supper, etc.,
and a good night's sleep. I sent for Jack Widdring-
ton when at breakfast, who immediately gave us
what money we wanted ; and we, who had been so
penurious for three days, became suddenly extravagant. Adam bought a £20 horse, and the rest
of us what trinkets we thought we wanted—
Robertson for his wife and children at Gladsmuir,
and Home and I for the children at Polwarth manse.
As we drew nearer home, our motion became acceler-
ated and our conversation duller : we had been in
two parties, which were formed about five or six
miles from London; for having met with a cow, with
a piece of old flannel tied about one of her horns,
pasturing on a very wide lane on the road, Home
and Robertson made a sudden tack to the left,
to be out of reach of this furious wild beast : I

jeered them, and asked of what they were afraid. They said a mad cow—did I observe the warning given by cloth upon her horn? " Yes," says I, " but that is only because her horn was hurt ; did you not see how quiet she was when I passed her ? " Adam took my part, and the controversy lasted all the way down, when we had nothing else to talk of. There were so many diverting scenes occurred in the course of our journey, that we often regretted since that we had not drawn a journal of it. Our debates about trifles were infinitely amusing. Our man Anthony was at once a source of much jangling and no small amusement. He was never ready when we mounted, and went slowly on, but he was generally half a mile behind us, and we had to halt when we wanted anything. I had got a hickory stick from Jackson, not worth 1s. 6d., which I would have left at the first stage had not Home and Robertson insisted on my not doing it ; but as I had less baggage, and an equal right in Anthony and his horse, and was treasurer withal, which they were afraid I would throw up, I carried my point ; and this stick being five feet long, and sometimes, by lying across the clothes-bag, entangled with hedges, furnished him with a ready excuse. It was very warm weather in May, and we rode in the hottest of the day : we seldom got on horseback before ten o'clock, for there was no getting Robertson and Home to bed, and Jamie Adam would not get up, and had, besides, a very tedious toilet. Our two

friends wanted sometimes to go before us, but I
would not pay the bill till James and Anthony were
both ready, and till then the ostler would not draw
or lead out the horses from the stable. As I perceived that Robertson and Home were commenting
on all my actions, I, with the privacy of James Adam,
did odd things on purpose to astonish them : as,
for instance, at the inn near Studley, where we
breakfasted, having felt my long hair intolerably
warm about my neck, I cut off five or six inches of
a bit of ragged green galloon that was hanging down
from a chair-back in the room, with which I tied my
hair behind. This made a very motley appearance.
But when we came to take horse, in spite of the
heat I appeared with my greatcoat, and had fastened the cape of it round my head ; and in this
guise I rode through the town of Ripon, at the
end of which I disengaged myself from my greatcoat, and my friends saw the reason of this masquerade. Another day, between twelve and one,
riding through very close hedges near Cornhill, we
were all like to die of heat, and were able only to
walk our horses. I fell behind, pulled my greatcoat
from Anthony, put it on, and came up with my
friends at a hard trot. They then thought that I
had certainly gone mad, but they did not advert to
it, that the chief oppression of heat is before the
perspiration. My receipt had relieved my frenzy,
and I reined in my horse till they came up to me.
Soon after we left Cornhill, we separated. Home

and I stopped at Polwarth manse for a night, and Robertson and Adam went on by Longformacus to Gladsmuir, Robertson's abode. James Adam, though not so bold and superior an artist as his brother Robert, was a well-informed and sensible man, and furnished me with excellent conversation, as we generally rode together. Thus ended a journey of eighteen days, which, on the whole, had proved most amusing and satisfactory.

We got to our respective abodes by the 22nd of May, and were in time for the business week of the General Assembly, of which Robertson and I were members, and where we came in time to assist in sending Dr. Blair to the New Church, to which he had a right, and of which a sentence of the Synod of Lothian and Tweeddale unjustly deprived him. This was the only occasion on which he ever spoke in the General Assembly, which he did remarkably well.

CHAPTER X

1758–1759 AGE, 36–37

IT was in the month of August this summer that
Robertson and I passed two days at Minto with Sir
Gilbert Elliot, who was very open and communicative. About the middle of October I rode to Inverary, being invited by the Milton family, who always
were with the Duke of Argyle, and who generally remained there till near the end of the year. I got the
first night to my friend Robin Bogle's, at Shettleston,
near Glasgow, where I found him very happy with his
wife and family. He was an honest, gentlemanly
man, but had been very dissipated before his marriage. From Glasgow I went all night to Roseneath,
where, in a small house near the castle, lived my
friend, Miss Jean Campbell of Carrick, with her mother,
who was a sister of General John Campbell of
Mamore, afterwards Duke of Argyle, and father of
the present Duke. Next day, after passing Loch
Long, I went over Argyle's Bowling-Green, called so
on account of the roughness of the road. As my
horses were not frosted, and the ice was strong, I had

396

to walk about six miles. This made me late in getting to St. Catherine's, directly opposite to Inverary. I wished very much to get across the loch, as it was but six in the evening ; but the mistress of the house, wishing to detain me and my servant and horses all night, pretended that the boatmen were out of the way and the oars a-seeking, and that I could not get across that night. This vexed me, as it was a miserable house to sleep in ; however, I called for a mutchkin of whisky, and prevailed with the good woman to taste it without water. As she became so familiar as to ask where I was when I was at home, I told her I was a schoolfellow of M'Callum More, and was much disappointed at not crossing the lake, as I had letters of importance to deliver to his Grace. She stared, and said I was a stalwart carl of such an age : my grisly undressed hair favoured this deception. I added that, if I could cross the loch, I intended to leave my servant and horses all night to her care, to come round by the head of the loch in the morning ; but if I could not cross, I must venture to ride the nine miles round, dark as it was. She took another sip of the whisky, and then left the room. In five minutes she returned and told me that the boatmen had appeared and were seeking for their oars, and would be ready in a few minutes. This was good news to me, as I knew the inn at Inverary to be pretty good, as I had been there two nights when I went to their country, in 1754, with Jamie Cheap of Sauchie. I was very soon summoned to the boat, and after recommending my man, John M'Lachlan, to the care of the landlady, I bid her farewell. We got very soon over, the night being calm, and the distance not much more than two miles.

I did not go that night to the Duke's house, as I knew I could not have a bed there (as he had not yet got into the Castle), but I went in the morning, and was very politely received, not only by the Milton family, but by the Duke and his two cousins, the present Duke, and his brother Lord Frederick, who were there. His Grace told me immediately that Miss Fletcher had made him expect my visit, and that he was sorry he could not offer me lodging, but that he would hope to see me every day to breakfast, dinner, and supper.

It would be quite superfluous to say anything here of the character of Archibald, Duke of Argyle, as the character of that illustrious person, both as a statesman and an accomplished gentleman and scholar, is perfectly known. I was told that he was a great humorist at Inverary, and that you could neither drink his health nor ask him how he did without disobliging ; but this was exaggerated. To be sure, he waved ceremony very much, and took no trouble at table, and would not let himself be waited for, and came in when he pleased, and sat down on the chair that was left, which was neither at the head nor foot of the table. But he cured me of all constraint the first day, for in his first or second glass of wine he drank my health and welcomed me to Inverary, and

hoped that as long as I stayed, which he wished to be
all the week at least, I would think myself at home.
Though he never drank to me again, I was much more
gratified by his directing much of his conversation to
me. His colloquial talent was very remarkable, for
he never harangued or was tedious, but listened to
you in your turn. We sat down every day fifteen
or sixteen to dinner ; for besides his two cousins and
the Fletcher family, there were always seven or eight
Argyleshire gentlemen, or factors on the estate, at
dinner. The Duke had the talent of conversing with
his guests so as to distinguish men of knowledge and
talents without neglecting those who valued themselves more on their birth and their rent-rolls than on
personal merit. After the ladies were withdrawn and
he had drunk his bottle of claret, he retired to an
easy-chair set hard by the fireplace : drawing a black
silk nightcap over his eyes, he slept, or seemed to
sleep, for an hour and a half. In the mean time,
Sandie M'Millan, who was toast-master, pushed about
the bottle, and a more noisy or regardless company
could hardly be. Milton retired soon after the ladies,
and about six o'clock M'Millan and the gentlemen
drew off (for at that time dinner was always served at
two o'clock), when the ladies returned, and his Grace
awoke and called for his tea, which he made himself
at a little table apart from that of the company. Tea
being over, he played two rubbers at sixpenny whist,
as he did in London. He had always some of the
ladies of his party, while the rest amused themselves

at another table. Supper was served soon after nine, and there being nobody left but those with whom he was familiar, he drank another bottle of claret, and could not be got to go to bed till one in the morning. Jack Campbell of Stonefield,* who had lately married his niece, Lady Grace Stuart, came to us on the second day. I may add that the provisions for the table were at least equal to the conversation; for we had sea and river fish in perfection, the best beef and mutton and fowls and wild game and venison of both kinds in abundance. The wines, too, were excellent.

I stayed over Sunday and preached to his Grace, who always attended the church at Inverary. The ladies told me that I had pleased his Grace, which gratified me not a little, as without him no prefer- ment could be obtained in Scotland.

The Duke had a great collection of fine stories, which he told so neatly, and so frequently repeated them without variation, as to make one believe that he had wrote them down. He had been in the battle of Sheriffmuir, and was slightly wounded in his foot, which made him always halt a little. He would have been an admirable soldier, as he had every talent and qualification necessary to arrive at the height of that profession ; but his brother John, Duke of Argyle,†

* John Campbell of Stonefield was raised to the Bench as a judge in 1763, and took the title of Lord Stonefield. He married Lady Grace Stuart, fourth daughter of James, second Earl of Bute, and sister of John, third Earl.

† " The one was, properly speaking, a hero ; the other altogether a man of the world. The Duke [John] thought Lord Islay

having gone before him with a great and rising reputation, he was advised to take the line of a statesman. I may add here, that when he died in spring 1762, it was found that he had marked my name down in his private notebook for Principal of the College of Glasgow, a body in whose prosperity he was much interested, as he had been educated there, and had said to Andrew Fletcher junior, to whom he showed the note, that it would be very hard if he and I between us could not manage that troublesome society. This took no effect, for the Duke died a year or two before Principal Campbell, when Lord Bute had all the power ; so that when the vacancy happened in the end of 1761, or beginning of '62, Professor Leechman was preferred to it, who was the friend, and had been the tutor, of Mr. Baron Mure.

I slept all night at Levenside, as I had promised to Stonefield, and got home the second day after.

In the end of this year, 1758, I was tempted, by the illiberal outcry that was raised against the Minister, William Pitt, on the failure of General Bligh, on the affair of St. Cas, on the French coast, to write the pamphlet, " Plain Reasons for Removing the Right Honourable William Pitt from His Majesty's Councils for ever, by O. M. Haberdasher ; " which was published in London in the beginning of 1759,

[Duke Archibald] undignified and time serving : Lord Islay thought the Duke wrongheaded and romantic. Yet both were assuredly superior men." Lady Louisa Stuart's *Memoir of John, Duke of Argyle.*

26

and had a great run. I had wrote it in the ironical style of Dean Swift, like that about burning the tragedy of *Douglas*, and thought I had succeeded pretty well. Besides panegyric on that great man, who had raised us from a very low state of political depression, not only in the eyes of all Europe, but in our own opinion, to make rapid progress to the highest state of national glory in which ever we had been,—it contained likewise much satire against the Minister who had reduced us so low.

After I returned from Inverary, I visited my friend Mrs. Wedderburn, whom, to my great grief, I found low and dejected. The Captain had been obliged to join his regiment in the West Indies in the spring, where there was much fighting, and she had not heard of him for some time. She was brought to bed of a daughter early in December, and died of a fever at that time, universally regretted, and never to be forgotten by those who were intimately acquainted with her.

Thus ended a year of greater variety than any in my life ; for though I had been in London before, and had rode to Edinburgh likewise on horseback, yet I had not till then seen such a variety of characters, nor had I acquired such a talent for observation, nor possessed a line for sounding the depths of the human character commensurate to that purpose as I now had. On this tour I had seen great variety of characters, with many of whom having been very intimate, the defect was in myself if I had not been able to sound all the depths and shallows through which I passed.

In this year, 1759, in the beginning of which I enjoyed the success of my ironical pamphlet in defence of William Pitt, afterwards Lord Chatham, I was encouraged to take my pen again occasionally, when anything should occur that suited it. Two or three years after this period, our neighbourhood was enriched by the residence of a very valuable man, Lieutenant-Colonel Robert Campbell of Finab, a man of the first-rate understanding and ability. He had been in the Duke of Cumberland's war, and was captain of grenadiers in the 42nd regiment, but had been much disgusted with the Duke of Cumberland, and not having good health, he left the army, I think, with major's rank ; and some time thereafter having bought the estate of Drumore, he came to live there with his family. As he had been at college with me, and in the same class, and having had a boyish intimacy together, it was not difficult to renew my acquaintance, and to make it more intimate. He was very sociable, and liked golf, the sport in which I excelled and took much pleasure.*
The Colonel had read very little, but he had taken a more comprehensive view of men and affairs than almost any person I ever knew. Adam Ferguson and he had been very intimate, and had a mutual regard for each other. This gentleman was truly

* A note in the original MS. of the Autobiography states that " Dr. Carlyle was captain of the golfers at Musselburgh."

a great addition to our society. He had been member of Parliament for Argyleshire, and was Receiver-General of the Customs for many years before his death. He left no son but Lieutenant-General Alexander Campbell of Monzie, the heir of his father's sagacity and talents, with more experience in war.

There was nothing very material before the General Assembly of this year, unless it was an explanation and extension of the Act against simoniacal practices, which had become necessary on account of some recent transactions. Dr. Robertson had been translated to Edinburgh this year, but did not yet take any particular charge of the affairs of the Church, because, not being yet Principal, he could not be a member of Assembly every year, as he afterwards was.

My father had gone to London in the month of March, to visit his daughter, Mrs. Dickson, and I had rode with him to Berwick. He was very much pleased and amused at London, where, besides his daughter and her infant, his first grandchild, he had his sisters, Paterson and Lyon, still alive, which gave him great satisfaction. As he had never been in London before, he enjoyed it very much, though now in his seventieth year. But being fresh and vigorous, and remarkably cheerful, he was a very great favourite with all his new acquaintances. But as he would needs ride down in midsummer, and had been unlucky in the purchase of a horse, which was very hard set, and still more so in his choice of a companion—one of his daughter's disappointed lovers, who paid no regard to his age in the length of his day's journey—he was so much overheated that, as my mother alleged, the fever never afterwards left him, which concluded his life in the year 1765 on the 8th of March. A more kind and affectionate parent and relation or more benevolent neighbour, or more faithful pastor, never existed.

It was near the end of summer this year that Charles Townshend and Lady Dalkeith, with her daughter, Lady Frances Scott,* then above eight years of age [came to Dalkeith], and remained there for two months. As they had two public days in the week, according to the ancient mode of the family, they drew a great deal of company to the house; and as I was considered as chaplain in ordinary to the family, the minister of Dalkeith for the time being not much in favour, I was very frequently there. Charles Townshend was a rising statesman, who aspired at the highest offices. A project he conceived after he came here much increased our intimacy : this was to offer himself a candidate for the seat in Parliament for the city of Edinburgh. The state of the city at that time made it not improbable that he might succeed. A Mr. Forrester, a counsellor-at-law, of Irish birth, and quite a

* Married in 1783, Archibald, Lord Douglas, and died in 1817.

stranger here, had been recommended by Baron
Maule to the Duke of Argyle, to whom he was
known, and to Lord Milton. Forrester was by no
means popular in Edinburgh, and Charles Townshend had bewitched Lord Milton with his seducing
tongue, which made him more sanguine in his project. He discovered that I had much to say with the
Baron and his lady, whom he cajolled and flattered
excessively.

He took me for his confidant and adviser in this
business. I had many conferences with him on the
subject, and endeavoured to convince him that if he
was not master of his wife's uncle, the Duke of Argyle,
as he pretended to have his own uncle, the Duke of
Newcastle,* he would never succeed ; for though Milton seemed to govern Argyle in most things, which
was necessary for the support of his credit as well as
for the Duke's ease, yet there were points in which
Milton could not stir a step without the Duke, and in
my opinion this was one of them. On this he fell into
a passion, and exclaimed that I was so crusty as never
to be of his opinion, and to oppose him in everything.
On this I laughed full in his face, took to my hat, and
said that if this was the way in which he chose to
treat his friend and adviser, it was time I were gone,
for I could be of no use to him. He calmed on this,
and asked my reason for thinking as I did. I an-

* " Charles Townshend has turned his artillery upon himself :
He says ' Silly fellow for silly fellow, I don't see why it is not as
well to be governed by my uncle with a blue ribband, as by
my cousin with a green one.' "—Walpole to Chute.

swered that the Member of Parliament for the city of Edinburgh was of great consequence, as whoever held that was sure of the political government of the country, and without it no man would be of any consequence ; that his lady, being the Duke's niece, was against him ; for as in political business no regard was paid to blood, that very circumstance was hostile to his design ; for it was not to be supposed that the Duke of Argyle would allow a young nobleman from the south, who had made himself a man of importance in the north by having obtained the guardianship of the heir of one of our greatest families in his minority, to take the capital of Scotland by a *coup-de-main*, and thereby undermine or subvert his political interest, for without his viceroyalty in Scotland, His Grace was of no importance in the State. I added that it was impossible to conceive that the Duke would be so blind as not to see that a young man of his aspiring temper and superior talents would [not] think of making himself member for Edinburgh, merely to show his address in political canvassing, to lay himself at the feet of his wife's uncle. This, with much more that I represented to him, seemed to open his eyes ; yet he still went on, for he could not desist from the pleasure of the courtship, though he had little prospect of success.

He came at last to be contented with the glory of driving Forrester off the field, which was not difficult to do ; for when Charles had the freedom of the city presented to him, and a dinner given him on the occasion, he lessened the candidate so much in their eyes by his fine vein of ridicule, that the dislike of the Town Council was increased to aversion. But Charles, while he effected one part of his purpose, failed in another ; for though he drove away his rival, he gained no ground for himself. He was imprudent and loose-tongued enough to ridicule the good old King George II., which, though it was not unusual among young noblemen, and indeed wits of all ranks, yet could not be endured by the citizens of Edinburgh, who, seeing their King far off and darkly, were shocked with the freedoms that were used with him. Besides this, Milton, who had been dazzled at first by Charles's shining talents and elegant flattery, began to grow cold, and drew off. He had sounded the uncle, and found in him a strong jealousy of the nephew, mixed with some contempt, the effect of which discovery was the gradual alienation of Milton, who had really been enamoured of Charles, and perhaps secretly thought he could manage him, if he had success, with more absolute sway than he did the Duke of Argyle.

After Charles returned to England he did not for some time desist, and I had much correspondence with him on the subject ; some of his letters I have still, but I kept no copies of my own, which I have since regretted, as they were wrote with anxiety and exertion. When I was in London in 1770, there was a gentleman who pressed me to pay a visit to Lady Townshend, his mother, who having many letters of mine to her son, was desirous to see me ; but not choosing to be introduced anywhere by that gentleman, I missed the opportunity of recovering my letters, which I have since understood are burnt, with all Charles's correspondence. The end of all was that Forrester having retreated from the field, having no friend but Baron Maule, and a caveat being entered against Charles Townshend, the good town of Edinburgh were glad to take an insignificant citizen for their member.*

While Mr. Townshend was here, we had him chosen a member of the Select Society in one sitting (against the rules), that we might hear him speak, which he accordingly did at the next meeting, and was answered by Lord Elibank and Dr. Dick, who were superior to him in argument and knowledge of the subject. Like a meteor, Charles dazzled for a moment, but the brilliancy soon faded away, and left no very strong impression, so that when he returned to England at the end of two months, he had stayed long enough here.

I must not forget, however, to mention an anecdote or two of him, which will explain his character more. Nothing could excel the liveliness of his parts, nor the facility with which he made other people's thoughts his own in a moment.

I called on him one morning at Dalkeith, when he said I had come most apropos, if not engaged, for that he was going to ride to Edinburgh to make some calls ; and his wife being engaged to dine with

---

* The citizen was the Lord Provost, the Rt. Hon. George Lind.

the Duchess of Gordon, he would be very glad of a small party in a tavern. I agreed, and we rode to Edinburgh together. When we drew near that city, he begged me to ride on and bespeak a small dinner at a tavern, and get a friend or two if I could to join us, as he must turn to the left to call on some people who lived in that direction. I went to town directly, and luckily found Home and Ferguson in Kincaid's shop,* and secured them, and sent a cady† to Robertson to ask him to meet us at the Cross Keys soon after two o'clock, who likewise came. During dinner, and for almost an hour after, Charles, who seemed to be fatigued with his morning visits, spoke not a single word, and we four went on with our kind of conversation, without adverting to Mr. Townshend's absence. After he had drunk a pint of claret, he seemed to awaken from his reverie, and then silenced us all with a torrent of colloquial eloquence, which was highly entertaining, for he gave us all our own ideas over again, embodied in the finest language, and delivered in the most impressive manner. When he parted from us, my friends remarked upon his excellence in this talent, in which Robertson agreed with them, without, perhaps, being conscious that he was the most able proficient in that art.

It was in the second week of August when the school at Musselburgh was publicly examined, and

---

* Kincaid the bookseller. His shop was that formerly occupied by Allan Ramsay, in the eastmost tenement of the Luckenbooths.

† Caddie—a messenger.

when the magistrates gave what was called the Solan
Goose Feast.   I took this opportunity of inviting Mr.
Townshend to visit the school, and to dine with the
magistrates, as he was tutor to His Grace the Duke
of Buccleuch, the lord superior of the town.   Mr.
Townshend sent them a fine haunch of venison, and
Mr. Cardonnel, who was magistrate at this time, took
care to assemble a brilliant company of men of letters
to meet Mr. Townshend, among whom were Home,
Robertson, Ferguson, and William Wilkie.*   There
was a numerous company, and the best dinner they
could make.   Cardonnel, in his anxiety to have the
venison properly roasted, had directed the cook to
put a paste round it ; but she not having given it
time enough, it came up to the table half raw, to the
great disappointment of the company, but chiefly of
a Colonel Parr, whose serious affliction made the rest
of the company quite easy on the occasion, for he
literally wept and shed bitter tears, and whined out
what an unfortunate fellow he was, that the only
haunch of venison he had met with in Scotland, and
the only one he had any chance of seeing while here,
should be served up raw !   This set the whole table in
a roar of laughter, and reconciled them to their fate.
After a little time, the Colonel recovered from his
disaster by the use of the gridiron to the venison,
and having got up his spirits with half-a-dozen glasses

* As to Cardonnel, see above, p. 228.   In the Wilkie who figures
in the scene the reader will recognise the great Greek scholar, and
author of the *Epigoniad*.—J. H. B.

of good claret, began to talk away with some effect ; for excepting his effeminacy about venison, he was not a bad fellow.

He was unlucky, however, in one of his topics ; for, Wilkie having begun to open, Parr, addressing himself to him, said something rude about the professors of St. Andrews (of which university Wilkie had very recently been chosen a member), and wished they would keep their students and professors within their walls, for that his corps had lately enlisted one of them, who was not only the most awkward beast, but the most unruly and debauched rascal that ever wore a red coat. Wilkie, who was indignant on this attack, and a very great master of horse-play raillery, and in scolding feared neither man nor woman, replied with witty and successful tartness, which, however, did not silence the Colonel ; when the company took sides, and there ensued a brawling conversation, which lasted too long. Mr. Townshend had interposed, with an intention to support Wilkie against his countryman ; but Wilkie, being heated, mistook him, and after two or three brushes on each side, silenced him as he had done the Colonel ; and the report afterwards went that Wilkie had completely foiled the English champion at his own weapons—wit and raillery.* But this was

* Sir Robert Liston in a letter to Henry Mackenzie says :— " He [Wilkie] talked indeed a great deal, and loved disquisition and debate ; but there was nothing overbearing or offensive, or even stiff in his manner of urging his arguments ; on the contrary he was always calm, placid, perfectly master of his temper—and often lively, jocular, and full of merriment."

a mistake, for Mr. Townshend had not the least desire to enter the lists with Wilkie, but whispered to me, who sat next to him, that as Wilkie grew brutal, he would put an end to the contest by making no answer. A silence ensued, which Cardonnel, one of the best toast-masters, took advantage of by giving us three bumpers in less than two minutes ; all contest for victory was at an end, and the company united again. Townshend said to me afterwards, when he came to take his carriage at my house, that he had never met with a man who approached so near the two extremes of a god and a brute as Wilkie did.

Soon after this, Mr. Townshend, and the Countess and her daughter Lady Frances Scott, set out for London. This was a very clever child, whose humour and playfulness Mr. Townshend's good-nature had to encourage and protect against maternal discipline carried too far. He continued to protect and instruct her, and frequently employed her as his amanuensis, as she has frequently told me since ; and added, that if he had not died when she was only sixteen, he would have made her a politician.

In the middle of September this year I went to Dumfries to meet my friends, as I usually did, and to accompany my friend Dr. Wight, who had come from Dublin to Dumfries, and forward to Musselburgh to visit me. While Wight was here, we supped one night in Edinburgh with the celebrated Dr. Franklin at Dr. Robertson's house, then at the head of the Cowgate, where he had come at Whitsunday, after his being translated to Edinburgh. Dr. Franklin had his son with him ; and besides Wight and me, there were David Hume, Dr. Cullen, Adam Smith, and two or three more. Wight and Franklin had met and breakfasted together in the inn at [   ] without learning one another's names, but they were more than half acquainted when they met here. Wight, who could talk at random on all sciences without being very deeply skilled in any, took it into his head to be very eloquent on chemistry, a course of which he had attended in Dublin ; and perceiving that he diverted the company, particularly Franklin, who was a silent man, he kept it up with Cullen, then professor of that science, who had imprudently committed himself with him, for the greatest part of the evening, to the infinite diversion of the company, who took great delight in seeing the great Professor foiled in his own science by a novice. Franklin's son was open and communicative, and pleased the company better than his father ; and some of us observed indications of that decided difference of opinion between father and son which, in the American war, alienated them altogether.

On our journey he [Dr. Wight] told me that he was heartily tired of his situation as a dissenting clergyman, and of the manner of life in Dublin, which, though social and convivial to the last degree, yet led to nothing, and gave him no heartfelt satisfaction, there being but a very few indeed with whom he could unite in truly confidential friendship. As I knew that the University of Glasgow were resolved to vacate Mr. Ruat's professorship if he remained much longer abroad, and as I happened likewise to know that he would not return during the life of Lord Hope, who was in a slow decline, I formed the plan of obtaining his professorship, which was that of History, and in the gift of the Crown, for Dr. Wight, and I set about it to secure it immediately. This was easily done, for I had access to His Grace the Duke of Queensberry, not only by writing to him myself, but by interesting John M'Kie Ross in the business, with whom both Wight and I were related, and also by means of Sir Gilbert Elliot we could secure Lord Bute ; while I, through Lord Milton, could gain the consent of the Duke of Argyle. I had favourable answers from everybody, and had no doubt of getting the place if it was vacated.

Before I left Dumfries, I was witness to an extraordinary riot which took place there on Michaelmas, the day of the election of their magistrates. Provost Bell had been two years dead, and the party which he had established in power, when he brought them over to their natural protector, the good Duke of Queensberry, being desirous to preserve their influence, did not think they could do better than to raise John Dickson, that Provost's nephew, to be their chief magistrate. As this man was at present Convener of the Trades, who are powerful in Dumfries, and was popular among them, he thought his ambition would be easily gratified. But there were sundry objections to this measure. Andrew Crosbie, advocate, the son of a Provost of that name who had been a private supporter of Provost Bell, in opposition to the party of the Tories, thought this a proper time to attempt an overturn of the present magistrates and managers, and put his own friends in their room, who would either be directed by Crosbie's maternal uncle, Lord Tinwald, then Justice-Clerk, and far advanced in years, or gain the credit and advantage of governing the town under the Duke of Queensberry. As Crosbie was a clever fellow, and young and adventurous, and a good inflammatory speaker, he soon raised the commons of the town almost to a pitch of madness against Dickson.* On the day of election, which happened to be on Saturday, they rose in a tumultuous manner, and took possession of the stair leading up to the Town Hall, and would not allow the election to proceed. But, supposing no election could take place after the day was elapsed, when twelve o'clock struck they allowed the magistrates and Council to depart. They came down separately and by backways to the George Inn, where Dr. Wight and I were waiting to see the issue of this day's riot. Dickson had married a sister of Wight's for his second wife. We waited

---

* Andrew Crosbie was a distinguished advocate, in great practice ; but little is now known of him except a few convivial anecdotes.† He is supposed to be the prototype of Pleydel in *Guy Mannering.*—J. H. B.

† A sketch of Crosbie's career will be found in Ramsay's *Scotland and Scotsmen of the Eighteenth Century.*

in an adjacent room till the election was over, and then joined them for half an hour, to drink the health of the new Provost.

The Deputy-Sheriff Kirkpatrick had come down from his house, ten or twelve miles off, with several country gentlemen, but there being no soldiers in the town, had not attempted to disperse the mob by any other method than remonstrance.   This affair ended in a very expensive lawsuit, and Dickson's right to be provost was established.   Wight was on his return to Dublin, and I on mine home; so I took leave of my friends on Monday, that I might see our grandfather, who by that time had an assistant.

On Tuesday morning, October 2, on my return from this visit to Dumfries, I got to Moffat, where I knew John Home was, as he usually passed two or three weeks every season there.   He introduced me to M'Pherson in the bowling-green, as I have narrated in a letter to the Highland Society.   He was good-looking, of a large size, with very thick legs, to hide which he generally wore boots, though not then the fashion.   He appeared to me proud and reserved, and shunned dining with us on some pretence.   I knew him intimately afterwards.*

---

* The letter referred to is in the Report of the Highland Society on the authenticity of the *Poems of Ossian*, p. 66.   He states that Macpherson showed some unfinished fragments, and continues— " Mr. Home had been highly delighted with them ; and when he showed them to me, I was perfectly astonished at the poetical genius displayed in them.   We agreed that it was a precious discovery, and that as soon as possible it should be published to the world."—J. H. B.

27

The Duke of Argyle made his usual visit to Argyle-shire in October, and stopped for a week or two at Brunstane, Lord Milton's, as he now seldom occupied his lodging in the Abbey, not caring to be troubled with too many visitors from the city of Edinburgh. I was sent for to him, and passed a very agreeable day. He rallied me on my friend Charles Towns-hend's attempt to steal the city of Edinburgh, and said he was not a very dutiful nephew. His Grace knew perfectly my intimacy with him, and so did not push the conversation.

It was after this that I was persuaded by William Johnstone, advocate, now Sir William Pulteney, and Adam Ferguson, to write what was called the Militia Pamphlet, under the signature of " A Freeholder of Ayrshire," which I chose, because that was said to be the only shire in Scotland out of which there had not issued a single rebel in 1745.* After an hour's con-versation with the two gentlemen I have mentioned, I undertook to write the pamphlet, and finished it in

* The pamphlet here referred to is called *The Question relating to a Scots Militia considered, in a Letter to the Lords and Gentlemen who have concerted the form of law for that establish-ment.*—By a Freeholder. The Act which placed the militia of England nearly in its present position, had been passed by the exertions of the author's friend, Charles Townshend, in 1757. When a proposal for extending the system to Scotland was suggested, ministers were afraid to arm the people among whom the insurrection of 1745 had occurred, and the feud between Jacobite and Revolutionist was still fresh. It is curious that, for a reason almost identical, Ireland has been excepted from the Volunteer organisation of a century later. It was not until 1793 that the Militia Acts were extended to Scotland.—J. H. B.

a fortnight, and carried it to Johnstone, who was highly pleased with it, and, after showing it to Ferguson, had it transcribed by his own clerk, and then shown to Robertson, who believed it to be of Johnstone's writing, as he had told him that the author's name was to be concealed. Robertson was well pleased, though he took no great concern about those kind of writings, and added a short paragraph in page [   ], which he laughingly alleged was the cause of its success, for great and unexpected success it certainly had ; for it hit the tone of the country at that time, which being irritated at the line which was drawn between Scotland and England with respect to militia, was very desirous to have application made for it in the approaching session of Parliament. Much honour was done to this pamphlet, for the Honourable George, now Marquis Townshend,* had it republished at London, with a preface of his own writing, as a Provost Ferguson of Ayr had done here. I had likewise a very flattering note from Sir Gilbert Elliot, who moved for the Scotch militia in the next session of Parliament, for he wrote me that he had only spoken the substance of my pamphlet in the House, and had got more praise for it from friends than for any speech he had formerly made ; but this did not happen till spring 1760, when a bill having been ordered and brought in, was rejected. Robert Dundas, then Lord Advocate, opposed it keenly, and it was said in party publications that this speech was the price paid for

* First Marquis Townshend, uncle of Charles Townshend.

his being made President immediately after. But my belief is, that as political principles were formed in the school of the disciples and followers of Sir Robert Walpole, whose ostensible motive, if not his governing one, was a fear of the family of Stuart, Dundas sincerely thought that arming Scotland was dangerous, though he rested his argument chiefly on a less unpopular topic—viz. that a militia would ruin our rising manufactures. Ferguson had published a very superior militia pamphlet in London a year or two before, in which all the genuine principles of that kind of national defence were clearly unfolded. The parties here were so warm at this time that it was necessary to conceal the names of authors, to which I had an additional motive, from a hint of Dr. Cullen's; for, supping one night with him, Dr. Wight being only in company, after praising the pamphlet, he added that he did not know the author, and was glad of it, for he who occasionally saw so many of the superior orders, could assure us that those pamphlets, which were ascribed to clergymen, had raised a spirit of envy and jealousy of the clergy, which it would not be easy to stand. As, since the days of the faction about the tragedy of *Douglas*, three or four of us were supposed to be the authors of all the pamphlets which raised public attention, we sheltered ourselves in the crowd ; and it was a good while before the real writers were found out.

CHAPTER XI

THIS year [1760] was the most important of my life,
for before the end of it I was united with the most
valuable friend and companion that any mortal ever
possessed. My youth had been spent in a vain pursuit ; for my first love, which I have mentioned as
far back as the year 1735, had kept entire possession till 1753, by means of her coquetry and my
irresolution. She was of superior understanding as
well as beauty. In this last she would have excelled
most women of her time, had she not been the worst
dancer in the world, which she could not be prevailed on to leave off, though her envious rivals
laughed and rejoiced at her persevering folly.
Though she had a bad voice and a bad ear, she was
a great mistress of conversation, having both wit
and humour, and, with an air of haughty prudery,
had enough of coquetry both to attract and retain
her lovers, of whom she had many.

An early inclination she had to a young gentleman who was prevented from marrying her, and

was soon after killed at the battle of Fontenoy, made her difficult to please. I had never fairly put the question to her till about the year 1752, when she expressly refused me. This made me lessen the number of my visits, and made her restrain her coquetry. Soon after another came in my way, whose beauty and attractions made me forget the former, to whom, though she was inferior in sense and even in beauty, yet being ten years younger, and having gaiety of spirit, I became deeply enamoured, and was in full belief that I had gained her affections, when I was informed that she had suddenly given her hand to a young man in every respect, except in birth perhaps, beneath her notice. In both those ladies I believe their vanity prevailed against affection. They could not think of being wife of a minister. The first attempted after this to ensnare me again, but I escaped. To have done with her, and to justify me—two gentlemen of my friends addressed her vehemently, Adam Ferguson, and Robert Keith the ambassador. The first, who pleased her much, was rejected for the same reason I was : he had been a clergyman, and though in a more lucrative profession now, it was not higher. Her rejection of the second, I believe, was owing chiefly to principle. Though he was twenty-four years older than her, his rank was an attraction which balanced that ; but she could not bear the idea of quarrelling with his daughters, some of whom were her companions, and not much younger than herself. At last, after having

rejected rich and poor, young and old, to the number
of half a score, she gave her hand, at forty-five, to
the worst-tempered and most foolish of all her lovers,
who had a bare competency, and which, added to her
fortune, hardly made them independent. They led
a miserable life, and parted ; soon after which he died,
and she then lived respectably to an advanced age.

I owed my good fortune to the friendship of John
Home, who pointed out the young lady to me as a
proper object of suit, without which I should never
have attempted it, on account of the inequality of
her age and mine, for she was then just past seventeen when I was thirty-eight. I was well acquainted
with her sister and her as children, and saw that
they were very remarkable ; the eldest, Sarah, for
beauty and elegance, accompanied with good sense
and a grave and reserved demeanour ; the second
for an expressive and lively countenance, with a fine
bloom, and hair of a dark flaxen colour. She had
excellent parts, though uncultivated and uncommon,
and a striking cheerfulness and vivacity of manner.
After nine months' courtship, at first by silent and
imperceptible approaches, and for three months by
a close though unwarlike siege, I obtained her heart
and hand, and no man ever made a happier conquest ;
for, with a superior understanding and great discernment for her age, she had an ease and propriety of
manners which made her to be well received, and indeed much distinguished, in every company. Having
lost her father and mother when her sister was five

years of age and she only two — the father, on
Christmas Day 1744, and the mother on the same
festival in 1745, of the small-pox — each of their
trustees (for they were co-heiresses of Heathpool in
Northumberland, Kirknewton parish, then only £180
per annum), Mr. Collingwood of Unthank, cousin-
german of their mother, took the eldest under his
care; and Mr. William Home, minister of Polwarth,
who had married their father's sister, Mary Roddam,
had the charge of the youngest. By this division,
Sarah, the eldest, had seemingly many advantages
above her sister, for she lived with superior people,
who frequented, and were indeed allied to, the best
families in their county, attended the best schools in
Newcastle, and was one year in the first boarding-
school in Edinburgh; and accordingly turned out an
elegant and well-bred woman, speaking perfectly good
English, without the roughness peculiar to the local
dialect, and was admired, courted, and respected
wherever she went. Yet Mary, the younger, with
no advantage but that of living with an aunt of
superior understanding and great worth, though
much uneducated, and having only one year of the
Edinburgh boarding-school, soon had her mind enlarged and her talents improved by some instruction,
and the conversation of those who frequented us, insomuch that in not more than one year after our
marriage, she appeared not only without any seeming
defect in her education, but like a person of high en-
dowments. Indeed, the quickness of her parts and the

extent of her understanding were surprising, and her talent both in speaking and writing, and in delicacy of taste, truly as admirable as any woman I ever knew. Add to this that she was noble and generous in the highest degree, compassionate even to weakness, and, if her friends were in distress, totally forgetful and negligent of herself. I do not think it is possible I could derive greater satisfaction from any circumstance in human life than I did from the high approbation which was given to my choice by the very superior men who were my closest and most discerning friends, such as Ferguson, Robertson, Blair, and Bannatine, not merely by words, but by the open, respectful, and confidential manner in which they conversed with her.

On the 14th of October was made the important change in my situation, in John Home's house, in Alison's Square, when he was absent at Lord Eglintoun's, who had become a favourite of the Earl of Bute's, very much by John's means. He was, indeed, a very able as well as an agreeable man, though his education had been sadly neglected. We had sundry visits next day, and among the foremost came Sir Harry Erskine and Mr. Alexander Wedderburn. I was not then much acquainted with the first, but as he was older than me by several years, and Fanny Wedderburn,* of whom he was then in full pursuit, was as much older than my young wife, I guessed that the real motive of this visit, as my friend

* Daughter of Peter Wedderburn, Lord Chesterhall.

Wedderburn seldom did anything without a reason, was to see how such an unequal couple would look on the day after their marriage.

We remained in Edinburgh till Tuesday the 21st of October, when Baron Grant's lady came in her coach to carry us to Castlesteads, some necessary repairs in the manse not being yet finished. There I had the pleasure to find that my wife could acquit herself equally well in all companies, and had nothing to wish for in the article of behaviour. We went home on Saturday morning, and the Grants followed us to dinner, and were met by the Cardonnels.

While I was busy with this important change in my domestic state, I was applied to by a friend to write a satirical pamphlet in my ironical style against the opposers of the Scotch Militia Bill, which had been rejected in the preceding session. Being too much engaged to attempt anything of that kind at the time, I proposed that it should be intrusted to Adam Ferguson, then living at Inveresk, preparing his academical lectures. My friend answered that he was excellent at serious works, but could turn nothing into ridicule, as he had no humour: I answered, that he did not know him sufficiently, but advised him to go and try him, as he would undertake nothing that he was not able to execute. This happened about the month of August, and Ferguson having undertaken it, executed that little work called *Sister Peg*, in the style of Dr. Arbuthnot's *John Bull*, which excited both admiration and animosity. The real

author was carefully concealed, though it was generally ascribed to me, as I had written two small
pieces in the same ironical style. The public had no
doubt but that it was the work of one out of four of
us, if not the joint work of us all. The secret was
well kept by at least ten or a dozen males and females.
This pamphlet occasioned a very ludicrous scene between David Hume and Dr. Jardine, who was in the
secret. David was a great blab, and could conceal
nothing that he thought for the honour of his friends,
and therefore it had been agreed to tell him of none
of our productions, except such as might have been
published at the Cross. He sent for Jardine, whom
he first suspected of being the author, who denying
his capacity for such a work, he fixed on me (never
dreaming of Ferguson); and when Jardine pretended
ignorance, or refused to gratify him, he told him he
had written it himself in an idle hour, and desired
Jardine to mention him as the author everywhere,
that it might not fall on some of us, who were not so
able to bear it. This I could not have believed, had
not David himself written me a letter to that purpose,
which I shall transcribe in the margin.*

His Majesty George II. died on the 25th of October, which put the whole nation in mourning. John
Home came to town for a night or two, on his way to
London, with Lord Eglinton, when began his greatness, for he might really have been said to have been

* The letter will be found in the *Life and Correspondence of
David Hume*, ii. 88.—J. H. B.

the second man in the kingdom while Bute remained in power, which influence he used not to his own advancement to wealth or power—for he never asked anything for himself, and, strange to tell, never was offered anything by his patron—but for the service of his friends, or of those who, by flattery and application, acquired the title of such, for he was easily deluded by pretences, especially to those of romantic valour. The celebrated Colonel Johnston, afterwards Governor of Minorca, owed to him his being restored to the line of preferment of which the late King had deprived him, for his insolent behaviour to a country gentleman in the playhouse ; and George Johnstone likewise.*

Towards the end of December I went to Polwarth with Mr. Home, my wife's uncle, and one of her guardians, and went to Unthank to visit Mr. Collingwood the other, with Forrester the attorney, to settle our affairs—a trusty fellow, who had already made a large fortune, and, what amused me much, taken the tone of a discontented patriot so strongly against the ministry of his Grace, that they were obliged in a year or two to let him have a share in the management. Alexander Collingwood of Unthank, Esq., the cousin-german of my wife's mother, was weak and vainglorious, proud of his family, and in all, and above all, of his wife, whom he obliged us to visit,

* The former, James Johnston, became subsequently Governor of Quebec. George Johnstone was Governor of West Florida, and author of *Thoughts on our Acquisitions in the East Indies.*— J. H. B.

and whom we found very handsome and very clever —too much so for the squire.

We returned by Langton, as we had come, where lived Alexander Davidson and his wife—two worthy people, who had acquired an independent estate by farming, which had not been frequently done at that time. [Heathpool], our estate, lies three miles from Langton, south-west, up Beumont Water, and is a beautiful Highland place. I had not been absent above five or six days, and found my wife at my father's, where she was the joy and delight of the old folks. At that time, indeed, she was irresistible ; for to youth and beauty she added a cheerful frankness and cordiality in her manner, which, joined with an agreeable elocution and lively wit, attracted all who saw her, which was not relished by my old flame, who, in the midst of forced praise, attempted a species of detraction, which was completely foiled by the good-humoured indifference, or rather contempt, with which it was received. This young lady, of uncommon parts and understanding, but a degree of vanity on account of trifling or imaginary qualities, ended her career at last in a very exemplary manner, as I have before stated.*

Early in this year (1761) my wife's elder sister, Miss Roddam, paid us a visit, and remained with us till she was married. She was a beautiful and elegant young woman, somewhat taller than her sister, and was a finer woman ; but she was grave and reserved ;

* See p. 423.

and though she had good sense, and was perfectly hearty, she was not only inferior to her sister in point of understanding, but in that lively and striking expression of feeling and sentiment which never failed to attract.

They were knit together with the most sisterly love, in which, however, the younger surpassed, not having one selfish corner in her whole soul, and being at all times willing to sacrifice her life for those she loved. This young lady soon attracted our friend Dr. Adam Ferguson's warmest addresses, to the ardour of which she put an end as soon as he explained himself, for, with a frankness and dignity becoming her character, she assured him that, had she not been inviolably engaged to another gentleman, she would not have hastily rejected his addresses, as his character and manner were very agreeable to her, and therefore prayed him to discontinue his suit to her, as she could not listen to him on this subject, but would be happy in his friendship, and the continuance of a society so pleasing to her. With this he reluctantly complied, but frequented our house as much as ever till she was married.

The gentleman she was engaged to was John Erasmus Blackett, Esq., the youngest brother of Sir Edward Blackett, Bart., of Malfen,* in Northumber-

* Matfen : inherited by Sir Edward Blackett through his marriage with Anne, daughter of Oley Douglas of Matfen. Sir Walter Blackett Coverley should read Sir W. B. Calverley. Mr. Calverley was heir to a baronetcy in his own right, and complying with his uncle's (Sir William Blackett) wishes, he married his

land—a man of large fortune, who represented the elder branch of the Blackett family, then in Sir Walter Blackett Coverley, who was the nephew of the late Sir William Blackett of Newcastle. John E. Blackett was a very handsome young man, of about thirty, who had been bred at Liverpool with Sir [   ] Cunliffe, and was now settled partner with Mr. Alderman Simson, an eminent coal-dealer in Newcastle. John Blackett was called Erasmus after Erasmus Lewis, who was secretary to Lord Oxford in Queen Anne's time, and an intimate friend of his father's, John Blackett, Esq. of [   ], in Yorkshire, who never was baronet, having died before his uncle, Sir Edward Blackett. John Erasmus was at this time a captain and paymaster in his brother's regiment of Northumberland Militia, lately raised, and quartered at Berwick since March or April 1760. As Miss Roddam was not of age till March, the marriage was delayed till after that time, when she could dispose of her moiety of the estate. As this did not shake Miss Roddam, that quieted a suspicion which some of her friends entertained that he meant to draw off. But he came and visited us in the end of January, when every shadow of doubt of his fulfilling his engagement was dissipated.

I was only afraid that a man so imperfectly educated as he had been, and of ordinary talents, could not long predominate in the breast of a young lady

cousin (see p. 435), assumed the name of Blackett and latterly became Sir Walter Calverley Blackett.

who had sense and sensibility enough to relish the
conversation of the high-minded and enlightened
philosopher, who had enough of the world, however,
to be entitled to the name of the Polite Philosopher.

I returned with Mr. Blackett in the beginning of
February to Berwick and Wooler, where I met the
trustees, where the estate was let to Ralph Compton,
the second son of our former tenant, for the usual
term, and rose from £180 per annum to £283. Before
we parted, Mr. Blackett settled with me that he would
come to us in April, and complete his engagement.
He went on from Alnwick, and I to the roup at
Wooler.

He came, accordingly, at the time appointed, from
Berwick, attended by a brother captain, Edward
Adams, whose mother was a Collingwood, a grand-
aunt of the young ladies. They came first to my
house for a day, and went to Edinburgh, where we
followed them two days after, where the young couple
were married by Mr. Car of the English chapel, as
they were both Episcopalians.

The day after the marriage Blackett gave us a
handsome dinner at Fortune's, for which he only
charged half-a-crown a-head, and said he then never
charged more for the best dinner of two courses and
a dessert which he could set down. Mr. Ferguson
dined with us. Next day they came to Musselburgh
for two days, and then departed for Newcastle through
Berwick, where the regiment still was. There was
one thing very remarkable of that regiment, which,

though six hundred strong, from all parts of the county, yet lost not one man for one year and four months. So much for the healthiness of Berwick.

My younger sister, Janet, a beautiful, elegant, and pleasing young woman, was married at London, where she had gone to be with her sister, on August 30th, 1760, with Captain Thomas Bell, a nephew of Provost Bell's, who had been captain of a trading vessel in the Mediterranean, and having been attacked by a Spanish privateer, took her after a short engagement, and got £1000 as his share of the prize. He was a very sensible, clever man, much esteemed by his companions, and had become an insurance broker.

On the first of July this year my wife brought me a daughter, and my sister gave a son to Thomas Bell on the 6th of the same month. He was the first of eight sons she had, seven of whom were running, of whom Carlyle, whom we took in 1782 at two years old, is the youngest, who are all alive in 1804, and eight daughters all well married, and have many children.

His Grace Archibald Duke of Argyle died early in spring, as suddenly almost, and at the same age of seventy-seven, as His Majesty, George II., had done in October preceding. On this occasion Lord Bute wrote a very kind letter to Lord Milton, the friend and sub-minister of Argyle, lamenting his loss, and assuring him that there should be no change in respect to him. Adam Ferguson was with Milton

28

when he received this letter, to whom he gave it after reading it, saying, " Is this man sincere ? " to which Ferguson, on perusal, " I have no doubt that he was so when he wrote it." Milton declined being longer employed ; and it was well, for he soon fell into that decline of mental powers which lasted till his death in 1766. Lord Bute tried to make his brother, Stuart M'Kenzie,* succeed Milton, but he neither had talents nor inclination. Baron Mure, who was a man of business and of sound sense, was employed while Lord Bute was in power.

In this year I lost my grandfather and grandmother Robison, truly respectable people in their day. He died first, at the age of eighty-six, and she, who was half a year younger than him, gave way to fate just six months after him.

When my wife was perfectly recovered, I found myself under the necessity of carrying her to New-

* James Stuart Mackenzie was Lord Bute's only brother, who married Lady Elizabeth Campbell, second daughter of John Duke of Argyle, and sister of the Countess of Dalkeith (see p. 313). Mr. Mackenzie was minister at Turin, and on the death of Archibald Duke of Argyle was recalled by his brother to take up the government of Scottish affairs. " He has been described as most amiable, remarkably cheerful and pleasant in society, with very simple tastes and no ambition." With reference to his position as " sub-minister " for Scotland, Mr. Stuart Mackenzie wrote —" They [the ministers headed by Grenville] demanded certain terms, without which they declined coming in ; the principal of which was, that I should be dismissed from the administration of the affairs of Scotland, and likewise from the office of Privy Seal. His Majesty answered that as to the first, it would be no great punishment, he believed, to me, as I had never been very fond of the employment ; but as to the second, I had his promise to continue it for life."—*Mitchell MSS.*

castle to visit her sister, to whom she was most tenderly attached. Mr. Blackett was then living in Pilgrim Street, a small but very pleasant house near the gate. This was in the beginning of October, when the judges were in town, and a great crowd of company. Mr. Blackett's brother Henry, the clergyman, was then with him, who was an Oxonian, a good scholar, and a very agreeable man of the world. We were visited by all their friends in Newcastle and in the neighbourhood, and made many agreeable acquaintances. Sir Walter Blackett was one who lived in a fine old house, directly opposite to Mr. Blackett. He was a very genteel, fine-looking man, turned of forty, who had not been happy with his lady, the daughter (natural) of his uncle, Sir William Blackett, who had left him and her heirs of his estate, provided they intermarried. He fulfilled the will most cordially, for he was in love with his cousin ; but she reluctantly, because she did not care for him. By report she was of superior understanding to him ; for he was not a man of remarkable parts, but strong in friendship, liberality, and public spirit ; and he had a great fortune, not less than £20,000, with which he amply gratified his own disposition. He was ostentatious, and fond of popularity, which he gained by his public charities ; but lived to lose it entirely. He was long member from the town of Newcastle, but never would ask any favours of ministers, while in the mean time he brought in a clever colleague, a Mr. Ridley, who got all the favours from ministers, having both Sir Walter's interest and his own, by which the credit of the former with his townsmen was much shaken.

Our sister, Mrs. Blackett, luckily proved a great favourite of Sir Walter's, as his cousin, John Erasmus, had been before, to whom he gave the payment of his lead mines, which being very productive, was a place of profit.

Mr. Collingwood of Chirton was another valuable acquaintance : he was Recorder of the town, and a lawyer of great ability. Though but the second brother, he had acquired the family estate in consequence of the dissipation of the elder, who was representative of an ancient family, and whose son is Vice-Admiral Collingwood, the husband of Mrs. Blackett's eldest daughter.* The Recorder had acquired Chirton by marriage ; for a laird of Roddam, one of the five families in the county who were proprietors before the Conquest, having been an attorney at Newcastle, had purchased the estate of Chirton, which he left to his two daughters, Mary and Elizabeth, one of whom married a Mr. Hilton Lawson, and the other Mr. Collingwood, while the ancient manor of Roddam went by entail to his nephew, Admiral Roddam.

* In the *Recollections* occurs this interesting note regarding Admiral Collingwood's family, written in 1804 :—" To amuse myself I am going from home first to my niece Mrs. Admiral Collingwood's at Morpeth and her two daughters, who are among my nearest cousins. She is an excellent person with plain good sense and such an excellent heart that it can be no effort to love her, had even her near relation to, and her most affectionate filial love for, the person I loved best not recommended her to my choice."

There were two houses at Chirton, only divided from each other by a road; and by far the best was the possession of Mary, the eldest sister, and her husband Lawson, which had, in the end of the seventeenth century, belonged to Archibald, the first Duke of Argyle, who had built or repaired it as a convenient place between London and Inverary on his journey to and from the capital. It was at this house that he died, on one of those journeys. This house is now the possession of Adam de Cardonnel Lawson, Esq., which was left to his mother, Ann Hilton, by her cousin Hilton Lawson ; because if her brother, a Rev. Mr. Hilton, had not died, he would have fallen heir to that and several other estates of Mr. Lawson's. This gentleman is the son and heir of my old friend Mansfelt de Cardonnel, formerly mentioned.*

Those families adopted our two wives as their relations, as their father was a descendant of the family of Roddam, and their mother of that of Collingwood of Unthank, who was related to both.

At this period there were not many conversible gentlemen in Newcastle, which made one value Mr. Collingwood the more ; for the men were in general very ill educated, while the ladies, who were bred in the south, by their appearance and manners, seemed to be very unequally yoked. The clergy at the time were almost all underbred, there being only one vicar in the town, and the rest only curates or lecturers. Sometimes a neighbouring clergyman of university

* See above, p. 228.

education accepted of a lectureship for the sake of living in town in the winter, though the salaries were no more than £100 ; yet, had it not been for the ladies, the state of society would have then been disagreeable.   For many years past it has been totally different.

At a grand dancing assembly our ladies were gratified as much as they could be, for Mrs. Blackett had the honour of dancing with the Duke of Portland, and her sister with Viscount Torrington, and had the approbation of a very numerous company for their genteel appearance and good looks.

His Grace had come down to take care of his parliamentary interest, having great estates in the northern counties.   He was opposed in Cumberland by Sir James Lowther, who, after a ten years' war, drove the beaten Duke, with infinite loss of money, out of the north.   Lowther went off conqueror, but more detested than any man alive, as a shameless political sharper, a domestic bashaw, and an intolerable tyrant over his tenants and dependents.   John Home cried him up as the bravest and most generous of men ; and he flattered and obliged John because he had the ear of Lord Bute, whose eldest daughter, an amiable and patient woman, he had married and abused.   Home prevailed with him to prefer George Johnstone, the Governor of Florida, to Admiral Elliot, for one of his seats in Parliament, though he was by no means the best man of the two ; but what was still more flattering to John, in two duels he was involved in (neither of which, however, took place), he took him for his second. John cried him up for every good quality, while Ferguson, who had seen him often, said he thought him a very stupid man. Bob Hume, who lived nine months in his house in London, attending his cousin, Sir Michael Fleming, with whom he went to Groningen, thought him a capricious, and sometimes a brutal, head of a family. Robert Adam told me many stories of him, which made me conclude that he was truly a madman, though too rich to be confined.

As Mrs. C. had never been in that country before, we made several excursions in the neighbourhood, such as to Tynemouth and Durham ; and on our return home visited the Roddams, though there were only there the old lady and her two daughters. The Admiral, who succeeded his elder brother in a few years, built himself a handsome house, and improved the place. He had three wives, but no children.

In the beginning of 1762 was instituted the famous club called " The Poker," which lasted in great vigour down to the year 1784. About the third or fourth meeting, we thought of giving it a name that would be of uncertain meaning, and not be so directly offensive as that of Militia Club to the enemies of that institution. Adam Ferguson fell luckily on the name of " Poker," which we perfectly understood, and was at the same time an enigma to the public.* This club consisted of all the literati of Edinburgh

* An instrument for stirring up the militia question.—J. H. B.

and its neighbourhood, most of whom had been members of the Select Society, except very few indeed who adhered to the enemies of militia, together with a great many country gentlemen, who, though not always resident in town, yet were zealous friends to a Scotch militia, and warm in their resentment on its being refused to us, and an invidious line drawn between Scotland and England. The establishment was frugal and moderate, as that of all clubs for a public purpose ought to be. We met at our old landlord's of the Diversorium, now near the Cross, the dinner on the table soon after two o'clock, at one shilling a-head, the wine to be confined to sherry and claret, and the reckoning to be called at six o'clock. After the first fifteen, who were chosen by nomination, the members were to be chosen by ballot, two black balls to exclude the candidate. There was to be a new preses chosen at every meeting. William Johnstone,* Esq., now Sir William Pulteney, was chosen secretary of the club, with a charge of all publications that might be thought necessary by him, and two other members with whom he was to consult.

* William Johnstone was the third son of Sir James Johnstone, third baronet of Westerhall. The eldest son James (see p. 188) succeeded to the baronetcy, and William by his marriage with the only daughter of Daniel Pulteney assumes that name, and on his wife's death acquired the property. He was created Sir William Pulteney, and on the death of his brother Sir James Johnstone, succeeded him as fifth baronet of Westerhall. At his death in 1805 Sir William was reputed one of the wealthiest men in the British Empire ; but according to the Rev. Thomas Somerville (*Memoir of my Life and Times*), the baronet did not live according to his position.

In a laughing humour, Andrew Crosbie was chosen
Assassin, in case any officer of that sort should be
needed ; but David Hume was added as his Assessor,
without whose assent nothing should be done, so that
between *plus* and *minus* there was likely to be no
bloodshed.

This club continued to be in great perfection for
six or seven years, because the expense was moderate,
while every member was pleased with the entertainment as well as the company. During these seven
years, a very constant attendant told me that he
never observed even an approach to inebriety in any
of the members. At the end of that period, by means
of an unlucky quarrel between one or two of the
members and our landlord, who was an absurd fool,
the club left his house and went to Fortune's, the
most fashionable tavern in town, where the dinners
were more showy, but not better, and the wines only
dearer ; but the day's expense soon came to three
times as much as the ordinary bill at Thomas Nicholson's, which made many of the members, not the
least conversible, lessen the number of days of attendance ; and what was worse, as the club had long
drawn the attention of the public, many members
were admitted whose minds were not congenial with
the old members. When this change seemed to be in
danger of essentially hurting the club, a few of us had
recourse to a plan for keeping the old members together, which was that of establishing a new club, to
be called the " Tuesday," to meet on that day, and

dine together, without deserting the Poker. This lasted for two years at Sommer's tavern ; for we did not go to Nicholson's, for fear of giving offence. In the mean time, the Poker dwindled away by the death or desertion of many of the members who had lately been brought in, and then we broke up the Tuesday, and frequented the Poker. I found in the hands of Ferguson a list of this club, taken in 1774, and wrote by Commissioner James Edgar, to which, in other hands, were added the new members as they were elected. I have seen no list previous to this ; but from 1762 to '84, sundry members must have died, two of whom I remember—viz., Dr. Jardine and Ambassador Keith ; Dr. Gregory, too, might be added, but he did not attend above once or twice. The amount of the whole on this list is sixty-six.* When James Edgar was in Paris with Sir Laurence Dundas, his cousin, during the flourishing state of this club, he was asked by D'Alembert to go with him to their club of literati at Paris ; to which he answered that he had no curiosity to visit them, as he had a club at Edinburgh, with whom he dined weekly, composed, he believed, of the ablest men in Europe. Similar to this was a saying of Princess Dashcoff, when disputing one day with me at Buxton about

* The list has been already printed in the Supplement to Tytler's *Life of Kames*, with some inaccurate extracts from Carlyle's MS. This is the best extant account of this curious institution, and nothing of value could be added to it even from the minutes of its proceedings, which the Editor saw in the hands of the late Sir Adam Ferguson.—J. H. B.

the superiority of Edinburgh, as a residence, to most
other cities in Europe, when, having alleged sundry
particulars in which I thought we excelled, none of
which she would admit of—" No," says she, " but I
know one article which you have not mentioned, in
which I must give you the precedency ; which is, that
of all the sensible men I have met with in my travels
through Europe, yours at Edinburgh are the most
sensible." Let me add one testimony more, that of
the Honourable General James Murray, Lord Elibank's brother, a man of fashion and of the world.
Being at the Cross (the 'Change) one day, just before
the hour of dinner, which by that time was prolonged
to three o'clock, he came up to me, and asked me if I
had yet met with his brother Elibank. I answered,
" No ; was he expecting him in town that day ? "
" Yes," said he ; " he promised to come, and introduce me to the Poker." " If that is all your business," replied I, " and you will accept of me as your
introductor, I shall be glad of the honour ; and perhaps your brother may come late, as he sometimes
does." He accepted, and the club happened to be
very well attended. When we broke up, between
seven and eight o'clock, it being summer, and I was
proceeding down street to take my horse to Musselburgh, he came up with me, and exclaimed, " Ah,
Doctor ! I never was so much disappointed in all my
life as at your club, for I expected to sit silent and
listen to a parcel of pedants descanting on learned
subjects out of my range of knowledge ; but instead

of that, I have met with an agreeable, polite, and lively company of gentlemen, in whose conversation I have joined and partaken with the greatest delight." As Murray was a very acute and sensible man, I took this as a very high compliment to the manners as well as the parts of our club.*

In April this year Mrs. C. went to Newcastle, to attend her sister, who was to lie-in of her first child. I went with her to Langton in Northumberland, and returned home, Mrs. B. having met her there.

I attended the Assembly of which I was a member, for the first time out of my course, when Dr. Trail of Glasgow was Moderator. He put upon me the three addresses which were sent up from this Assembly to the King, the Queen, and the Princess-Dowager of Wales, on the marriage of their Majesties, which were thought to be well composed, especially that to His Majesty. This even met with the approbation of the Commissioner,† though not pleased with me, when on one of the preceding years I had helped to raise bad humour against him for inviting Whitefield to dine at his table, and another year he had entertained [a design] of dissolving the Assembly before the second

* " Although the great object of these meetings was national, of which they never lost sight, they had also happy effects on private character by forming and polishing the manners which are suitable to civilised society, for they banished pedantry from the conversation of scholars, and exacted the ideas and enlarged the views of the gentry and created in the several orders a new interest in each other which had not taken place before in the country."—Graham's *Scottish Men of Letters* (Carlyle MSS.).

† Charles, Lord Cathcart.

Sunday. To be sure, the business before us was but slack, yet had we allowed the precedent to take place, we should never have recovered that Sunday more.

On the last day of this Assembly I learned, to my great joy, that my friend Dr. William Wight was presented by the King to the vacant chair of History at Glasgow. As he was my near relation, his advancement, in which I had a chief hand, was very pleasing ; and as he was the most agreeable of all men, his coming near me promised much enjoyment.

Towards the end of June I was earnestly requested by William Johnstone, Esq., now Pulteney, to accompany his uncle, Lord Elibank, on some jaunt, to take him from home, as he had just lost his lady, and was in bad spirits. I agreed, on condition that he would take the road which I wished to go, which was to Newcastle, to bring home Mrs. Carlyle. This was agreed to, and I went to him in a day or two, and we set out on the 27th of June ; and as he travelled with his own horses, we did not arrive there till the 29th to dinner. My fellow-traveller was gloomy, and lamented his wife very much, who had been a beauty in her youth, and was a Dutch lady of fortune, the widow of Lord North and Grey. He himself was now turned sixty, and she was ten years older. She was a weak woman, but very observant of him, and seemed proud of his wit and fine parts, and had no uneasiness about his infidelities, except as they affected his prospects in a future world. She had a large jointure, which he lost, which added to his affliction.   But she had brought a large sum besides, and, falling in with his humour of saving, from being a very poor lord she had made him very wealthy.   When he arrived at Newcastle, he was at first overcome with the sight of my wife, who was well acquainted with his lady ; but her sympathy, and the gentle manners of her sister, attracted his notice.   He had by nature very great sensibility ; he admired, and had once loved, his wife, whom he was conscious he had injured.   In this tender state of vexation, mixed with grief and penitence, he met at Newcastle with a very hand-some young lady, Miss Maria Fielding, a niece of Sir John Fielding, whose manners, softened by his recent loss and melancholy appearance, so much subdued him, that he fell suddenly in love, and was ashamed and afflicted with his own feelings, falling into a kind of a hysterical fit.   Mrs. Carlyle told me afterwards that she had made him confess this, which he said he did because he saw she had found him out.   Hearing that some of his friends were at Harrogate, he left us on the fourth or fifth day, and went there : at this place there was plenty of gay company, and play, and every sort of amusement for an afflicted widower, so that his lordship soon forgot his lady and her join-ture, and Maria Fielding, and all his cares and sorrow, and became the gayest man in the whole house before the month of July elapsed.

As we were to go round by Dumfries to visit my sister Dickson, who had fallen into a decline, and was

drinking goats' whey in the neighbourhood, we proposed to take the road to Carlisle from Newcastle;
and Mrs. Carlyle not being very strong, we got Mr.
Blackett's chaise for the first day's journey. After
you have got ten or twelve miles west from Newcastle, the country becomes dreary and desolate,
without a single interesting object but what employs
the curious research of the antiquarian—the remains
of that Roman wall which was constructed to prevent
the inroads of the barbarians on the Roman provinces or the defenceless natives. The wall in many
parts is wonderfully entire; and while it demonstrates the art and industry of the Romans, brings
full in our view the peace and security we now enjoy
under a government that unites the interest and pro-
motes the common prosperity of the whole island.
We slept at Glenwhilt, a paltry place, and got to
Brampton early next day, but had to send to Carlisle
for a chaise, as I did not choose to carry Mr. Blackett's any further. This place, as is noted in an account of Dr. Wight, is remarkable for the birth of
three persons in the same year, or nearly so, who got
as high in their respective professions as they possibly
could—Dr. Thomas, a son of the rector of the parish,
who came to be Bishop of Rochester; Mr. Wallace,
a son of the attorney, who arrived at the dignity of
Attorney-General, and would have been Chancellor
had he lived; and Dr. William Wight, the son of the
dissenting minister, who lived to be Professor of
Divinity in Glasgow.

It was late in the afternoon before the chaise came from Carlisle, for which I had sent, so that we not only breakfasted but dined here, when the cheapness, not less than the goodness, of our fare was surprising, as 4s. 6d. was the whole expense for Mrs. Carlyle's dinner and mine, and Blackett's servant, and two horses, mine having gone on to Carlisle. The environs of Carlisle are beautiful, and Mrs. Carlyle was much pleased with them. The road from thence to Dumfries is through a level country, but not very interesting, being at that time unimproved, and but thinly inhabited. The approach to Dumfries on every side is pleasing.

My sister Dickson was down at Newabbey, ten miles below Dumfries, on the west side of the Nith, for the sake of goats' whey. We went down next day, but found her far gone in a decline, a disorder which had been so fatal to our family. She was well acquainted with Mrs. Carlyle's character before she met her, which she did with the most tender and cheerful affection. Her appearance, she told me, even surpassed all she had heard ; and for the two days they remained together, there never was a closer union of two superior minds, softened by tenderness and adorned with every female virtue. It was difficult to part them, as they were sure they would meet no more : many confident promises were made, however, to lighten as much as possible the melancholy parting, which my sister performed with such angelic gaiety as led Mrs. Carlyle into the belief that she thought herself in little danger. I knew the contrary. One thing she did—which was, to confirm me in the opinion of what an excellent mind it was to which I was united ; but this needed no confirmation. After this scene, Dumfries and the company of our other friends was irksome, so we made haste to meet my mother, who had taken the road home from Penrith, having been so long absent from my father. We found our little girl in perfect health.

It was this year, in September, that on the death of Hyndman I succeeded him in the place of Almoner to the King, an office of no great emolument, but a mark of distinction, and very convenient, as my stipend was small, for I kept my resolution to defer a prosecution for an augmentation till my patron was of age.* I had reason to expect this office, not only by means of John Home, now having much of Lord Bute's ear, but from the friendship of Sir Gilbert Elliot and Sir Harry Erskine, who were friends of Lord Bute. Charles Townshend, too, had made application at this time, though he failed me before.

The death of Hyndman was a disappointment to Robertson in the management of the Church, which he had now in view. By his preference of Hyndman,

---

* " When Dr. Carlyle got what was described as an exorbitant augmentation, Lord Gardenstone, who differed in almost every respect from his brother Auchinleck, told the Court that the Doctor was a fine fellow, in whose company their Lordships would be delighted ; but in order to enable him to give them a dinner, it would be proper they should give him something handsome, which the tithes could well afford."—Ramsay's *Scotland and Scotsmen.*

29

he had provoked Dick, who was a far better man, and
proved a very formidable and vigorous opponent ;
for he joined the Wild or High-flying party, and by
moderating their councils and defending their measures as often as he could, made them more embarrassing than if they had been allowed to follow their
own measures.   Hyndman was a clever fellow, a
good preacher, and a good debater in church courts.
Cuming had adopted him as his second, and had
helped to bring him from Colinton to the West Church.
Being unfortunate in his family, he had taken to
tippling and high politics.   He finished his constitution, and became apoplectic.   Cuming and he had
quarrelled, and Robertson, without adverting to his
undone constitution *

It was in about the end of this year that my sister
Bell, and her two children then born—William and
Jessie—came down to pay my father and mother a
visit, and stayed between their houses and ours till
the month of June 1763.

Thomas Cheap, consul at Madeira, my friend, came
to Edinburgh in the beginning of the year [1763], to
visit his friends and look out for a wife.   After having been plied by two or three, he at last fixed on
Grace Stuart, a very pretty girl, and carried her.

* The sentence is left unfinished : the intention seems to have
been to say, that Robertson made him second in command to
himself as leader of the Church.   Hyndman is referred to in Chap.
III., and on several other occasions.   A notice of him will be
found in Morren's *Annals of the General Assembly*, ii. 402.—
J. H. B.

This pleased his sister well, who was always looking after quality ; for her mother, Lady Ann, was
a sister of the Earl of Murray. This courtship occasioned several pleasant meetings of private parties
at Chrystal's, a tavern in the parish, where Dr.
Robert Finlay, now possessor of Drummore, displayed such qualities as he had ; for he was master of
one of the feasts, having lost a dinner and a ball to
the Consul's sister. Ann Collingwood made a good
figure in the dance, but Grace Collingwood surpassed
her.

About the end of April, my sister, and my wife, and
[I, paid] a visit to our friends in Glasgow, where we
were most cordially received by my old friends, Mr.
Dreghorn and sundry other merchants, who were con-
nected with Mr. Bell in Airdrie, particularly Robin
Bogle and the Dunlops. Dr. Adam Smith and
Dr. Black, as well as Dr. Wight, were now here,
though the last had not yet got into his house. We
had many agreeable meetings with them, as well as
with our mercantile friends. It was there that I saw
No. 45, when just published by Wilkes, of which
Smith said, on hearing it read, " Bravo ! this fellow
will either be hanged in six months, or he will get
Lord Bute impeached." * Supping with him in a

---

* " The plot thickens : Mr. Wilkes is sent to the Tower for the
last *North Briton* [No. 45], a paper whose fame must have reached
you. It said Lord Bute had made the King utter a great falsehood in his last speech. This hero is a bad fellow as ever hero was,
abominable in private life, dull in parliament, but they say very
entertaining in a room, and certainly no bad writer, besides

company of twenty-two, when a certain young peer
was present, after a little while I whispered him that
I wondered they had set up this man so high, as I
thought him mighty foolish.   " We know that perfectly," said he ;   " but he is the only lord at our
college."   To this day there were not above two or
three gentlemen's chaises in Glasgow, nor hackney-
coaches, nor men-servants to attend at table ; but
they were not the worse served.

Soon after we returned home in the beginning of
May, my sister and her children returned to London,
but took the way by Dumfries to visit their friends
there.

Dr. Robertson was Moderator of the Assembly this
year, and being now Principal of the University of
Edinburgh, had it in his power to be member of
Assembly every year.   He had lost Hyndman, but he
had now adopted Dr. John Drysdale, who had married his cousin, one of the Adams, a far better man in
every respect ; for he had good talents for business,
though his invincible modesty prevented his speaking in public.   He now managed the Highland correspondence, and became extremely popular in that
division of the Church.   Robertson had now Dr.
Dick as his stated opponent, who would have been
very formidable had he not been tied up by his own
principles, which were firm in support of presentations, and by his not having it in his power to be a

having had the honour of contributing a great deal to Lord Bute's
fall."—Walpole to Mann.

member of Assembly more than once in four or five years, on account of the strict rotation observed by the Presbytery of Edinburgh.

Andrew Crosbie, the advocate, was another constant and able opponent of Dr. Robertson and his friends, though hampered a little by the law of patronage. His maternal uncle, Lord Tinwald, the Justice-Clerk, who was his patron, being dead, he wished to gain employment by pleasing the popular side. Fairbairn, the minister of Dumbarton, was another opponent—brisk and foul-mouthed, who stuck at nothing, and was endowed with a rude popular eloquence ; * but he was a mere hussar, who had no steady views to direct him. He was a member of every Assembly, and spoke in every cause, but chiefly for plunder—that is, applause and dinners— for he did not seem to care whether he lost or won. Robertson's soothing manner prevented his being hard-mouthed with him.

Dr. Robertson had for his assistants [not only] all the Moderate party in Edinburgh and the neighbourhood, but many clergymen annually from the most distant Synods and Presbyteries ; who, now that the debates of the Assembly were carried on with freedom, though still with great order, were very good

* " A plain country clergyman, but of infinite native humour, Fairbairn, minister of Dumbarton, whose talent for enlivening a debate by pleasantry, or turning the laugh against his adversary by sarcasm, not rude, though keen, I have seldom heard equalled by any debater whatever."—Henry Mackenzie's *Life of Home*.

speakers and able debaters.   There were very few of
the lay elders of much consideration who opposed
him ; and Henry Dundas (Lord Melville), who was
in himself a host, coming next year to our aid, [added
greatly to our strength, and made the business fashionable, for till then] many of the superior elders
deserted the Assembly, insomuch that I remember
one year, that when a most important overture was
debated there was neither one of the Judges nor of
the Crown lawyers in the Assembly.*

In May this year we had a visit from the Blacketts,
who did not stay long ; and having an appointment
with Dr. Wight to go for a few weeks to Harrogate,
we set out in the beginning of July, and on our way
passed some days in Newcastle, where Wight, who
was a stranger, made his usual impression as one of
the most agreeable men they had ever seen.   When
we arrived at the Dragon, in Harrogate, however,
Wight's vivacity was alarmed at the shyness of the
English, who are backward to make up to strangers
till they have reconnoitred them a while.   Wight
was much enraged at this, and threatened either to
leave the place, or to breakfast in a private room.   I
prevailed with him to have his table set in the long
room, where our demeanour being observed by the
company, we were soon relieved from our awkward
situation by an invitation from two ladies, who had
no men with them, to come to their breakfast-table,

* The passage in brackets is in the MS., but not in the Author's
hand.

according to the custom of the place at this time. We found them very agreeable, and were envied for our good-luck. When we entered the dining-room at two o'clock, we were no longer strangers, and took our places according to the custom of the house. There were two tables in the dining-room, which held between thirty and forty apiece, and our places were at the bottom of that on the right hand, from whence we were gradually to rise to the top of the room as the company changed, which was daily.

Harrogate at this time was very pleasant, for there was a constant succession of good company, and the best entertainment of any watering-place in Britain, at the least expense. The house we were at was not only frequented by the Scotch at this time, but was the favourite house of the English nobility and gentry. Breakfast cost gentlemen only 2d. apiece for their muffins, as it was the fashion for ladies to furnish tea and sugar ; dinner, 1s. ; supper, 6d. ; chambers, nothing ; wine and other extras at the usual price, and as little as you please ; horses and servants at a reasonable rate. We had two haunches of venison twice a-week during the season. The ladies gave afternoon's tea and coffee in their turns, which, coming but once in four or five weeks, amounted to a trifle. The estates of the people at our table did not amount to less than £50,000 or £60,000 per annum, among whom were several members of Parliament ; and they had not had the precaution to order one newspaper among

them all, though the time was critical ; but Andrew
Millar, the celebrated bookseller, supplied that defect,
for he had two papers sent to him by every post, so
that all the baronets and great squires—your Sir
Thomas Claverings, and Sir Harry Grays, and Drummond of Blairdrummond—depended upon and paid
him civility accordingly ; and yet when he appeared
in the morning, in his old well-worn suit of clothes,
they could not help calling him Peter Pamphlet ; for
the generous patron of Scotch authors, with his city
wife and her niece, were sufficiently ridiculous when
they came into good company. It was observed, however, that she did not allow him to go down to the well
with her in the chariot in his morning dress, though
she owned him at dinner-time, as he had to pay the
extraordinaries.

As Wight had never been in York, we went down
early on a Sunday morning, when we heard that the
Archbishop and the Judges were to be in the Cathe-
dral. We had Dr. Hunter, M.D., who at that time
frequented Harrogate, for our guide ; but he was kept
in such close conversation that he mistook the road,
and led us two miles out of our way, so that we had
but just time to breakfast before we went to church,
when the service being begun, we entered the choir,
where it was crowded to the door. Our eyes were
delighted with such a magnificent show, but our ears
were not so highly pleased, for no part of the service
seemed to us to suit the grandeur of the scene. We
were invited to dine with Mr. Scott from Madeira,

Thomas Cheap's partner ; but Wight had engaged
to dine with the Honourable Archdeacon Hamilton,
whose education he had superintended for a year at
Glasgow, and with whom he was well acquainted in
Ireland, where his preferment lay. His beautiful
wife had eloped from him with a Sir George Warren,
and he had received her again, and was living privately at York till the story became stale. Wight extolled her beauty and her penitence—and, if I remember right, they continued to live together, and
had sons and daughters. We passed the evening
with Mr. Scott, who had with him a large party of
Americans—Mr. Allen, Justice-General of Pennsylvania, and his two sons and daughters, fine young
people indeed, the eldest of them not yet twenty
years of age : with them there was also a Mr. Livingstone, and, I think, a sister of his also. Mr. Allen
was a man very open and communicative, and as he
was of Scottish extraction, his grandfather having
fled from Stirlingshire to escape the cruel persecu-
tions of the Presbyterians by Lauderdale and James
II., he seemed partial to us as clergymen from Scotland. He said he intended to have gone as far as
Edinburgh, but found he should not have time at
present, but was to leave his sons in England to complete their education. He wished us to stay all next
day, and come an hour in the forenoon to examine his
lads, to judge to what a length young men could now
be brought in America. This we declined, but agreed
to dine next day, and bring on such conversation as

would enable us to judge better of the young men than any formal examination.

There was a circumstance that I shall never forget, which passed in one of our conversations. Dr. Wight and I had seen Dr. Franklin at Edinburgh, as I have formerly related : we mentioned this philosopher to Mr. Allen with the respect we thought due, and he answered, " Yes, all you have said of him is true, and I could add more in his praise ; but though I have now got the better of him, he has cost me more trouble since he came to reside in our State than all mankind besides ; and I can assure you that he is a man so turbulent, and such a plotter, as to be able to embroil the three kingdoms, if he ever has an opportunity." Franklin was after this for several weeks in Edinburgh with David Hume, but I did not see him, having been from home on some jaunt. In 1769 or '70 I met him at an invited dinner in London, at John Stuart's, the Provost's son I think it was, where he was silent and inconversible, but this was after he had been refused the office of Postmaster-General of America, and had got a severe dressing from Wedderburn, then Solicitor or Attorney-General. We returned to Harrogate in the evening, where Mr. Scott and his wife joined us next day.

It was my good fortune at dinner to sit next Mr. Ann, a Roman Catholic gentleman of Yorkshire, who was very agreeable, and knew the whole company ; but it was our misfortune to lose our new friends very fast, for at the end of a fortnight I was at the head of

a table, above thirty, and, I remember, had to divide
a haunch of venison among fifteen of them without
getting any portion of fat for myself—" but what
signifies that, when you have an opportunity of obliging your friends ? " as Sir J. Dalrymple said to me
one day when we had a haunch at the Poker, flattering me for a good piece, for he was a gourmand.   But
it was wonderful to observe how easily we united
with our new friends who took the places of the
deceased, for most of them were in reality so to us.
We fell in by accident with a very agreeable man, a
Colonel Roberts, who was lieutenant-colonel of the
Royal Irish, and had been in that country for three
years, and had so completely caught the brogue that
it was impossible at first to think him an Englishman
born and bred, which he nevertheless was, and nephew
to Lord Egremont, Secretary of State at the time.
This gentleman, by ill-luck, had been directed to the
Salutation Inn, which was the Quakers' house, of
excellent entertainment, but indifferent company.
He took much to Wight and me, and we would fain
have drawn him to our house, but he would not for
the world affront the good people, with whom he had
lived a week.   So we compromised the matter, and
went sometimes to dine at his house, and he returned
the visit and came to ours.   He was truly a man of
sense, and of much reading, and a great master of
conversation : he was the first whom I met with who
struck out an idea that has been followed since ; for,
talking much of Hume's and Robertson's Histories,

he said that Hume appeared to him to be the Homer and Robertson the Virgil of British historians,—a criticism that has of late been confirmed by Dugald Stewart's quotation.

Our friend Captain Francis Lindsay was at the Granby, who sometimes dined with us, as we did one day with him, when we understood that Lord Clive and his train were to dine there ; and he had arrived the evening before, of which Lindsay informed us, and we went in due time to dinner. Clive was an ill-looking man, with the two sides of his face much unlike, one of them seeming distorted as with the palsy. When we entered the long room, he was sitting at a table in a window with a great many papers before him, which he had received with that day's post.   It was by those despatches that he had learned that his jagire * was taken from him.   Lindsay had watched his countenance from the moment he got them, but could perceive no change in the muscles of his face, which were well suited to bad news.   But he must have known before this time what had happened. He sat at some distance from me on the opposite side, but he seemed to converse with nobody during dinner, and left the table immediately after.   There were

* " A rent-charge which had been granted him by the Nabob, and which on the seizure of the territory on which it was charged, by the East India Company, Lord Clive insisted that the Company should continue to pay.   It was about twenty-five thousand pounds per annum."   Note by Croker to the following reference by Walpole.   " The East India Company, yesterday, elected Lord Clive—Great Mogul ; that is, they have made him Governor-General of Bengal and restored his jaghire."

half-a-dozen people with him, among whom were his favourite secretaries, both jolly fellows, who loved a glass of claret, which Lindsay recommended to them, and which was truly good.

Thomas Cheap, my friend from Madeira, who had been married at Inveresk with Grace Stuart, came to Harrogate, according to his promise, to visit Lindsay and me. He came to the Dragon, and remained four days with us. She was very handsome and spirited, and made a great impression. Robert Berry and his beautiful wife were there at the same time, and it could not be doubted that she was the finer woman of the two ; yet our fair Caledonian had so much frankness and spirit, and danced so exquisitely, that she carried off all hearts, insomuch that there was a sensible degree of regret and gloominess in the company for a quarter of an hour at least after she left it.

Wight and I rode one day to Hackfell, a place of the Aislabies, a few miles beyond Ripon, through a most delightful country, no part of which is finer than Ripley. Hackfell consists of a few wooded hills on both sides of a valley, terminating in a fine village on the banks of a small river, called Masham. There are fine walks cut through the woods, which make the place very delightful. Many such are now in Scotland, since our great proprietors have found the way to lay open the secret beauties of their romantic domains to strangers. Not being able to reach Harrogate to dinner, we tried to get something at Grewelthorpe, the adjacent village ; but there was no fire in the house, nor anything indeed, but very bad oat bread and some ordinary cheese. Rummaging about in the awmry, however, I found at last about two pounds' weight of cold roast-veal, which was a great prize, especially now that two gentlemen had joined us, an Hanoverian nobleman, and a Dr. Dod from London—not he of infamous memory, but another of perfect good character and very agreeable manners. We visited many fine places in the neighbourhood, and particularly Harewood, the seat of Squire Lascelles, now Lord Harewood, where there is a very fine house built by Robert Adam, and then not inhabited. The house might have had a finer site, had it been a quarter of a mile more to the north, where there is a full view of one of the finest vales in Yorkshire. Next year I visited this place again with my wife and the Blacketts, and having been rebuked by Sir David Dalrymple [Lord Hailes] for having omitted it before (because I was ignorant of its curiosity), I went into the village church and saw the monument of the Chief-Justice Gascoigne, a native here, who had arrested Henry V., when Prince of Wales, for a riot.

Harrogate abounded with half-pay officers and clergymen. The first are much the same at all times, ill educated, but well bred ; and when you now and then meet with a scholar such as Colonel Roberts, or my old friend whom I knew when Lieutenant Ward at Musselburgh—a little stuttering fellow, about the year 1749, who had read Polybius and Cæsar twice over, and who rose to be a general and commander of the cavalry in Ireland—you will find him as intelligent as agreeable. Of the clergy I had never seen so many together before, and between this and the following year I was able to form a true judgment of them. They are in general —I mean the lower order—divided into bucks and prigs ; of which the first, though inconceivably ignorant, and sometimes indecent in their morals, yet I held them to be most tolerable, because they were unassuming, and had no other affectation but that of behaving themselves like gentlemen. The other division of them, the prigs, are truly not to be endured, for they are but half-learned, are ignorant of the world, narrow-minded, pedantic, and overbearing. And now and then you meet with a *rara avis* who is accomplished and agreeable, a man of the world without licentiousness, of learning without pedantry, and pious without sanctimony ; but this *is* a *rara avis*.

This was the first time I had seen John Bull at any of his watering-places, and I thought it not difficult to account for his resort to them. John is an honest and worthy person as any in the world, but he is seldom happy at home. He has in his temper a shyness that approaches to timidity, and a deference for the opinion of his servant that overawes him, and keeps him in constraint at home, while he is led into unreasonable expense. At his watering-places he is free from these shackles ; his reserve is

overcome by the frankness of those he meets ; he is
master of his servants, for he carries only two with
him ; and the man of £10,000 per annum can spend
no more than the man of £500, so that the honest
man finds himself quite unfettered, and is ready to
show his kind and sociable disposition ; he descends
from his imaginary dignity by mixing with those who
are richer than himself, and soon shows you what he
really is, viz. the very best sort of man in the world.
The late wars have been very favourable to the im-
proving and disclosing his character, for instead of
going into France, where he was flattered, laughed at,
and plundered, he is now obliged to make all his summer excursions round his own country, where his heart
expands ; and, being treated as he deserves, returns
home for the winter happy and much improved.

At this period everything was cheap and good at
Harrogate, except wine, which, unless it was their
claret, which was everywhere good and reasonable,
was very bad indeed. John Bull, however, has little
taste, and does not much care ; for provided he goes
to bed muzzy, whether it be with his own native
drink, ale, or sophisticated port, he is perfectly contented.

As I designed to convey Wight to Dumfries, and
Captain Lindsay was going by Lochmaben to visit
his brother James, the minister, we agreed to set
out together, and made a very agreeable journey.
Some part of the road was dreary after we passed
Sir Thomas Robertson's, which is a fine place, and

where there is an inscription fairly acknowledging that the family took its rise from a Scotch pedlar. When we approached Appleby, we were delighted with the appearance of the country, which, being a mixture of hill and dale, of wood and water, of cultivated and uncultivated, is far more pleasing to the eye and the imagination than those rich plains which are divided into small squares or parallelograms, which look like bleach-fields for cotton, on the banks of the Clyde or Leven. At Penrith we resolved to stop a day, to rest our horses, and to take the opportunity of going to visit the lake Keswick, of which we had heard so much. Next morning we took a post-chaise and four and drove thither, over a rough road, through a barren country to the village, at a distance of eighteen miles. We were unlucky, for it proved a rainy afternoon, so that we could not sail on the lake, and saw everything to great disadvantage. We returned to Penrith, where we had good entertainment and excellent claret.

Next morning we set out northwards, and separated from Captain Lindsay when we came to Longtown, for he went to Lochmaben, and we took the road to Dumfries, where, after staying a few days, I took the road home by Moffat, and Wight went over to Ireland, once more to visit his friends there. I found my wife and little daughter in good health, with a fair prospect of another ere long. My wife had supposed that I had some scorbutic symptoms, which had been removed by Harrogate waters.

30

The remainder of the season passed on as usual, but I was not any more from home, except now and then in Edinburgh at the Poker Club, which ceased to meet by the 12th of August, and reopened on the 12th of November.

Luke Home, our aunt Home's youngest son, came to us to be at the school a year or two before, and remained four years. Their daughter, Betty, came after, and stayed two or three years. On the first day of December this year my wife brought me a second daughter, which, after trying in vain to nurse, she gave to a very faithful and trusty woman in Fisherrow, who, after remaining one quarter with us, we allowed to take the child to her own house, where she continued to thrive to our entire satisfaction.

CHAPTER XII

It was in February this year, I think, that Mrs. Carlyle, being perfectly recovered, and I accompanied her uncle and aunt, Mr. and Mrs. Home, to Glasgow, to see their son Walter, who was in quarters there with his regiment, the 7th Foot. Dr. Wight had by that time got into his house in the College, and had got his youngest sister to keep his house, who was remarkably handsome, had very good parts, with the frank and open manner of the Dumfriesians. Her brother did not disappoint her turn for social entertainment, for he loved company, and the house was not without them almost any day. Here we and our friends were handsomely entertained, as well as at Mrs. Dreghorn's, where we lodged ; and at her brother's, Mr. Bogle's, who never relaxed in his attachment to me. Walter Home, then only a lieutenant, whose chum was a Mr. Mainwarring, a very agreeable man, had made himself very respectable in Glasgow, to which he was well entitled, as much from his superior sense and knowledge as

from his social turn. John Home, by one of his
benevolent mistakes, had put him about James
Stuart, Lord Bute's second son, whom he was
engaged to attend daily while he lived with Dr.
Robertson in Edinburgh.

At this time Henry Dundas, the most strenuous
advocate for the law of the land respecting presentations, and the ablest and steadiest friend to Dr.
Robertson and his party that ever appeared in
my time, became a member of Assembly. He
constantly attended the Assembly before and after
he was Solicitor-General, though when he rose to
be Lord Advocate and member of Parliament he
was sometimes detained in London till after the
meeting of Assembly. He was more than a match
for the few lawyers who took the opposite side,
and even for Crosbie, who was playing a game, and
Dr. Dick, who was by far the ablest clergyman in
opposition.* I am not certain whether Henry
Dundas did not excel more as a barrister than he
did as a judge in a popular assembly—in the first,
by his entering so warmly into the interest of his
client as totally to forget himself, and to adopt all
the feelings, sentiments, and interests of his employer ;
in the second, by a fair and candid statement of the
question, and followed it by strong and open reasoning in support of his opinion. For a few years at

* " On the other side was Dr. Dick, one of the most powerful
speakers in point of eloquence and impression that had ever
appeared in that, or any other, popular [assembly."—Henry
Mackenzie's *Life of Home*.

this period there was a great struggle in the General Assembly against the measures supported and carried through by Robertson and his friends, and we had to combat the last exertions of the party who had supported popular calls ; and it must be confessed that their efforts were vigorous. They contrived to bring in overtures from year to year, in which they proposed to consult the country, in the belief that the result would be such a general opinion over the kingdom as would oblige the General Assembly to renew their application for the abolition of patronage, or at least for some more lenient exercise of it. Those endeavours were encouraged by a new schism in the Church, which was laid by a Mr. Baine, minister of Paisley, which in a few years produced a numerous body of new seceders called the Presbytery of Relief, who had no fault to anything but presentations. This faction was supported for several years by a strange adventurer, a Mr. William Alexander, the second son of the provost of that name, who of all the men I have known had the strongest propensity to plotting, with the finest talents for such a business. As his attempts to speak in the Assembly were unsuccessful, and drew nothing on him but ridicule, he actually wrote to Dr. Blair (I have seen the letter), offering him a thousand pounds if he could teach him the art of speaking in public. As Blair was Professor of Rhetoric and Belles-Lettres, he thought he was the most likely person to comply with his request ;

but he had not observed that Dr. Blair never spoke in public himself, but from the pulpit, from whence he might have gathered that the knowledge of rhetoric was different from the practice.

It was in this year that Dr. Drysdale was translated from Kirkliston to Edinburgh after a long struggle with the popular body, the General Session of Edinburgh, who, with the Town Council, had for many years elected all the ministers. The Magistrates and Council reassumed their right of presentation in this case, and after much litigation established it, much for the peace of the city. During the contest, which was violent, my friend Dr. Jardine rode out to me, and requested me to draw up a paper in their defence, which I did on his furnishing me with the facts, and published under the title of *Faction Detected*. This I mention, because Mr. Robertson, the Procurator, asked me once if it was not of his father's composing, for so it had been said to him. But I told him the fact, and at the same time gave him the reasons of dissent from a sentence of the Commission in 1751 or '52, which had been originally drawn by Dr. Robertson, though corrected and enlarged by a committee. This pamphlet had so much effect that the opposition employed their first hand, Dr. Dick, to write an answer to it; and yet neither the provost, nor any of the magistrates, nor Drysdale himself, ever thanked me for it. Dr. Jardine perhaps never told his father-in-law, Drummond, and I never asked him about it.

Lindsay, who was restless, for whom John Home had obtained Lochmaben, now got Kirkliston, and Lord Bute sent Dicky Brown to Lochmaben, for which he had no thanks from the neighbourhood, for though Lindsay's temper was not very congruous to his brethren and neighbours, yet he was a gentleman, whereas the other was the contrary, and sometimes deranged.

In the end of summer I went again with Mrs. Carlyle to Harrogate, as her health was not good, and as the [change], if not the waters, might be good for her. I got an open chaise with two horses— one before the other, and the servant on the first. As many of the roads through which we went were not at all improved, we found this an excellent way of travelling. We visited our friends in the Merse and in the north of England by the way, and stayed some days at Newcastle. As Mr. Blackett and his lady were going soon to Ripon to visit his mother, they agreed to come on for a week to Harrogate, after which we would return with them by York, where Mrs. Carlyle had never been.

The assizes were at Newcastle while we were there, and Alexander Wedderburn was attending as a counsellor.* He had been there the preceding year, but had not a cause. Mr. ————, an old counsellor, who had left London and settled at Leeds, had

* The reader need hardly be reminded that the Alexander Wedderburn so frequently mentioned became Lord Chancellor Loughborough.—J. H. B.

become acquainted with him, and had discovered the superiority of his talents. He got him two or three briefs this circuit, and his appearances were such as insured him future success. This very gentleman pointed out his first lady to him, with whom he got £10,000. When the assizes were over he dined with us at Mr. Blackett's, where his talent for conversation not being equal to that at the bar, being stiff and pompous, he made not such an impression on the company as they expected. The appearance of self-conceit always disgusts the ladies. He came to Harrogate during the first days of our residence there and stayed two nights, when Mrs. Carlyle had some difficulty in getting him a partner.

It will not be improper here to state, that on a future occasion I had the good fortune to save a man for that time from the gallows. There was a man of the name of Robertson, who lived near Belford, who was accused of having stolen a heifer, and killed it at his own house. The heifer had belonged to a person several miles distant from Belford, and was killed and skinned before it was seen by anybody ; but the proof on its marks, and the colour of its skin, made it very like the one amissing. The man had no advocate, and being put on the boards, was asked by the judge (Yates) if he had any defence to make. He answered, that he was in use of going annually to Dunse fair, where he generally bought a beast or two for his own use, and this was one he had got there.

The judge summed up the evidence and charged the jury, observing in his conclusion, that the only defence the man made was, that he bought the heifer at Dunse fair. Now it having been proved that this heifer was of English breed, which could not be bought at Dunse, that defence would go for nothing. I was amazed at the ignorance of the judge, and the carelessness of the grand jury, and said to Colonel Dickson of Belford that the judge had gone quite wrong in his charge. He answered that Robertson was a great rascal, and deserved to be hanged. I answered that might be true, but that he ought not to suffer for the ignorance of the judge or jury, for he knew as well as I did that cattle of Northumberland were to be bought at Dunse fair —nay, that half the cattle in Berwickshire were of that breed, so that if he would not explain this to the judge, I would. I at last prevailed with him to go round and whisper the judge, who, calling in the jury, retracted what he had said. He sent them out again, and in a few minutes they returned and gave in their verdict, " Not guilty." I am afraid such mistakes must frequently happen in England, in spite of the perfection of their laws.

When we arrived at Harrogate, the Dragon was not full, and the first person we saw was the late General Clerk, whom, though younger by at least a year than me, I had known at college, and had sometimes met when I was last in London. This was a very singular man, of a very ingenious and active intellect, though he had broke short in his education by entering at an early age into the army ; and having by nature a copious elocution, he threw out his notions, which were often new, with a force and rapidity which stunned you more than they convinced. He applied his warlike ideas to colloquial intercourse, and attacked your opinions as he would do a redoubt or a castle, not by sap and mine, but by open storm. I must confess, that of all the men who had so much understanding, he was the most disagreeable person to converse with whom I ever knew. The worst of him was that he was not contented with a patient hearing, nor even with the common marks of assentation, such as yes, or certainly, or to be sure, or nodding the head, as Charles Townshend, and William Robertson, and other great talkers were ; you must contradict him, and wrangle with him, or you had no peace. Elibank had something of the same humour, but he was better bred. Clerk was truly the greatest siccatore in the world. Like some of the locusts that blast the vegetable world, and shrivel to dust everything that is green, he was of the caterpillar kind, who have a particular species of food, on which alone they fasten, and leave the rest untouched. I un-luckily happened to be the only person of that species at this time in the Dragon whom he knew, and he fastened on me like a leech. Mrs. Carlyle and I breakfasted at a table by ourselves, not caring to join with anybody, as we expected our

friends from Newcastle. In vain I hinted this to
him as an excuse for not asking him to breakfast.
That, he said, he never did, as he wished to be
independent. On the third day, however, after
our arrival, having been much taken with Mrs. Carlyle's manner of conversing, and her not being
alarmed at his paradoxes, but only laughing at
them, he ordered his tea-table to be set down close
by hers, and kept up a noisy palaver which attracted
the attention of the whole room ; and had it not
been for the lady's entire possession of herself, and her
being a general favourite of the company who were
there, might have let loose the tongue of scandal.
He told me that he expected Adam Ferguson from
Edinburgh immediately, who was to take the two
brothers of Lord Grenville, who were with Dr.
Robertson at Edinburgh, under his care, and that
he looked every day for his arrival. Ferguson had
told me this before, and I now ardently wished for
his coming. In about four or five days Ferguson
came, and most happily relieved me from my post
of fatigue ; for when everybody went a riding or
walking in the forenoon, the first of which he could
not do, as he had no horse,—would you believe it ?
he patiently walked backwards and forwards within sight of the door, so that I could not possibly
escape him, and was obliged to submit to my destiny,
which was to walk and wrangle with him for three
hours together. About the fourth evening I had
a little relief by the arrival of two gentlemen, whom,

as we met driving to the inn in such a carriage as mine, as we were walking on the heath, Clerk, having stopped and spoken to them, returned to me and said that we were now lucky, for those were hands of the first water. They were ⸻ Hall, Esq., the author of *Crazy Tales* ; and the famous Colonel Lee, commonly called Savage Lee.* As Clerk expected Ferguson, and Charles, and Robert Grenville, we had agreed to keep at the foot of one of the tables that we might have them near us ; and he requested me to remain in the same position, as the two newly-arrived would be glad to sit by us. I acquiesced, and found the first a highly-accomplished and well-bred gentleman ; not so the second, but he might have been endured had it not been for the perpetual jarrings between Clerk and him, which, if it had not been for the mild and courteous manner of his companion Hall, must have ended in a quarrel ; for the moment after the ladies rose from table, which was very soon, the two soldiers fell a wrangling and fighting like pugilists, which made their company very disagreeable.

In a day or two Ferguson arrived, which effectually took Clerk off me, except at our meal-time, which I could now endure, as his fire was divided. Before Ferguson came, the house began to be crowded, and

---

* The *Crazy Tales* were published in 1762 anonymously. They appear (1795) in the collected works of John Hall Stevenson, who died in 1785. Charles Lee was afterwards celebrated as the rival of Washington for the command of the American army. He was one of the reputed authors of Junius.—J. H. B.

he was put into a very bad lodging-room, near where the fiddlers slept, and very noisy. On the third day he was seized with a fever, of which he was very impatient, and said it was entirely owing to his bad room. I brought Mrs. Carlyle to him, who thought him very feverish. I went to the landlady to procure him a better room, and when Kilrington, the M.D. from Ripon, who attended the house daily, arrived before dinner, I carried him to him, who prescribed nothing but rest and sack whey. After two days more, Kilrington, who saw him twice a-day, told me to go to him, for he was better. I sat with him a few minutes, and as the dinner-bell rang, I left him, saying I would send Clerk after dinner. " God forbid," said he, in a voice of despair, " as you regard my life." This explosion left me no room to doubt what was the true cause of his fever. In two days more he was able to join us.

Soon after this there was a party made out which amused us much. The Laird of M'Leod, with his wife and daughter, afterwards Lady Pringle, arrived after dinner ; and as we were their only acquaintance, and they had arrived after dinner, we waited on them to tea in their parlour, when they asked us [to a concert] they were to have there an hour or two later, which was to be private, but we might bring one or two of our friends. We attended accordingly, and took Messrs. Hall and Lee and two ladies with us. Miss M'Leod was at this time in

the prime of her beauty, and a few months past
sixteen. She was truly very striking and attractive.
When the Savage saw her, he seemed astonished
with her beauty ; when she sang a Scottish song,
he was delighted ; but when she finished with an
Italian song of the first order, he was ravished, and
fell into a silly amazement, how a young lady from
the barbarous coast of the Isle of Skye could possibly
be such a mistress of the Italian music and Italian
tongue. He spake not another word all that night
or the next morning, when he had several opportunities of drinking deeper in the Cyprian goblet ;
but when he saw them preparing to leave us after
dinner, the conquered hero could not stand the
mortifying event, but retired from the company,
and was seen no more that night. The fit lasted
for several days, and he bore the raillery of Hall and
Clerk with a meekness which proved the strength
of his passion. M‘Leod had only looked in at
Harrogate to observe the state of gaming there ;
but as he found nothing higher than a guinea whist-
table, he thought to stay would be losing time, and
made the best of his way to a town about forty miles
off, where there were races to begin next day.

Mrs. Carlyle had never been at any watering-place
before, and, considering that she was only twenty-
four, she conducted herself with surprising propriety, many proofs of which I had, to my great
delight—one proof was, the great joy that appeared
when she won the chief prize in a lottery which was

drawn for the amusement of the company. There was another lady from the south, of popular manners, a Mrs. Maxwell, who had the good wishes of a few of the ladies ; but our party beat hers both in numbers and sincere attachment.

Our friends, the Blacketts, had now been for some days at Ripon with his mother, a fine hospitable old lady, the daughter of Mr. Wise of the Priory at Warwick. By a message they invited us to dine there next day, and desired us to bespeak their lodging, as they were to come to Harrogate with us. This we accordingly did, and passed a very agreeable day with the old lady and our friends. She had a fine haunch of venison for us from Studley Park, besides many other good things. Ripon is a delightful village to live at, not merely on account of the good provisions for the table and a plentiful country, but because there is a dean and chapter, and generally excellent musicians. The dean and prebendary are well endowed, and they and their families furnish a good society. The Blacketts returned with us to Harrogate, and we passed our time very pleasantly. On the last night Clerk and Hall asked me in the evening to go to the Queen's Head to see some of our acquaintance there, and to shun our own ball. We went accordingly, and met with a ball there, of which we tired, and that we might be quiet, went to the Granby, where there was no ball, and where there was excellent claret. As Lee had refused to come abroad that evening, Hall was at liberty, and so, taking Kilrington the doctor with us as a fourth hand, we went there to supper, when Hall and Clerk fell a-debating so tediously and so warmly about Lord Bute's character and fitness for the place of minister, that we did not return to the Dragon till six in the morning. I was diverted to see how Clerk, who generally took part against Lord Bute, that night became his zealous friend, and not only contended that his being a Scotchman was no bar, but that his talents were equal to any high situation. Hall allowed him private virtues, but no public ability.

This conference was very tiresome, and lasted too late for me, who was to set out soon next morning. Ferguson's young gentlemen were not yet arrived, and he remained a week longer without being able to shake off his dear friend Clerk, who had procured for him the charge of those boys, and who, through his friendship to Lady Warwick, took a fatherly charge of them.

Our company got to York before dinner, where we stayed most part of next day, and got to Newcastle in two days, and in a few days more arrived at home. Blackett's horse was very heavy, and my tandem far outran them. When we came home, we found our children in perfect health, which was a great delight to us, and proved the fidelity of Jenny's nurse, with whom we had trusted them both.

Ambassador Keith had returned home, and having a handsome pension settled on him, he lived

handsomely for some time in Edinburgh, and after
a while at Hermitage, on Leith Links. He was a
man, though without wit and humour, yet of good
sense and much knowledge of the world. He had
been absent from Scotland for twenty-two years as
private secretary to Mareschal Lord Stair, Envoy
at Holland, and Ambassador at Vienna and Petersburg. He complained that the society of Edinburgh
was altered much for the worse. Most of his old
companions were dead. The Scottish lairds did
not now make it a part of their education to
pass two years at least abroad, if they had but £300
per annum, from whence they returned polished in
their manners ; and that portion of them who had
good sense, with their minds enlarged and their
manners improved. They found themselves now
better employed in remaining at home, and culti-
vating their fields ; but they were less qualified for
conversation, and could talk of nothing but of
dung and of bullocks. The lawyers had contented
themselves with studying law at home. The medical
tribe had now the best school of physic in Europe
established in Edinburgh, and a rising infirmary,
which promised the students an ample field of
practice, so that very few of that profession went now
to Leyden or Paris. Keith complained of the dulness
of the society, in which he was confirmed by his son,
afterwards Sir Robert Murray Keith, who had come
down to stay for three months, but returned by the
end of one, not finding the state of society to his

mind.   The Ambassador had recourse to our order, who had, till lately, never been thought good company; so that finding Blair and Robertson and Jardine and myself, to whom he afterwards added Ferguson, good company for him, he appointed us ambassador's chaplains, and required an attendance at least once a week to dinner at his house, and was to return our visits when we asked him.   He was soon chosen a member of the Poker Club, which was entirely to his taste.   Baron Mure and Lord Elliock were also much in his society, especially the first, who having been intimate with Lord Bute during the ten years he resided in Bute, previous to 1745, was, after serving in Parliament for some years for Renfrewshire, promoted to the place of Baron of Exchequer.   When Milton's infirmities made him retire from business, Baron Mure was the man who was thought fit to supply his place, after Lord Bute's brother, who tried it for one season, but finding his being sub-minister not agreeable to the country, and very irksome to himself, he prudently declined it, when Mure became the confidential man of business, for which he was perfectly well qualified; for though his manner was blunt and unattractive, yet as, at the same time, he was unassuming, of excellent understanding and great ability for business, he continued to be much trusted and advised with as long as he lived.*   Elliock was an excellent scholar,

* William Mure of Caldwell, Baron of the Exchequer, held a high social place among the men of letters of that day in Scotland ;

and a man of agreeable conversation, having many curious anecdotes in his store ; and to his other fund, had the good fortune to be well acquainted with Frederick the Great of Prussia, when he retired into Holland from his father's tyranny, and visited him at least once by invitation, after he came to the throne.*

This was the year, too, when Dr. John Gregory, my Leyden friend, came to settle in Edinburgh, a widower, with three sons and three daughters.† He soon came to be perfectly known here, and got into very good business.　Dr. Rutherford, Professor of the Practice of Physic, beginning to fail, and being afraid of Cullen becoming his successor, whom he held to be an heretic, he readily entered into a compact with Gregory, whom he esteemed orthodox in the medical faith, and resigned his class to him.　In a year or two that doctor died, when Cullen and Gregory, agreeable to previous settlement, taught the two classes the theory and practice by turns, changing every session. I got Gregory elected into the Poker, but though very desirous at first, yet he did not avail himself of it, but desisted after twice attending, afraid, I suppose, of

he was the intimate friend and the correspondent of David Hume.　His correspondence is contained in " the Caldwell Papers," edited for the Bannatyne Club by his descendant, the late distinguished scholar and author, Colonel Mure.—J. H. B.

* James Veitch, advocate, was raised to the bench in 1760, when he took the title of Lord Elliock.　He enjoyed a reputation in his day, from the circumstance, alluded to in the text, of Frederic the Great having taken a fancy to him, and conferred on him the rank of Correspondent.—J. H. B.

† See above, p. 176.

disgusting some of the ladies he paid court to by falling in sometimes there with David Hume, whom they did not know for the innocent good soul which he really was. Professor Ferguson told me not long ago that he was present the second time Dr. Gregory attended the Poker, when, enlarging on his favourite topic, the superiority of the female sex, he was so laughed at and run down that he never returned.

Gregory had met with Old Montague * at the Royal Society in London, who was fond of all mathematicians, and had made himself master of his mind. Montague introduced him to his wife, a fine woman, who was a candidate for glory in every branch of literature but that of her husband, and its connections and dependencies. She was a faded beauty, a wit, a critic, an author of some fame, and a friend and coadjutor of Lord Lyttleton. She had some parts and knowledge, and might have been admired by the first order of minds, had she not been greedy of more praise than she was entitled to. She came here for a fortnight, from her residence near Newcastle, to visit Gregory, who took care to show her off ; but she did not take here, for she despised the women, and disgusted the men with her affectation. Old Edinburgh was not a climate for the success of impostures. Lord Kames, who was at first catched

* Edward Montagu. He was much older than his celebrated wife. His interest lay in agriculture and mathematics, while his wealth was largely derived from coal mines in Northumberland.

with her Parnassian coquetry, said at last that he
believed she had as much learning as a well-educated
college lad here of sixteen. I could have forgiven
her for her pretensions to literary fame, had she not
loudly put in her claim to the praise and true devotion of the heart, which belongs to genuine feelings
and deeds, in which she was remarkably deficient.
We saw her often in the neighbourhood of Newcastle,
and in that town, where there was no audience for
such an actress as she was, her natural character
was displayed, which was that of an active manager
of her affairs, a crafty chaperon, and a keen pursuer
of her interest, not to be outdone by the sharpest
coal-dealer on Tyne ; but in this capacity she was
not displeasing, for she was not acting a part. Mrs.
Montague was highly delighted with " Sister Peg,"
which Ferguson had written, and congratulated Mrs.
Carlyle on having a husband whose conversation must
be a constant source of entertainment. She did not
advert to it, that in domestic life the scene did not
always lie in the drawing-room.

We had a sight of the celebrated poet Gray at
Dr. Gregory's, who passing through Edinburgh to
the Highlands with my friend Major Lyon for his
conductor, six or seven of us assembled to meet him,
and were disappointed. But this eminent poet had
not justice done him, for he was much worn out with
his journey, and, by retiring soon after supper,
proved that he had been taken at a time when he
was not fit to be shown off.

(1765.)—Early in March this year I lost my worthy father, at seventy-five years of age. He had been for some years declining, and of late had strong symptoms of dropsy, a disease of worn-out constitutions ; for though seemingly robust and very active, he had been afflicted all his life with sundry disorders of an alarming nature, such as an universal rheumatism, and spasms in his stomach at regular hours every night for three months together. He died with the utmost calmness and resignation, and ordered all his affairs with a prudence and foresight that were surprising, amidst frequent effusions of the most fervent piety. Though long expected, I felt this a severe blow, as every man of common feelings must do—the loss of a respectable parent. The sincere grief of his parish, and the unaffected regret of all who knew him, raised pleasing sensations in the minds of his family. I had withdrawn my wife from this afflicting scene, by letting her yield to the importunity of her sister, and go to Newcastle in the beginning of March. This ascendance which her sister had on her affections accounted perfectly for our not growing rich, as some of our free-judging neighbours alleged we must certainly be doing ; for though our income was tolerable, yet these frequent visits to the south—not less than twice in a year—put it only in our power to pay our accounts at the end of the year. I went to Newcastle before the end of April to bring my wife home, on which or some such occasion we brought with us Dr.

Gregory's two daughters, Dolly and Anne, very fine girls, who had been staying with Mrs. Montague. As there were none of my father's family now alive but my sister Bell, who was the youngest, and Sarah, who was one or two years older, and unmarried, my father had the satisfaction that my mother would be independent, but advised her to come close to me, which she did at the Michaelmas term.

Lord Prestongrange, the patron of the parish, who was my father's friend and old companion at college, was generous to my mother, by giving her a grant of the glebe, which was partly sown, and a considerable part of the vacant stipend, to which she was not entitled. The two next successors to my father died in four years, so that his place was not well filled up, nor the regret of the parishioners lessened for his loss, till Dr. Joseph M'Cormick succeeded in 1768 or '69.

In the General Assembly this year there was a strong push made to bring in an overture to all the presbyteries of the Church to inquire into the causes of schism, etc., from whence those in opposition to patronages believed there would come such a report as would found and justify a fresh application to the Legislature for their abolition. It was thought best on our side not directly to oppose this motion, but to propose a committee of Assembly rather than agree to the transmission, which was agreed to, and a large committee appointed, who, strange to tell, in spite of all their zeal, met only once, and did nothing, though they had full power, and made no report to next Assembly.*

It was in the months of August and September this year that Dr. Wight and I made our tour round the north, where neither of us had ever been, from whence we derived much amusement and satisfaction. We went on horseback by Queensferry, Perth, Dundee, Arbroath, etc. We stayed four days and nights at Aberdeen on account of Dr. Wight's horse having been lamed in crossing the ferry at Montrose ; but we passed our time very agreeably between the houses of our friends Drs. Campbell and Gerard.†

When I returned—for Wight went to Dumfries from Edinburgh—I found the children well, but their mother suffering from a very severe rheumatism in her teeth, owing to their being cleaned too much. A fresh call from Newcastle carried Mrs. Carlyle there again in the beginning of November. I did not go with

* The reader will recognise in these and subsequent passages some interesting incidents of the great contest, which, beginning with the Patronage Act of 1710, threw off two dissenting bodies— the Secession and the Relief—in the eighteenth century, and ended in the construction of the Free Church in 1843. The nature of the proceedings will be understood by keeping in view that the " overture," or opening of a measure (a term taken by the Parliament of Scotland from French practice), required, in conformity with one of the fundamental regulations of ecclesiastical procedure in Scotland, called the " Barrier Act," to be transmitted to the local presbyteries for adoption by a majority before being passed and carried into effect by the General Assembly.—J. H. B.

† Dr. George Campbell, Principal of Aberdeen University and author of *A Dissertation on Miracles* in answer to Hume's *Philosophy of Rhetoric*. Dr. Gerard, Professor of Divinity in King's College, Aberdeen, author of *An Essay on Taste*, etc.

her, but went for her at the end of the year, and carried a Miss Wilkie with me from Ingram's, and a Rev. Mr. Forbes, who married a grand-aunt of Mrs. Carlyle's.

(1766.)—I have not mentioned some visits we had from our friends in Newcastle, nor do I exactly [remember] the dates of their coming. *He* soon tired, and had always business to carry him back. Not so his lady, who loved our society better than that of Newcastle. In April I made a tour with Mary to Berwick, Langton, and Fogo, for her health, and to visit our friends.

John Home was now always in London from October till May, when Lord Bute parted with him, for most part to come to the General Assembly, as, being Lord Conservator, he was now a constant member, and, though no great debater, gave us a speech now and then.

In the Assembly this year there was the last grand effort of our opponents to carry through their Schism Overture, as it was called, as it proposed to make an inquiry into the causes and growth of schism. On the day before it came before the Assembly we had dined at Nicholson's. Before we parted, Jardine told me that he had examined the list of the Assembly with care, and that we should carry the question—that it would be nearly at par till we came as far on the roll as Lochmaben, but that after that we should have it hollow. I have mentioned this on account of what happened next day, which was Friday the 29th.

There was a very long debate, so that the vote was not called till past seven o'clock. Jardine, who had for some time complained of breathlessness, had seated himself on a high bench near the east door of the Assembly House, there being at that time no galleries erected. He had, not half an hour before, had a communication with some ladies near him in the church gallery, who had sent him a bottle of wine, of which he took one glass. The calling of the roll began, and when it had passed the presbytery of Lochmaben, he gave a significant look with his eye to me, who was sitting below the throne, as much as to say, " Now the day's our own." I had turned to the left to whisper to John Home, who was next me, the sign I had got ; before I could look round again, Jardine had tumbled from his seat, and, being a man of six feet two inches, and of large bones, had borne down all those on the two benches below him, and fallen to the ground. He was immediately carried out to the passage, and the roll-calling stopped. Various reports came from the door, but, anxious to know the truth, I stepped behind the Moderator's chair and over the green table, and with difficulty made the door through a very crowded house. When I came there, I found him lying stretched on the pavement of the passage with many people about him, among the rest his friend and mine, James Russel the surgeon. With some difficulty I got near him, and whispered was it not a faint ? " No, no," replied he, " it is all over." I returned to the house, and, resuming my place, gave out that there were hopes of his recovery. This composed the house, and the calling of the roll went on, when it was carried to reject the overture by a great majority. This was a deadly blow to the enemies of presentations, for they had mustered all their strength, and had been strenuous in debate. Henry Dundas, however, had now come to our aid, who was himself a match for all their lay forces, as Robertson and a few friends were for all the bands of clergy. I was not a member. A party of us had been engaged to dine with Mr. Dundas, but could not now go, as Dr. Jardine was a near relation of his lady, who was delivered of her first child that night.

Robertson was much dejected, as he had good reason. I immediately proposed to him and J. Home to send for a post-chaise and carry them out to Musselburgh, which was done directly, and which relieved us from all troublesome company. This death of Jardine was not only a breach in our society which we long felt, as John Jardine was one of the pleasantest of the whole, who played delightfully on the unbounded curiosity and dupish simplicity of David Hume, but was a great support to Robertson and our friends in the management of ecclesiastical affairs, as he was the son-in-law of Provost Drummond, and kept him steady, who had been bred in the bosom of the Highflyers. And having had the management of the burgh of Lochmaben for Charles Erskine of Tinwald at twenty-nine years of age, he acquired early that address and dexterity in managing men which could easily be applied to Edinburgh politics, though they were on a much greater scale. In politics he was artful, in other affairs quite trusty.*

As Jardine, however, had one-third of the deanery, Robertson availed himself of the vacancy to obtain it for Dr. Drysdale, whose wife was one of the Adams' and Robertsons' cousin-german. This attached Drysdale more to him, and made him apply assiduously to the correspondence with the distant clergy, which opened up to him a view of the clerkship of the Church, which he afterwards obtained.

I said that the Schism Overture which we defeated was the last blow that was aimed at patronage, for whatever attempts were afterwards made were feeble and ineffective. There still remained, however, in the Assembly's instructions to their Commission, an article which was a constant reproach to the General Assembly—viz., That they should watch for a convenient opportunity of applying to the King and Parliament for redress from the grievance of patronage. This was too much, at a time when

---

* Dr. John Jardine, minister of the Tron Church parish, was born in Dumfriesshire in 1716. He was an active leader in the church courts, and intimate with the great literary circle of Edinburgh ; but the only things he is known to have written are contributions to the short-lived *Edinburgh Review*, commenced in 1755.—J. H. B.

almost every clerical member of Assembly had been settled by a presentation. This, however, was not left out till Dr. Robertson had retired from the conduct of our affairs, when, in the Assembly 1784, I got it proposed by some of the elders, when, after some debate, it was carried to leave it out by a great majority. Next year there was a feeble attempt to restore the article in the Instructions, but this did not even raise a debate, and we heard no more of it.

CHAPTER XIII

AGE, 44–46

IT was this year, in the month of August, that Dr. Robertson having solicited me strongly to be of a party to the west country with him and the Honourable James Stewart Montague, who was then attending the College of Edinburgh, and lived in his house, I could not set out on the same day with them, but followed in the end of the week, and got to Dr. Wight's, at Glasgow College, on Saturday, where I remained all next day, having got a little cold. He had now been for some time in the house allotted to his office, which, though one of the old ones, was convenient, and had several apartments, so that he could have room for two or three boarders. His youngest sister had now been with him for more than a year, and they lived very comfortably, which she, though but just turned of twenty, managed very well. I remained with them all Tuesday, and next day got to Caldwell (Baron Mure's) before dinner. We went next day to Lord Glasgow's, where we were joined by Mr. Oliphant, afterwards Postmaster, who, with Baron Mure and

Alexander M'Millan, Esq., W.S., were Lord Bute's commissioners or trustees for the management of his estate. We had rode through a very hilly part of Renfrewshire to Kelburn, Lord Glasgow's seat, finely situated on the Clyde, almost opposite to Bute, about five or six miles distant, where the expanse of water is finely broken by the two islands of Cumbray, the first of which is not more than a mile distant, while the channel for ships sailing up or down the Clyde lies between that island and the shore of Cunningham. We were very late of dining for that period, when the usual hour was two o'clock, but we sat long enough after dinner to loosen out landlord's tongue, who, being in general a reserved and silent man, partly through modesty and partly through flat spirits, yet, after a long repast, became not only open and free, but truly eloquent. Baron Mure, though a very sensible man, was yet too great a friend of Lord Bute's to hear William Pitt extolled to the skies, which Lord Glasgow had casually done ; on which Mure made some tart remarks. This fired his lordship, who gave us a panegyric at last on Mr. Pitt's character and administration, with as much force, energy, and eloquence as that great man himself could have done, had he dealt in panegyric. His lordship was beginning to flag, and his audience to tire, when luckily we were called to supper. Robertson whispered me, in going to the dining-room, that his powers had perfectly astonished him. The presence of the ladies put an end to our political debate. We passed next day with his lordship, when we had such another exhibition in the evening. We agreed among ourselves, that had it not been for his invincible modesty, which debarred him from ever entering the drawing-room at St. James's, where he was sure of a good reception, for he had been wounded at the battle of Fontenoy, he might have made a very conspicuous appearance in the House of Lords. He was now the Lord High Commissioner to the Assembly, and was a great favourite with us, not merely for his obliging manners and improved entertainment at his table, but for his attention to the business of the house, and his listening to and entering into the spirit of every debate. His lordship did not attend us to Bute, to which we sailed next day.*

We remained six days in Bute, and passed our time very agreeably. Alexander M'Millan was one of the best landlords for a large company, for he was loud and joyful, and made the wine flow like Bacchus himself. We passed the mornings (which were not so long as now, for they extended only to two o'clock, when dinner was on the table) in riding about the island, which we found very beautiful, though but little cultivated ; for besides a plantation around the house of Mount Stuart, of very fine trees, of a square mile, every little cottage had a dozen of trees around it. A Lady Bute, while a widow, had got

* John Boyle, third Earl of Glasgow, of whom what was heretofore known is so scanty as to give much value to this sketch.—J. H. B.

them planted in every kailyard, as their little gardens are called, and they make a pleasing ornament. There is nothing like a hill but on Lord Bannatyne's estate on the north-east, where it is separated by a narrow strait called the Kyles of Bute. Rothesay, where stand the ruins of the old castle which gives a ducal title to the Prince of Wales, as it did anciently to the Prince of Scotland, is a finely-situated port, and has thriven amazingly since that period. We had to take an early dinner one day, and ride down there to be made free of the burgh, which cost us a hard drink of new claret. Mount Stuart is truly a fine place, with a charming view of the islands and opposite coast. The soil everywhere lies on sea-shells, so that they have the means of improvement at hand; and being in shape like the convex of a Roman shield, where the rain cannot lie, seemed everywhere capable of tillage. What was done about Mount Stuart and Rothesay gave great encouragement. We went to Kingarth Church on Sunday, where I lectured and Robertson preached. There are three parishes in the island, in two of which the ministers must have the Erse language.

Our conversation at table was liberal and lively, as might be expected where there were so many sensible men; for besides our company there were several other very able men, particularly a Mr. Dunlop, a son of the Greek Professor's, at Glasgow, who was remarkably knowing and good-humoured. The wine was excellent, and flowed freely. There was the best

cyprus I ever saw, which had lain there since Lord
Bute had left the island in 1745. The claret was of
the same age, and excellent.

After we had been four days there, Robertson took
me into a window before dinner, and with some
solemnity proposed to make a motion to shorten the
drinking, if I would second him—" Because," added
he, "although you and I may go through it, I am
averse to it on James Stuart's account." I answered
that I would willingly second whatever measure of
that kind he should propose, but added that I was
afraid it would not do, as our toastmaster was very
despotic, and, besides, might throw ridicule upon us,
as we were to leave the island the day after the next,
and that we had not proposed any abridgment to the
repast till the old claret was all done, the last of which
we had drunk yesterday. " Well, well," replied the
Doctor, " be it so then, and let us end as we began."

We left the island on the day we proposed, I
in a boat, for Port-Glasgow, with the Postmaster, Oliphant, as we could not join the rest to pass two days
more at Lord Glasgow's (Kelburn) on their return,
as they had promised. We got very rapidly to
Port-Glasgow in the customhouse yacht, and to
Glasgow on horseback early in the evening, where
he visited his friends, and I remained with mine at
the College that night and all next day.

I was Moderator of the Synod this year. Webster
having made it fashionable for even the Moderators
of that court to give handsome suppers, it cost me

five guineas ; but there being very few who could afford such expensive repasts, after having gone through six or seven of us, this entertainment ceased, and the Moderators of the Synods were contented with small committees and meagre suppers, as they had been heretofore, and Webster, of course, absented from them.

In December this year we made another journey to Newcastle, Mrs. Carlyle being absolutely necessary to her sister when she lay in, or was at all ill. Blackett was but a dull man, and his cousin, Sir Walter B., no better, though rich, magnificent, and generous. The company about them were not very agreeable ; some of their bucks had humour, but they were illiterate and noisy. Two or three of their clergy could be endured, for they played well at cards, and were not pedantic. John Withrington was then almost the only man who had any literature. Mr. Moyse, a clergyman, was now master of the grammar-school, and being able and diligent in his profession, soon made a great change on the young natives of Newcastle ; insomuch, that soon after there issued from it several distinguished characters, such as Mr. Chambers, a judge, I think, in India, or a professor of law at Oxford ; and the two Scotts, Sir William and his younger brother, the Chancellor of England.* Dr. Akenside was also a native of that town, and had studied physic in Edinburgh in the years 1744-5. As he was of low descent, his father being a butcher,

---

* Viz., Lord Stowell and Lord Eldon.—J. H. B.

he stole through his native town *incog.* as often as
he had occasion to pass, and never acknowledged his
relation to it.

(1767.)—This year nothing remarkable happened
for several months. In the month [of August], Mrs.
Carlyle not being very well, we went in our open chaise
to visit our friend Mr. Alexander Glen, at Galashiels,
with our friend Dr. Wight.   I had been there before,
but Mrs. Carlyle never had, and was much delighted
with the amenity of the place, as well as the kindness
and hospitality of our landlord, who was not yet
married.   We visited Melrose Abbey to gratify Mrs.
Carlyle.   The fine pastoral stream of Gala falls into
the Tweed a mile below the church and village,
from whence four miles down the river stands the
famous abbey of Melrose, the exquisite beauty of
whose ruins is well supported by the romantic scenery
around it.   About a week before we arrived here, a
waterspout had fallen into the mountain stream
Slitterick, which joins the river Teviot at Hawick,
which occasioned a great alarm there ;   had broken
down a bridge which joined the town to a street where
the church stands ;   had ruined a mill on the rivulet,
and drowned one of the millers, and threatened the
whole town with inundation ;   but as it had come
down in the night, it abated early in the forenoon.

This phenomenon, so uncommon in this country,
excited our curiosity, and were solved to proceed to
Hawick to see the effects of it.   Mr. Glen gladly accompanied us, Wight and he being great companions.

We set out in the morning, after an early breakfast, that we might reach Hawick some time before dinner. We had given notice to Laurie, the minister there, that we would dine with him and stay all night; which information was necessary, as there were so many of us, although the fashion of men's sleeping in the same bed together was not yet at an end. After we passed the Tweed, near Selkirk, where the delightful streams of Ettrick and Yarrow fall into it from the fine pastoral valleys or glens which run parallel to each other to the summit of the country, the scenery was by no means interesting. Selkirk was then a very paltry town, and the fields around it very poorly cultivated, though now there is a very different face on both. Hawick is beautifully situated, and though but an ill-built town, very much resembles the famous city of Bath in its situation, being a close warm-looking nest in the midst of surrounding hills, all but the openings made to the south and north of the town by the beautiful river Teviot, which runs within a quarter of a mile of it, and whose clear untroubled stream, except when great rains descend, glides gently by, and like a mirror reflects the adjacent pastoral scenery. We visited the devastations made by Slitterick, which falls from the mountain in a tremendous torrent into Teviot, which was quite unmoved, as the two channels lay at right angles from each other.

We passed the day very pleasantly with Laurie and his wife, who was an old acquaintance of Mrs. Carlyle's

when they lived at Langton, the next parish to
Polwarth, where she passed her infant years.   Wight
rallied Laurie not a little for his having delayed
calling the people to prayers on the morning of the
inundation, till he saw from his garden the flood a
little abating ; and then continuing so long in prayer
(for a full hour), when it had fallen so much that a
man on horseback could pass below the mill, which
the good people ascribed to the fervency of their
pastor, and would have continued to believe in the
efficacy of his prayer, had not the surviving miller
assured them that the inundation had fallen six inches
before the church-bell rang.   Laurie was perfectly
pleased with so much address being ascribed to him,
though he lost a little in the article of interest in
heaven which was imputed to him.

Laurie was an uncommon character.   Dr. John
Armstrong and he were at college together, and one
year, during the vacation, they joined a band of
gypsies, who in those days much infested the Border.
This expedition, which really took place, as Armstrong informed me in London, furnished Laurie
with a fine field for fiction and rhodomontade,
which was so closely united to the groundwork,
which might be true, that it was impossible to dis-
compound them.   After Armstrong had settled in
London for some time, Laurie went to visit him about
1739 or '40; on that he founded many marvellous
stories of his intimacy with secretaries of state and
courtiers, with whom he pretended he had been quite

familiar. When he alleged that he had been quite at his ease with the Chancellor and the Speaker of the House of Commons at that time, and could call on them at any hour, and remain to dinner or supper without being invited, we used to call to him, " Halt there, Laurie ; if you don't know the boundary between truth and falsehood, you should draw the line between what is probable and what is not so." As, like a snowball, we gathered as we rolled along, he fixed himself upon us for the rest of the journey.

We set out in the morning after breakfast, that we might reach Langholm, twenty-two miles off, in time for dinner, and travelled over a beautiful pastoral country, eleven miles to the top of the ridge beyond which the waters run south, whereas before their course is north and east.   The road had been finished some time before, and was so perfectly good and well laid out that in my open chaise I could keep at the trot both down and up the whole way.   The first place we passed was the seat of Dr. Langlands, M.D., a very pleasing place, about a mile above Hawick on the Teviot ; of late it was in possession of Lord Napier, and much improved by him, and is now bought by James Anderson, Esq., a younger brother of St. Germains.   In a mile or two further we reached the fine seat of the family of Buccleuch, the Castle of Branxholm, which an ancestor of that family ex-changed.   When we got to the top of the ridge, we stopped to feed our horses at a rural inn, kept by a curious fellow called Rob Achison, with whom we had not conversed many minutes when we discovered the cause of his being reduced from the condition of an opulent farmer to that of the keeper of a mere halting-place to divide a long stage. Robert had been a Border rake or buck of the first head in his younger days, and to wit and humour, of which he had abundance, he added a sufficient portion of address and impudence, which he carried with an air of careless indifference. He had eloquence enough, however, to make us both eat and drink in his house, for the first of which he was but ill provided ; but he soon made us understand, by the scurrility which he poured out against those who had passed his house without calling for something besides corn for their horses, how we should be treated for the entertainment of the next who came, so we took a sorry repast with Robert, and drank of his liquors.

The slope from this to Langholm is just eleven miles, and the road excellent ; the country was exceedingly picturesque, though then without trees, and full of sheep, which, as the young Duke of Buccleuch and his Duchess were daily expected, had been taught to line the road daily through which they were to pass, that they might see wherein the riches of the land consisted. As it was now in the beginning of August, the fields had a fine variegated cloak of verdure ; for as the ferns, or brackens, as they are called here, were now in perfection, and of a different shade from the grass, they looked like a large curtain or mantle of green silk damask.

We arrived in the evening at Langholm, where the village is situated at the confluence of the two streams of Ewes and Wauchope with the Esk, which from thence flows, after being almost doubled by the Liddel, through delightful scenery, to the Solway Firth, which with it makes the western boundary between England and Scotland.

It was too late to attempt to see the castle, so we sent immediately for John Dickie the minister, who was an old bachelor, and who had such a mixture of odd qualities in his composition, such as priggism and pedantry, with the affectation of being a finished gentleman ; very sanctimonious in his manners, with a desire of being thought free and liberal in his sentiments ; not without a portion of knowledge, but more proud of it than Dr. Bentley, or Purdie the schoolmaster.   As Mrs. Carlyle had never seen him before, she was highly diverted with him ; and having in a moment discovered all his weaknesses, she met them in so caressing and encouraging a manner that he would have leapt over the house to serve her ; and before he left us at twelve to go home, he became her sworn knight-errant.   To make her conquest complete over the little man, she would not let him go till a horse was got ready for an ostler to conduct him through the water.   Laurie and Glen thought this carrying her coquetry too far, but Wight and I knew better ;   for she was of that turn of mind, that if anything had befallen the little man, as he had got enough of wine, and had no better seat than a clue on a horse, she would never have forgiven herself. With all his imperfections he was good-natured and social, which after a banquet never failed to appear. He had a young mare which he wished to sell, and was going to send it to be sold at Hawick or Jedburgh, when, hearing there was to be a fair at Carlisle next day, and that we were deliberating about going or not, when somebody happened to say that Carlisle was the best place, and that we would all go there ;—Mrs. Carlyle immediately said, " I will consent to go if you will be so good as accompany us." The honest soul instantly yielded, and we all resolved to go, now amounting to five gentlemen and a lady, with only one servant.

We set out next morning, and had a very agreeable ride down the river Esk for seven or eight miles, through a valley finely covered with young plantations. We stopped at Longtown, where there is a fine bridge over the Esk, which has saved many a life which was annually lost in passing very dangerous fords of the river a mile or two lower down ; and, crossing some sands in the channel of the Frith of Solway, where the traveller was frequently overtaken by the rapidity of the tide, we arrived at Carlisle before dinner, and found the town as much crowded as curious travellers could wish, as there was not only a great fair holding on this day, but the Judges were in town, and a set of players to entertain the company. The King's Arms was so much crowded that we were obliged to resort to the large dining-room, which was crowded like a coffeehouse. But as the company, consisting chiefly of country lads and lasses, were all to disperse in the evening, we were able to secure beds, which was the chief point in view.

After strolling about the town a while I attempted to go into the court-house, which was so much crowded and so hot that I only remained a few minutes in the outskirts, where I heard my friend Wedderburn pleading as well as he could under a severe hoarseness. We returned to the inn, where we found Governor Johnstone, and John Scotland, minister of Westerkirk, with our friends. Johnstone was employed in canvassing the citizens, and Scotland had come with a Dunfermline friend on purpose to see Mr. Wedderburn. The Governor told us of the players, and we all set out immediately to try for places, but it was so much crowded that we were disappointed, and obliged to return. Laurie, however, remained after the rest, when he had a quarrel with a very drunken squire of the name of Dacres, who had insulted him with foul language, which Laurie returned with a blow, forgetting that he was now in a country where a breach of the peace is much more dangerous. Dacres attempted to have him committed, but Laurie made his escape, and Johnstone having interfered and said it was only a drunken Scotch parson who had been riotous, and was ignorant of English laws, who had broken the peace, he got Dacres pacified, and we heard no more of it.

The Governor had promised to sup with us, and I

proposed sending to Mr. Wedderburn ; but Scotland said it was needless, as he had seen him, and found him preparing to go to bed, as he was very hoarse.   I wrote him a note, however, telling him that Mrs. Carlyle and Wight and I were there, and that Governor Johnstone had promised to sup with us, and that I would infallibly cure his hoarseness before to-morrow morning.   His answer was that he would be with us in half an hour.   He was as good as his word, but was very hoarse.   The supper was good enough, but the liquors were execrable—the wine and porter were not drinkable.   We then made a bowl of the worst punch I ever tasted.   Wedderburn said, if we would mix it with a bottle of the bad porter, it would be improved.   We did as he directed, and to our surprise it became drinkable, and we were a jolly company.   The counsellor did not forget the receipt to cure his hoarseness.   This was nothing more than some castile soap shaven into a spoon and mixed with some white wine or water, so that it could be swallowed.   This he took, and returned to us at nine next morning perfectly cured, and as sound as a bell.

Dickie having sold his mare, we returned by the road we came, and, passing one night at Hawick, and one at Galashiels, arrived at home with Wight next night, and found all well.   It is remarkable that I remember very exactly most of the circumstances on going from home even on a long journey, but that on returning I can seldom find any trace of them on my memory, and all seems a blank.   Is this owing to the imagination being fully occupied with the thoughts of home, which are always agreeable ? Or is it owing to the eagerness and curiosity with which one begins a journey, and the rising hopes of new pleasures and amusements, and the drowsy and inactive state of the imagination as you return ?

The young Duke and Duchess of Buccleuch were expected at this time to arrive in Scotland to take possession of their fine estate in the south, and their palace at Dalkeith as their chief residence. They were eagerly expected over all the country where we had been, great part of which, from Tweedside to the borders of Cumberland, was the property of that noble family. There had been a long minority, for this duke's grandfather had died in 1752, and his son, Lord Dalkeith, two years before him. The family had been kind to their tenants, and the hopes of the country were high that this new possessor of so large a property might inherit the good temper and benevolence of his progenitors. I may anticipate what was at first only guessed, but came soon to be known, that he surpassed them all as much in justice and humanity as he did in superiority of understanding and good sense.

The Duke and Duchess, with Lady Frances Scott, the Duke's sister, arrived at Dalkeith in the beginning of September, where his Grace had never been before, being withheld by Charles Townshend, his father-in-law, lest he should become too fond of Scotland. This stratagem was defeated by the Duke's sagacity, for he discovered on his journey through his own great estate, from the marked attention of the people, that he would be a much greater man in this country, and would have a much more extensive range for his benevolence than he could possibly have in the south, where his own estates were small, and where there was such a number of more opulent lords, his rivals in all the attributes of true nobility.

In order to make the Duke and Duchess feel more impressively the attachment of their vassals and tenants in the south, I wrote a copy of verses on the birthday of the former, which I had copied in another hand, and sent on the morning of that day. It was some time before they could guess that I was the author ; and one of their tenants had for a while the credit of it. I had by good-luck truly predicted, by way of advice, what her Grace became, but no prediction could then reach the extent of her merit. The verses were sent to the *Scots Magazine*, where Dr. Gregory read them, and suspected me for the author. When I next saw him, he asked me, and I owned them, when he said they were very good—too good for the subject, for they would never act up to the strain of praise in that poem. " Do you know them, Doctor ? " " No," answered he, " but Mrs. Montague does ; and she says that, though very good young people, they have no energy of character, and will remain obscure and insignificant." " Mrs. Montague's line, then, is too short, my good Doctor : you may trust me to measure their depth, and you will live to see that her discernment on this occasion has failed her." Gregory, with many good qualities, had so much of the apothecary about him, that he did not think much of anybody who was not likely to frequent his shop. He knew that Smith would recommend both Cullen and Black to be their physician in ordinary rather than him.*

Between their arrival at Dalkeith and his Grace's birthday, the 13th of September, the Right Honourable Charles Townshend died, after an illness of a few days, of an inflammation in his bowels. This event obliged them to postpone the celebration of the birthday, when they were to have had an entertainment for all their friends. This sudden death affected the Duke and his sister very differently. She, who had been bred up under him from the fourth or fifth year of her age, and had found in him an enlightened instructor and a kind protector, felt all the grief which a dutiful child feels for an indulgent parent ; but the Duke, who had been very little at home during Mr. Townshend's marriage with his mother, and whose more ripened discernment had probably disclosed to him his father-in-law's defects as well as his shining qualities, was much less afflicted on this melancholy occasion, and was heard to say, a few days after the news, that though he sincerely regretted Mr. Towns-

* For information about Cullen, Black, and the other eminent men of the medical school of Scotland often mentioned in these pages, it is fortunate that the *Life of Cullen*, begun by Dr. John Thomson, and continued by his son, has now been completed by Dr. Craigie, 2 vols. 8vo, 1859.—J. H. B.

hend's premature death, yet to him it was attended
with the consolation that it left him at liberty to
choose his own line of life, for had Mr. Townshend
survived he might have been drawn into the vortex of
politics much against his will.   Such was the soundness of this young nobleman's mind at an early age,
from whence a discerning observer might predict the
excellence of that character which gradually evolved
on his admiring countrymen.

In two or three weeks the day came when they
were to see company, and when they assembled by
cards about fifty ladies and gentlemen of their friends
and the neighbourhood, of whom few indeed were
ladies, as they were hardly yet acquainted with anybody.   The fare was sumptuous, but the company
was formal and dull. Adam Smith, their only
familiar at table, was but ill qualified to promote the
jollity of a birthday, and their Graces were quite inexperienced.   The Duke, indeed, had been more than
two years in France, and four months in London since
he came home, but he was backward at that time to
set himself forward, and showed a coldness and reserve which often in our superiors is thought to be
pride.   Had it not been for Alexander M'Millan, W.S.,
and myself, the meeting would have been very dull,
and might have been dissolved without even drinking
the health of the day.   After that health and a few
more toasts had gone round, and the ladies had
moved, and M'Millan and his companions at a by-
table had got into the circle, we got into spirits that

better suited the occasion. The Duchess at that time was extremely beautiful ; her features were regular, her complexion good, her black eyes of an impressive lustre, and her mouth, when she spoke, uncommonly graceful. The expression of her countenance was that of good sense and serenity ; she had been bred in too private a way, which made her shy and backward, and it was some time before she acquired ease in company, which at last enabled her to display that superiority of understanding which led all the female virtues in its train, accompanied with the love of mirth, and all the graces of colloquial intercourse. Her person was light, though above the common height, but active and elegant.

Smith remained with them for two months, and then returned to Kirkcaldy to his mother and his studies. I have often thought since, that if they had brought down a man of more address than he was, how much sooner their first appearance might have been ; their own good sense and discernment enabled them sooner to draw round them as familiars a better set of people of their own choosing, than could have been picked out for them by the assistance of an aide-de-camp.

By means of an established custom of their predecessors, they had two public days in the week, when everybody who pleased came to dine with them. But that on Thursday was soon cut off, and Saturday was their only public day. But it would have been far better if that day had been also abolished, and if, in

33

place of that, they had taken to invited companies, which might have been well assorted, and might have prevented all that dulness, and even solemnity, which overclouded large companies little acquainted, and seldom capable of making a company of a score tolerably agreeable. I must aver, however, without pretending to uncommon discernment, that I soon discovered in both that superior understanding, and that uncommon degree of humanity, as well as the highest sense of probity and virtue, which have made them a blessing and honour to their country for many years past. For the Duke's uncommon abilities, as well as his public spirit, became ere long as conspicuous in the exercise of more honourable offices of trust, which fell on him unsought, as his unassuming and familiar manners made him appear a complete gentleman in all the intercourse of private life. The family, though rich and great, had long been in a state of obscurity through want of talents and long minorities. In this Duke was revived the character which Sir James Melville gave his renowned predecessor in Queen Mary's reign—" Walter Scot of Buccleugh, wise and true, stout and modest." *

No two characters I ever have known are so free of defects as that noble pair, while each in their department displayed such talents and virtues as made their numerous descendants not only happy in them-

* "Quhilk Lard of Bahclouch was a man of rare qualites, wyse, trew, stout, and modest.—MELVILLE's *Memoirs*, 240.— J. H. B.

selves, but also trained them up in the habitual disposition to become blessings to all their own connections to the latest posterity.

The Duke's sister, Lady Frances, though far from
handsome, or in any respect attractive in her person,
though then only seventeen, showed the opening of
that character which she has since so fully displayed
as Lady Douglas. She had taste and knowledge in
the belles-lettres, a pleasant vein of ridicule, without
the least grain of malignity; for she, like her brother,
was the very milk of human-kindness.

As I had been intimately acquainted with Charles
Townshend, her father-in-law, who protected her
from domestic tyranny, and had even opened her
mind by his instructions, she took readily to me, and
I soon became intimate with her, and kept up a
correspondence with her, both in prose and verse,
which conduced to our amusement. The prosperity
and happiness of Lord Douglas's family, which consisted of three sons and one daughter, demonstrated
the excellence of her domestic character. It was remarkable that she was the first female descendant of
the Duchess of Monmouth and Buccleuch who was
married.

I had been Moderator of the Synod in November
1766, and opened the Synod in May 1767 with a
sermon, which was printed. The window-tax was
now levied, which gave a serious alarm to the clergy:
there was a standing committee of Assembly, which
had hitherto done nothing effectual. As I had been

the champion for resisting payment of the tax, I was obliged to bestir myself very much about it ; and as Dr. Robertson was of opinion we ought to submit to it, I had uphill work with it.

(1768.)—Towards the end of January this year it was that Mrs. Carlyle and I accompanied her aunt and uncle to visit their son Walter Home, then a lieutenant in the 7th Regiment, and lying at Glasgow. Walter had a chum of the name of Mainwaring, a very agreeable young man. As Dr. Wight was now fully established in Glasgow, and had one of his sisters for his housekeeper, he was very hospitable and popular, and we met daily several of the Professors, who were able men, and had agreeable conversation,—such as Alexander Stevenson and John Millar. This last had even begun to distinguish himself by his democratical principles, and that sceptical philosophy which young noblemen and gentlemen of legislative rank carried into the world with them from his law-class, and, many years afterwards, particularly at the period of the French Revolution, displayed with popular zeal, to the no small danger of perversion to all those under their influence. I had a hint of this from Dr. Wight before 1782, when he died, who added, that though some sound heads might find antidotes to this poison before they went into the world, and see in the British constitution all that is valuable in a democracy, without its defects and faults, yet, as it was connected with lax principles in religion, there might be not a few of such a contexture of understanding as could not be cured. Millar lived to the end of the century.*

I met with a strong proof of what is contained in the above paragraph respecting Professor Millar a long time afterwards, when dining with Robert Colt, Esq., then residing at Inveresk. I don't exactly remember the year, but I think it was before the war of 1798. There was nobody with Mr. Colt but a brother-in-law of his, when we were joined by the late Sir Hew Dalrymple of North Berwick, who had dined in Edinburgh. After consenting to stay all night, Sir Hew said, " Colt, was not you a student of law for two years with Millar at Glasgow ? " " Yes, I was," answered Mr. Colt. " Then," replied Sir Hew, " I find I am right ; and as my Hew has been four years at St. Andrews, and seems now desirous of following the law, I have been advised to send him to Millar, and have come to consult you about it." " We'll talk about that coolly to-morrow morning, Sir Hew ; in the mean time, give me your toast." I knew well the meaning of this reserve ; and a few days afterwards meeting Mr. Colt, " Well," said I, " did you settle your friend Sir Hew's mind about sending his son to Glasgow ? " " Yes," answered he, " and you'll hear no more of that project." This Mr. Colt was an able and a worthy man, but he was shy and reserved, and died, unknown but to a few, in

* Author of the once very celebrated *Historical View of the English Government*, and of *Observations Concerning the Distinction of Ranks.*—J. H. B.

the year 1797. He had overcome many disadvantages of his education, for he had been sent to a Jacobite seminary of one Elphinstone at Kensington, where his body was starved, and his mind also.* He returned to Edinburgh to college. He had hardly a word of Latin, and was obliged to work hard with a private tutor. At Glasgow, to be sure, he learned public law, but took in poison with it, which he had strength of understanding to expel, as well as to overcome many other disadvantages.

Lieutenant Walter Home, before the end of the American war, was major of the 42nd Regiment, was an able man and an excellent officer ; he was the ablest of all the family, except Robert the clergyman, although his third brother Roddam, the admiral, got to a higher rank. By means of my old connections at Glasgow and Dr. Wight's friends, we were feasted and every way well entertained there. Nothing could surpass the satisfaction Mr. and Mrs. Home had in seeing their son so well received in the best society in Glasgow. In those days the members of the ministry, excepting a very few indeed,

* " The character of Mr. Elphinstone is to my knowledge most erroneous. He was a worthy and excellent man, an able scholar, and most attentive to his pupils, both as a teacher and as a guardian of their morals. Whatever were his political opinions his only care was to make his pupils good men and good subjects, and it was probably owing to the instruction and sound principles which he then imbibed that Mr. Colt attained that reputable character for which he is here justly praised." Note to original MS. by Colonel Alex. Ferguson, author of *Henry Erskine and His Time*, etc.

were the only people of liberal conversation in that city.

Drs. Blair and Robertson were at London this year during the time of the Assembly—the first to visit London for the first and only time in his life ; the second to transact with his bookseller for his History of Charles V., Emperor of Germany and King of Spain, and to enjoy the fame of his former publication. Dr. Robertson was introduced to the first company in London, as all the people of fashion, both male and female, were eager to see the historian of Queen Mary, who had given them so much pleasure. He did not disappoint their expectation, for though he spoke broad Scotch in point of pronunciation and accent or tone, his was the language of literature and taste, and of an enlightened and liberal mind. Dr. Blair exhibited in a much narrower circle, for nothing of his having been yet published but his Dissertation on *Ossian*, he had raised but little curiosity ; and excepting the family of Northumberland, a son of which, Lord Algernon Piercy, had been three years under his roof at the university, he hardly was known to any of the English nobility or gentry, and depended chiefly for his entertainment there on such literary people as he had seen at Edinburgh, or was introduced to by Dr. Blair of Westminster, or James M'Pherson, the translator of the *Ossian*.*

* His " Lectures on Rhetoric," as delivered to his class, though not then published, had obtained considerable colloquial celebrity. It was not until 1777 that he became famous by the publication of his Sermons.—J. H. B.

Blair had taken charge of Lord Glasgow, the King's Commissioner, during the General Assembly, who, though he was a very able man, had so much distrust in himself that he could not compose his own speeches. This service was laid upon me, and I had much pleasure in the close communication which this gave me with his lordship, as it opened to me a near view of uncommon talents and exalted mind, of the service of which the world was in great measure deprived by the most insuperable diffidence and modesty.*

I was a member of the Assembly this year, in which there was little business of any consequence. Henry Dundas, who was now well known there, took an attentive charge of it, and leaned on me as his best clerical assistant.

* See above, p. 495.

CHAPTER XIV

THE window-tax alarmed the clergy more and more, and as I had been the great champion in maintaining on every occasion that the Scottish clergy by our law ought to be exempted from this tax, on the same grounds on which they are exempted from paying the land-tax for their glebes, while one of our meetings were deliberating what was to be done, I told them that as I intended to be in London in the spring on private business, I would very gladly accept of any commission they would give me, to state our claim to the King's Ministers, and particularly to the Lords of the Treasury ; and at least to prepare the way for an application for exemption to the Parliament in the following year, in case it should be found expedient. Robertson, who had thought it more advisable to pay rather than resist any longer, was surprised into consent with this sudden proposal of mine, and frankly agreed to it, though he told me privately that it would not have success. The truth was, that Mrs. Carlyle's health was so indifferent that I became uneasy, and wished to try Bath, and to visit London, where she never had been, on our way. The clergy were highly pleased with my offer of service without any expense, and I was accordingly commissioned, in due form, by the Committee on the Window-Tax, to carry on this affair. We prepared for our journey, and set out about the middle of February. We had the good fortune to get Martin, the portrait-painter, and Bob Scott, a young physician, as our companions on our journey. This made it very pleasant, as Martin was a man of uncommon talents for conversation. We stopped for two days with the Blacketts at Newcastle, and then went on by Huntingdon, and after that to Cambridge. As I had not been there when I was formerly in London, I was desirous to see that famous university; and besides, had got a warm exhortation from my friend Dr. Robertson, to diverge a little from the straight line, and go by Hockwell, where there were the finest eels in all England. We took that place in our way, and arrived long enough before dinner to have our eels dressed in various ways; but though the spitch-cocked had been so highly recommended by our friend, we thought nothing of them, and Mrs. Carlyle could not taste them, so that we had all to dine on some very indifferent mutton-broth, which had been ordered for her. I resolved after this never to turn off the road by the advice of epicures.

We got to Cambridge in the dark, but remained all next forenoon, and saw all the public buildings, some of which are very fine, particularly King's College Chapel. As none of us had any acquaintances there that we knew of, we were not induced to stay any longer, and so made the best of our way to London.

My youngest sister Janet, a beautiful, elegant, and pleasing young woman, having gone to London to visit her married sister, had herself married, in 1760, a gentleman who had been captain of a trading vessel in the Mediterranean, and, having been attacked by a French or Spanish privateer, took her after a short engagement.* He was a very sensible clever man, much esteemed by his companions, and had become insurance-broker. On our arrival in London, therefore, which was on the 11th February, we took up our residence at their house, which was in Aldermanbury. They had also a country-house, where their children resided the whole year, and where they spent the summer months ; and being only nine miles from London, with a very good road, my brother-in-law could easily ride every day to attend to his business, and return to dinner. Merton was a very agreeable place. The house had been originally built by Lord

* See *Scots Magazine*, December 1759 :—
" CAPTURES BY PRIVATEERS, ETC.
" By the *Dragon*, Bell, and the *Greyhound*, Dewar, both from London, *Le Pendant*, Jos. Geruhard, from St. Domingo ; carried into Gibraltar."
See also the *Caledonian Mercury*, 15th December 1759 :—
" The *Dragon*, Bell, and the *Greyhound*, Dewar, both from London, are arrived at Gibraltar, and have carried a French prize with them."—*Note appended to the MS.*

Eglinton, and soon after forsaken and sold. There was a large garden of three acres, divided into three parts, and planted with the best fruit-trees, on which, when I afterwards saw it in the season, I said there were more peaches and apricots than grew then in Midlothian ; for I well remember that [there were very few] till we had hothouses here, which had then only had a beginning, by Lord Chief-Baron Ord, at the Dean, and Baron Stuart Moncrieff, and were not in great numbers till 1780.

About the third night after we came, we went with the Bells to the Scotch dancing assembly, which then met in the King's Arms Tavern, in Cheapside, where we met many of our acquaintance, and were introduced to several others with whom we were not before acquainted. I was glad to find from them all that my brother-in-law was in high esteem among them as a man of business, not only for his integrity, but his aptitude for business. My sister was much admired as a fine woman, and no less for the elegance and propriety of her manners than for her handsome face and fine person. He had the good luck to be called Honest Tom, in distinction to another who frequented Lloyd's Coffeehouse, who was not in so much favour, and was besides a very hot Wilkite. After a few days more we were invited to a fine subscription-dinner in the London Tavern, where there was a company of about fifty ladies and gentlemen. The dinner was sumptuous, but I was not much delighted with the conversation. The men, especially, were vulgar and uneducated ; and most of the English among them violent Wilkites, and gave toasts of the party kind, which showed their breeding where the majority were Scotch. It was with some difficulty that I could get Honest Tom to treat their bad manners with ridicule and contempt, rather than with rage and resentment.

Having now been near a week in London, it was proper that I should give a commencement to the business which I had undertaken ; I therefore applied myself to making the necessary calls on Dr. Gordon of the Temple, a Scotch solicitor-at-law, and the Lord Advocate for Scotland, and whoever else I thought might be of use. I had drawn a short memorial on the business which Dr. Gordon approved, but wished it to be left with him for corrections and additions. This I did, but was surprised to find, when he returned it several weeks after as fit to be sent to the press, that there was hardly any change on it at all. But I was still more surprised, when calling on the Lord Advocate (James Montgomery, Esq.), and opening the affair to him, to hear him answer that he wished me success with all his heart, but could give me no aid ; for, he added, that when the clergy were lately in four years' arrears, the payment of which would have greatly distressed them, Dr. Robertson had come to him in Edinburgh, and had strongly interceded with him to get that arrear excused, and he would answer for the punctual payment by the clergy in future. He had, accordingly, on this promise, applied to the Duke of Grafton, then First Minister, and obtained what the Doctor had asked on the condition promised. In this state of things it was impossible that he could assist me as Lord Advocate, but that, as a private gentleman, he would do all he could ; that was, to introduce me to the Minister, to speak of me as I deserved, and to say that he thought the petition I brought very reasonable, and agreeable to the law of Scotland. All this he punctually fulfilled, for he was an honourable man.

The Church of Scotland had been at all times very meanly provided ; and even when they were serving their country with the utmost fidelity and zeal at the time of the Restoration, and ever afterwards supporting that part of the aristocracy which resisted the encroachments of the Crown and maintained the liberties of the people—even then their most moderate requests to be raised above poverty were denied.* After the union of the crowns, and even after that of the legislatures, they have, on every application for redress, been scurvily treated. The history of our country bears the strongest testimony of their loyalty to the king, while they warmly opposed every appearance of arbitrary power even to persecution and death. They were cajoled and flattered by the aristocracy when they wanted their aid, but never relieved, till Cromwell considered their poverty, and

* Whether or not the author meant to say *Reformation*, the word Restoration must have been a slip.—J. H. B.

relieved them for the time. Yet, after Presbytery was finally settled at the Revolution, the clergy were allowed almost to starve till, down in our own time, in the year 1790, a generous and wise man was raised to the President's chair, who, being also President of that Court when it sits as a committee of Parliament for the augmentation of ministers' stipends, with the concurrence of his brethren had redressed this grievance, and enabled the clergy and their families to survive such years of dearth as the 1799 and 1800, which, but for that relief, must have reduced them to ruin. This happened by good luck while the land estates in Scotland were doubled and tripled in their rents, otherwise it could not have been done without a clamorous opposition.*

It is observable that no country has ever been more tranquil, except the trifling insurrections of 1715 and '45, than Scotland has been since the Revolution in 1688—a period of 117 years; while, at the same time, the country has been prosperous, with an increase of agriculture, trade, and manufactures, as well as all the ornamental arts of life, to a degree unexampled in any age and country. How far the steady loyalty to the Crown, and attachment to the constitution, together with the unwearied diligence of the clergy in teaching a rational religion, may have contributed to this prosperity, cannot be exactly ascer-

* The Lord President of the Court of Session here referred to is Sir Islay Campbell. This matter is again alluded to, p. 554.— J. H. B.

tained ; but surely enough appears to entitle them to
the high respect of the State, and to justice from the
country, in a decent support to them and to their
families, and, if possible, to a permanent security like
that of the Church of England, by giving the clergy a
title to vote on their livings for the member of Parliament for the county, which would at once raise their
respect, and, by making them members of the State,
would for ever secure their interest in it, and firmly
cement and strengthen the whole.

Before I began my operations relative to the window-tax, I witnessed something memorable. It being
much the fashion to go on a Sunday evening to a
chapel of the Magdalene Asylum, we went there on the
second Sunday we were in London, and had difficulty
to get tolerable seats for my sister and wife, the crowd
of genteel people was so great. The preacher was Dr.
Dodd, a man afterwards too well known. The unfortunate young women were in a latticed gallery,
where you could only see those who chose to be seen.
The preacher's text was, " If a man look on a woman
to lust after her," etc. The text itself was shocking,
and the sermon was composed with the least possible
delicacy, and was a shocking insult on a sincere penitent, and fuel for the warm passions of the hypocrites.
The fellow was handsome, and delivered his discourse
remarkably well for a reader. When he had finished,
there were unceasing whispers of applause, which I
could not help contradicting aloud, and condemning
the whole institution, as well as the exhibition of the

preacher, as *contra bonos mores*, and a disgrace to a Christian city.*

On the day after this I went to the House of Peers, and heard Sir Fletcher Norton's † pleading on the Douglas Cause, on the side of Douglas, but in a manner inferior to what I expected from his fame : but this was not a question of law, but of fact. I dined and supped next day with Colonel Dow, who had translated well the *History of Hindustan*, and wrote tolerably well the *Tragedy of Zingis*. As James M'Pherson, the translator of *Ossian*, and he lived together, and as his play, in point of diction and

---

* Compare Dr. Carlyle's attitude towards this notorious man and that of Walpole in the following extract from one of his letters to George Montague :—" A party was made up to go to the Magdalene house . . . Prince Edward, Colonel Brudenel his groom, Lady Northumberland, Lady Mary Coke, Lady Carlisle, Miss Pelham, Lady Hertford, Lord Beauchamp, Lord Huntingdon, old Bowman, and I . . . Lord Hertford at the head of the Governors with their white staves met us at the door, and led the prince directly into the Chapel, where before the altar was an armchair for him, with a damask blue cushion, a *prie-Dieu*, and a footstool of black cloth with gold nails. . . . At the west end were enclosed the sisterhood, about one hundred and thirty in all in greyish-brown stuffs. As soon as we entered the chapel the organ played, and the Magdalens sang a hymn in parts ; you cannot imagine how well. . . . Prayers then began, psalms, and a sermon : the latter by a young clergyman, one Dodd.[1] . . . He apostrophised the lost sheep, who sobbed and cried from their souls; and so did my Lady Hertford and Fanny Pelham, till I believe the city dames took them both for Jane Shores. . . . In short it was a very pleasing performance, and I got the *most illustrious* to desire it might be printed."

† Elected speaker of the House of Commons in 1770, and created Baron Grantley of Markenfield in 1782.

---

[1] The Rev. William Dodd; was executed in 1770 for forgery.

manners, had some resemblance to the poems of Ossian, there were not a few who ascribed the tragedy to M'Pherson ; but such people did not know that, could M'Pherson have claimed it, he was not the man to relinquish either the credit or profits which might arise from it, for the tragedy ran its nine nights.

Dow was a Scotch adventurer, who had been bred at the school of Dunbar, his father being in the Customs there, and had run away from his apprentice-ship at Eyemouth, and found his way to the East Indies, where, having a turn for languages, which had been fostered by his education, he soon became such a master of the native tongue as to accelerate his pre-ferment in the army, for he soon had the command of a regiment of sepoys. He was a sensible and know-ing man, of very agreeable manners, and of a mild and gentle disposition. As he was telling us that night, that, when he had the charge of the Great Mogul, with two regiments under his command, at Delhi, he was tempted to dethrone the monarch, and mount the throne in his stead, which he said he could easily have done :—when I asked him what prevented him from yielding to the temptation, he gave me this memorable answer, that it was reflecting on what his old schoolfellows at Dunbar would think of him for being guilty of such an action. His company were Dr. John Douglas and Garrick, the two M'Phersons, John Home, and David Hume who joined us in the evening.*

* Colonel Alexander Dow is known as the translator and con-tinuer of the Persian History of Hindostan, and the writer of

I have before, I believe, given some account of them all but Robert M'Pherson, the chaplain, whom I had not known till now. Though not a man of genius, he was a man of good sense, of a firm and manly mind, and of much worth and honour. He was a younger brother of M'Pherson of Banchors, a man near the head of the clan in point of birth, but not of a large fortune. He had been bred at Aberdeen for the Church, but before he passed trials as a probationer, he had been offered a company in his regiment of Highlanders by Simon Fraser, and had accepted. But when the regiment rendezvoused at Greenock, he was told, with many fair speeches, that the captains' commissions were all disposed of, much against the colonel's will, but that he might have a lieutenancy, or the chaplainry if he liked it better. M'Pherson chose the last, and took orders immediately from the Presbytery of Lochcarron, where he returned for ten days. He soon made himself acceptable to the superiors as well as to the men, and after they landed in Nova Scotia, in every skirmish or battle it was observed that he always put himself on a line with the officers at the head of the regiment. He was invited to the mess of the field officers, where he continued. On hearing this from General Murray, I asked him (M'Pherson) if it was true. He said it was. How came you to be so foolish? He answered,

Tales from the Persian, and of another tragedy besides his Zingis, called Sethona. The editor is not aware, however, of any other source of information about the personal adventures referred to in the text.—J. H. B.

that being a grown man, while many of the lieutenants and ensigns were but boys, as well as some of the privates, and that they looked to him for example as well as precept, he had thought it his duty to advance with them, but that he had discontinued the practice after the third time of danger, as he found they were perfectly steady.

Dining with him, and General James Murray and one or two more, at the British one day, I put him on telling the story of the mutiny at Quebec, when he had the command after the death of Wolfe. He told us that the first thing he had done was to send and inquire if Mac had taken advantage of the leave he had given him to sail for Britain the day before, for if he had not sailed, there would have been no mutiny. But he was gone, and I had to do the best I could without him ; and so he went on. Not being certain if this anecdote might not have been much exaggerated, according to the usual style of the *windy Murrays*, as they were styled by *Jock at the Horn*, I asked Mac, when the company parted, how much of this was true ? He answered, that though the General had exceeded a little in his compliments to him, that it was so far true, that he, being the only Highland chaplain there—he of Fraser's regiment having gone home—he had so much to say with both of them that he could have persuaded them to stand by their officers and the General, in which, if those two regiments had joined, they would have prevented the mutiny.

One anecdote more of this worthy man, and I shall

have done with him. In one of the winters in which
he was at Quebec he had provided himself in a
wooden house, which he had furnished well, and in
which he had a tolerable soldier's library. While he
was dining one day with the mess, his house took fire
and was burned to the ground. Next morning the
two serjeant-majors of the two Highland regiments
came to him, and, lamenting the great loss he had
sustained, told him that the lads, out of their great
love and respect for him, had collected a purse of four
hundred guineas, which they begged him to accept of.
He was moved by their generosity, and by and by
answered, " That he was never so much gratified in
his life as by their offer, as a mark of kindness and
respect, of which he would think himself entirely unworthy if he could rob them of the fruits of their wise
and prudent frugality ; " and added, " that, by good
fortune, he had no need of the exertions of their
generosity." The annals of private men I have often
thought as instructive and worthy of being recorded
as those of their superiors.

Having formerly given some account of James
M'Pherson and Garrick, I shall say nothing more of
them here, but that in their several ways they were
very good company. Garrick was always playsome,
good-humoured, and willing to display ; James was
sensible, shrewd, and sarcastic. Dow went a second
time out to India, and after some time died there.

By this time I had discovered that I should have
no need to go to Bath, as Mrs. C. had fallen with

child, which left me sufficient time to wait even for
the very slow method of transacting Treasury business, which made me sometimes repent that I had
undertaken it. I had found Sir Gilbert Elliot at last,
who both encouraged and assisted me. I had also
met Mr. Wedderburn, who was not then in the line of
doing me much service. Mr. Grey Cooper,* who had
been brought forward by the Honourable Charles
Townshend, and was then a Secretary of the Treasury,
frankly gave me his services. But the only person
(except Sir G. Elliot) who understood me perfectly
was Mr. Jeremiah Dyson. He had been two years
at Edinburgh University at the same time as Akenside and Monckly, and had a perfect idea of the
constitution of the Church of Scotland and the nature
and state of the livings of the clergy. Of him I
expected and obtained much aid. Broderip, secretary to the Duke of Grafton, on whom I frequently
called, gave me good words but little aid.

On the 23rd of this month I went with John Home
to the first night of his tragedy of the *Fatal Discovery*, which went off better than we expected.
This was and is to my taste the second-best of Home's
tragedies. Garrick had been justly alarmed at the
jealousy and dislike which prevailed at that time
against Lord Bute and the Scotch, and had advised
him to change the title of *Rivine* into that of the
Fatal Discovery, and had provided a student of

* Afterwards Sir Grey Cooper, Secretary of the Treasury and a
Privy Councillor.

Oxford, who had appeared at the rehearsals as the author, and wished Home of all things to remain concealed till the play had its run. But John, whose vanity was too sanguine to admit of any fear or caution, and whose appetite for praise rebelled against the counsel that would deprive him for a moment of his fame, too soon discovered the secret, and though the play survived its nine nights, yet the house evidently slackened after the town heard that John was the author. Home, however, in his way, ascribed this to the attention of the public, and especially of the Scotch, being drawn off by the Douglas Cause, which was decided in the House of Lords on the 27th, forgetting that this took up only one night, and that any slackness derived from that cause could not affect other nights.

To finish my account of this play, I shall add here that Garrick still continued to perform it on the most convenient terms. Mrs. Carlyle, John Home, and I, dined with Mr. A. Wedderburn at his house in Lincoln's-Inn Fields, and went to the *Fatal Discovery* with him and his lady and his brother, Colonel David Wedderburn, when we were all perfectly well pleased. We returned with them to supper, Wedderburn having continued cordial and open all that day ; his brother was always so.

We became acquainted with my wife's uncle and aunt, Mr. Laurie and Mrs. Mary Reed, brother and sister of her mother by another wife. Mr. Reed was a mahogany merchant in Hatton Wall, a very worthy and honourable man ; and his sister, whom I had seen once or twice before in Berwick, was a handsome and elegant woman, though now turned of thirty, with as much good sense and breeding as any person we met with. Mr. Reed was not rich, but between an estate of £250, which he had near Alnwick, and his business, he lived in a very respectable manner. Their mode of living was quite regulated, for they saw company only two days in the week ;— on Thursday, to dinner, when you met a few friends, chiefly from Northumberland ; and here, if you pleased, you might play cards and stay the evening. On Sunday evening they likewise saw their friends to tea and supper, but they were too old-fashioned to play cards, which was very convenient for me. The uncle and aunt were proud of their niece, as they found her, in point of conversation and manners, at least equal to any of their guests ; and the niece was proud of her uncle and aunt, as in him she found as honest a man as Mr. Bell, and in her a woman who, for beauty and elegance, could cope with my sister, who was not surpassed by any lady in the city. Here I met with many old acquaintances, and made some new ones, such as Sir Evan Nepean and his lady, then only in their courtship, and A. Collingwood, a clever attorney, said to be nearly related to the family of Unthank—indeed, a natural son of my wife's grandfather. To this very agreeable place we resorted often ; and when I came the next year alone, I availed myself of it, especially on Sunday nights.

I was much indebted to my hospitable friend, Dr. Blair of Westminster, at whose house also I met with sundry people whose acquaintance I cultivated. On the 26th of this month I met him at Court, after having attended service in the Chapel Royal and in the chaplain's seat, and was by him introduced in the drawing-room to Lord Bathurst, then very old, but extremely agreeable ; Dr. Barton, Dean of Bristol, Rector of St. Andrew, Holborn, etc., and to Dr. Tucker, Dean of Gloucester—very excellent people, whose acquaintance I very much valued.*

On the 27th I attended the House of Peers on the Douglas Cause. The Duke of B[uccleuch] had promised to carry me down to the House ; but as I was going into Grosvenor Square to meet him at ten o'clock, I met the Duke of Montague, who was coming from his house, and took me into his chariot, saying that the Duke of B. was not yet ready. He put me in by the side of the throne, where I found two or three of my friends, among them Thomas Bell. The business did not begin till eleven, and from that time I stood, with now and then a lean on the edge of a deal board, till nine in the evening, without any refreshment but a small roll and two oranges. The heat of the house was chiefly oppressive, and Lord Sandwich's speech, which, though learned and able, yet being three hours long, was very intolerable. The Duke of Bedford spoke low, but not half an hour.

* Josiah Tucker, whose works on Trade anticipated some of the established doctrines on political economy.—J. H. B.

The Chancellor and Lord Mansfield united on the side of Douglas ; each of them spoke above an hour. Andrew Stuart, whom I saw in the House, sitting on the left side of the throne, seemed to be much affected at a part of Lord Camden's speech, in which he reflected on him, and immediately left the House ; from whence I concluded that he was in despair of success. Lord Mansfield, overcome with heat, was about to faint in the middle of his speech, and was obliged to stop. The side-doors were immediately thrown open, and the Chancellor rushing out, returned soon with a servant, who followed him with a bottle and glasses. Lord Mansfield drank two glasses of the wine, and after some time revived, and proceeded in his speech. We, who had no wine, were nearly as much recruited by the fresh air which rushed in at the open doors as his lordship by the wine. About nine the business ended in favour of Douglas, there being only five Peers on the other side. I was well pleased with that decision, as I had favoured that side : Professor Ferguson and I being the only two of our set of people who favoured Douglas, chiefly on the opinion that, if the proof of filiation on his part was not sustained, the whole system of evidence in such cases would be overturned, and a door be opened for endless disputes about succession. I had asked the Duke of B., some days before the decision, how it would go ; he said that if the Law Lords disagreed, there was no saying how it would go ; because the Peers, however imperfectly prepared to judge, would follow the Judge they most respected. But if they united, the case would be determined by their opinion ; it being [the practice] in their House to support the Law Lords in all judicial cases.

After the decision, I persuaded my friends, as there was no coach to be had, not to attempt rushing into any of the neighbouring taverns, but to follow me to the Crown and Anchor in the Strand, where we arrived, Thos. Bell, Alderman Crichton, Robert Bogle, junior, and I, in time enough to get into a snug room, where we wrote some letters for Scotland, the post then not departing till twelve ; and after a good supper, Bell and I got home to Aldermanbury about one o'clock, where our wives were waiting, though not uninformed of the event, as I had despatched a porter with a note to them immediately on our arrival in the tavern.

The rejoicings in Scotland were very great on this occasion, and even outrageous: although the Douglas family had been long in obscurity, yet the Hamiltons had for a long period lost their popularity. The attachment which all their acquaintances had to Baron Mure, who was the original author of this suit, and to Andrew Stuart, who carried it on, swayed their minds very much their way. They were men of uncommon good sense and probity.*

* Andrew Stuart, often mentioned by Carlyle, had devoted the whole energies and prospects of his life to the Hamilton side of the cause. He challenged Thurlow, the leading counsel on the opposite side, and they fought. His bitter " Letters to Lord

Mrs. Pulteney being still living, we had a fine dinner at Bath House, after which, Mrs. Carlyle and I paid an evening visit to Mrs. Montague. Pulteney * at this time had fallen much under the influence of General Robert Clerk, whom I have mentioned before. I happened to ask him when he had seen Clerk ; he answered he saw him every day, and as he had not been there yet, he might probably pay his visit before ten o'clock, and then enlarged for some time on his great ability. Clerk had subdued Pulteney by persuading him that there was not a man in England fit to be Chancellor of Exchequer but himself. Mrs. Pulteney's good sense, however, defeated the effect of this influence. Pulteney was unfortunate in not taking for his private secretary and confidential friend Dr. John Douglas, who had stood in that relation to the late Lord Bath, and was one of the ablest men in England. But on Pulteney's succession he found himself neglected, and drew off. Clerk came at ten, as Pulteney had foretold, and I saw how the land lay.

On this first mission to London I was much obliged

Mansfield " have often been read, like those of Junius, as a model of polished vituperation.—J. H. B.

When the Douglas case was decided in the Court of Session by the casting vote of the Lord President " some one asked Boswell why all the people of extraordinary sense were Hamiltonians ? "   " I cannot tell," he answered ;   " but I am sure all persons of common sense are Douglassians."—Ramsay's *Scotland and Scotsman*.

* Already referred to (pp. 296, 418, etc.) as Sir William Johnstone or Sir William Pulteney. He was not made a baronet until 1794.

to Sir Alexander Gilmour, who was a friend of the Duke of Grafton's. He knew everybody, and introduced me to everybody. One day he carried me to the Archbishop of Canterbury (Cornwallis), who received me graciously; in short, I called on all the Scotch noblemen and Members of Parliament, many of whom I saw, and left memorials at every house where I called. Lord Frederick Campbell * was particularly obliging. At this time I dined one day with Sir A. Gilmour on a Sunday, after having been at Court; General Graham and Pulteney, and Colonel Riccart Hepburn, dined there. In the conversation there, to my surprise I found [Graham] talking strongly against Administration for not advising the King to yield to the popular cry. Gilmour opposed him with violence, and I drew an inference, which proved true, that he had been tampering with her Majesty, and using political freedoms, which were, not long afterwards, the cause of his disgrace. Graham was a shrewd and sensible man, but the Queen's favour and his prosperity had made him arrogant and presumptuous, and he blew himself up.†   Not long

* Second son of John, fourth Duke of Argyle, was appointed Keeper of the Privy Seal of Scotland, and in 1768 Lord Clerk Register of Scotland, in which capacity he laid the foundation stone of the Register House in Edinburgh in 1774. He was instrumental in recovering from London many valuable records of the Scottish Parliament.

† This is probably the " Colonel Græme " who, according to Walpole (who says he was a notorious Jacobite, and out in the '45), negotiated the marriage of George III., having been " despatched in the most private manner as a traveller, and invested with no character, to visit various little Protestant courts, and

after this time he lost his office near the Queen, and re-tired into obscurity in Scotland for the rest of his days.

My connection with physicians made me a member of two of their clubs, which I seldom missed. One of them was at the Horn Tavern in Fleet Street,* where they had laid before them original papers relating to their own science, and had published a volume or two of Essays, which were well received. Armstrong, who took no share in the business generally, arrived when I did, about eight o'clock ; and as they had a great deference for him, and as he was whimsical, they delayed bespeaking supper till he came, and then laid that duty on him. He in complaisance wished to turn it over on me, as the greatest, or rather the only stranger, for I was admitted *speciali gratia* ; but I declined the office. The conversation was lively and agreeable, and we parted always at twelve. There was another club held on the alternate Thursday at the Queen's Head in St. Paul's Churchyard, which was not confined to physicians, but included men of other professions. Strange the engraver † was one, a very sensible, ingenious, and modest man.

In the course of my operations about the window-tax, I had frequently short interviews with Lord

make report of the qualifications of the several unmarried princesses."—See *Mem. of Geo. III.*, ch. v.—J. H. B.

* Now represented by Anderton's Hotel.

† The father of line engraving in Great Britain. He was born in Orkney in 1721. A staunch Jacobite, he served throughout the insurrection of 1745 in the Prince's Life Guards. He married Miss Lumisden, sister of Andrew Lumisden, who was one of the Prince's household at Rome. Strange was knighted in 1787.

Mansfield. One day he sent for me to breakfast, when I had a long conversation with him on various subjects. Amongst others, he talked of Hume and Robertson's Histories, and said that though they had pleased and instructed him much, and though he could point out few or no faults in them, yet, when he was reading their books, he did not think he was reading English : could I account to him how that happened ? I answered that the same objection had not occurred to me, who was a Scotchman bred as well as born ; but that I had a solution to it, which I would submit to his lordship. It was, that to every man bred in Scotland the English language was in some respects a foreign tongue, the precise value and force of whose words and phrases he did not understand, and therefore was continually endeavouring to word his expressions by additional epithets or circumlocutions, which made his writings appear both stiff and redundant. With this solution his lordship appeared entirely satisfied. By this time his lordship perfectly understood the nature of our claim to exemption from the window-tax, and promised me his aid, and suggested some new arguments in our favour.

I made a very valuable acquaintance in the Bishop of London, R. Jerrick, having been introduced to him by his son-in-law, Dr. Anthony Hamilton, whom I met at Dr. Pitcairn's. I found the Bishop to be a truly excellent man, of a liberal mind and excellent good temper. He took to me, and was very cordial in wishing success to my application, and was very friendly in recommending me and it to his brethren on the bench. He never refused me admittance, and I dined frequently with him this year and the next. He was then considered as having the sole episcopal jurisdiction over the Church of England in America. He was so obliging to my requests that he ordained, at my desire, two Scotch probationers, who, having little chance of obtaining settlements here, were glad to try their fortune in a new world. As I was unwilling to forfeit my credit with this good man, I had not recommended them but with perfect assurance of their good characters. The first, whom I think he had sent to Bermudas, he gave me thanks for when I saw him a year after, as, he told me, he had fully answered the character I had given him. He [the Bishop] was a famous good preacher, and the best reader of prayers I ever heard. Being Dean of the Chapel Royal, he read the communion service every Sunday. Though our residence was at my sister's in Aldermanbury, as I had occasion frequently to dine late in the west end of the town, I then lodged in New Bond Street with my aunt, and resorted often at supper to Robert Adam's, whose sisters were very agreeable, and where we had the latest news from the House of Commons, of which he was a member, and which he told us in the most agreeable manner, and with very lively comments.

My good aunt Paterson's husband, a cousin of Sir Hew Paterson, took care to have us visit his son's widow, Mrs. Seton, the heiress of Touch, whose first husband was Sir Hew's son, who had died without issue. There we dined one day with a large company, mostly Scots, among whom were Mrs. Walkinshaw *—who had a place at court, though she was sister of the lady who was said to be mistress to Prince Charles, the Pretender's son—and David Hume, by that time Under-Secretary of State. The conversation was lively and agreeable, but we were much amused with observing how much the thoughts and conversation of all those in the least connected were taken up with every trifling circumstance that related to the Court. This kind of tittle-tattle suited Dr. John Blair of all men, who had been a tutor to the King's brother, the Duke of York, and now occasionally assisted Dr. Barton as Clerk of the Closet to the Princess Dowager of Wales. It was truly amusing to observe how much David Hume's strong and capacious mind was filled with infantine anecdotes of nurses and children. Mr Seton was the son of a Mr. Smith, who had been settled at Boulogne, a wine merchant, was a great Jacobite, and had come to Scotland in the time of the Rebellion, 1745. Poor Mrs. Seton, whose first husband, Paterson, was, by his mother, a nephew of the

* Katherine, third daughter of John Walkinshaw of Barrowfield and Camlachie (who was uncle to Lord Kames) and Katherine, daughter of Sir Hugh Paterson of Bannockburn. Katherine was bed-chamber woman and afterwards housekeeper at Leicester House to the Princess Dowager of Wales, mother of George III. John Walkinshaw had ten daughters, the youngest of whom was Clementina, the reputed mistress of Prince Charles Edward.—Tweed's Edition of McUre's *History of Glasgow*.

35

Earl of Mar, had fallen a sacrifice to that prejudice, for Seton possessed no other charm. I call her a sacrifice, because his bad usage shortened her days. She was a very amiable woman. His future history is well known.*

At this time we had a dinner from Dr. Gartshore, whose wife, the heiress of Rusco, in Galloway, was my cousin.† Besides Drs. Blair and Dickson, there were several dissenting parsons, such as Drs. Price, Kippis, and Alexander, who were very bad company indeed, for they were fiery republicans and Wilkites, and very pedantic, petulant, and peremptory. Blair and I, however, with the help of Dickson, kept them very well down. Gartshore himself acted the part of umpire, with a leaning to their side, as they had an ascendant over many of his patients.

John Home, who was very obliging to us, when I was at liberty, in the middle of April, went with Mrs. Carlyle and me to see Hampton Court and Windsor. After we had seen the first, we went and showed Mrs. Carlyle Garrick's villa in Hampton Town, which she was highly pleased with. The family had not yet returned to the country. We went all night to Wind-

---

* Archibald Seton successively filled several high offices in the Indian service, and died in 1818.—*Gentleman's Magazine*, vol. lxxxviii. p. 184. The mansion of Touch, long the abode of one of the old Seton families, is a venerable square tower, with later adjuncts, on the slope of the Gargunnock Hills, about three miles from Stirling.—J. H. B.

† Dr. Maxwell Gartshore, a native of Kirkcudbrightshire, died after a long and successful professional career in London, in 1812. —J. H. B.

sor. In the morning we called on Dr. Douglas and his lady, a granddaughter of Sir George Rooke, of Queen Anne's reign, then in residence. He engaged us to dine with him. We went to church and heard him preach an excellent sermon, though ill delivered. His conversation was always instructive and agreeable. He had a greater number of anecdotes, and told them more correctly, than any man I ever knew. In going through his library, which was pretty full of books, he selected one small elegant French novel, and gave it as a keepsake to Mrs. Carlyle, which she and I were much pleased with, as a token of regard.

We had passed one day with Mrs. Montague by invitation, which did not please us much, as the conversation was all preconceived, and resembled the rehearsal of a comedy more than the true and unaffected dialogue which conveys the unaffected and unstudied sentiments of the heart. What a pity it was that she could not help acting ; and the woman would have been respectable had she not been so passionately desirous of respect, for she had good parts, and must have had many allurements when she was young and beautiful.*

John Home went with us to see Sion House, the inside of which had been most beautifully adorned by Robert Adam. We dined with Mr. and Mrs. Barry, who had been old friends of John's, and Barry had been his military companion at Falkirk, and escaped with him from Doune Castle. John was

* See above, p. 484.

much attached to him, and he deserved it. His wife was very amiable. There dined with us M'Pherson and Blair, besides Home. Our stay in London drew to a close, and having obtained all I expected from the Treasury, which was encouragement to apply to Parliament next year, I made haste to show Mrs. Carlyle what she had not seen.

We went to Greenwich in the morning, and the same day dined again with Mr. and Mrs. Seton, and supped with my old friend, Lady Lindores.

I sat to Martin for the large picture that went next year into the Exhibition : this was for the third time. Another sitting in January thereafter did the business. We went to the opera with my sister. We stayed for our last fortnight at my aunt's, as my business at the Treasury made it more convenient, and my wife had to make all her farewell visits. She had not seen Garrick, who was at last to play for three nights. With difficulty and bribery we got places ; but Mrs. C. felt sick, and we were obliged to leave it in the middle. We went to see Westminster Abbey, and dined with our kind friends, the Blairs, who had engaged us. My sister being now gone to Merton with her children, we took aunt and passed a day there. On the last day we went into the city, and took leave, and dined at uncle Reed's.

We dined on the 25th April at the Brand's Head with some friends, and set out on our journey northwards at five in the evening. Mr. Home had got a partner, a young man of the name of Douglas, going

to Berwick. This lad being fantastic and vain, because he had an uncle who was under-doorkeeper to
the House of Commons, diverted us much. To enjoy
him, Home and I took him stage about. My wife
was delighted with him in the inns, but she did not
choose him to go in the chaise with her, as she was at
this time apt to be sick. My wife's condition made
me resolve to travel slow, though we were to halt
some time at Newcastle.

We had agreed, for my wife's amusement and our
own, to take the middle road, and go down by North-
ampton and Nottingham, where we had never been ;
and were much amused with the beauty of the country, and the variety of its scenery. When we came
to Nottingham, however, as the road was rough,
which did not suit Mrs. Carlyle's present condition,
and the houses and horses inferior, [we thought] it
would be better to turn into the east road again, and
make the best of our way to Doncaster. When we
drew near that place, Mrs. Carlyle found out that
we had changed our route, and was well pleased.
We had come by Mansfield and Welbeck (the Duke
of Portland's), and the Duke of Norfolk's, places well
worth seeing. The road goes through the trunk of a
famous oak tree. The woods in that part of the
forest of Willingham are very fine, and the oaks are
remarkably large. We arrived at Wallsend, a very
delightful village about four miles below Newcastle,
on the road to Shields, where Mr. Blackett had a
very agreeable house for the summer. There were

other two gentlemen's houses of good fortune in the
village, with a church and a parsonage-house.   Next
day, the 1st of May, was so very warm that I with
difficulty was able to walk down to the church in
the bottom of the village, not more than two hundred
yards distant.

Mary Home, a cousin-german of Mrs. Blackett's
and my wife's, was residing here at this time, and had
been for several months at Newcastle.   This was
the young lady who John Home married, who was
then a pretty lively girl, and reckoned very like
Queen Charlotte. She unfortunately had bad health,
which continued even to this day ; for she is now
sixty-seven, and is still very frail, though better than
she has been for several years.   It was in some respects an unlucky marriage, for she had no children.
Lord Haddington, however, said she was a very good
wife for a poet ; and Lady Milton having asked me
what made John marry such a sickly girl, I answered
that I supposed it was because he was in love with
her.   She replied, " No, no ; it was because *she* was
in love with *him*."

We stayed here for eight or ten days, and visited
all the neighbours, who were all very agreeable, even
the clergyman's wife, who was a little lightsome ;
but as her head ran much on fine clothes, which she
could not purchase to please her, but only could
imitate in the most tawdry manner, she was rather
amusing to Mrs. B., who had a good deal of humour
—more than her sister, who had a sharper wit and

more discernment. The husband was a very good sort of man, and very worthy of his office, but oppressed with family cares. Mr. Potter, I think, was an Oxonian.

We did not fail to visit our good friend Mr. Collingwood of Chirton, and his lady, Mary Roddam, of both of whom my wife was a favourite. We went down together to Berwickshire in the middle of May, where we remained some days at Fogo Manse, the Rev. Mr. William Home's, where, leaving John with his bride, we came on to Musselburgh about the 27th of May, near the end of the General Assembly.

I had been persuaded to buy a young horse from a farmer near Mr. Home's, an awkward enough beast, but only four years old, which, if he did not do for a riding-horse, might be trained to the plough, for I had, at the preceding Martinmas, entered on a farm of one hundred acres of the Duke of Buccleuch's. On the Saturday morning after I came home, I unfortunately mounted this beast, who ran away with me in my green before the door, and was in danger of throwing me on the railing that was put up to defend a young hedge. To shun this I threw myself off on the opposite side, in sight of my wife and children. I was much stunned, and could not get up immediately, but luckily, before she could reach the place, I had raised myself to my breech, otherwise I did not know what might have befallen her in the condition she was in. No harm, however, happened to her ; and the new surgeon who had come in our absence, a John Steward or Stewart, a Northumbrian, an apprentice of Sandy Wood's, was sent for to bleed me. I would not be bled, however, till I had made my report on the window-lights ready for the General Assembly, which was to be dissolved on Monday, lest I should not be able to write after being bled, or not to attend the Assembly on Monday. But it so happened that I was little disabled by my fall, and could even preach next day.

When we returned from the south, we were happy to find our two fine girls in such good health ; but my mother, and unmarried sister Sarah, had lived for some time close by us, and saw them twice every day. Sarah, the eldest, was now eight years of age, and had displayed great sweetness of temper, with an uncommon degree of sagacity. Jenny, the second, was now six, and was gay and lively and engaging to the last degree. They were both handsome in their several kinds, the first like me and my family, the second like their mother. They already had made great proficency in writing and arithmetic, and were remarkably good dancers. At this time they betrayed no symptoms of that fatal disease which robbed me of them, unless it might have been predicted from their extreme sensibilities of taste and affection which they already displayed. It was the will of Heaven that I should lose them too soon. But to reflect on their promising qualities ever since has been the delight of many a watchful night and

melancholy day.   I lost them before they had given
me any emotions but those of joy and hope.

On the 25th of September this year, Mrs. Carlyle
was delivered of her third daughter, Mary Roddam,
and recovered very well.   But the child was un-
healthy from her birth, and gave her mother the
greatest anxiety.   She continued to live until June
1773, when she was relieved from a life of constant
pain.   In 11th November that year she had her
son William, who was very healthy and promising
till within six or eight weeks of his death, when he
was seized with a peripneumony, which left such a
weakness on his lungs as soon closed his days.

On Monday I went to Edinburgh, and rendered
an account of my mission at the bar of the General
Assembly.   I received the thanks of the General
Assembly for my care and diligence in the management of this business, and at the same time was
appointed by the Assembly their commissioner, with
full powers to apply to next session of Parliament for
an exemption from the window-tax, to be at the
same time under the direction of a committee of
Assembly, which was revived, with additions.   This
first success made me very popular among the clergy,
of whom one-half at least looked upon me with an
ill eye after the affair of the tragedy of *Douglas*.
There is no doubt that exemption from that tax was
a very great object to the clergy, whose stipends
were in general very small, and besides, was oppos-
ing in the beginning any design there might be to

lay still heavier burdens on the clergy, who, having only stipends out of the tithes allocated, together with small glebes and a suitable manse and offices free of all taxes and public burdens, would have been quite undone had they been obliged to pay all that has since been laid on houses and windows.

For as much use as the clergy were at the Reformation, and for as much as they contributed to the Revolution, and to preserve the peace and promote the prosperity of the country since that period, the aristocracy of Scotland have always been backward to mend their situation, which, had it not been for the manly system of the President (Islay Campbell), must have fallen into distress and contempt. As it is, their stipends keep no pace with the rising prosperity of the country, and they are degraded in their rank by the increasing wealth of the inferior orders. Had the nobility and gentry of Scotland enlargement of mind and extensive views, they would now, for the security of the constitution, engraft the clergy into the State, as they have always been in England, and by imparting all the privileges of freeholders, except that of being members of Parliament, on their livings, they would attach them still more than ever to their country ; they would widen the basis of the constitution, which is far too narrow, without lessening their own importance in the smallest degree, for there could be no combination of the clergy against their heritors ; on the contrary, they would be universally disposed to unite with their heritors, if they behaved well to them in all political business ; but I know very few people capable of thinking in this train, and far less of acting on so large and liberal a plan. In the mean time, on account of many unfortunate circumstances, one of which is, that patrons, now that by help of the Moderate interest, as it is called, there is no opposition to their presentations, have restored to them that right they so long claimed, and for most part give them the man they like best ; that is to say, the least capable, and commonly the least worthy, of all the probationers in their neighbour-hood.* The unfitness of one of the professors of divinity, and the influence he has in providing for young men of his own fanatical cast, increases this evil not a little, and accelerates the degradation of the clergy. His cousin, Sir James H. Blair, never re-pented so much of anything as the placing him in that chair, as he soon discovered the disadvantage to the Church that might [arise] from his being put in that situation. It is a pity that a man so irreproachable in his life and manner, and even distinguished for his candour and fairness, should be so weak ; but he does more harm than if he were an intriguing hypocrite.

During the summer 1769, after I had given the clergy such hopes of being relieved from the window-tax, they set about a subscription (the funds of the Church being quite inadequate at any time, and then very low) for defraying the expense of their commis-sioner, and of procuring an Act of Parliament.

* The sentence seems incomplete, but *sic* in MS.—J. H. B.

Nearly two-thirds of the clergy had subscribed to this fund, for a sum of about £400 was subscribed, if I remember right, by subscriptions from five shillings to one guinea, and put into the hands of Dr. George Wishart, then Principal Clerk of the Church.

Mrs. C. having recovered from her late inlying, I now prepared to go to London to follow out the object of my commission ; and lest I should be too late, I set out in such time as to arrive in London on the 21st of December. I had a Major Paul as my companion in the chaise, and though we took five days to it, the expense in those days was no more than £10, 8s. 7d. As my business lay entirely in the west end of the town, I took up my lodging in New Bond Street, and engaged the other apartment for John Home, who was to be there in a fortnight. But I immediately took Neil [   ], a trusty servant, who had been with him last year, and could serve us both now, as I required but very little personal service. The very day after I came to London, I had wrote a paper signed Nestor, in support of the Duke of Grafton, who was then in a tottering state. This paper, which appeared on the 23rd of December, drew the attention of Lord Elibank and other Scotch gentlemen who attended the British Coffeehouse, which convinced me that I might continue my political labours, as they were acceptable to Administration. At this time I did not know that the Duke of Grafton was so near going out, but soon after I discovered it by an accident.

On one of the mornings which I passed with Lord Mansfield, after he had signified his entire approbation of my measures to obtain an exemption for the clergy of Scotland, I took the liberty of saying to him in going downstairs, that his lordship's opinion was so clear in our favour, that I had nothing to wish but that he would be so good as to say so to the Duke of Grafton. His answer surprised me, and opened my eyes. It was, " I cannot speak with the Duke of Grafton ; I am not acquainted with his Grace ; I never conversed with him but once, which was when he came a short while ago from the King to offer me the seals. I can't talk with the Duke of Grafton ; so good morning, Doctor. Let me see you again when you are further advanced." I went instantly with this anecdote to my friend Mrs. Anderson, at the British, and we concluded almost instantly, without plodding, that the change of the ministry was nigh at hand. When I saw her next day, she told me she had seen her brother, Dr. Douglas, who was struck with my anecdote, and combining with it some things he had observed, concluded that the fall of the Duke of Grafton was at hand, which proved true.

This accordingly took place not long after, when Charles York, the second son of the Chancellor Hardwick, having been wheedled over to accept the seals, and being upbraided severely for having broken his engagements with his party, put himself to death that very night ; which was considered a public loss, as he was a man of parts and probity. Pratt was appointed Chancellor, and Lord North became minister. I was in the House of Commons the first night that he took his place as Premier. He had not intended to disclose it that night ; but a provoking speech of Colonel Barré's obliged him to own it, which he did with a great deal of wit and humour. Barré was a clever man and good speaker, but very hard-mouthed.* I was the first person at the British after the division ; and telling Mrs. Anderson the heads of North's speech, and the firmness and wit with which he took his place as First Minister, she concluded with me that he would maintain it long. Lord North was very agreeable, and, as a private gentleman, as worthy as he was witty ; but having unluckily got into the American war, brought the nation into an incredible sum of debt, and in the end lost the whole American colonies. He professed himself ignorant of war, but said he would appoint the most respectable generals and admirals, and furnish them with troops and money ; but he was weak enough to send the Howes, though of a party opposite to him, who seemed to act rather against the Ministers than the Americans. They were changed for other commanders ; but the feeble conduct of the Howes had given the Americans time to become warlike, and they finally prevailed.

* See the debate in the *Parl. Hist.*, xvi. 705 *et seq.*—The name of Colonel Isaac Barré, so conspicuous in its day, is so completely excluded from ordinary biographical works of reference, that it may be useful to refer to a curious notice of him by Walpole in his *Memoirs of George III.* (i. 109). Colonel Barré gives an account of his own services in a speech reported in *Parl. Hist.*, xxiii. 156. —J. H. B.

North maintained his ground for no less than twelve years through this disgraceful war, and then was obliged to give way that a peace might be established. This at first was thought necessary to Great Britain ; but Lord North's attempt to make a coalition with his former opponents having failed, and Charles Fox's scheme of governing the nation by an aristocracy, with the aid of his India Bill, being discovered and defeated, made way for Mr. Pitt's * first Administration in 1783, which soon restored national credit and promised the greatest prosperity to the British empire, had it not been interrupted by the French Revolution in 1789, and the subsequent most dangerous war of 1798. It was discovered early in this period that the revolt and final disjunction of our American colonies was no loss to Great Britain, either in respect of commerce or war. I have been led to this long digression by Lord North's having become Premier in the beginning of the year 1770.

Although the discharge of my commission required attention and activity, yet the Lords of the Treasury having frequently referred me for an answer to a distant day, I took the opportunity of making frequent excursions to places where I had not been.

One of the first of them was to Bath with John Home, to pay a visit to his betrothed, Mary Home, whom he married in the end of summer. He had sent her to Bath to improve her health, for she was very delicate. We set out together, and went by the common road, and arrived on the second day to dinner.

* William the Younger.

Miss Home had taken a small house at Bath, where she lived with a Miss Pye, a companion of hers, and a friend of Mrs. Blackett's. They lived very comfortably, and we dined with them that day. Bath is beautifully built, and situated in a vale surrounded with small hills cultivated to the top; and being built of fine polished stone, in warm weather is intolerably hot; but when we were there in the beginning of March it was excessively cold. The only thing about it not agreeable to the eye is the dirty ditch of a river which runs through it.

On the morning after we arrived, we met Lord Galloway in the pump-room, who having had a family quarrel, had retired to Bath with one of his daughters. The first question he asked me was, if I had yet seen our cousin, Sandie Goldie, his wife being a sister of Patrick Heron's. I answered no, but that I intended to call on him that very day. "Do," said his lordship, "but don't tell his story while you are here, for he is reckoned one of the cleverest fellows in this city, for being too unreasonable to sign receipts for above £1000, the produce of the reversion of his estate. He makes a very good livelihood at the rooms by betting on the whist-players, for he does not play." Lord Galloway engaged us to dine with him next day.* We went to the rooms at night, and to a ball, where I was astonished to find so many old acquaintances.

* Alexander Stewart, sixth Earl of Galloway. He died in 1773.

We had called on Goldie, who engaged us to dine with him. The day after we were to dine at Lord Galloway's. We met with Dr. Gusthard, M.D., who had the charge of Miss Home's health. He was the son of Mr. Gusthard, minister of Edinburgh, and being of good ability and a winning address, had come into very good business. Lord Galloway, though quite illiterate by means of the negligence of his trustees or tutors, was a clever man, of much natural ability, and master of the common topics of conversation. We dined next day at Alexander Goldie's, where we had the pleasure of his lordship's company. In our landlord we discovered nothing but an uncommon rapidity of speech and an entertaining flow of imagination, which perhaps we would not have observed if we had not known that he had been cognosced at Edinburgh, and deprived of the management of his estate.

Next day we made a party to Bristol hot wells, and added to our company a Miss Scott, of Newcastle, a very pleasing young woman, who afterwards married an eminent lawyer there ; and another lady, whose name I have forgot, who was a good deal older than the rest, but was very pleasant, and had £30,000, by which means she became the wife of one of the Hathorns. This place appeared to me dull and disagreeable, and the hot wells not much better. Next day we dined at Dr. Gusthard's, and the day after set out on our return to London. We resolved to go by Salisbury Plain and Stonehenge, as neither

36

of us had ever been there, both of which raised our
wonder and astonishment, especially Stonehenge, but
as we were not antiquarians, we could not form any
conjecture about it.   We got to London next day
before dinner.

SUPPLEMENTARY CHAPTER

By JOHN HILL BURTON

AT this point the Autobiography stops, the pen having literally dropped from the dying Author's hand. It would be vain and presumptuous to attempt to carry out his purpose—the intended remainder must be counted among the world's literary losses. But it may be considered proper that the Editor should briefly notify, for the reader's instruction, the subsequent events of Carlyle's life, uttering them, as far as possible, in his own words, by enlivening the narrative with such passages from his letters and other writings as make the nearest approach to the characteristics of his Autobiography. The project he had undertaken for the relief of his brethren from the window-tax was a tedious and tortuous affair, and cost him much travelling, talking, and writing before it was effected. If he had lived to tell the story of his labours, we would have had vivid sketches of many a little scene and character, so adorning as almost to conceal the train of unimportant and uninteresting transactions. But no one would be thanked in the present day for extracting the tenor of the narrative out of the official despatches, committee minutes, and other like documents in which it is imbedded.

It is not until the year 1782 that this matter is wound up, in a letter to Dundas, thanking him for the assistance, "without which," he says," I could not have so satisfactorily concluded my little affair in London;" and as this letter, after some news about the General Assembly and the new Moderator, breaks in upon some larger political transactions, a passage from it may not be unacceptable. It refers to a project for sending Dundas out as Governor-General of India.

" I don't know well whether to be glad or sorry, to hear it repeated again and again that you are going out supreme governor of the East Indies, with full powers. I am sorry you should disappear at this time from our hemisphere, as I have a chance of being set myself before your return. I am much more sorry that Britain should lose the advantage of your virtue and abilities at so critical a period. At the same time, I must own that this is but a partial view of the subject ; for when I consider how many millions of the human race look for a guardian angel to raise and perfect them, I see a shining path in the East that leads to a pinnacle of glory and virtue. Go, then, and pursue the way that Providence points out. Your health may be in danger, but, with a principality, who thinks of health ? besides, a sore throat or a collic is as dangerous in obscurity."

The window-tax discussion does not, however, afford many extracts so good as this ; and, indeed, the greater portion of Carlyle's existing correspondence lies under a like disqualification to be the companion of his animated Autobiography. The letters which the world would pick out from the correspondence of a man of rare gifts are those written to his familiar friends ; but he himself is apt to preserve as the more important the correspondence upon business affairs affecting public or private interests at the moment. Hence, among the stores placed at the

Editor's disposal, by far the larger portion refer to matters of local interest—literally parochial affairs, which called for dutiful and laborious attention in their day, but cannot be resuscitated with either profit or pleasure at the present time.   There are, for instance, the proceedings of a presbytery or a synod to be watched and managed : Some leading man in the Church court has got into bad hands, and must be rightly advised, otherwise harm will come of it : The right man must be thoroughly backed for this perferment—the wrong man will get that if So-and-so be not spoken to, and so forth.   Such affairs had their little world of living interest, now no more.

It is sufficient to say that Carlyle had a great voice in the selection of the men who were either to be brought into the Church by ordination to charges, or who were to be advanced as leaders from having proved themselves worthy in the ranks.   No one will expect an inquiry to be here pursued into the manner in which he exercised in each case the influence he possessed.   If the lighter motives had some effect the heavier would have a greater ; and it would be wrong to suppose that his patronage was exercised on no better ground than what is stated in the following little characteristic passage, though he no doubt thought the considerations stated in it should have their own weight :—

   " Lord Douglas is here and well.   A church of his in the Merse, called Preston, is vacant just now.   The incumbent was so very old that it is more than probable that he may be engaged, otherwise perhaps your Grace might take the opportunity of providing for Mr. Young, the handsome young man and fine preacher, who is a native of Dalkeith. My presentiment in his favour has been confirmed by inquiry. If Lord Douglas should be engaged, suppose you should try for Bothwell, which can't be long of being vacant ? I think it of great consequence to a noble family, especially if they have many children, to have a sensible and superior clergyman settled in their parish. Young is of that stamp, and might be greatly improved in taste, and elegance of mind and manners, by a free *entrée* to Lady Douglas. The late Lord Hopetoun, who was a man of superior sense, was very unfortunate in his first lady's time. By some accident the high-flying clergy were chiefly admitted about them. Weak heads and warm imaginations lie open to the zeal of fanaticism or the arts of hypocrites. He found his error when it was too late, and was sorry he had not encouraged the Wisharts and Blairs to come about him."

Carlyle's influence in ecclesiastical promotion appears not to have been entirely limited to Scotland. Occasionally his distinguished friends would find a place for a student who could not get on with the Presbyterian system, in the more manageable Church of England and Ireland ; as, for instance :—

" There is an old assistant of mine, J—— W—— by name, who, having grown impatient at not obtaining a church here, took orders in the Church of England—sold a little patrimony he had, and bought a chaplaincy to a regiment. Since that time he has been always unhappy. He was for some years in Minorca, where he lost his health. He followed the regiment to Ireland, where he lost his sight. He came to Bath and recovered his health and sight, but lost his substance. He applied to me for God's sake to get him a curacy anywhere, that he might be able to pay for a deputy-chaplain. I recommended him to a friend of mine in London, who procured the curacy of Hertford for him. Soon after he wrote me from thence that he was so much despised in that town that he was in danger of hanging himself."

He was to have got this hopeful personage on the Chancellor's list, but there were technical obstacles ; and now if the correspondent would obtain for " my poor despised friend a small living of £100 a-year or so," it would be " to serve a worthy creature, humble as he is."

There are more pleasing associations connected with a scrap of writing—undated, but of course belonging to a late period of life. Every one will recognise him who is its object, though he is more aptly remembered as the venerable pastor and philosopher than as the young Oxonian.

" Dr. Carlyle begs leave to recommend Mr. Alison * to Mr. Dundas's best offices, as a young divine bred in the Church of England, of uncommon merit and accomplishments. After the usual academical education at Edinburgh, Mr. Alison studied two years at Glasgow, and from thence was sent as an exhibitioner to Baliol College in Oxford, where he resided for nine or ten years, and where he received ordination."

In another letter we find him thanking Dundas for taking " Archy " by the hand, and explaining that it will thus, in this instance, be unnecessary to draw upon the patronage of Sir William Pulteney, with whom also Carlyle had corresponded about his young friend.†

In the same letter in which he thus holds out a

* Rev. Archibald Alison returned to Edinburgh in 1800 to become senior clergyman of the Episcopal Chapel in the Cowgate —at that time the most fashionable church in the City. He removed to St. Paul's, York Place, when the congregation built that church, where he ministered till 1831. An interesting sketch of Mr. Alison is given in Lord Cockburn's *Memorials*.

† It has been said, however, on good authority, that it was to Pulteney that Alison owed his promotion in England. See *Memoir of Alison* in the fragment of a Biographical Dictionary by the Society for the Diffusion of Useful Knowledge. In a letter by Pulteney, dated 22nd June 1784, there is this pleasant account of Alison's marriage to the daughter of Dr. John Gregory :—" Andrew Stewart and I accompanied Mr. Alison to Thrapston, and the marriage took place on the 19th by a licence

hand to a young aspirant, he pleads at greater length
and with deeper earnestness the cause of his old friend
Adam Ferguson, whom he expected to die before he
had been paid the debt of fame and fortune which
the world owed to him, or even realised the means of
securing his family from destitution.   It so happened
that Ferguson, though attacked with hopeless-look-
ing symptoms in middle life, wore on to a good old
age ; and that, through various chances, he became
wealthy in his declining years.   That the world had
done gross injustice to *The History of the Roman
Republic*, was a fixed opinion with Carlyle ; and, in
pleading for its author's family, he says :—

" I do not know by what fatality it is that the best and most
manly history (with some imperfections, no doubt) of modern
times, has been so little sought after.   The time will come when
it will be read and admired.   That time, I hope, is not at a great
distance.   Germany is the country where it will receive its
name ; and when the report returns from the learned there, the
book will begin to be prized.   But Ferguson may be dead by that
time, and an Irish edition may glut the market.   I was always
in hopes that some of you would have quoted it in the House
of Commons, as Charles Fox did Principal Watson's *Philip*, for
some of his purposes in the time of the American War.   I am
sure Ferguson's contains ten times more instruction for the
statesman and legislator than the other does ; but I have been
disappointed."

from the Archbishop of Canterbury.   I conducted them afterwards to their residence, and we left them next morning after
breakfast as happy as it is possible for people to be.   Mr. Alison
was obliged to come round by London in order to take an oath
at granting the licence, and I was glad of the opportunity which
the journey afforded me of making an acquaintance with him ;
for though I had little doubt that Miss G. had made a proper
choice, yet I wished to be perfectly satisfied ; and the result is
that I think neither you nor Mr. Nairne have said a word too
much in his favour."

By far the greater portion of Carlyle's letters which have been preserved relate, as has been said, to matters of business—such as those dealt with in the preceding quotations, or even affairs of still less interest. Some bundles of epistles, addressed to him, show that he had a wide correspondence of a lighter cast ; and he is reported to have been famous as a fashionable letterwriter—a highly-prized accomplishment in his day. Much of this correspondence was with the female aristocracy, including members of the two great Scottish ducal families, Argyle and Buccleuch. He was, indeed, as he said his parishioners hinted against him when he became their clergyman, partial to the company of his superiors. But if he liked the aristocracy, the aristocracy liked him ; the two met half-way, and he was a man who could hold his own with them. Thus he occupied the happy though often rather precarious position, of one who is alike removed, on the one hand, from the tuft-hunter, possessing nothing but sycophancy to give for the countenance he seeks ; and on the other hand, from the surly cynic, who cannot trust that his independence will hold good beyond the circuit of his tub. No doubt, whatever society one keeps, one must give a deference to its laws and customs—which is a different thing from paying undue deference to its individual members. There was, in that day, among the enlightened women of rank who cultivated men of genius, a propensity to get the most out of them, by drawing upon their talents, in conversation and correspondences of a peculiarly allegorical, or, as he terms it, "Parnassian" character, a little like the euphuism of the seventeenth century, though not so absolutely hard and unnatural. Moderate as it was, however, it is difficult to suppose a person of Carlyle's acute and sarcastic character well adapted to it ; and we can suppose him as little at home in it, as his friend David Hume, when he had to perform the Sultan between two rival beauties in Madame de Tessé's salon. Such efforts of this kind as he unbent himself to, appear, however, to have been very acceptable. Here, for instance, follows a letter to his amiable friend, Lady Frances Scott. In pursuance of some jocular fiction, of which the point is not now very obvious, he had been addressing her as the ghost of Mrs. M'Cormick—an elderly female, whose death has been brought about by the neglect and cruelty of the lady—characteristics, of course, entirely the reverse of her true qualities. She writes back " from the Elysian fields," where " we have never ceased gliding about the heavens with the happy spirits our companions ; for you must know that the chief source of happiness here arises from the power which our wings give us of never being two minutes in a place." There is a certain materiality, however, in the elysium, for the angels or goddesses are looking after affluent gods with broken constitutions ; while impoverished deities of the male sex worship where there is neither youth nor beauty, but plenty of wealth, to attract. Olympian Jove is but a master of the ceremonies, and " Juno is neither endowed with celestial loveliness nor awe-inspiring dignity." This is the way of stating that the family are at the Bath waters, then in their pride, with the successor of Beau Nash playing the part of Olympian Jove. Carlyle's answer, instead of aiding and developing the allegory, is apt rather to scatter its filmy texture by outbreaks of practical sagacity and homely wit.

" At my return from the south, ten days ago, I found your ladyship's, dated from Elysium, which transported me so, that I had to receive sundry twinges in the region of the heart, by the daily decline of a child and the grief of her mother, who is the greatest martyr to sensibility that ever was born, and at last to get a great knock on the pate by the sudden death of Dr. Gregory, who was our chief stay and support, before I could recollect that I was still in the body. Were I to wait till I could answer yours from the abodes of the happy in the manner it deserves, millions of more ghosts might have time to pass the Stygian ferry. But why should I be mortified, that as much as heaven is above hell, your ladyship's description should surpass mine ? Though I dare say by this time you imagine that I am to behave to you as an old humourist, a friend of mine, did long ago to me. We were in use of corresponding together, and many a diverting letter I had from him. At last he took a panic about his son, who was at school here, and wrote me a long letter, complaining of what he was well informed—viz., that the schoolboys had got gunpowder, and were in daily use of firing pistols and carabines, and that they made squibs and crackers, to the infinite danger of their own lives ; and then he quoted me an hundred fatal accidents that had happened by means of gunpowder, and prayed my interposition to save the life of his son. As I knew it was impossible to prevent the evil of which he complained, as three regiments of foot, with a train of artillery, were encamped in the Links, I first read one of the most extravagant chapters in all *Rabelais*, and then wrote him a letter assuring him that he had not heard the hundred part of the truth ; for that the boys were arrived at the most dangerous and incorrigible use of powder, and then gave him instances—such as that they came to church every Sunday with swivel-guns screwed on their left arms, with which they popped down everybody whom they disliked, etc. The effect of this letter was that the old gentleman found himself so far outdone, that it entirely broke up our correspondence. And when I employed somebody to ask him the reason of his silence, he said that the young folks nowadays (this was fifteen years ago) went such lengths in fiction, that it was impossible to answer them.

"But your ladyship shall see that I am not in the least mortified by your letter, but that, on the contrary, I am highly delighted with it, and value it more than I would do a new volume of the *Arabian Nights Entertainments*. Before I left the shades below, I had a peep into Elysium myself; and though I did not find things exactly in the same state your ladyship did, as I happened not to be in the same region of heaven, that can be no objection; for surely there can be no Elysium without variety; but that may possibly be the subject of another letter. In the mean time, I may give your ladyship some intelligence of what is going on here.

"By the by, though I have no great taste now for that part of bliss, which your ladyship says consists in everlasting fleeting about by means of the wings that make a part of the celestial body, yet I remember the time when I should have thought such a power very material to happiness. Bless me! how I envied the happy in some island in the Pacific Ocean—not Atlantic—whom Peter Wilkins represented as having most powerful and trusty pinions. But in those days I used to be in love, and thought that wings would make me everywhere present with my mistress.

"I am very glad to hear that Jupiter is henpecked, since he suffers the name of angel to be prostituted for gold in his dominions. I suppose he draws a good round sum by way of tax for liberty to go by that name. We have known titles of honour sold upon earth, you know, and why not the privilege of being angels? When they have once given their hands, they'll not long boast of their angelic appellation.

"No; really we are very much imposed upon. Happiness does not consist in the place—it resides in the disposition of the person, and the company. The material difference in your abode and mine consisted in the long stories that were such a torment to me, and that you were free of.

"But to return to sublunary things. First, as to public diversions: I have neither had time nor inclination to mix with the conversable world in the capital, near which I reside; so that I can entertain your ladyship with a very few pieces of news of any kind. You would hear, no doubt, of the mock masquerade they had some time in January. That piece of mummery was carried on so ill, that I daresay they won't attempt another in haste. The two Turks met with rather hard usage, considering the natural as well as assumed gravity of their characters. The one was excluded his own house all night by the custom-house porter, being mistaken for a vagrant Turk who had been begging on the streets all winter; and the other got a sad curtain-lecture from his wife for having embraced a religion, even but in disguise, that allows no souls to women, and allows of four wives and innumerable concubines.

"The playhouse has been much frequented since Mrs. Yates arrived, who receives infinite applause. For though she often appears on the stage more than half-seas-over, she's not the less agreeable to all the male part of her audience, who come there a little disguised themselves; and in this land of obsequious wives, you know, there is no disputing the taste of the men.

"With respect to the fine arts, I have reason to believe that cookery is still the favourite; and as we were a little behind in that article, it is very right that it should continue to be progressive for some time. The men of genius and taste who frequent that temple of pleasure that goes by the name of Fortune's, have subscribed very handsomely to enable the chief priest there to hire a French cook of the first accomplishments. There are hundreds of people, indeed, on the point of starving, but the eminent critics have observed that there is the greatest race of genius, and that the fine arts thrive best, in the time of public calamities—such as civil war, pestilence, or famine.

"General Scott, who is here this winter looking out for another wife to make him uneasy, gives the most superb, elegant, and refined entertainments that ever were in this northern region. Poor Mr. Stuart Moncrief, who had no other department in the Temple of Fame but that which is allotted to the makers of great feasts, after witnessing one of the General's most magnificent repasts—for you're certain he could not be a partaker—went home and wept for two hours over his vanquished reputation, sickened, and went to bed, and died, for anything I know, next day. Dead, he certainly is, to glory! M'Queen the lawyer, who felt a very different passion from envy, after having devoured of twenty-seven several dishes, attacked at last ancient pye with so much vivacity, that he had nigh perished in the cause—at least he was able to attend no other cause for a fortnight.

"We are to propose to next General Assembly that a certain

deadly sin, for which both men and women used to do penance and be severely rebuked in the Church, shall be blotted out of our Statute-Book, and the sin of Gluttony put in its place.

" As to the state of learning this winter, I am told there are many poorer students than usual. But they say they are better boys, and mind the ladies less than they used to do. The English of that is, I fancy, that as there are but few men of fortune among them, the aunts and the mothers don't mind them. The misses, dear angels, I hope, are above valuing any man but for his personal merit. Lord Monboddo, one of the most learned judges, is just about publishing a book, in which he demonstrates that mankind walked originally on all-fours, like other animals, and had tails like most of them ; that it was most likely 5000 years before they learned to walk in an erect posture, and 5000 more before they could learn the use of speech. The females, he thinks, might speak two or three centuries sooner."

Here is a specimen of what may be considered the same order of composition, although it is varied to suit the taste of a male correspondent. It is taken from the

" Scroll of a Letter to Sir JOHN MACPHERSON, Bart. 1797.

" Although one's correspondence with one's friend should be never so much interrupted by business or idleness, there are certain occasions when they must not be neglected, such as marriages and births, and even death itself. As the last has lately befallen me, though I am happily restored to life, I think it is proper to announce to you, my very good friend, my return to this world, and to give you some account of the slight peep I had into the other. About a month ago I was suddenly seized, after a hearty dinner, with a dreadful collic, which lasted for fifty hours, which threatened immediate dissolution, and actually sent me out of the body for a few minutes. During that short period (like Mahomet in his dream) I had a view of Elysium, hanging, as I thought, on the brink of a cloud, and every moment ready to descend. But, as I saw clearly before me, the first group I perceived was David Hume, and Adam Smith, and James Macpherson, lounging on a little hillock, with Col. James Edmonstone standing before them, brandishing a cudgel, and William Robertson at David's feet in a listening posture. Edmonstone was rallying David and Smith, not without a mixture of anger, for having contributed their share to the present state of the world ; the one, by doing everything in his power to undermine Christianity, and the other by introducing that unrestrained and universal commerce, which propagates opinions as well as commodities. The two philosophers, conscious of their follies, were shrunk into a nutshell, when James the bard, in the act of raising himself to insult them, perceiving my grey hairs hanging over them in the cloud, exclaimed, ' Damn your nonensical palaver ; there is Carlyle just coming down, and John Home and Ferguson cannot be far behind, when I shall have irresistible evidence for the authenticity of Ossian. Blair, I daresay, is likewise on the road, and I hope he'll bring his dissertation on my works along with him, which is worth a thousand of his mawkish sermons, which are only calculated to catch milk-sops and silly women.' Upon this Robertson rose to his feet, and seemed to be in act to speak one of his decisive sentences in favour of the winning side, when Joseph Black, and Charley Congalton, and Sandy Wood, who had hold of the skirts of my coat, fearing I should leap down at the sight of so many of my friends, and carry them after me, made a sudden and strong pull altogether, and jerked me back into life again, not without regret at being disappointed in meeting with so choice a company."

The social habits of Carlyle were, doubtless, like other men's, much influenced by his domestic position. It was his lot to taste of more than the average amount of human sorrow, for he lost all his children at an early period, and while there were yet above thirty years of his own earthly pilgrimage to be performed. The last, his son William, born in 1773, died in 1777. Had it been otherwise, perhaps his memoranda might not have left traces of so continued a succession of visits and receptions of guests. While they show him to have been much in the world, however, they bear no trace of his being addicted in later life to the social convivialities where males only can be present ; for his faithful partner,

Mary, is his almost constant companion, whether his visits be to a ducal mansion in London, or to the quiet manse of some old companion. How it continued to fare with him and with his chosen friends may best be told in one or two extracts from the letters in which he communicates the passing news to his correspondents. One of his early companions—a John Macpherson—had been signally fortunate in life. Getting into the service of the East India Company, he rose by stages, though not without unpropitious casualties, until he became Sir John Macpherson, and the successor of Warren Hastings as Governor of British India. To him Carlyle thus reports, in 1796, about some of their common friends:—

" Now for an account of your old friends, which, if you saw Ferguson as he passed, which I think you did, I might spare.

" To begin with Robertson, whom you shall see no more. In one word, he appeared more respectable when he was dying than ever he did even when living. He was calm and collected, and even placid, and even gay. My poor wife had a desire to see him, and went on purpose, but when she saw him, from a window, leaning on his daughter, with his tottering frame, and directing the gardener how to dress some flower-beds, her sensibility threw her into a paroxysm of grief ; she fled upstairs to Mrs. Russell and could not see him. His house, for three weeks before he died, was really an anticipation of heaven.

" Dr. Blair is as well as possible. Preaching every Sunday with increasing applause, and frisking more with the whole world than ever he did in his youngest days, no symptom of frailty about him ; and though he was huffed at not having an offer of the Principality, he is happy in being resorted to as the head of the university.

" John Home is in very good health and spirits, and has had the comfort, for two or three winters, of having Major Home, his brother-in-law, a very sensible man, in the house with him, which makes him less dependent on stranger company, which, in advanced years, is not so easy to be found, nor endured when it is found.

" With respect to myself, I have had many warnings within these three years, but, on the whole, as I have only fits of illness, and no disease, I am sliding softly on to old age, without any remarkable infirmity or failure, and can, upon occasions, preach like a son of thunder (I wish I were the Bold Thunderer for a week or two against the vile levelling Jacobins, whom I abhor). My wife, your old friend, has been better than usual this winter, and is strong in metaphysics and ethics, and (can) almost repeat all Ferguson's last book of Lectures, which do him infinite honour. I say of that book, that if Reid is the Aristotle, Ferguson is the Plato of Scotch philosophers ; and the Faculty of Arts of Edinburgh have adopted my phrase."

The following, from a letter to Principal Hill, dated 25th September 1801, gives an account of a visit to Lord Melville when he had retired with Pitt on the formation of the Addington Administration:—

" We had Jesse Bell and her husband, Mr. Gregg, and their son from London, for ten days, in the middle of August, which gratified and amused us : and about the end of it John Home and I had a fine jaunt to Duneira. We set out on the 25th of August, and returned on the 1st of September, and were much pleased with our reception everywhere, as well as with the country, which was then in the highest beauty, and where we had never been before.

" Our great object, no doubt, was the retired statesman, whom it delighted us to see so well and so happy, and as easy and *dégagé* as he was in his boyish days.

" I was afraid that, like most of ex-ministers, his gaiety might be put on to save appearances. However, as his was not a fall, but a voluntary and long-projected retreat, and as he is conscious that his great exertions have not only saved his own country, but put it in the power of Europe to save themselves, while the applauses of his country, universal and unreserved, at once resound his uncorrupted integrity, as well as his unbounded capacity,—I believe him genuine and sincere.

" I compared his place to an eagle's nest, which pleased him. But I did not add, that he was like the thunder-hearing bird of Jove, whom his master had allowed to retire awhile, after his war with the giants, to recreate himself from the toils of war, and

37

sport with his own brood ; but who, in the midst of carelessness and ease, still throws his eyes around him, from his airy height, to descry if the regions of the air are again disturbed, and to watch the first nod of the Imperial King, to take wing and resume his place in the Chariot of War.

" We passed three days and three nights with him, one at Ochtertyre and another at Monzie, and fain would I have gone down the country, as I had never been farther up before than at Lord Kinnoul's. But my partner, in spite of all his heroic tragedies, was too much afraid of the water to take any other road than Stirling Bridge. The country was truly rich and yellow with grain, and the harvest far advanced for the 1st of September.

" Plenty, thank God, has returned, but I am afraid peace is still at a distance.

" Buonaparte is entirely governed by personal considerations, and he has still the chance of an invasion in Ireland to establish his throne awhile. I can hardly think he will venture to invade Britain. Yet, if Admiral de Winter should fight an obstinate battle off our coast, and, in the mean time, a few transports should land with 2000 men anywhere between this and Newcastle, it might prove very troublesome, while their main effort was made on Ireland. In the interval left us, we are in high preparation here, and our camp, with the force in Edinburgh, are put in condition to act together with effect on the shortest warning.

" There was a fine show on Tuesday, as you would see in the papers, and there is to be a repetition of it on Braid Hills next week.

" Major Elliot, of the Lanarkshire, said to me that their Tuesday's work was worth all they had been taught before, and he is a soldier of name."

The reader will have noticed the keen zest with which Carlyle always watched the politics of the time, whether home or foreign. It is infinitely to be regretted, therefore, that he did not bring down his Autobiography through the French Revolution and the Great War. He would have spoken, no doubt, entirely on one side, but with that breadth and fixity of opinion which partakes more of devotion than of mere partiality or prejudice, and is both respectable

and interesting in the eyes of those who think otherwise. His politics, indeed, were a political faith that
never swerved. While many of his friends were
frightened into their Conservative opinions by the
terrors of the French Revolution, he took and kept
his position calmly in the very front of his party, like
a soldier at his post. The resoluteness of the resistance offered by such men, not only to innovation, but
to the mere raising of the faintest question of the
necessity of matters being as they are, is a thing
which it is difficult for men of any party to realise
in the year 1860.

By the Test Act, the members of the Church of
Scotland were in England placed legally in the same
position as other dissenters from the Church. Loving
and admiring his own Church as he did, it might have
been anticipated that he would rather further than
repress a remonstrance by the General Assembly of
1791, in which they represented that the members of
the Church of Scotland were unequally dealt with,
since they could not hold any office in England without taking the communion according to the Church
of England ; while, on the other hand, no similar
compliance was required of Episcopalians holding
office in Scotland. But he was not to be caught by
this bait, nor was he to remain silent while it was held
out to the weak and inexperienced. He came forth
not merely in favour of the Test, but in strong
championship of it. It was to be supported upon
grounds of toleration towards the Established Church

of England, which well merited such protection. " In this enlightened and liberal age, when toleration has softened the minds of men on religious opinions, it would disgrace the General Assembly to do anything that might seem to separate the two Established Churches farther from each other. Their doctrines are nearly the same ; and he must be but a very narrow-minded Presbyterian who, in the various circumstances in which he might be placed, could not join in the religious worship of the Church." This doctrine must have been a little startling to those brethren who inherited even but a small portion of the doctrine prevalent in his youth—that the bare toleration of Episcopacy in any shape, and in any portion of the empire, was one of the great national sins for which Divine vengeance might be anticipated. Nor is it easy to realise the feelings with which the representatives of the Covenanters would receive this climax of a speech delivered in 1791 :—

"Nay, Moderator, had I the talents of, etc., I think I could show that the Test Act, instead of an evil, is a blessing. The Test Act has confirmed the Union. The Test Act has cured Englishmen of their jealousy of Scotsmen, not very ill-founded. The Test Act has quieted the fears of the Church of England. The Test Act has enlarged and confirmed the principles of toleration ; so far is it from being a remnant of bigotry and fanaticism as the memorial would represent. The Act, sir, has paved the road to office and preferment. The Test Act, sir, for there is no end of its praises, is the key that opens all the treasures of the south to every honest Scotchman."

But, in small matters, the keenness of his antipathy to any innovation or interference with established authorities might perhaps be even more distinctly exemplified. For instance, in 1795, a Lady Maxwell represented to him that certain Highland soldiers at Musselburgh were in religious destitution from want of a clergyman speaking Gaelic. She calls them " well-disposed officers, sergeants, and privates," though it is difficult to suppose that there could then be commissioned officers unacquainted with the general language of the empire. She offers the services of an enthusiastic youthful missionary for the occasion, and this suggested interference with the established order of things in his Majesty's army and the parish of Inveresk calls from its minister the following severe rebuke :—

" Dr. Carlyle presents respectful compliments to Lady Maxwell. He received her ladyship's card, in answer to which he has to observe, that she proceeds on misinformation. The officers who command the several regiments encamped are too conscientious, and understand their duty too well, to let their soldiers be without the ordinances of religion in a tongue they understand. Two chaplains, men of respect and of standing in the Church, have performed public worship in the Gaelic language every Lord's day in camp since ever it was established.

" With respect to her ladyship's design, of the purity of which Dr. Carlyle has not the smallest doubt, it belongs to the commanding officers to approve of it or not, and not to him ; but perhaps, on being better informed, Lady Maxwell may not think it necessary to employ her student in theology, however well qualified she may hold him to be, to interfere officiously with the duty of the two clergymen of mature age and acknowledged ability. The young man, at least, seemed not to abound in prudence, when he pressed so earnestly as he did to be allowed to visit the condemned prisoners, whom two clergymen had been anxiously and diligently preparing for their fate for the whole preceding week.

" Those times of sedition and mutiny seem to require that every person in office should be left to do his own duty, and that strangers should be cautious of intermeddling with the religious tenets or principles of any set of people, especially those of the army.

"*Mussb., July* 17, 1795.

"To Lady Maxwell, Dowager of Pollock,
"at Rosemount, near Edinburgh."

If there be something a little incongruous to the small occasion in the tone of this rebuke, it will perhaps be admitted that there is something sublime in the following brief testimony to his principles, delivered to the General Assembly in 1804—two years after he had passed his eightieth year, and one before his death :—

"Note of what I said (Assembly 1804), when an address to his Majesty was read, in which was an expression, *the awful state*, or the *awful situation of this country* :—

"MODERATOR,—I was so unlucky as not to be able to attend the committee who drew up this address, and consequently have heard it now for the first time. In general I am well pleased with the address. But there is one phrase in it, which has just now been read, that I do not like. I do not like to have it known to our enemies, by a public act of this Assembly, that we think our country in an awful state, which implies more terror and dismay than I am willing to own. When the Almighty wields the elements, which are His instruments of vengeance on guilty nations—when heaven's thunders roll and envelop the world in fire—when the furious tempest rages, and whelms triumphant navies in the deep—when the burning mountain disgorges its fiery entrails and lays populous cities in ashes ;—then, indeed, I am overawed : I acknowledge the right arm of the Almighty : I am awed into reverence and fear : I am still, and feel that He is God : I am dumb, and open not my mouth. But when a puny mortal, of no better materials than myself, struts and frets, and fumes and menaces, then am I roused, but not overawed ; I put myself in array against the vain boaster, and am ready to say with the high-priest of the poet, *I fear God, and have no other fear.*"

The year 1789 became disagreeably memorable to Carlyle, from his having then been defeated in an object of ambition, which was near his heart, and, as he thought, fairly within his reach. This was the appointment to the office of Clerk to the General Assembly, become vacant by the death of Dr. Drysdale in whose appointment he had been largely instrumental. The salary, £80 a-year, was an object to a clergyman of the Church of Scotland, but the position and influence towards which the office might be rendered available were of far higher moment. To understand this, it is only necessary to keep in view, that the constitution of that Church admits of no heirarchy or gradation of offices. Every body of men, acting in a collective or corporate capacity, must, however, have some person presiding over them to regulate their proceedings, and represent them in their communications with the rest of the world. For the preservation of the Presbyterian polity from the encroachments of any such officer, however, the " Moderator," who presides over the proceedings of each Church Court, is elected periodically, or for the occasion. Permanent appointments are given to subordinate officers only, and each Church Court, from the General Assembly downwards, has thus its clerk, who is the servant of the collective body. It will naturally happen, however, under such arrangements, however skilfully devised, that where one kind of man really is what he professes to be, a servant, another kind of man becomes a master. Hence, it is often, on the occasion of such appointments, a question of more consequence, Who can be kept out ? than, Who can be put in ?

Carlyle not unnaturally concluded that he had done services to the Church at large, and to many of its ministers, which entitled him to expect this small recompense at their hands.

On the other hand, for reasons which the tenor of his Autobiography reveals with sufficient distinctness, there was a large party among the clergy determined to do all that their strength enabled them to do to defeat him. The public eminence and extensive social influence on which his claims rested were, in their eyes, the strongest motives for resistance. He represented what to them were hostile interests. These interests were as yet outside ; by endowing him with an office of place and trust among them, they would be bringing the enemy within the gates. The taking of the vote was a great field-day for which the forces had been long mustered and disciplined on both sides—the friends of Government, with Dundas at their head, taking the part of Carlyle ; while the cause of his competitor, Dr. Dalzel, was led by Harry Erskine, the great jester. It was, however, a question, not merely of ecclesiastical politics, but of soundness in opinion and teaching, and on this matter his enemies occupied the strong position of professing to be sounder in faith and stricter in conduct than his friend. When such an element as this affects a contest, it is sure to disturb the original numerical strength of the parties, by a sort of intimidation. The side professing greater sanctity frightens its more timid opponents into a compromise. They are afraid of bringing on themselves the suspicion of heterodoxy ;—they are often conscious of something about themselves that would not easily endure a hostile scrutiny, and so they purchase peace by compliance with their natural opponents, or by keeping out of the way : so Carlyle found it.

The vote stood at first 145 for Carlyle, and 142 against him, so that he was elected by a majority of three. He took his place as clerk, and delivered an address, in which he stated that it had ever been his object in ecclesiastical courts to correct and abate the fanatical spirit of his country,—an allusion by no means likely to mitigate the wrath of his opponents. But the matter was by no means decided. It had been arranged that there should be a scrutiny of the foundation of each voter's right of membership, and that the decision of the Assembly should be as the relative numbers stood after the bad votes were struck out. It was as if a division of the House of Commons at the beginning of a session, should stand subject to the deduction of the votes of all the members who may be afterwards found by an election committee to be unduly elected. It would be useless to describe the technicalities of such a process ; but it is pretty clear that, like the contemporary controverted elections in the House of Commons, there was no rigid law to govern it, and much of it was decided rather through casual victories than the application of fixed general principles. The contest was long and keen, and apparently not quite decorous, as we may infer from the following short account of it, in a very moderately-toned work—Dr. Cook's *Life of Principal Hill* :—

" In canvassing the claims on the Commissions to which objections were made, there was displayed ingenuity that would have done credit to a more important cause ; but with this there was mingled a degree of violence, unworthy of the venerable court in which it was exhibited. The debates were protracted to a most unusual length, and upon one occasion, after all regard to order had been cast aside, the Moderator, with unshaken firmness, exercised the power which he conceived to be vested in him. He turned to the Commissioner, and having received his consent that the Assembly should meet at a certain hour next day, he adjourned the house. Amidst the loudness of clamour, this step, which none but a man of courage and nerve would have taken, was applauded ; and it probably was useful in putting some restraint on the angry passions which had before been so indecently urged. Previous to the scrutiny, the Moderator, having been asked to declare for whom, in the event of an equality, he would vote, *he replied that he now voted for Dr. Carlyle* ; thus unequivocally showing whom he was eager to support, although he might have avoided thus explicitly giving his voice against Mr. Dalzel,* for whom he had a high esteem, and with whom, as Professor of Greek, he had maintained such kindly intercourse."

Carlyle found his opponent gaining so surely, that he abandoned the contest. The result irritated him at first, and his anger was naturally directed less against his avowed enemies than those who, though ranked of his own party, had, for the reasons already explained, voted against him or stayed away. But while the voice of his friends was still for war, to be carried on in a new Assembly or in the Court of Session, he wrote to the all-influential Dundas, recom-

* See Cockburn's *Memorials* for a pen portrait of Professor Dalzel and of the leading churchmen of this period.

mending peace. "Although the court," he says, "should sustain themselves judges—and I suppose they would—yet the suit might prove so very tedious as to render it totally unworthy of all the trouble, were we even certain of being victorious in the end. Some people think that next Assembly may, on the ground of the protest, take up the business and re- verse what has been done by the last ; but, God knows, this is not worth while ; for it would oblige me to exert every species of power or interest we have to bring up an Assembly stronger on our side than the last, which it would be very difficult to do, as our opponents would exert themselves to the utmost." In a letter to Dr. Blair, as the representative of the more zealous of the party, Dundas, while explaining with his usual practical sagacity the impolicy of con- tinuing the contest, says—" If Mr. C. were a young man, and the office £500 a-year instead of £80, I would undertake the cause, and would certainly carry it ; but for such a paltry object it is scarce worth while to renew such a disagreeable contest."

Two years later, Carlyle engaged in a contest, in which the clergy as a body were on his side, against the landed gentry of Scotland. It was inaugurated, indeed, in 1788, by Sir Harry Moncrieff Wellwood, the most distinguished member of the opposite party in the Church, in a pamphlet called *Sketch of a Plan for Augmenting the Livings of the Ministers of the Established Church of Scotland*. Since the first deliberate disposal, after the Reformation, of the ecclesiastical property of Scotland, there existed a certain amount of revenue or rent charge, which was stamped with the legal character of being available to the Church, while it remained in the hands of the landowners, who were enabled to make their possession fully nine-tenths of the law. Much of the ecclesiastical history of Scotland, in fact, clusters round the efforts made on one side to keep, and on the other to take, this fund. From the beginning, the zealous protesting barons who had got possession of the property of the old Church, when desired to give it up for the purposes of the new, said that such an idea was a fond imagination; and in the same spirit, modified to the condition of the times, their successors had treated all efforts to enlarge the incomes of the clergy out of the " unexhausted teinds," as the chief substance of the fund was technically termed.

In the General Assembly, Carlyle adopted the tone that the Church was entitled to what it demanded; and that by the help it had given—first, in establishing the Hanover succession, and next, in supporting law and order—it had well earned the frank assistance of the Government and the aristocracy in securing its rights. The following passage is taken from one of his speeches on this matter:—

" I must confess that I do not love to hear this Church called a poor Church, or the poorest Church in Christendom. I doubt very much that, if it were minutely inquired into, this is really the fact. But, independent of that, I dislike the language of whining and complaint. We are rich in the best goods a Church can have —the learning, the manners, and the character of its members. There are few branches of literature in which the ministers of this

Church have not excelled. There are few subjects of fine writing in which they do not stand foremost in the rank of authors, which is a prouder boast than all the pomp of the Hierarchy.

" We have men who have successfully enlightened the world in almost every branch, not to mention treatises in defence of Christianity, or eloquent illustrations of every branch of Christian doctrine and morals. Who have wrote the best histories, ancient and modern ?—It has been clergymen of this Church. Who has wrote the clearest delineation of the human understanding and all its powers ?—A clergyman of this Church. Who has written the best system of rhetoric, and exemplified it by his own orations ?—A clergyman of this Church. Who wrote a tragedy that has been deemed perfect ?—A clergyman of this Church. Who was the most profound mathematician of the age he lived in ?—A clergyman of this Church. Who is his successor, in reputation as in office ? Who wrote the best treatise on agriculture ? Let us not complain of poverty, for it is a splendid poverty indeed ! It is *paupertas fecunda virorum.*"

The Government brought in a bill for " the Augmentation of Stipends," but they found the country gentlemen of Scotland too strong for them, and it was abandoned. In the General Assembly Carlyle took the opportunity of dropping some sharp remarks on the ingratitude thus shown to the Church, and did not spare his friend Dundas. A jocular country clergyman remarked that nothing better could come of sycophancy to the aristocracy ; and told a story how a poor neighbour of his own, after a course of servility, had got nothing but castigation in the end, and found no better remonstrance to make than that which had been addressed to Balaam—" Am not I thine ass, upon which thou hast ridden ever since I was thine to this day ? " The allusion took, and was improved by Kay the caricaturist. The Government promised still to do justice to the clergy, but they had

to wait for it until the year 1810, when the Act was
passed for bringing all stipends up to a minimum of
£150 a-year.

On the establishment of the Royal Society of Edinburgh in 1783, Carlyle made, through its Transactions,
a very acceptable gift to literature.   Johnson, in his
Life of Collins, referred to the loss of an ode on the
Superstitions of the Highlands, which Dr. Warton
and his brother had seen, and " thought superior to
his other works, but which no search has yet found."
A poem so wild and sweet—so far beyond the bounds
of the conventionalities of the day, and so full of
imagery drawn direct from nature in her highest and
most wayward flights—was not likely to be quite forgotten by any one who had seen it.   Carlyle remembered having read it in 1749 with Home, to whom it
was addressed, and John Barrow, who had been one
of Home's fellow-prisoners in Doune Castle.*   After
a search, Carlyle found the actual manuscript of the
ode in an imperfect state.   He and Henry Mackenzie set themselves to filling up the *lacunæ*, and
presented it in a complete shape to the Royal Society.
Soon afterwards the ode was published from what
was said to be an original and complete copy, which
of course deviated from the other on the points where

* Barrow was " the cordial youth " referred to in the concluding stanza.   One might suppose that he was the same " Barry "
whom Carlyle met in London in 1769, also one of the fugitives
from Doune (page 547).   But *Barrow*, according to Carlyle's
letter in the " Transactions," died paymaster of the forces in the
American War of 1756.

Carlyle and Mackenzie had completed it. This copy was, however, printed anonymously, and its accuracy has not passed unsuspected. The editor of Pickering's edition of Collins (1858) says : " The Wartons, however, had read and remembered the poem, and the anonymous editor dedicated the ode to them, with an address. As this called forth no protest from the Wartons, it is to be presumed that they acknowledged the genuineness of the more perfect copy ; and it has for that reason, though not without some hesitation, been adopted for the text of this edition."

The Royal Society version has, however, its own interest on the present occasion, as Carlyle's interpolations afford some little indication, if not of his poetical capacity, at least of his taste. Here, for instance, is the concluding stanza, with the words supplied by Carlyle printed between commas :—

" All hail, ye scenes that o'er my soul prevail ;
    Ye ' spacious ' friths and lakes which, far away,
  Are by smooth Annan filled, or pastoral Tay,
    Or Don's romantic springs, at distance hail !
  The time shall come when I, perhaps, may tread
    Your lowly glens, o'erhung with spreading broom,
  Or o'er your stretching heaths by fancy led :
    Then will I dress once more the faded bower,
  Where Johnson sat in Drummond's ' social ' shade,
    Or crop from Teviot's dale each   classic flower,'
  And mourn on Yarrow's banks ' the widowed maid.'
  Meantime, ye powers that on the plains which bore
    The cordial youth on Lothian's plains, attend ;
  Where'er he dwell, on hill or lonely muir,
    To him I love your kind protection lend,
  And, touched with love like mine, preserve my absent
      friend."

Here is another specimen of the interpolated passages :—

> " 'Tis thine to sing how, framing hideous spells,
>   In Skye's lone isle the gifted wizard ' sits,'
>   ' Waiting in ' wintry cave ' his wayward fits,'
> Or in the depths of Uist's dark forest dwells." *

Scott said of Carlyle, that " he was no more a poet than his precentor," a rather hard saying, about which it is curious to consider that Scott must certainly have had his mind under the influence of the passage just cited when he drew his own seer Bryan in the *Lady of the Lake*—

> " 'Midst groan of wreck and roar of stream
>   The wizard waits prophetic dream."

It is observable that Carlyle's interpolated version has considerably more resemblance to this than the other has.

We find Carlyle's contemporary, Smollett, giving him credit in his earlier days for poetical efforts which cannot be traced home to him. Writing in 1747, Smollett says :—

" I would have been more punctual had it not been for Oswald the musician, who promised from time to time to set your songs to music, that I might have it in my power to gratify the author in you, by sending your productions so improved. Your gay catches please me much, and the Lamentations of Fanny Gardner has a good deal of nature in it, though, in my opinion, it might be bettered. Oswald has set it to an excellent tune, in the Scotch style ; but as it is not yet published, I cannot regale you with it at present."

---

* In the other version it stands—

> " 'Tis thine to sing how, framing hideous spells,
>   In Skye's lone isle the gifted wizard seer,
>   Lodged in the wintry cave with fatal spear,
> Or in the depth of Uist's dark forest dwells."

Whether the "gay catches" were of Carlyle's composition or not, there seems to be little doubt that the ballad of "Fanny Gairdner" was written by his friend Sir Gilbert Elliot. If Carlyle had been the author, it is likely that some trace of such a fact would have been found in his Autobiography, and so, perhaps, of the "gay catches." There is a small heterogeneous bundle of manuscript verses among Carlyle's papers—some of them in his own handwriting and some in others. They are all, so far as the editor is aware, unknown to fame, and, on consideration, he thought it the better policy not to meddle with them, since attempts to settle the authorship of manuscript literature of this kind are apt to be unsatisfactory,—the conclusions adopted on the most subtle critical induction, being often upset by some person who has been pottering among old magazines and newspapers.

It would have been extremely interesting if Carlyle had brought down his Autobiography, to have had his remarks on the new literary dynasty of which he lived to see the dawn. The letters written to him show that he interested himself in the *Lay of the Last Minstrel*, and in Southey's early poems, but we have not his own criticisms on them. The following on Wordsworth, however, is surely interesting. It is in a letter addressed by Carlyle to " Miss Mitchelson : "

" I must tell you, who I know will sympathise with me, that I was very much delighted indeed, on the first sight of a new species of poetry, in ' The Brothers,' and ' The Idiot Boy,' which were pointed out to me by Carlyle Bell, as chiefly worthy of admira-

38

tion. I read them with attention and was much struck. As I call every man a philosopher, who has sense and observation enough to add one fact relating either to mind or body, to the mass of human knowledge, so I call every man a poet, whose composition pleases at once the imagination and affects the heart. On reading ' The Brothers,' I was surprised at first with its simplicity, or rather flatness. But when I got a little on, I found it not only raised my curiosity, but moved me into sympathy, and at last into a tender approbation of the surviving brother, who had discovered such virtuous feelings, and who, by his dignified and silent departure, approached the sublime. After being so affected, could I deny that this was poetry, however simply expressed ? Nay, I go farther, and aver that, if the narration had been dressed in a more artificial style, it would hardly have moved me at all.

" When I first read ' The Idiot Boy,' I must confess I was alarmed at the term as well as the subject, and suspected that it would not please, but disgust. But when I read on, and found that the author had so finely selected every circumstance that could set off the mother's feelings and character, in the display of the various passions of joy and anxiety, and suspense and despair, and revived hope and returning joy, through all their changes, I lost sight of the term *Idiot*, and offered my thanks to the God of Poets for having inspired one of his sons with a new species of poetry, and for having pointed out a subject on which the author has done more to move the human heart to tenderness for the most unfortunate of our species, than has ever been done before. He has not only made his Idiot Boy an object of pity, but even of love. He has done more, for he has restored him to his place among the household gods whom the ancients worshipped."

It may here be proper to say a few words on a matter not likely to have been directly alluded to by Carlyle himself—his personal appearance and deportment. They are of more than usually important elements in his biography, since, according to the tenor of some traditions and anecdotes, his remarkable personal advantages exercised a great influence both on himself and others. The portrait after Martin, engraved by W. Roffe, represents a countenance eminently endowed with masculine beauty. His appearance has been hitherto chiefly known to the present generation through the *Edinburgh Portraits* of Kay. This limner had the peculiar faculty while preserving a recognisable likeness, of entirely divesting it of every vestige of grace or picturesqueness which nature may have bestowed on it. In this instance he is not, however, quite successful ; for even from his flat etchings, the "preserver of the Church from fanaticism " comes forth a comely man with a rather commanding presence.

Sir Walter Scott has left a colloquial sketch of him, which, though of the briefest, is broad and colossal as a scrap from the pencil of Michael Angelo. He is discoursing of the countenances of poets ; some that represented the divinity of genius, and others that signally failed in that respect. "Well," said he, " the grandest demigod I ever saw was Dr. Carlyle, minister of Musselburgh, commonly called *Jupiter Carlyle*, from having sat more than once for the king of gods and men to Gavin Hamilton ; and a shrewd clever old carle was he, no doubt, but no more a poet than his precentor." * The sitting to Gavin Hamilton is improbable. Had Carlyle been accustomed to meet this great painter, something would certainly have been said about him in the Autobiography. In what is probably a variation of the same tradition, it is said that a sculptor accosted him on the streets of London and requested him to sit for Olympian

* Lockhart's *Life*.

Jove. The late Chief Commissioner Adam, in a few anecdotes, called *The Gift of a Grandfather*, which he printed at a press of his own for private distribution, says, " On some particular occasion, I don't exactly recollect what, he was one of a mission upon Church affairs to London, where they had to attend at St. James's in the costume of their profession. His portly figure, his fine expressive countenance, with an aquiline nose, his flowing silver locks, and the freshness of the colour of his face, made a prodigious impression upon the courtiers ; but," adds the Commissioner, " it was the soundness of his sense, his honourable principles, and his social qualities, unmixed with anything that detracted from, or unbecoming, the character of a clergyman, gave him his place among the worthies."

Besides the picture already referred to, Martin painted another portrait of him, far more ambitious, but not so pleasing. In the Autobiography he mentions his sitting for it, much as Sheridan spoke of his having undergone two operations—the one sitting for his portrait, the other getting his hair cut (p. 548). Of the completion of this work he writes to his wife, on the 7th of April 1770 : " My picture is now finished for the exhibition. It looks like a cardinal, it is so gorgeously dressed. It is in a pink damask night-gown, in a scarlet chair. Martin thinks it will do him more good than all the pictures he has done." Besides the likenesses by Kay and Martin, there was a portrait by Skirving, of which an engraving—not of much merit—is in the hands of some collectors. In an undated letter Lord Haddington says : " I am much obliged to you for recollecting your promise of sitting to Raeburn, and beg that it may be a head done on canvas of the ordinary size. I mean it to hang as an ornament in my new library, and that size will answer best." Accordingly, there are two entries in the Diary : " 1796, *May* 19.—Began to sit to Raeburn for Lord Haddington." " 9*th June*.— Sat with Raeburn for last time." A letter from Lady Douglas (his old friend, Lady Frances Scott), written in February 1805, a short time before his death, refers to a likeness by an artist who was living within the past twelve years. " I have received your bust from Henning, and think it very strikingly like ; but I do not think that he has quite done justice to the picturesque appearance of your silver locks, which, ' in wanton ringlets, wave as the vine casts her tendrils.' If I have time, I will go and see his drawing while I am at Dalkeith."

His Autobiography was the great occupation, and apparently also the great enjoyment, of the concluding years of his life. He began it, as the opening announces, in the year 1800, when he was entering on his seventy-ninth year ; and he appears to have added to it from time to time, until within a few weeks of his death. The last words written in his own handwriting, which became very tremulous, are about " Lord North's having become Premier in the beginning of the year 1770 " (p. 559). The few remaining paragraphs have been written to dictation.

It will naturally have surprised the reader that, at so advanced an age, a man who had not done much in early life to give him the facilities of a practised composer, should have written with so much vigour, eloquence, and point. At the same time, the sort of contemporary-like freshness with which he realises scenes over which long years, crowded with other recollections, had passed, looks like a phenomenon unexampled in literature. But there are reasons for these characteristics. The editor has convinced himself that the favourite scenes and events which Carlyle describes had been from the first forming themselves in his mind, and even resolving themselves into sentences, which would become mellowed in their structure and antithesis, by the more than obedience to the *nonumque prematur in annum*. The habit acquired by a clergyman of the Church of Scotland, who had to preach sermons committed to memory, would form the practice of retaining finished pieces of composition in the mind. This view of the literary growth of the work, though originating in a general impression from its whole tenor, can be supported by a few distinct incidents of evidence. The chief of these is the repetition at considerable intervals of the same scene or anecdote, in almost the same words, and with the more characteristic and emphatic expressions identical. Farther ; there is a separate manuscript of his Autobiography, down to the year 1735, cited in the notes as *Recollections*. These were written at different times, and partly, it would seem, before he began the present work. They were prepared for the amusement of his friend Lady Frances Douglas ; and, expanding into rhetorical decorations and jocular allusions— probably intended to enhance their interest in the special eyes for which they were destined—they are far inferior, except in a few passages, to the corresponding portion of the Autobiography. It is evident, however, that they are substantially the same material inflated for the occasion.

In fact, the amount of repetition in the Autobiography, and the absence of general order throughout, show that the author did not retain the full faculty of arranging the collection of finished compositions stored up in his mind. When there is virtually verbatim repetition, the duplicate of the passage has been omitted in the printing. But it was impossible, without depriving the work of its racy charms, to obliterate every second going over of the same ground, or even to group together the dispersed passages which bear upon the same matter, and which might, had the author written at an earlier and more active time of life, have been fused by him into each other. For the precision with which he notified dates and places he seems to have been indebted to a series of accurate diaries. There exists at least a succession of diaries, from the sojourn in London in the midst of which the Autobiography stops, down to the time when he could no longer write. It is likely enough that these had predecessors ; they may have been lost sight of from his having taken them out of their repository for the purpose of consulting them in the composition of his Autobiography. The diaries which exist are of the very briefest kind, intended evidently for no other eye but his own, and containing no more words or even letters than might be sufficient to recall to memory the dates and sequence of the events of his life.

The existence of this Autobiography has been well known, and there have been many expressions of surprise by authors, from Sir Walter Scott downwards, why it had not been made public. Perhaps it is better that it should have waited. It is easy to sympathise with a reluctance to have published some portions of it half a century ago. When a man leaves behind him his experience and opinions as to his contemporaries in an outspoken book—as this certainly is—the manuscript is apt to be dismantled of one ornament after another, to spare the feelings of the surviving kindred. In this way records of individual conduct, which it might be cruel to publish immediately, are lost to the world ; while, if they were preserved until the generation liable to be distressed by their publication have departed, they might be given forth without offence. What at one time is personal, irritating, and even cruel, becomes, after a generation or two has departed, only a valuable record of the social and moral condition of a past

period.   Though the popular expectation about such
records is, that they only exist to remind the later
generation of pristine times and departed virtues, yet
the account of personal follies and vices which they
may contain have their own weight and value as part
of the history of the period.

While he was struggling through increasing years
and infirmities with his too long postponed task, the
last and greatest of his domestic calamities overtook
him in the death of his wife, on the 31st day of January 1804.   For once the hard brevity of the diary is
softened by a touch of nature.   " She composed her
features into the most placid appearance, gave me her
last kiss, and then gently going out, like a taper in
the socket, at 7 breathed her last.   No finer spirit
ever took flight from a clay tabernacle to be united
with the Father of all and the spirits of the just."

All was done to brighten his few remaining days
that the affectionate solicitude of relations and dear
friends could do.   His nephew, Mr. Carlyle Bell, was
all to him that a son could be, and held that place in
his affection.   Besides the scanty remnant of his old
contemporary friends, there rose around him a cluster
of attached followers among the younger clergy, foremost and best beloved of whom was John Lee, the
late learned and accomplished head of the University
of Edinburgh, who has himself just passed from
among us, well stricken in years.   Addressing his
good friend Lady Frances at this time, he thus alludes
to his nephew and Lee : " I, who have now acquired

a kind of personal greatness, by means of the infirmities of age, which make me dependent, have by that very means acquired all the trappings of greatness. For, besides my nephew,* who is my governor, nurse, and treasurer, I have got likewise a trusty friend and an able physician, an uncommonly good divine and an eminent preacher—all in the person of one young man, whom I have taken to live with me." He then touches on a matter which still afforded him an interest in the world—the completion of the new church for his parish. Its slender spire is a conspicuous object for many miles around. " By the first Sunday of August I intend, God willing, to gratify my people by opening my new church, if it were only with a short prayer (for Othello's occupation's gone), when I shall have been 57 years complete minister of this parish." But it was not to be. Among the last entries in his brief diary in 1805, are, " 25th July—John Home and Mrs. Home ; 27th— George Hill called going east." Next day, the entry is " very ill ; " for some days afterwards, " no change ; " and the last entry, as distinct as any, is " August 12th and 13th, the same." He died on the 25th. So departed one who, if men are to be esteemed, not by the rank which external fortune has given them or the happy chances they have seized, but by the influence they have imparted from mere personal character and ability, is certainly one of the

* Carlyle Bell, W.S., for twenty-five years joint city-clerk of Edinburgh (see page 433).

most remarkable on record. Born in a simple manse, he remained all his days that type of humble respectability—a village pastor ; nor does he seem ever to have desired a higher sphere. His lot was not even cast on any of those wild revolutionary periods which give men in his position a place in history ; nor did he attempt any of those great ventures for literary distinction in which many of his comrades were so successful. It seems to have been his one and peculiar ambition that he should dignify his calling by bringing it forth into the world, and making for it a place along with rank, and wealth, and distinction of every kind. This object he carried through with a high hand ; and scarcely a primate of the proud Church of England could overtop in social position and influence the Presbyterian minister of Inveresk.

He was laid beside his long-departed children and the faithful partner of his days, in his own churchyard, which he had always loved for the beauty of the prospect it overlooks. The following inscription, composed by his friend Adam Ferguson, was engraved upon his tomb :—

ALEXANDER CARLYLE, D.D.,
FIFTY-SEVEN YEARS MINISTER OF THIS
PARISH ;
BORN ON THE 26TH JANUARY 1722,
DECEASED ON THE 25TH AUGUST 1805 ;
HAVING THUS LIVED
IN A PERIOD OF GREAT LUSTRE
TO THE COUNTRY,
IN ARTS AND ARMS,
IN LITERATURE AND SCIENCE,
IN FREEDOM, RELIGIOUS AND CIVIL :
HE TOO WAS WORTHY OF THE TIMES ;
LEARNED AND ELOQUENT,
LIBERAL AND EXEMPLARY IN HIS MANNERS,
FAITHFUL TO HIS PASTORAL CHARGE,
NOT AMBITIOUS OF POPULAR APPLAUSE,
BUT TO THE PEOPLE A WILLING GUIDE
IN THE WAYS OF RIGHTEOUSNESS
AND TRUTH :
IN HIS PRIVATE CONNECTIONS,
A KIND RELATION,
AN ASSIDUOUS FRIEND,
AND AN AGREEABLE COMPANION ;
NOT IMMERSED IN SPECULATION,
BUT EARNEST IN ACTION,
TO PROMOTE THE MERIT HE ESTEEMED,
OR THE PUBLIC CAUSE HE ESPOUSED ;
AND, WHEN FULL OF YEARS,
CALMLY PREPARED
TO DIE IN PEACE.

INDEX

605

FOUR CLASSICS OF SCOTTISH LIFE

AUTOBIOGRAPHY OF
DR. ALEXANDER CARLYLE

of INVERESK (1722–1805). Edited by J. HILL BURTON. New Edition, with many additional notes, Frontispiece in Colour, and 32 Portraits in Photogravure of the Eminent Men of the Time. Extra crown 8vo, 600 pp., buckram, **6s. net**.

"Jupiter" Carlyle was the friend of most of the eminent literary men of his day, and one of the chief figures in Scottish society at the time when Scotland was at the height of its fame as a centre of literary and social activity. His Autobiography, first issued in 1860, now re-edited and republished after being many years out of print, is one of the most interesting and valuable contemporary documents of the time.

MEMORIALS OF HIS TIME.

By LORD COCKBURN. New Edition, with Introduction by his Grandson, HARRY A. COCKBURN. Containing 12 Portraits in Colour by Sir HENRY RAEBURN, and many other Illustrations. Ex. Cr. 8vo, 480 pp., buckram, **6s. net**; velvet calf, **12s. 6d. net**.

An admirable and living record of the men and manners of Scotland two or three generations ago, written by one of the most able of that brilliant coterie to which Scott, Jeffrey, and Lockhart belonged. Not only is it a valuable contribution to history, but its humorous descriptions of the quaintly coloured society and manners, make it " one of the pleasantest fireside books of the century."

ANNALS OF THE PARISH.

By JOHN GALT. New Edition. With Sixteen Illustrations in Colour by HENRY W. KERR, R.S.A. Extra crown 8vo, 300 pp., buckram, **5s. net**; velvet calf, **10s. 6d. net**.

" Certainly no such picture of the life of Scotland during the closing years of the last century has ever been written. He does what no other can do so well. He shows us with vivid directness and reality what like were the quiet lives of leal folk, burghers and ministers, and country lairds a hundred years ago."—S. R. CROCKETT.

The notable feature of this edition is the new illustrations by Mr. Henry W. Kerr, which should meet with a great reception.

REMINISCENCES OF
SCOTTISH LIFE & CHARACTER.

By DEAN RAMSAY. New Edition. With 16 Illustrations in Colour by HENRY W. KERR, R.S.A. Crown 8vo, 400 pp., buckram, **5s. net**; bound in velvet calf, **10s. 6d. net**.

This work, unrivalled as a storehouse of Scottish humour and anecdote, is recognised as the finest book on Scottish life and character ever written. Mr. Kerr's world-famed pictures of old Scottish life are reproduced in this new edition, which is an ideal gift book.

Complete List of Publications and Books for Presentation

T. N. FOULIS, 15 Frederick St., Edinburgh; and London

IMPORTANT NEW ART BOOKS

ARTS AND CRAFTS OF OUR TEUTONIC FOREFATHERS

By Professor G. BALDWIN BROWN, Author of "The Fine Arts," "The Arts in Early England," etc. With many Illustrations, some in colour. Small 4to, 300 pp., buckram, **5s. net.**

The aim of this important work is to describe the little-known artistic achievements of the Teutonic peoples before they overthrew the Roman Empire and founded the political systems of the modern world. Much attention is paid to the interesting question of the materials and technical processes used by these early craftsmen.

MATERIALS OF THE PAINTER'S CRAFT

From the Earliest Times to the End of the Sixteenth Century. By A. P. LAURIE, M.A., D.Sc., F.R.S.E., Principal of the Heriot-Watt College, Edinburgh. With many Illustrations, including seven in colour. Small 4to, 300 pp., **5s. net.**

This work gives a comprehensive account of the methods of preparing and using painter's materials from the time of their use in Egyptian tombs to that of the oil paintings of the 16th-century masters. The methods employed during these centuries for the illumination of MSS., the painting of walls, panel pictures, and frescoes are fully described.

ARTS AND CRAFTS OF ANCIENT EGYPT

By Professor W. M. FLINDERS PETRIE, Author of "A History of Egypt," etc. With 45 Full-page and other Illustrations. Small 4to, buckram, **5s. net.**
Second Impression.

This volume, written by one of the most eminent Egyptologists of the day, contains a very fully illustrated survey of Egyptian Arts and Crafts—the beauty and wonderful craftsmanship are almost unknown in this country.

ARTS AND CRAFTS OF OLD JAPAN

By STEWART DICK. Containing 30 full-page and other illustrations. Small 4to, 166 pp., buckram, **5s. net.**
Fourth Impression.

" We know of no book that within such modest limits contrives to convey so much trustworthy information on Japanese Art."—Literary World.

ARTS AND CRAFTS OF OLDER SPAIN

By LEONARD WILLIAMS, Author of "The Land of the Dons." With over 150 full-page Illustrations. 3 Vols., small 4to, buckram, **15s. net per set.**

The only available work in English on Spanish Arts and Crafts, full of suggestion and interest for artworkers and connoisseurs.

Complete List of Art and Presentation Volumes, post free

T. N. FOULIS, 21 Paternoster Square, London; and Edinburgh